THE FAILURE
OF WALL STREET

ALSO BY ERIK BANKS

Working the Street. Palgrave Macmillan, 2004.
The Financial Lexicon, Palgrave Macmillan, 2004.
Liquidity Risk. Palgrave Macmillan, 2004.
The Credit Risk of Complex Derivatives, 3rd edition. Palgrave Macmillan, 2003.
Corporate Governance. Palgrave Macmillan, 2003.
Alternative Risk Transfer. John Wiley, 2004.
Exchange-Traded Derivatives. John Wiley, 2003.
The Simple Rules of Risk. John Wiley, 2002.
e-Finance. John Wiley, 2000.
The Rise and Fall of the Merchant Banks. Kogan Page, 1999.
The Credit Risk of Complex Derivatives, 2nd edition. Macmillan, 1997.
Asia Pacific Derivative Markets. Macmillan, 1996.
Emerging Asian Fixed Income Markets. Macmillan, 1995.
The Credit Risk of Complex Derivatives. Macmillan, 1994.
The Credit Risk of Financial Instruments. Macmillan, 1993.

AS CO-AUTHOR

Practical Risk Management (co-written with R. Dunn). John Wiley, 2003.
Weather Risk Management (edited/co-written with XL/Element Re). Palgrave
    Macmillan, 2001.

THE FAILURE
OF WALL STREET

How and Why Wall Street Fails—
And What Can Be Done About It

Erik Banks

THE FAILURE OF WALL STREET
Copyright © Erik Banks, 2004.

All rights reserved. No part of this book may be used or reproduced in any
manner whatsoever without written permission except in the case of brief
quotations embodied in critical articles or reviews.

First published 2004 by
PALGRAVE MACMILLAN™
175 Fifth Avenue, New York, N.Y. 10010 and
Houndmills, Basingstoke, Hampshire, England RG21 6XS.
Companies and representatives throughout the world.

PALGRAVE MACMILLAN is the global academic imprint of the Palgrave
Macmillan division of St. Martin's Press, LLC and of Palgrave Macmillan Ltd.
Macmillan® is a registered trademark in the United States, United Kingdom and
other countries. Palgrave is a registered trademark in the European Union and
other countries.

ISBN 1-4039-6402-5 hardback

Library of Congress Cataloging-in-Publication Data
Banks, Erik.
    The failure of Wall Street : how and why Wall Street fails—and what can be
done about it / by Erik Banks.
        p. cm.
    Includes bibliographical references and index.
    ISBN 1-4039-6402-5
    1. Wall Street.   2. Securities—United States.   3. Stock exchanges—United
States.   4. Investments—United States.   I. Title.
HG4572.B28   2004
332.64'273—dc22

                                                                      2004045507

A catalogue record for this book is available from the British Library.

Design by Letra Libre, Inc.

First edition: September 2004
10 9 8 7 6 5 4 3 2 1
Printed in the United States of America.

Contents

Acknowledgments   vii

Bio   viii

Part I
How Wall Street Fails

Chapter 1   Wall Street and Its Role   3

Chapter 2   When the Intended Role Fails   17

Chapter 3   Problems Raising Capital   29

Chapter 4   Bad Corporate Advice   51

Chapter 5   Bad Personal Financial Advice   87

Chapter 6   Breaching Trust   111

Chapter 7   Bad Risk Management   165

Part II
Why Wall Street Fails

Chapter 8   Internal Breakdown   203

Chapter 9   External Weakness   229

Part III
Overcoming Failure

Chapter 10   Getting the House in Order   247

Chapter 11   Shoring Up the Defenses   265

Chapter 12   Summary: What's Next?   279

Notes   285

Index   289

Acknowledgments

I would like to thank Toby Wahl, senior editor at Palgrave Macmillan in New York, for his valuable support and guidance throughout the project. Thanks are also due to Donna Cherry, production editor, and the production and marketing teams at Palgrave for assistance in creating the book.

And my biggest thanks, as always, go to my wife Milena.

—EB
Redding, Connecticut, 2004
Ebbrisk@netscape.net

Bio

Erik Banks spent sixteen years on Wall Street, most of it at a major global investment bank. After training and early job experience in New York, he spent eight years running departments in Tokyo, Hong Kong, and London, and then returned to New York as a managing director. Mr. Banks retired from Wall Street in 2002 to write; he is the author of more than a dozen books on banking, risk, derivatives, and governance, including the Palgrave titles *Working the Street, The Credit Risk of Complex Derivatives (3rd edition),* and *Corporate Governance.*

"Hell is empty and the Devils are all here."

—Shakespeare, *The Tempest*

Part I

HOW WALL STREET FAILS

Chapter 1

WALL STREET
AND ITS ROLE

Wall Street is the center of the financial machinery that makes the global economy work. Though Wall Street exists physically—the nexus of Wall and Broad, the location of the New York Stock Exchange (NYSE), within eyesight of the New York Federal Reserve, the American Stock Exchange (AMEX), and the gleaming headquarters of powers like Goldman Sachs, Merrill Lynch, Lehman Brothers—we refer to Wall Street in its conceptual and functional sense. Wall Street as a financial conduit exists as much in lower Manhattan as in midtown Manhattan, or London, or Tokyo, or the electronic sphere. In this sense of Wall Street, physical location is irrelevant, but function is not, because it's what propels companies and clients.

Wall Street is a large industry, made up of thousands of institutions employing hundreds of thousands of people all over the world. But at the center there is a remarkably small group that drives everything. The top dozen banking firms play a pivotal role in arranging the world's commercial and financial transactions. The list of a dozen changes periodically as banks merge, get bought out, or fade away, or as smaller firms develop strength in an area and leapfrog some of the larger institutions, but the core always remains quite small. These banks are joined by a few of the largest mutual fund groups and the major stock and futures exchanges. The power of the Street is thus extremely concentrated. What the sector says and does helps decide the financial fate of companies, countries, and individuals. And that, as we'll see, has far-reaching implications.

The Street, which has performed its pivotal role for decades, can lay claim to many successes. It does many things exceptionally well: mobilizing and placing capital, creating new and innovative financial products, buying and selling physical and financial assets, and advising institutional and personal clients on a range of transactions. It has proved to be remarkably flexible and resilient, adapting to change and weathering crises and dislocations. Its role in global economic growth has been, and remains, unique and vital. There can be little doubt that without Wall Street's creativity and leadership, financing and innovation would be brought to a standstill and economic progress stifled. Let us not underestimate the tremendous benefits the Street has brought, and still brings, to modern economic society.

But the Street, for all of its importance and strengths, for all of the benefits it is capable of delivering, often fails to do what it's supposed to do. Perhaps this failure is a by-product of the free market system: the very forces that have allowed the creation of such a sophisticated and adaptable financing framework leave it exposed to misuse and abuse. The economic profit incentives that lead to financial innovation, capital mobilization, and wealth and risk transfer can also skew action and behavior, meaning the system doesn't always function as intended. Unfortunately, we don't have to look far to find evidence of failure. The headlines of the past few decades tell it all: bad deals, mistreated clients, poorly managed risks, conflicts, fiduciary breaches, fraud. And these aren't isolated problems that appear once in a blue moon. They happen so frequently that they can't be dismissed as an aberration or an exception. The Street is routinely in the spotlight for having done something wrong: it's in court or in front of arbitration panels trying to defend some wayward action; it's in the news for having lost lots of money; it's negotiating settlements to appease angry corporate or personal clients; it's plea-bargaining with regulators for having breached some rule. In fact, it's hard to think of another industry that stumbles as often and badly. Of course, other industries in the corporate world have problems of their own, including excess inventories, bad acquisitions, flawed strategies, and product recalls. But their misadventures seem to lack the scope and scale of the Street's and certainly don't appear with the same frequency.

With just a little digging we find that the Street makes lots of mistakes in its core areas of expertise. Whether it's raising capital, giving advice, managing risk, or looking after customers, it regularly falls short of its potential and its responsibilities. And most of the failures are financially and reputationally damaging. Insiders and outsiders get hurt when things go wrong: employees and managers, personal and corporate clients, investors, creditors, regulators, and sometimes even industries, municipalities, or sovereigns. Worse, the Street often seems unable (perhaps unwilling) to learn from its mistakes, to recognize and resolve some of the underlying problems.

Naturally, Wall Street doesn't fail at everything all the time. If that were true, the global economic picture would look decidedly different: stifled growth, limited capital flows, mismanaged investments, excess risks. Happily, the Street is still quite successful at handling much of its business on a pretty even keel: it has been instrumental in building up a $14 trillion global capital market, arranging thousands of worthwhile mergers and acquisitions, funding lots of start-up ventures, creating smooth trading conditions, helping millions of investors manage their wealth, and coming up with clever ways of coping with risks. When it is focused and diligent, the Street can work wonders. And we are by no means condemning Wall Street or issuing a blanket critique of every institution or person working there. There are lots of talented professionals on the Street trying to do a good job; they improve the quality of business dealings and make the place more efficient and secure. Many deserve credit for their efforts because without them things would be far worse.

But Wall Street can do much, much better. For all of the good the Street does and all the triumphs it can claim, should we really look the other way when banks defraud governments or companies to the tune of billions, when they leave institutional and personal investors holding the bag on bad deals or failed strategies, when they put their own interests ahead of everyone else's? Should we be satisfied when they misrepresent facts and information in order to earn fees, when they sell clients things they don't need just to generate commissions, or when they don't do what they are supposed to do to protect clients and investors? Why should we be satisfied with any of these behaviors? These are all elements of Wall Street's failure; they represent serious flaws and shouldn't be swept under the carpet or glossed over—yet they often are.

Why does the Street fail in these areas? Largely because it is focused on maximizing profits, sometimes at any cost. How does it fail? Through flawed governance, bad management, poor strategies, conflicts of interest, inadequate skills, poor controls, and weak external checks and balances. And why doesn't the Street doesn't fix the problems? Primarily because it is reluctant to alter the profitable status quo and jeopardize revenues and compensation. With diffuse accountabilities and negligible penalties, there seems to be little reason to reform.

My aim in this book is to explore the Street's failures—how and why key financial intermediaries fall down on the job. Like others who have spent many years on Wall Street, I am concerned with what I see happening. But I'm not despairing, and I'm not interested in condemning. I prefer to be constructive and advance the agenda by proposing ways in which aspects of Wall Street's less savory behavior can be improved, so that there are more winners and fewer losers, and the triumphs of Wall Street can shine through more often. I'll explore all of these points in the coming chapters, but first I'd like to set the stage by reviewing a little bit about Wall Street's role and the nature of its key players.

WALL STREET'S ROLE

Though the Street does lots of things, most of them revolve around five basic tasks: raising capital, giving corporate advice, giving personal financial advice, performing fiduciary duties, and managing risks. We'll look at how these functions operate, and sometimes fail, in practice in the next few chapters, but let's start with an overview on how they're supposed to work.

Raising capital

At its core, Wall Street is about raising capital. In fact, though all of the Street's functions are important, this one is primus inter pares, because it has a direct impact on everything else that happens: acquisitions, takeovers, and investments occur because of capital. Companies use capital to fund productive assets that generate revenues. Without capital companies cease to function, and economic growth gets choked off. So if the national and global economies are going to produce and expand, companies need access to capital. Though some of this can be generated internally through retained earnings, most of it has to come from two external sources: debt and equity. Debt capital, which represents a corporate liability, is nothing more than a borrowing, an IOU. Equity capital, in contrast, represents a corporate ownership stake. Of course, debt and equity come in many different flavors. Debt includes short-term notes, commercial paper, and deposits; medium-term notes and bonds; secured and unsecured loans; subordinated debentures; and so forth. Equity in its pure form is issued as common stock, but there are a plethora of equity-related hybrids: preferred stock (of various types, including cumulative preferred, noncumulative preferred, redeemable preference shares, and so on) and convertible bonds (again, in lots of varieties, including standard convertibles, mandatory convertibles, reverse convertibles, as well as a stable full of hybrids with clever acronyms, like LYONS, PRIDES, FELINE PRIDES, TOPRS, DECS, PERCS—most just subtle tax- and conversion-related variations on the theme).

So Wall Street firms try to raise capital for their institutional clients. The typical sequence finds relationship managers or investment bankers calling on corporate treasurers, chief financial officers (CFOs), state treasurers, or finance ministers, pitching various ideas, demonstrating the effects of an initial public offering (IPO), equity add-on, or bond on the balance sheet and cash flow of the firm. If there's some interest, product specialists might join in and start hammering out details (i.e., where to price the deal, whether some aspect of it can be hedged or packaged with a derivative to lower costs, where it will be placed, what kind of aftermarket support will be necessary, whether it should be done on a best-efforts or fully underwritten basis, what kind of research coverage is necessary, and so forth). This stage completed, the company might award the bank a mandate or seek offers from other banks; indeed, the astute corporate treasurer or CFO always shops around, playing banks against one another in order to get the best deal possible. But once a bank has the green light, the syndicate team prepares to launch through premarketing and book-building (i.e., establishing preliminary allocations); this helps identify a proper launch spread (for debt) or price (for equity). Research enters a quiet period (i.e., no disclosure), and on deal date the issue is priced and launched. If it's a best-efforts deal the bank will place what it can through its institutional/retail sales force and deliver funds to the company. So if the deal is targeted at $100 million but only $75 million can be raised, that's all the company gets. But if the deal is underwritten (if it is a bought, or fully committed, deal) the bank delivers $100 million to the company and then pumps whatever it can through its sales force. If it gets the pricing right by making it look attractive to the investor base, it'll get rid of the full $100 million; if it doesn't, it'll get stuck with some of the securities—a hung deal. Regardless of the success of the initial placement, the bank is likely to provide research coverage and some amount of secondary trading support, so that there is liquidity in the issue; the secondary trading forms part of the bank's risk activities, noted below.

If all of this works as it should, *everyone wins:* a company gets the capital it needs, at a price that is fair and competitive; investors get an investment they find attractive, backed by dependable liquidity and research support; and, banks get fees for the work they've done. Fees vary tremendously: from 6–7 percent for US equity issues (3–4 percent for international issues) down to 1 percent for bonds and maybe 0.1–0.5 percent for loans. (Little wonder that all the bankers chase IPOs and equity add-ons and are loath to make loans.) Sometimes, though, Wall Street gets ahead of itself and tries to bring deals to market when it shouldn't: IPOs that aren't ready and bonds or loans for companies that are already highly leveraged. We'll talk more about this in chapter 3.

Giving Corporate Advice

Wall Street also gives companies (and countries) advice on a range of issues, including corporate finance transactions (e.g., mergers and acquisitions (M&A), spin-offs, recapitalizations, privatizations, leveraged buyouts (LBOs), tax shelters), and investment management strategies (e.g., asset allocations, derivative-based speculation).

Companies are constantly changing their stripes: they expand by acquiring or merging at home or abroad, they succumb to outside pressures and sell themselves to a competitor, or they spin off pieces of the firm that they no longer want. Wall Street is on hand to help them arrange these transactions. Most banks have dedicated teams that handle different aspects of the process: relationship managers to build and maintain ties with corporate clients, so that they can provide advice on a range of strategies; corporate finance generalists to help arrange the nuts and bolts of simple (or "vanilla") transactions; and, specialists to take care of the very tricky structures that might require an added degree of legal, tax, accounting, or financial expertise. The process is extremely involved and typically starts with analysis of potential corporate finance opportunities for client companies. Ideas are pitched to executives, and when a company decides to move ahead, the intense work gets under way: number crunching by teams of junior bankers and analysts, due diligence, preparation of valuations and fairness opinions, arrangement of capital (if needed), and drafting of legal documentation and regulatory disclosures. Everything culminates in the final deal execution (which also includes bankers from the other side of the transaction). Wall Street firms have also found that it can be lucrative to help corporate clients arrange offshore tax structures that help them minimize the size of the checks they send the IRS every year. They have dedicated experts with intimate knowledge of the tax code that dissect client financials to determine potential tax plays that might generate savings; then they go calling on prospective clients with relationship managers to see if transactions can be arranged.

Of course, not all of the Street's institutional advice is based on corporate finance or tax strategies. Much of it relates to the essential management of balance sheets and income statements: what to do with liquid assets and the investment portfolio, how to manage liability and funding flows, how to alter operating and financial cash flows and, ultimately, how to boost returns. Again, Wall Street has cadres of specialists that help corporate clients arrange suitable deals. Some of them service the investment management sector by marketing deals and products that are geared for mutual funds, pension funds, and other institutional asset managers—lots of vanilla stocks and bonds, usually nothing too spicy. Others take care of hedge funds and sophisticated corporations that are keen to use derivative instruments (off-balance sheet financial contracts that derive their value from other market references) to create customized investment opportunities, hedge financial risks, lock in funding costs, or just punt. Derivative marketers come up with clever ways to get an institution as much juice as possible on investments, or to squeeze out every possible basis point from funding costs. Some of the instruments are pretty complex, so diligent salespeople take time and effort to explain upside and downside scenarios so that clients can understand what can go right and what can go wrong.

When all of this corporate advice works as it should, *everybody wins:* companies (and their investors) get good acquisitions, tax hedges, or investment/speculative opportunities, while banks get very handsome fees, commissions, spreads, and trading profits. Unfortunately, some of the M&A deals, tax plays, and investment transactions that appear good on the surface are actually disasters in the making, as we'll discover in chapter 4.

Giving Personal Financial Advice

Many Street firms cater to the legions of private clients—the Moms and Pops on Main Street—that require investment and wealth management guidance. The biggest houses on Wall Street each have between five thousand and fifteen thousand brokers around the globe, wooing clients and their assets, making investment recommendations (on a security-specific commission basis), and offering wealth advice, such as asset management and retirement planning (on a fee basis). Brokers (or "financial consultants," as they like to be called) are given "top pick lists" by research analysts, and it's their job to press clients into buying them. And as the investing population ages, the biggest firms offer clients a variety of retirement-related services, like estate and tax planning, retirement and annuity programs, and so forth. Most of the big banks even run their own mutual funds (a very popular form of investment for individuals) to generate additional revenues and compete with the established mutual fund companies. A great deal of retail business is still driven by commission-based advice and trading, though some banks are trying to migrate to recurring fee business; this helps insulate revenues when the markets turn down, retail players head for the sidelines, and volumes dwindle. Far better for a bank to take 50 or 100 basis points of annual fees on the assets in a client's account (letting them do free or very cheap trades in the process) than charge higher commissions and pray for strong markets and high volumes. Because even when volumes dry up, the assets tend to stay put, meaning revenues remain relatively buoyant.

Financial consultants are part of the distribution mechanism that gives Street firms their strength. Though lots of securities are sold through institutional sales forces to professional investors (e.g., the pension and mutual funds, hedge funds, and companies mentioned above), a large volume flow through retail networks to Moms and Pops. Banks with retail distribution power have a competitive advantage over those with a strict institutional focus, as the capital sitting with individuals is considerable; indeed, an ability to sell into this base of investors is a powerful calling card when pitching a stock or bond deal to a corporate treasurer.

Again, when the role is working as it should, *everybody wins:* clients get sound advice and recommendations on how to manage their finances, and their portfolios perform as they should (it doesn't mean all the investments are winners, of course, just that there aren't any nasty surprises); banks, in turn, get fair commissions and fees for their efforts. The retail business, however, doesn't always function smoothly and is periodically the scene of some rather horrific problems, as we'll see in chapter 5.

Performing Fiduciary Tasks

Street firms are also responsible for various other client-related duties, some of them a bit intangible. Though it's easy to understand an M&A transaction, a bond trade, or a retail client sales ticket, it is far more difficult to get one's arms around trust and fiduciary duties—functions like unbiased advice, safe custody of assets, ethical treatment, proper due diligence, accurate fairness opinions—things that are meant to be done correctly if the interests of clients and stakeholders are to be properly served. Since this can be a bit nebulous—but is absolutely critical to the smooth functioning of the marketplace—it's easier to think about it in terms of examples. A client of a Wall Street firm wants complete confidence that it is being treated fairly in business dealings, advice, and execution. This means the bank has to be honest and independent in providing investment research and M&A fairness opinions, and thorough in performing due diligence. It must be very clear regarding the riskiness of deals and be sure securities and confidential information are held in safekeeping. It needs to execute trades according to the client's precise instructions, and provide timely and correct information on positions, valuations, and deals. When given discretionary power, a bank has to use that power with the utmost care. In short, the Street must provide all of the duties that you would expect a diligent, honest professional or company to provide. This is especially critical in an industry like financial services that lacks a base of hard assets to fall back on; the core of the function is based on intangibles like goodwill, trust, and intellect.

And, of course, when it all works as intended, *everybody wins:* the client is treated properly and has confidence in the advice, service, or information it is receiving, and the bank earns fees from its specific fiduciary duties; more important, it strengthens its reputation for "doing the right thing." But if these things go astray, the client loses and the bank's reputation can be damaged; we'll explore this in more detail in chapter 6.

Managing Risks

Though risk taking is tremendously important to Wall Street firms and the efficient working of the financial markets, it tends to be somewhat invisible to the person on Main Street (unless something blows up, in which case the episode might make the evening business news). Banks exist to take and manage risk. That is what they do for a living, and it's one of the key value-added services they provide. General Motors makes cars, Compaq makes computers, and banks make risk capacity. If they didn't, companies and individuals would have to fend for themselves, which would be inefficient, expensive, and dangerous.

Risk comes in lots of different forms. There is, for instance, market risk: the risk that markets might go up or down, or become more or less volatile, or that the shape of the yield curve will steepen or flatten, or that bond credit spreads will tighten or widen. There is credit risk, or the risk that a company won't make good on repaying its loans (or some other risky transaction, like a bond or derivative). And there is liquidity risk, or the risk that a firm won't be able to obtain funding or sell some of its assets quickly enough (and for enough money) to pay its bills. (There are other kinds of risks, like legal, suitability, model, and operational risks, which we'll introduce later in the book). All of these risks have to be dealt with, so the Street puts its creativity and capital to work to transfer, repackage, hedge, and otherwise manage things that might otherwise lead to losses. And they use the same techniques in their own operations to profit directly or manage downside risk of loss, or both.

Most Street firms have armies of traders who are responsible for buying and selling bonds, stocks, derivatives, and other things on behalf of clients and for their own accounts. Those who trade primarily for clients are agents, matching up buys and sells and taking a small spread in the middle but no direct risk. Those who take client positions straight on their books are dealers, and those who trade exclusively for themselves by risking the firm's capital are proprietary (prop) traders. Dealers and prop traders hope to generate profits by speculating (i.e., outright risk positions) or arbitraging (i.e., lower-risk combinations of positions). Indeed, that's where a lot of money is made and lost on Wall Street; banks that put on big positions tend to have very volatile profit and loss (P&L) from quarter to quarter and year to year. Regardless of the source and nature of risk, the results of a bank's activity are apparent every day through the revaluation (or mark-to-market, MTM) process; there is no hiding from the results. Away from the day-to-day trading and lending, some firms are involved in private equity investments, which involves allocating the firm's capital to start-up or established ventures as an investor—the classic merchant banking function pioneered and refined by the old British houses. These investments have elements of credit and equity risk and tend to be long term in nature—they are "buy and hold" positions that culminate in cash-out through an IPO or third-party sale several years down the line. Since equity investments are long-term positions they usually aren't marked-to-market, so there's no evidence of daily P&L swings.

And the same story exists here: when things go as planned, *everybody wins:* clients get liquidity, good market prices, tight execution and, most important, an appropriate risk hedge, while the bank gets a proper return for the risky positions it's taking (again, it doesn't mean that all positions are winners, just that they are priced commensurately with risks taken). However, since risk is a tricky beast, things don't always work out like they're supposed to; clients and banks can get sandbagged, as we'll see in chapter 7.

WALL STREET'S KEY PLAYERS

As we said earlier, Wall Street is a tight-knit community with a core group of institutions doing most of the business that needs to get done. We'll focus most of our discussion on the banks themselves, since they are the center of the process and drive lots of what happens in other areas, such as mutual funds, stock exchanges, and futures exchanges. But we'll touch on some of the other institutions in the sector from time to time, because they are part of the whole picture—the successes as well as the failures.

The structure, composition, and power rankings of the banking world change from time to time, but Wall Street is still largely an oligopoly of a dozen or so players that set the pace and direct most aspects of business. Niche players with established expertise can share in the spoils, but they are the exception, not the norm. Regional players (e.g., ex-New York houses) can be important in servicing the local communities in which they operate, but they tend to march to the beat set by Wall Street's major firms. Even the main powers abroad—mostly a few European behemoths—are powers because they've acquired other Wall Street firms (or sucked up a lot of the Street's homegrown talent). So it's the core group of a dozen that dominates the capital raising, corporate and private client advice, fiduciary services, and risk management/trading.

The key players are all starting to look very similar, since they are pretty much involved in the same lines of business. They are fierce competitors on virtually every front, though some of them have comparative advantages in specific areas (i.e., J.P. Morgan Chase in derivatives and syndicated loans, Goldman Sachs in investment banking and prop trading, Morgan Stanley in investment banking and consumer credit, Citibank in underwriting, lending, and foreign exchange trading, and so forth). This wasn't always the case, of course. Between the creation of the Glass-Steagall Act in 1933 and the passage of the Gramm-Leach-Bliley (GLB) Act in 2000 (which felled the bits of Glass-Steagall that remained), Wall Street was divided into commercial banking and investment banking—the businesses were separate and distinct. The separation arose in the aftermath of the Great Crash as a way of keeping Wall Street on the straight and narrow: regulators didn't want banks, having lent money unwisely to bad companies, to repay themselves by issuing securities to investors; this was just passing the buck from banks (and their investors) to unknowing capital markets investors. There were too many opportunities for abuse (as the system had learned), so a separation of powers was mandated. For the next six decades, commercial banks couldn't engage in securities underwriting, investment banks couldn't make loans, and neither group could write insurance. As the realities of modern finance changed in the 1980s and 1990s—through forces of deregulation, competition, and globalization, and growing demand for risk capacity and financing—some slippage occurred. Commercial banks were allowed to set up securities subsidiaries to underwrite debt issues (as long as overall revenues generated by the business were a small fraction of total revenues), investment banks could hold commercial banking licenses and both could dabble in insurance. By the time Gramm-Leach-Bliley came along, Wall Street firms were chomping at the bit to get into each other's businesses in a more significant way—and they did. Glass-Steagall is now gone, everyone can do everything, and they do. So J.P. Morgan Chase is a huge underwriter of debt and equity securities, Merrill Lynch has a commercial bank with a balance sheet of more than $100 billion, Citibank is part commercial bank, investment bank, asset manager, and insurer, Lehman Brothers owns a bank and a reinsurance company, and so forth. This model essentially replicates the universal bank and "bancassurance" blueprint that has existed in Europe for many decades.

It's hardly a surprise that the top banks on Wall Street drive so much of the world's financial business: they have the capital, distribution networks, technical skills, and marketing/trading prowess; they put the big deals together, help clients along, and try to cope with challenging, risky markets. We'll see most of these firms throughout the book because they are at the center of activity; and if they are at the center of activity, then they've almost certainly stumbled along the way—hurt some clients, made big mistakes in trading or lending, or failed to deliver to their shareholders. No one is immune on Wall Street! The cast of characters, in no particular order, includes:

- Citibank (incorporating the old Salomon unit, itself a 1990s merger of powerhouse trader Salomon and old-line retail firm Smith Barney).
- J.P. Morgan Chase (the granddaddy of the merged banks, featuring the remnants of Manufacturers Hanover, Chemical Bank, Chase Manhattan, J.P. Morgan, and Bank One)
- Morgan Stanley (the product of white-shoe investment bank Morgan Stanley and the Dean Witter retail shop [which was, for a little while, part of Sears])
- Merrill Lynch (the integrated institutional and retail firm, well represented on Main Street)
- Lehman Brothers (a bank that has come full circle—independent, then part of Shearson, then a combined part of American Express with Shearson and Hutton, then independent)
- Goldman Sachs (the prestigious investment bank that was the last major firm to convert from private partnership to public company, in the late 1990s)
- Bear Stearns (the proprietary trader and mortgage specialist)
- Credit Suisse First Boston (CSFB, the investment banking arm of Swiss-based Credit Suisse, incorporating the original First Boston entity, and retail and junk bond house Donaldson Lufkin and Jenrette [DLJ])
- Deutsche Bank (not a U.S. firm per se, but a major U.S. force through its acquisitions of Baltimore equity/M&A house Alex Brown and New York derivative bank Bankers Trust)
- Union Bank of Switzerland (UBS; again, not a U.S. firm, but a major U.S. force through its acquisitions of retail house Paine Webber and investment banking boutique Dillon Read)

We'll also be visiting some other Wall Street institutions in the book: a few second-tier securities firms that appear from time to time in particular segments of the market, including Lazard, A.G. Edwards, Piper Jaffray, and Schwab; a few big non–New York banks that try to have a go at it, such as Bank of America and Wachovia (with most of Prudential's brokerage force in tow); a couple of electronic trading platforms trying to challenge the status quo, including electronic communication networks like Archipelago and Instinet and on-line platforms like E-Trade and Ameritrade; the major exchanges, consisting of the NYSE, AMEX, Nasdaq, and the Chicago and New York futures exchanges; and, some of the big fund companies, like Alliance, Strong, Putnam, and Janus. We'll also check in on a few of the thousands of very small banks and brokers that get caught up in the maelstrom every so often, and a few that once existed but are no more: Drexel Burnham Lambert, Kidder Peabody, Gruntal, rest in peace. Most of our focus, though, is on the Street's big players—the leaders.

All of these institutions are important because they help tell our story and convey our theme. But it's worth remembering that they are simply the late-twentieth- and early-twenty-first-century embodiment of similar types of firms that have existed in the past, and a representation of those that will undoubt-edly exist in the future. Much of what I talk about in the book is a snapshot of the last few decades: the 1980s, 1990s, and early part of the millennium, a time when the Street's players have been involved in failures related to capital rais-ing, corporate and personal advice, fiduciary duties, and risk management. A time when problems like fraud, collusion, fiduciary breaches, mistreatment of clients, mispricing of deals, and risk losses seem to have become larger, more pronounced, and more egregious.

But the core problems aren't new. We could step back in time, to the late nineteenth and early twentieth centuries, and see J.P. Morgan, National City Bank, Kuhn Loeb, Seligman and Co., Goldman Sachs, Lehman, Speyer and Co., R. Whitney and Co., and others involved in similar problems: prejudicing shareholders and debtholders through the creation of steel and railroad trusts, pushing investors into leveraged pyramid schemes, urging excessive purchases of stocks on margin, repaying their bad loans by selling unwitting investors shiny new securities, engaging in collusive underwriting practices, ignoring due diligence and underwriting standards, allowing all manner of sales chicanery, spinning stocks to favored public officials, creating wash trades and fictitious orders, manipulating the markets through pool schemes and insider-driven bear raids, and so on. The banks of the modern era didn't create all the mis-behavior and abuse, just as they didn't invent poison pills, subordinated con-vertibles, payment-in-kind junk bonds, pool operators, market cornering, or interlocking trusts. The roots run deep.

So the issues we consider in this book aren't a sudden creation, they are simply the current manifestation of activities that date back many decades—new versions of old problems. But the issues are more vital than ever, because the Street's role is more significant and its failures more frequent and damag-ing. As we've said, the Street has demonstrated remarkable resilience over the years, overcoming mistakes, problems, and adversity to continue performing an effective role. But can it continue to do so if it ignores the problems? Harvard professor William Ripley, commenting on the state of Wall Street during the speculative 1920s, noted: "The first duty is to face the fact that there is something the matter . . . the house is not falling down—no fear of that! But there are queer little noises about, as of rats in the wall."[1] We can extend that observation to the industry of the millennium: we know there are rats in the wall, the question at hand is whether the population of rats will get so out of hand and do so much damage that the structural integrity of the house will actually be threatened. Many are rightly concerned about the integrity of the system. Some of those that have been involved in the industry for many decades view the Street's modern era problems as extremely significant: SEC Chairman William Donaldson (founder of DLJ and former head of the NYSE) has noted that Wall Street of the millennium is in a "legal and ethical quagmire. . . . [O]ccurrences [of problems] represent a fundamental betrayal of our nation's investors and are symptomatic of a disease that has afflicted far too many in the industry."[2] Former SEC Chairman Arthur Levitt echoes the view, noting that "the ethical loss is cataclysmic."[3] And Former Lazard partner Felix Rohatyn has observed: "We are, slowly but surely, causing serious damage to one of our greatest assets: the credibility of our financial system. . . . The last few years have shown that excess can come about when finance capitalism and modern technology are abused in the service of naked greed . . . our system cannot stand much more abuse."[4] It's not surprising that others inside and outside of the industry share similar views; the issues are serious and must be addressed.

With our stage now set, we are ready to explore the failure of Wall Street.

Chapter 2

WHEN THE INTENDED ROLE FAILS

Before we embark on the practical part of our Wall Street journey—the one that examines all the real problems—let's explore a bit of theory. This will help later on when we compare what's *supposed* to happen in the financial sector with what *actually* happens, and it will show us just how large the gap between the two can get. Let's start off by considering what happens, in a theoretical sense, when things go wrong. What happens when the five functions we just talked about aren't handled properly? What happens when the Street messes up? Since there is never a free lunch, someone has to pay. So who's paying?

SMOOTH SAILING

As we consider these questions, let's first think about what occurs when everything goes as planned. We mentioned in the last chapter that everyone wins when Wall Street is doing what it is supposed to do—a state we might term "smooth sailing."

The clients win because they get what they're looking for. In the corporate realm this might mean a properly priced stock or bond issue (e.g., cheap funding) that is well placed and trades nicely in the aftermarket. If it's an M&A deal, it could mean a nice target acquisition that's purchased at a fair premium and fits in with corporate plans. If it's an investment strategy based on derivatives, it'll mean a return that is commensurate with risk (it doesn't mean that it's a guaranteed money-winner—Wall Street doesn't usually guarantee returns on speculative deals—just that the strategy has the risk/return profile that the client expects). If it's risk management advice, then it could be a sound hedging strategy based on well-understood parameters and favorable execution levels. If we're talking about private clients, it could mean a well-balanced portfolio that performs as it should, sound research recommendations and financial advice, or great service in dealing with 401(k)s, retirement plans, and safe-custody issues.

The banks win because they earn good revenues on the deals they're putting together and the advice they're giving. They're servicing their clients properly, meaning they'll capture repeat business and win new business, generating more revenues. They're keeping their own houses in order, taking smart risks and earning the right returns, not stretching for extra basis points or ticks. They can trade and lend prudently and profitably, and they don't have to panic or play silly games. All of the folks working at the banks—from the executives down to the producers and controllers—are winning, too, because they've got a stable work environment and good compensation.

Bank shareholders win because they're seeing the value of their investments in Street firms rise steadily; if the banks are doing solid business, posting good earnings, keeping costs under control, treating the clients well, and not making mistakes, then investors will be encouraged, buy more shares, and push the stock prices up.

Creditors win because any money they've lent the Street is being repaid promptly, as agreed. The fact that banks are doing well means they're borrowing at the lower spreads accorded good credits, but that's fine because the money is being paid back with interest—there are no problem credits.

Regulators win because everyone is behaving like they're supposed to. No one is causing liquidity problems, generating excess volatility, or threatening the stability of the system, and no one is in financial jeopardy or trying to take advantage of clients. Everyone is obeying the letter and spirit of the law, and arbitration cases are the exception rather than the norm. There is no need for extra inspections, sanctions, fines, or censure—meaning no extra regulatory headaches.

And the economy wins. When Wall Street is doing well, other parts of the economy benefit. If banks are willing to lend and take risks, arrange good financing deals and acquisitions, and underwrite securities at the right price, they help companies grow. Corporate growth, in turn, fuels the economic expansion of a city, state, region, and country. Investors have a chance to put their savings and income to work in quality investments. A growing capital market generates more wealth for people and companies—meaning more savings, investment, reinvestment, consumption, and, ultimately, economic growth.

That's generally what happens when the sailing is smooth. But we know that the waters are rarely that calm or the wind speed that predictable. This idealized world is, unfortunately, a bit of a fabrication. So let's see what happens when the water gets rough.

CHOPPY WATERS

When a Street firm is not doing what it is supposed to, it is failing in one or more of its five core functions, and that means stakeholders are not receiving the value or service they expect. There are, of course, different kinds of failures; for our purposes we'll divide them broadly into "accidental stumbling" and "doing the wrong thing." The two may have the same unhappy ending, such as damaged clients, lost money. or tarnished reputations, but the causes are different: lack of capability on the one hand, and lack of ethics on the other. It's worth understanding the differences between the two because later in the book we'll be considering how to deal with their rather unique root causes.

Accidental Stumbling

A bank may not perform its duties properly as a result of accidental behaviors, such as mistakes or lack of knowledge. Someone takes his or her hand off the rudder and the boat runs aground. It's not malicious, conniving, or premeditated, but it's still a problem—and a common one at that. Given the complexity of the corporate world, companies make mistakes and can't be faulted for occasional slipups. Greater concerns arise when they happen repeatedly and, unfortunately, Street firms seem to suffer them frequently. Banks don't always learn lessons from the previous times they've run aground, so stakeholders suffer new losses—ones that are entirely avoidable. For instance, a bank can get the price of a transaction wrong and take a loss; that's no big deal, because a pricing mistake can happen. But if the bank gets it wrong five or seven times out of ten, week in and week out, then the problem is bigger. The same can happen on the client front: a bank may misvalue trades in a single client portfolio once or twice, but if it's doing the same thing with many client portfolios, month after month, then something is wrong. In either case problems may relate to lack of proper controls, discipline, or management attention. Again, the problems may be accidental, but the fact that they happen over and over raises serious questions.

Sometimes the evidence of accidental failure is relatively easy to spot. A bank, for example, misprices a junk bond deal. It may launch a deal for a risky company with an interest coupon that's far too low, causing would-be investors to walk away. If the bank has committed to underwrite the deal, it will get stuck with the bonds (i.e., the bought deal scenario we mentioned in chapter 1). It then has two options. It can swallow its pride and admit that it was wrong, take a big writedown by selling the securities at a discount to someone who sees value at the lower price, and show the loss in the daily P&L statement. Or it can keep believing that investors are wrong and its price is right, and that time (and maybe the market) will bail it out. It'll take the bank awhile to find a new clearing level, and, until it does, it has some "stuck inventory" on its balance sheet (which, incidentally, draws a capital charge and has to be funded); the bank's controllers will also require gradual writedowns of the bond every week or month, meaning a slow bleed in the P&L. Either way, the evidence of a stumble is there: an immediate hit to profits or a slow bleed and a bloated balance sheet.

Sometimes, though, it's hard to know when a bank has stumbled: some accidents never come to light (Wall Street has lots of dark secrets that are buried deep in the basement). For instance, a bank may have lots of losses from operational errors—bad trade confirmations, misdirected funds, accounts receivable reconciliation errors, suspense account problems, corporate action mistakes, and so on. You'll never hear about these failures (and they are failures, because they cost money and are avoidable). They're hidden from public view because they happen in small increments of $1,000, $10,000, or $100,000 rather than the $5 million or $10 million that the bond desk eats on the failed junk underwriting, which everyone gets to read about in the financial press. This is death by a thousand cuts—one in which a hundred or a thousand mistakes at $100,000 each adds up to real money.

Doing the Wrong Thing

Sometimes a bank fails by knowingly doing things that it shouldn't do. This moves beyond accidental stumbling into the more serious realm of doing the wrong thing: violating the spirit and/or the letter of the law, and demonstrating general disregard for clients, investors, and regulators. The losses aren't necessarily bigger than the accidental ones, but the causes and motivations can be more unsettling because they involve a breach of ethical behavior, and possibly even laws and regulations. It's like purposely navigating the boat through a treacherous shipping lane, knowing it's dangerous and illegal and that others are being placed in jeopardy, but wanting to come out ahead of all the rest. This sort of failure can take many forms: knowingly giving retail investors bad advice in order to boost commissions; persuading an unsophisticated company to purchase a highly toxic and completely inappropriate derivative; producing manifestly false company research in order to win more business for the bank;

stuffing unauthorized trade tickets in desk drawers to cover losses; misvaluing hard-to-price transactions internally to increase reported profits; and so on. The endgame in most instances seems to be money. In the search for revenues, profits, and bonuses, some overly aggressive Wall Streeters (and, sometimes, larger business units and whole firms) forget the basic tenets of good behavior and just loot and pillage wherever they can.

Spotting these types of failures can be difficult, because those involved usually have a vested interest in obfuscating for as long as possible. Though most folks tend to own up to mistakes and accidents, those who take advantage of clients or short-circuit internal controls will do their best to keep things buried for a long time (and again, it's not necessarily confined to individuals—groups and firms can be involved, too). Sometimes things don't come to light for many years, until losses or other problems have grown so large that they just can't be hidden anymore. And maybe not until the culpable parties are long gone (having pocketed generous compensation, of course). For instance, several years into a risky swap trade a client company may realize that it has lost buckets of money: only then does it question the bank, its sales practices, valuation procedures, risk disclosures—and decide it has been taken for a ride. The first time senior management at the bank learns what's going on is when it's served legal papers by the client's attorneys. Till then, no one, except the swap marketer, may even know that the client is bleeding. (We'll see examples of this in chapter 4 when we consider cases involving Bankers Trust, J.P. Morgan, and Merrill Lynch.) Or a crafty trader may slip a few trade tickets in the desk drawer, keeping one, two, or three steps ahead of risk managers, internal auditors, and controllers, especially if she knows how to circumvent aspects of technology, control, and reporting (and the crafty ones usually do). So unauthorized trades pile up for months or years, everyone oblivious until the losses are just too big to hide. (We'll see examples of this in chapter 7 when we take a look at Merrill Lynch, Barings, and Allfirst, each of which has lost lots of money through these kinds of infractions). Multiply these kinds of transgressions by a hundred or a thousand and you get whole departments or firms that are doing the wrong thing.

We'll explore many instances of accidental failure and unethical behavior in the next few chapters; these will show just how choppy the waters can actually get.

WHY DOES IT HAPPEN?

Why does the Street stumble or do the wrong thing? Why does it engage in activities that hurt or prejudice others? There are actually lots of reasons, some of them firm specific, others industry wide, and some fueled by a lax external environment. We'll talk more about specific reasons for failure in part II, but let's set the stage by briefly noting a few of the things that can cause problems.

At a micro level, a firm may be plagued by bad mismanagement, in which directors and executives don't know what's going on, don't care, or actually condone bad practices. They may chase ill-advised strategies, take too much risk, or put profits ahead of clients. A firm may also suffer from conflicts of interest, misaligned incentives, poor ethics, weak controls, or a dearth of skills and knowledge. Any one of these on its own can be enough to cause serious problems; put a few of them together and things can get really ugly (and, don't forget, this isn't a strictly theoretical discussion; it's grounded in real-life examples, as we'll soon see).

Of course, failure isn't confined to a single bank. Sometimes the whole industry has problems—the whole flotilla gets caught in the same churning water and churns it up even more. This isn't surprising when we realize that the Street has a strong herd mentality. When a number of banks (with huge balance sheets, risk appetites, and profit pressures) chase after the same business, you can bet broader shock waves will ripple through the system if they all run aground at the same time. Everyone will feel it: the financial industry, the corporate sector, the regulatory community, and the economy at large.

Wall Street commands formidable resources. The combined capital that the top firms put to work in trading, underwriting, lending, and speculating is breathtaking—meaning that if everyone is doing the same thing at the same time, the possibility of systemic dislocation arises if (or when) there is a misstep. For instance, if everyone is lending imprudently to the same industry simultaneously, they are introducing massive leverage into that sector, lowering its overall creditworthiness, and increasing the specter of widespread default (as was the case with emerging markets in the post-petrodollar recycling period of the 1970s and early 1980s, commercial real estate companies and junk-rated borrowers in the late 1980s, technology-media-telecom (TMT) companies in the late 1990s, and so on). When things reach a point of excess, a whole sector can collapse, meaning losses for stakeholders and concerns for regulators (e.g., a halt in production, massive layoffs, and economic contraction). It may trigger a knock-on effect that causes related industries to run aground. It may damage consumers, creditors, and suppliers and require bailouts or restitution. Similar herd moves can occur in other areas, too. If all of the banks are doing sloppy due diligence work and letting lots of weak issuers into the capital markets, default frequency could rise across the board. If all of the banks are producing hyped-up research to entice investors to jump back in the market, the investors are going to get hit en masse when the true financial colors of the companies come to light. If all of the banks are advising their corporate clients to buy up competitors in a particular industry, there may be significant overpayment and the creation of firms with much less enterprise value. If all of the banks are telling their institutional investors that they should buy souped-up exotic options on emerging markets, then all of the clients are going to blow up when the target countries head south.

Though failure by an individual firm to perform its role is concerning, the systemic angle is troubling because problems and losses are no longer confined to a firm and its immediate circle of stakeholders. A systemic dislocation can hurt those that are minding their own business and are completely unaware of what Street firms may be doing. And dislocations that result in bailouts of "too-big-to-fail" banks, hedge funds, or entire countries create moral hazards. If the deep pockets (read: taxpayers) are there to bail out Wall Street because it has lent too much, or taken too much risk, or failed to implement good controls, or advised its clients to do unwise things, then the behaviors continue unchecked and unabated, and the intended role continues to fail.

As we'll see later on, some of the Street's failures are permitted to occur because of problems in the external operating environment. Specifically, regulators and auditors, who are meant to act as checks and balances and to ensure fair play, accurate reporting and solid controls, sometimes fall down on the job. When they are no longer effective in providing that extra layer of oversight, Street firms have fairly wide discretion to behave as they choose, sometimes with unpleasant results. If regulations are inadequate or go unheeded, or if auditors aren't detecting internal control problems, then instances of failure can increase.

WHO PAYS?

When things go pear-shaped on Wall Street, someone's going to pay, and lots of the problems have large price tags. Who pays for these failures depends to a large degree on the kind of problem and the size of the loss. For starters, let's divide things into two camps: the outsiders and the insiders.

The Outsiders

The typical Wall Street bank has a number of external stakeholders that hope, and expect, to derive some benefit from the firm's activities and behavior. Benefits can take different forms: they can be financial (such as an increase in the share price or the successful completion of a deal), legal or regulatory (such as compliance with rules and regulations), or systemic (such as contribution to the wealth, welfare, and stability of the community). When a bank fails to do what it is supposed to, these benefits are placed in jeopardy. Wall Street firms don't operate in a bubble and shouldn't be oblivious to those around them, though they sometimes are. Let's see how some of these external parties may be forced to pay when the Street falls short.

We start by considering the impact on a bank's *investors,* since they can be the biggest losers when things go awry. Indeed, we'll see that they often draw the short straw, dipping into their pockets time after time to cover problems. Investors supply publicly held Wall Street firms with risk capital (and all the big firms are now public, Goldman having floated in 1999); that capital is used to fund operations. Though banks by definition are highly leveraged, (with balance sheet assets to equity of 20:1 (generally), 30:1 (sometimes), 50:1 (a breach of regulatory requirements and big trouble), they still need an adequate supply of equity capital as a financial cushion to take risks, underwrite business, and satisfy regulators. So investors supply funds if they believe a firm's prospects are good. In exchange for the capital, investors receive shares in the bank, which convey some legal (control) rights and some financial (rent) rights. Though legal rights (e.g., power to vote at the annual general meeting, right to bring direct and derivative lawsuits) are very important, we'll focus on financial rights for the moment.

An investor owning a share of stock is entitled to a prorata share of the future cash flows of a firm, discounted at some relevant rate, along with periodic dividends. If the firm is profitable, the share price rises and dividends grow, and the investor gets a fair return on capital invested. If the company's cash flows are riskier (more uncertain), the investor will demand a greater return. No rational investor will supply capital to a risky company in exchange for a risk-free return; he or she will just go buy some Treasury bonds. There is thus an expectation of proper return. Wall Street firms are risky entities: we've said they are highly leveraged and exposed to a host of risks (credit, market, liquidity, legal), and they are very dependent on the strength of economic cycles, business activity, and the financial markets. These variables combine to produce volatile revenues. Wall Street firms are also notorious for being sloppy with costs. Many banks have large cost bases (e.g., compensation accounts for more than 50 percent of revenues during boom times), meaning less money drops down to the bottom line and into the pockets of investors. In bad times most banks go through phases of cost cutting (slashing head count, pulling back on travel and entertainment, lowering compensation); but as soon as things start perking up, any modicum of expense discipline disappears, and it's back to wasting corporate resources. Bank investors know all of this, so they penalize financial firms by giving them lower valuation multiples and expecting higher returns to compensate for the unpredictable nature of the earnings streams.

Knowing all of this, it's not too difficult to figure out how shareholders wind up paying when Wall Street messes up. It can come in different forms, but it always hits the bottom line. If a firm accidentally stumbles, it's going to post lower revenues, operating income, and/or net income. It doesn't really matter what has happened: perhaps big deals have been lost to the competition through silly mistakes, some IPOs have been badly mispriced, a huge block trade has gone sour, some large model errors have been discovered, management has blown its expense budget, the firm has decided to close down some offices or subsidiaries or lay off a bunch of employees—the bottom line is going to be lower than it should be, meaning less for the investor. If a firm fails because it is doing something wrong and gets caught, it can mean all of the above *plus* loss of additional revenues from business that is redirected to competitors and an increase in onetime charges to cover lawsuits, settlements, and regulatory fines. The net to the bottom line is even lower than it should be, and the investor loses again. And if things are really bad—perhaps the firm has been sanctioned and penalized very severely, meaning creditors have grown nervous and pulled back on their liquidity lines, and the credit rating agencies have downgraded the firm's debt—then costs associated with financial distress rise (e.g., higher borrowing costs, greater employee retention expenses, poorer supplier terms), and even less money flows to the bottom line. Not only do investors lose out on the capitalized value of future earnings, they may suffer additional capital erosion if others start selling on the bad news; the brave investors who continue to hang tough suffer a negative return on capital. In fact, bank investors routinely bear the brunt of Wall Street's misadventures: lost revenues, trading losses, credit losses, excess costs, restructuring charges, fines, and settlements, which together add up to one big disappointment (and all of this ignores anything associated with the external environment, like poor economic conditions and low business volume).

Investors aren't the only ones who pay, of course. We also have to consider the *clients,* who are exposed to Wall Street's foul-ups very directly. Clients want good service at a fair price, and they expect to be treated properly. Not surprisingly, all kinds of things can wrong on the Street to work against these fundamental (and seemingly reasonable) client expectations, leading to some kind of loss: overcharging on trades, deals, or acquisitions; giving poor advice that leads to bad decisions; failing to properly perform a range of fiduciary duties, including due diligence and safe custody; prejudicing client positions by front-running or colluding on trades; and so forth. Sometimes clients eat the losses directly because they can't fight back, or it's not worth the hassle. Other times they decide to go to arbitration or court in hope of receiving some restitution; this can, of course, be an expensive and time-consuming process, meaning more costs for the client. There is a class-action system that permits lawsuits to be brought against firms that have done the wrong thing, and judgments can go in favor of the plaintiffs, but overall restitution is often a fraction of what has been lost. (Plus it still leaves losers: the investors we've just mentioned have to fork over more money because the bank failed in its duties and caused the clients to lose.[1])

Creditors are losers when things are dire enough to cause a Street firm to default. Fortunately, such defaults aren't terribly common. Though many small brokers have gone under since the mid-nineteenth century (e.g., Ketchum and Sons, Kenyon Cox, R. Whitney and Co., Pickard and Co., Gregory and Co., and so on), not many large Street firms have collapsed over the years (just a handful, like Drexel and Thomson McKinnon), meaning creditors (including Street firms who may, themselves, be lenders) haven't had to pay up. (Of course a different problem arises when Street firms are the ones lending imprudently to companies or sectors that default ([e.g., emerging nations, Enron, WorldCom, hedge funds]; that's when Street firms, as creditors, get hit through actions of their own making—but that's a problem for their investors, who bear the credit losses as a charge to earnings.)

Regulators can also be hurt by Wall Street's failures. The degree of damage depends on the depth and breadth of the problem. If problems are contained within a single firm (e.g., a bank is found to have abused clients, violated insider trading laws, reported false financial information, or performed bad due diligence), regulators don't suffer much at all. More serious issues arise when problems are endemic to the entire Street—when lots of firms have published bad research, taken excessive risk in illiquid markets or lent to unstable sectors, or sold clients nasty derivatives with the barest of warnings. That's when regulators can suffer significant damage to their reputations: they may be accused of falling down on the job, not detecting problems in the making or allowing them to grow to the point of significant damage, or being technically incompetent. Sometimes regulators are thrust in the uncomfortable role of having to contend with broader financial dislocations. If the Street's problems are significant enough to shatter investor confidence, push clients to the sidelines, and threaten liquidity, regulators may find themselves orchestrating or facilitating a bailout in order to calm market fears (as in 1984 with Continental Illinois Bank and 1998 with Long Term Capital Management [LTCM]). This is a pressure-filled exercise that has to be handled with extreme care, and it's one that typically winds up costing lots of money (sometimes funded by taxpayers, meaning a new set of losers).

The Insiders

The damage wrought when things go wrong is not confined to outsiders—Street firms have many internal stakeholders, including *employees* and *executives,* who can suffer as well. In fact, it's kind of ironic that with so much at stake these folks aren't even more diligent in making sure things don't blow up or the wrong behavior doesn't proceed unchecked. Every time a bank steps on a land mine and loses money or suffers a blow to its reputation, insiders lose. Again, what they lose, and how much, depends on the severity of the problem. At a minimum there's loss of compensation. When a bank repeatedly suffers excessively large credit or trading losses, or faces lawsuits and fines, its income gets squeezed—meaning bonus pools get cut (for mid- and lower-level employees, at any rate). If things are more serious—maybe the problems are larger and the infractions more flagrant, and the markets are heading into a downturn—then pink slips start circulating. Employees and managers are at real risk of losing their jobs, because when banks cut jobs they tend to cut deep: not 1 percent or 5 percent of the staff, but 10 percent, or 20 percent, or even more (meaning everyone is out of work at the same time, trying to find a job, compounding personal financial woes).

Interestingly, CEOs, COOs, presidents, and senior business heads often dodge the bullets. Even though they are supposed to be driving the firm's activities and should thus be responsible for the bad as well as the good, they often (though, granted, not always) escape scot-free when the hammer falls. Their punishment comes from having bonuses slashed from $15 million or $20 million to only $5 million or $7 million—real belt-tightening stuff. Curiously, board directors often escape unharmed as well. Even though directors are agents of the shareholders and are supposed to oversee and guide the corporation in its activities, they often plead ignorance or lack of knowledge when things go wrong (the see-no-evil, hear-no-evil approach to governance) and walk away unscathed, happy to pocket their director stipends but not to assume responsibility.

And in the final analysis, the firm's reputation also suffers when the intended role fails. If we think of reputation as an amalgam of all aspects of the firm—its activities, intellectual powers, experience, creativity, and web of contacts—then it is surely an internal party that winds up paying, just like employees and executives. We've already noted that Street firms have little to fall back on but their intangibles: brainpower, experience, trust, integrity, and goodwill. Accidental stumbling and doing the wrong thing can bruise the intangibles. Though goodwill is a bit nebulous and hard to pin down in dollar terms (though market cap can serve as a proxy), it's bound to get hurt when clients start suing over bad advice, bankers commit fraud, traders take unauthorized positions that lead to big losses, or sales desks lie to their clients about the riskiness of trades. All of these things cast a pall over the firm and its reputation. Creating goodwill is a long and arduous process that demands diligent and honest work by everyone inside the firm; damaging it can be done quickly, without much thought. In some instances it's even enough to drive away future business or propel a firm into much more dire straits (as was the case with Drexel, Bankers Trust, Prudential, Kidder Peabody, Salomon). When the firm pays for mistakes (or misbehavior) with its reputation, all of the insiders, and many of the outsiders, lose.

The bottom line is that Wall Street has an important function to perform. It is theoretically and practically responsible for doing the five things we talked about in the last chapter and tends to do them pretty well. But it also fails, through bad management, ethics, strategies, and controls. When it does, lots of parties—investors, clients, employees, regulators—can get hurt. And sometimes those who should get hurt—those who should take greater responsibilities for bad decisions, strategies, execution, and behavior—don't.

With this little background in hand we're now ready to explore actual instances of Wall Street's failure.

Chapter 3

PROBLEMS RAISING CAPITAL

We kick off our discussion on Wall Street's failures by looking at the process of raising capital. We've already said that the Street's single most important job is to raise debt and equity for companies (and supranationals and sovereigns) so that they can fund their operations, pursue investment and expansion plans, finance productive research and development, and buy up competitors. And capital is, of course, the raw material that investors need in order to put their money to work; without capital instruments like stocks and bonds, investors wouldn't have a way of earning a return. It's simple: if the Street isn't helping raise capital, financial flows stall and the global economy comes to a shuttering halt.

A bank's role in all of this is to act as an intermediary between various parties. It talks to the company to see how much capital it needs, it talks to the investor base to see what kind of returns they're looking for (and what kind of risks they might be willing to take), and it talks to other banks to see if they might be willing to chip in on a deal (though no sharing of the coveted "lead manager," "lead arranger," or "lead placement agent" roles appearing on the deal tombstones, of course—that's public relations gold). If all the stars align, the bank prints and places the deal, and then supports it with secondary trading and research coverage. As we said earlier, a bank sometimes has to put up its own capital to fund the deal: it makes the loan or buys the bonds or equity with its own cash, and then tries to unload what it can in the secondary market. This is obviously a riskier way of doing business, because if investors or syndicate banks disappear as the deal is being printed, the bank has to spend days, weeks, or months moving the paper, often at a loss. There are easily thousands (and probably more) of these "bought deal" horror stories, with lots of gory details that never make the light of day. Every bank on the Street has its battle scars, and in a competitive world in which other banks are willing to use their balance sheets to win business, it's an unfortunate, and perhaps permanent, reality. Indeed, the day of the civilized, low-risk best-efforts/book-building transaction may have come and gone (investors in Street firms, take note); companies know that they can get committed funding by playing the banks against one another, and banks are often so eager to win the deals that they're willing to play along.

Unfortunately, the capital-raising function is fraught with potential pitfalls. To put all of this into context, let's look at three things that can go wrong: raising too much capital, raising too little capital, and mispricing the capital that is actually raised.

TOO MUCH MONEY

Raising capital, whether debt or equity, is good for a company. But raising too much capital, more than is really needed, is not—it's dangerous. For instance, if a bank raises too much debt for a company, it jeopardizes that firm's financial position to the point of creating financial distress: excessively large interest payments, decreased financial flexibility, lower credit ratings. Though a bank should know better than to lend too much, it often ignores prudent behavior (and even its own internal credit policies) and lends recklessly. Why? To earn fees, climb higher in the league tables, or position itself for the client's future M&A business or equity offerings—or all of the above. And to keep up with the rest of the pack, who may be raising money for the same company. It's part of the Street herd mentality we mentioned in the last chapter: when one bank discovers a niche in which it can raise debt capital profitably, others quickly join in. The attractive spreads and fees that are available on Day 1 compress as more banks throw money at eager borrowers in the industry du jour. No matter—as long as there are takers for the money, the bankers seem to be able to persuade managers, credit committees, and investors to keep funding, till the risk/return is badly out of whack. How many times in the past few decades have we seen the banks acting like lemmings, all falling off the cliff at once as they rush to print more debt deals? Many times, in fact: way too much debt for emerging markets, commercial real estate, savings and loans, LBOs, technology, media, and telecom, energy, the airlines. A frenzy of lending proceeds till a point of excess is reached. Then borrowers can't pay their interest or principal anymore, they default, investors lose on the bonds, and banks lose on their loans.

The same is true in raising equity. If a bank tries to bring a company to the public markets through an IPO before that company is actually ready (i.e., too much equity for the wrong company), the end result may be a rotten apple for investors buying the stock—the price will plummet as everyone figures out that the company isn't all that it's cracked up to be. Or if a bank is issuing more equity for a company that's already gone public—just for the sake of expanding the company's paid-in capital account, and not because the firm actually needs it—then the company and its investors lose out, because equity capital is expensive and dilutive. If a bank tries to bring entire sectors to market at the same time, as is wont to happen, then things can get very treacherous; lack of discipline leads to too many questionable deals and competing alternatives, which together become the kindling for a speculative bonfire. So why would a Street bank print an IPO for a company that is decidedly not IPO material, or float new equity for a company that's already listed, or do the same for a whole sector? Same reasons—fees, league tables, future business (but especially the fees: 7 percent, versus sub 1 percent for debt).

The Street has fallen all over itself many times trying to lend lots of money to firms that can't always handle the interest burden, to print more IPOs for companies that aren't ready for the markets, or to do add-ons for those that don't need them. Which means excessive leverage, large interest burdens, financial distress, higher all-in capital costs, poor investor returns, and shareholder dilution—none of them particularly good.

Too Much Debt

The Street has been busy printing bonds and loans for eager borrowers for decades, and sometimes it just prints too much. It injects too much leverage into companies, industries, and the system at large, leverage that can be sustained only when market conditions are optimal: low rates, stable inflation, robust investment, active consumers. When things weaken and the operating environment is no longer benign, the leverage becomes a huge burden. Of course, Wall Street's job is to act as a capital conduit, transporting the money from "A," where it's in surplus, to "B," where it's in deficit. But Wall Street's real job is to be a *discriminating* capital conduit, making sure that B can handle the obligation to repay. This all goes way back, of course: in the 1920s Charles Mitchell, head of National City (one of Citibank's forefathers), directed his troops to underwrite lots of bonds for Latin American governments that couldn't really handle the debt burden, and to sell them to unwitting investors. Most of the bonds wound up in default, leaving investors with losses; no matter, the bank moved on to a new sector. National City wasn't alone in this business, of course; several other banks did similar things, with very similar results. Too much debt, courtesy of Wall Street.

During the 1970s newly found oil wealth coming out of the Middle East led to petrodollar recycling: oil producing nations deposited dollars with international banks and Wall Street firms, and the banking community lent the money on a LIBOR basis (e.g., London Interbank Offered Rate, a floating interbank rate) to a host of borrowers, including emerging nations in Latin America, Africa, and Asia. As financial volatility and inflation mounted in the late 1970s, global interest rates starting rising; because LIBOR floats, the petrodollar loans became more expensive for the emerging market borrowers to service. By the turn of the decade the credits looked decidedly shaky, and by the early 1980s the jig was up: in August 1982 Mexico, which was going through a few home-grown structural problems, told the world that it couldn't handle its debt load. Most other borrowers followed in lockstep. Brazil, Argentina, the Philippines, Morocco, Nigeria, and all the other recipients of oil largesse couldn't pay, so everything had to be restructured. Citi, J.P., Chase, Chemical, Bank of America, and others were forced to take massive reserves to cover all that excessive lending; the borrowers and the bank lenders (no, their investors) lost. Too much debt, courtesy of Wall Street.

And then it happened again. From 1980 until the eve of the 1987 crash, nonfinancial corporate debt arranged by the Street reached $1.8 trillion, an all-time record. The large absolute dollar amount and the high interest-rate environment meant that the average U.S. company was using half of its earnings just to service principal and interest. Wall Street was being as efficient and creative as possible in arranging all of these debt financings: it targeted a range of borrowers and offered access to debt capital through a slew of instruments. Corporate borrowers came in all shapes and sizes: small and large, unsophisticated and sophisticated, well meaning and greedy. Perhaps most notable was a significant decrease in the credit quality of the borrowers—the Street seemed to be less discriminating than ever before. In fact, the hostile takeovers, LBOs, reverse takeovers, greenmail, and other excesses of the "greed is good" movement drove lots of this leverage. The cycle spawned widespread use of junk bonds; banks such as Drexel, Merrill, Morgan Stanley, and DLJ underwrote bonds for all kinds of issuers, popularizing the instrument as never before. And greater amounts of subordination were introduced into the process, through instruments such as junior subordinated bonds, payment-in-kind (PIK) bonds (securities paying interest in the form of more bonds rather than cash), and reset PIKs (or death spirals, securities with a coupon that increases in order to keep the securities trading at par—meaning a growing interest burden as the borrower deteriorates and a near certain spiral to corporate death); increasingly subordinated investors suffered larger losses when issuers ultimately went under. Then came the October 1987 crash, a period of poor economic conditions, and the start of record debt defaults, which reached an all-time high in 1990–91. The end result: companies, bond investors, banks (no, bank investors) all lost. Too much debt, courtesy of Wall Street.

And then it happened again. Between 1990 and 2002 the outstanding debt capital of nonfinancial companies increased yet again, from $2.4 trillion to $4.9 trillion. Certainly some of this leverage was appropriate and justifiable; as we've said, the global economy needs capital to keep the wheels turning. But things got a bit frothy, as they always do, and the extra leverage again began looking unhealthy and unmanageable. When national economies and markets cracked in 2001 (and a couple of major corporate scandals brought about several record bankruptcies), global defaults hit new highs: $119 billion in 2001 and $178 billion in 2002, back up at levels not seen since the leverage binge of the early 1990s. Though lots of bondholders got hurt the banks (no, bank investors) had to eat their share of the losses, too: all those deals cost them an estimated $37 billion in 2002 alone.[1] Too much debt, courtesy of Wall Street.

Up to the Gills in Telecom Debt

Different sectors tap into the Wall Street debt machine during specific economic cycles and industrial phases: during the 1970s it was emerging nations, conglomerates, and transportation companies; in the 1980s it was commercial real estate firms, energy companies, and lower-rated credits from various industries; in the early 1990s it was airline and industrial companies. And from the mid-1990s till the dawn of the millennium, it was the telecom companies. The telcos were big, big borrowers—ready, willing, and able to borrow whatever they could, for at least three purposes: to buy up competitors, expand into optical networking and fiber optics, and purchase wireless spectrum/licenses. All three motivations appear good, reasonable, and justifiable—but only to a degree. Because there comes a time when it no longer makes sense for borrowers to borrow or lenders to lend. When there is too much capital chasing acquisitions, laying fiber, or bidding up finite spectrum, things can get ugly; when the acquisitions don't work out, the fiber stays dark or the economics of mobile telephony fall apart, the debt becomes burdensome. And that, of course, is just what happened in the telecom sector in the millennium.

Banks lent very aggressively to telcos, particularly during the key period of 1998 to 2000. All of the major firms were present, underwriting telecom bonds, acting as direct lenders, or both: Citibank, J.P. Morgan Chase, Deutsche, Barclays, Morgan Stanley, CSFB, UBS, Goldman Sachs, Merrill Lynch. The banks threw money at all sorts of firms: good ones, bad ones, established ones, unproven ones. In 1998, outstanding debt granted to telecommunications companies was $38 billion; by December 2000 that figure had risen to a staggering $250 billion. That was far too much debt, as it happens, because when things started heading south and the hypothetical "disaster scenarios" started becoming reality, telco defaults soared. In fact, by late 2000 things started looking so precarious that the Financial Stability Forum (a group of regulators and finance ministers from 11 countries), the United Kingdom's Financial Services Authority, and a few other agencies, cautioned the banks: reduce debt funding to the U.S. and European telecom sectors, because leverage is reaching unsustainable levels. (The FSA noted that 34 banks had very concentrated debt exposure in the sector; some had as much as 5 percent of their assets and 40 percent of their equity out to telecoms. Look out.)

Of course some of the borrowing was economically justifiable. Industry expansion, capital investment, and research and development, are all important aspects of what the telecommunications sector has to do to advance; that's how new technologies are created and new services offered. But at some point it all got way out of hand: banks were far too willing to lend against overvalued assets or very dicey revenue projections, and helped put some companies on a slippery slope. Telco CFOs and CEOs get some share of the blame, too, as they were unrealistic in their assessments and apparently couldn't say "no" to their friendly bankers. But banks lost all discipline in their pursuit of more business. Naturally, the orgy of debt ended badly. In 2001 and 2002 telecom companies defaulted in large numbers and dollar amounts, because their leverage was simply unsustainable in the business environment. Telcos accounted for 26 percent of dollar defaults in 2001 and an astonishing 56 percent in 2002. That's $29 billion of defaults in 2001 and $91 billion in 2002. Lots of major borrowers went under, including WorldCom, Qwest, Telewest, NTL, Marconi, United Pan European Communications (to be sure, in some instances there were other factors contributing to bankruptcy, e.g., WorldCom's revenue fraud—but the primary, if not sole, cause for all was massive leverage that was impossible to support in a weak operating environment).

Banks that lend or underwrite bonds are meant to be very conservative in their evaluation of a company's ability to repay debt. They are supposed to know whether payback can occur under a whole host of scenarios, including disasters; they are supposed to avoid overlending to a sector; they are supposed to identify two, and even three, sources of repayment so that their own books don't become burdened with credit losses and their own investors don't get burned. But it seems that a few of them forgot to do all of that, as evidenced by *a quarter-trillion dollars* of debt washing around the telecom sector. Loaded to the gills.

––––––––––––––––––

There are many, many examples of companies and nations that have borrowed far too much over the years, thanks mainly to Wall Street's willingness to loosen the purse strings and "make things happen": Mexico, Argentina, Brazil, Indonesia, Korea, Iridium, Global Crossing, WorldCom, Enron, Vivendi, Swissair, Marconi, RailTrack, Kirch, Daewoo, Xerox, Time Warner—we're going to run out of space and ink, so we'll stop. But you get the point. Of course borrowers have to bear some responsibility for their actions. It's unlikely that anyone from the Street is holding a gun to the head of some CFO or finance minister, demanding that he or she sign up for a revolving credit facility or issue some floating rate notes. Whatever leverage borrowers assume ought to be consistent with their strategic goals (acquisition, internal expansion, market share, infrastructure development, geographic footprint), as well as their budgets and cost of capital, and if it's not, then they have to be faulted. But let's face it, investment bankers, lending officers, and capital markets specialists are smooth talkers: their job is to sell products and services—including loans, bonds, reset PIKs—and sell they do.

As we've said, the Street needs to act as a conduit in raising debt capital: that is one of its jobs. But it should be raising funds for the right borrowers on the right terms, not for everyone who wants to take out a loan or tap the capital markets. A leveraged company can still be a good borrower and credit risk—as long as everything about a debt financing transaction is thoroughly analyzed, well understood, and appropriate, and the returns being earned by the bank are adequate. But maybe the Street shouldn't be pitching aggressively to raise funds for a mega-leveraged telecom company laying more dark fiber at the peak of the TMT boom, or an illiquid Indonesian conglomerate known to engage in graft and corruption, or a Russian energy company with shaky financials and half of its assets stripped away. And when the Street gets unsolicited requests for money, maybe it should perform extremely intensive investigations and due diligence to figure out whether the potential borrower is really worthy. Wall Street ought to know all of this, yet too often it prints deals anyway—because there are fees, league table ranking, and bonuses at stake. Remember, the loans banks raise or the securities they issue are going to wind up on their balance sheets or in the hands of investors—and if things go wrong, they'll get burned, and so will investors. Even though the Street should remember this lesson every time a borrower files for bankruptcy or declares a moratorium, it routinely seems to forget. Too much debt, too many clever leverage structures, and not enough really discriminating behavior mean lots of credit losses for banks, bank shareholders, and outside investors. Ex-Citibank CEO Walter Wriston once noted that "judgment comes from experience and experience comes from bad judgment." It seems that lending bankers are stuck on the latter part of that thought.

WorldCom's Debt Burden

WorldCom, the giant telecom company, became the largest bankruptcy in U.S. history when it filed for Chapter 11 in July 2002. At the time of its filing it listed a staggering $37 billion of debt (on par with the amount entire countries like Malaysia and Chile borrow externally). The company's downfall, reflected in a share price that slid from $72 to $1 in four years, came from an unhealthy combination of mismanagement, rumors of accounting manipulations, and excessive personal loans taken by the CEO. But it was aided and abetted by a spectacular, Street-arranged debt feast—one that reduced the company's financial flexibility dramatically. A syndicate of banks including J.P. Morgan, Citibank, and Bank of America led the charge in raising $29 billion of bond financing and $8 billion in loans for World-Com over a five-year span. That's $37 billion of debt. Much of it was used to pay for legitimate, if overpriced, acquisitions like MCI, UUnet, Skytel, and CompuServe, and some of it was used for "general corporate purposes," aka the great catchall slush fund. No matter: it was simply too much for the company to handle—it came far too quickly for the company to digest properly and created a huge interest tab.

Perhaps the lenders should have known better. Perhaps with each new request for funds from WorldCom's finance team the banks should have stopped to investigate just how much more debt the firm could absorb without seriously threatening its financial future (and the financial well-being of bond investors and other syndicate lenders). Or maybe they did, as they managed to offload a fair (though not total) amount of WorldCom credit exposure to mutual funds, pension funds, insurance companies and retail investors (and protected pieces of their remaining risk through the credit derivative market). Smart. For instance, when Citibank underwrote an $11 billion bond for WorldCom in the spring of 2001 it found big buyers in the form of CalPERS, Met Life, Deutsche Asset Management, Wellington, Vanguard, Alliance, Barclays, and Prudential. And guess where half of the bond proceeds went? Back to the bank syndicate, to repay short-term loans and commercial paper (freeing up bank-supplied backup lines in the process). So the bondholders wound up taking on more risk than the banks. Smart, and kind of reminiscent of some of the Street's behavior in the early twentieth century—the kind of behavior that led to the creation of Glass-Steagall (you know, issuing securities to investors in order to repay questionable bank loans—repaying loans by issuing securities is okay, but not if the banks know that the company is in trouble). But the bondholders aren't done with the bankers: they sued them for bad due diligence on the bond deal, which we'll talk about later in the book—that's failure of a different sort.

When WorldCom finally emerged from Chapter 11 under the MCI banner, it did so with a much cleaner balance sheet: only $4 billion of net debt, and a commitment from management to keep borrowing under control. Let's hope the firm remembers the damage all that leverage did—and can keep the bankers at bay when they come calling.

Too Much Equity

The danger isn't just debt, of course. Raising too much equity can be a problem as well. Though we typically think that more equity is better than more debt—who wants all that leverage, anyway?—that's true only when the equity issuance is being done for the right reasons and for the right companies. For instance, back in the 1920s the Street issued lots of stock, even for companies that were very dodgy; in a 12-month span before the Great Crash, the Street underwrote a record $5 billion of new equity issues, with lots of the proceeds going to no-name companies. Some deals were floated by second-tier brokers, to be sure, but even venerable J.P. Morgan (pre-Glass-Steagall, when it could still lend and underwrite securities), Kuhn Loeb, Goldman, and a few other big-name houses were in the thick of things, pushing shares of companies that had little or no track record and little or no chance of making it. In fact, lots of the companies could make it only for as long as their meager profits covered interest expenses (forget about dividends). So these were very dubious issues, and most of them hit the wall during the crash.

In the 1950s and 1960s there were several bouts of excessive equity issuance, mostly for the hot sectors of the moment, including computer companies, electronic manufacturers, conglomerates, franchisers, and fast-food chains. In 1968 the Street issued a hefty $4 billion of new stock, mostly for no-names or story stocks (e.g., Four Seasons Nursing Homes, International Leisure, National Student Marketing Corp.) and some of the go-go conglomerates of the period. Each of these cycles led to the flotation of way too much equity for companies that were decidedly not worthy. And, predictably, many tanked as soon as the markets turned, leaving behind lots of shell-shocked investors.

The same thing happened very dramatically at the turn of the millennium. In the aftermath of the Drexel–junk bond–hostile takeover phase a process of reequitization took hold, generally to good effect. Companies deleveraged their operations, cleaned up their balance sheets, reduced interest payments, strengthened cash flows, and boosted net income. They purged the debt excess of the 1980s and started looking healthy again. But the equity pendulum kept on swinging: lots of companies started tapping the equity markets. Little start-ups, many of them tied to the growing Internet, wireless, and fiber-optic frenzy, floated equity with the help of friendly investment bankers in search of 7 percent fees (most of the banks set up shops in Silicon Valley to be close to the action). Wall Street brought public some tiny outfits with a dozen people, a business plan, and some office space in Palo Alto in IPOs valued at unreal multiples of "future expected revenues" (not earnings), and most of them traded up to spectacular levels for periods of one, two, or three years. Banks also issued new equity for established companies that were funding fiber installations or acquiring media properties to play on the "content/delivery convergence platform"—and most did so despite massive oversupply of fiber capacity, extreme competitive pressures, and highly suspect strategic plans, suggesting that the business cases were not thoroughly investigated by anybody before deals were printed. In short, banks floated equity for virtually everybody: more than $1 trillion was raised for the telecom and technology sectors during the boom of late 1990s/early millennium (in February 2000 alone there were an astonishing 55 new equity issues—almost three per day). And we all know the unhappy ending: a massive collapse in stock prices from early 2001 through 2003 that extinguished some $6 trillion in market value. Institutional investors watched their capital funds get pulverized, and legions of private clients saw their life savings vanish. Morgan Stanley examined all of the U.S. technology IPOs launched between 1980 and 2002 (1,700+) and found that $1.6 trillion of value was created during the two decades[2]; but it also found that 5 percent of the IPOs (some 80 to 90 companies) generated most of that $1.6 trillion, suggesting that the other 95 percent may have been fairly worthless endeavors—bankers were basically issuing equity for anybody with a business plan and a placard on the door. There was just far too much equity that ultimately soured, and when we try to figure out what went wrong, we can only point to the Street.

Of course the issuing companies were willing participants, the venture capitalists helped sell the Street on the newest hot thing, the financial media helped tout the latest fly-by-night dot com, and institutional investors helped propel demand and inflate stock prices. And, yes, even retail investors did their part, getting swept up in the resurgence of "greed is good" that didn't really end with Gordon Gekko (you know it's bad when Moms and Pops have become CNBC junkies, "negative momentum swing traders," and paper millionaires). It takes lots of players to feed a true speculative frenzy, and all of them have to take their share of the blame. But at the end of the day it was Wall Street, with its persuasive investment banking talent, research gurus, and salespeople/traders that made the whole thing gel (sometimes they made it gel with questionable glue, like bad research, spinning, and laddering, but we'll save that for chapter 6). The banks should have been far more diligent and careful in screening out the wheat from the chaff, but they weren't. They didn't do their jobs properly, because they were just in it for the 7 percent, the league tables, and the bonuses. So, remember, too much equity can be a bad thing, too.

NOT ENOUGH MONEY

The flip side obviously appears when there's not enough money to go around—when the Street pulls back on lending or issuing bonds for companies, when it won't entertain new IPOs or equity add-ons, and when it turns its back on entire industries, sectors, or countries. This doesn't seem to happen quite as often as the excess capital scenario, since the Street likes "more" and is always eager to earn fees. But it can happen, because Wall Street has the keys to capital kingdom—certainly not in the sense of the near monopoly enjoyed by J.P. Morgan in the early twentieth century, but one that is only a few steps removed. Despite some competition and disintermediation, and a few substitutes/alternatives, the Street's major banks still set the pace when it comes to raising funds. So when Wall Street says "no" it usually means that companies (industries, countries) that deserve and need capital can't get it. The result is that corporate and economic growth are jeopardized and investors are barred access to what might otherwise be promising investment opportunities. Funds can be in short supply if investors, lenders, and Street firms aren't interested in taking risk or aren't in a position to do so, or the Street itself isn't eager to pursue a particular segment of the marketplace. Let's consider both scenarios.

If investors aren't feeling good about taking risk, they aren't going to buy bonds or equities, and if Street firms aren't feeling good, they aren't going to make loans or underwrite securities—regardless of price. In general, investors and Street firms feel skittish about risk when the economic or political picture is cloudy or the markets are in turmoil. But something nasty has to happen for banks to pull in their horns and stop raising capital for others—like losing so many dollars somewhere else that they've lost their desire, or ability, or authorization to raise funds. It's happened several times in the Street's history, often after speculative bubbles burst. Consider the Depression years following the Great Crash: during the early 1930s there was a "strike of capital," and borrowers and public companies were simply unable to look to the Street for debt or equity capital. Banks, some of which had been badly burned during the crash, couldn't or wouldn't lend money or issue equity—not even on a collateralized basis, not even for good firms. That capital vacuum last nearly five years. It's also happened in the modern era: it occurred in the aftermath of the 1980s Latin debt crisis (which crippled a number of money center banks), and in the early 1990s after record corporate defaults hit the system (hurting many investment banks). And it happened rather dramatically in August and September 1998, as Russia was imploding and hedge fund LTCM was falling apart (more on all of this later)—new debt and equity issuance ground to a standstill. Even great credits—AAA's and AA's—had trouble raising money. If they did manage to tap into the Wall Street conduit, they paid up—even very good firms had to pay 10, 20, even 50 basis points more than normal. Anyone rated below A couldn't raise a nickel. New equity issues were nowhere to be seen. For a period of two to four months, raising capital via Wall Street was virtually impossible. Why? Not because the AAA or AA credits were no longer good risks—they were pretty much as solid as they had been before the crisis (and were willing and able to pay their obligations), and not because legitimate equity issuers were any less promising than before. No, it was because many Street firms had been damaged by their credit and market risk exposures to Russia, emerging markets, LTCM and other hedge funds. They were bleeding profusely—losing, in some cases, hundreds of millions of dollars and more—so they became very risk averse (or were instructed by their directors to become risk averse). They were unwilling (and in some cases unable) to entertain new capital raisings. So, the lack of capital, even for the most creditworthy or promising companies, was driven to a significant degree by the Street's own risk losses. This means that if banks blow it in one area they may not be able to help out in another one, and begs the obvious question: should corporate access to capital be dependent on the trading or credit losses of Wall Street? If the answer is "yes" and this is a fact of the marketplace, then institutions (or countries) wanting to tap into the global markets when they need funds have two options: disintermediate Wall Street (as some sophisticated players have done, e.g., General Electric, General Motors, Ford, United Parcel Service) or pray that the Street isn't going through a bad patch of its own.

Of course, sometimes Wall Street just ignores an entire community, sector, or country, steadfastly refusing to give it access to capital regardless of the environment. This can happen if the Street just can't see enough profit potential in the business, when it feels it's just not worth the time and effort, when the business seems too risky, or when it doesn't want to deal with any additional headaches or aggravation. Fair enough. No one says Wall Street has to provide capital to everyone, especially if the economics aren't compelling or the risks are misbalanced. But are the reasons for not raising capital actually good ones, and are the banks really sure the economics aren't there? Do they know for certain that the risks and returns are not what they should be, or are they just being lazy or saving their energy for hunting the big game? For instance, for years a number of banks on the Street have ignored the small and medium enterprise (SME) sector. SMEs, many of them quite profitable and on an aggressive growth trajectory, have been forced to tap alternate sources of capital, such as loans from their small local bankers (at what may be unfavorable rates), venture capital, and medium-term funds from special government-financing programs. That's too bad, because some SMEs become LEs—large enterprises, the kind that Wall Street likes to bank. So banks may be missing opportunities to catch some of these outfits on the ground floor, to help nurture them from small platforms to global ones, solidifying relationships (read: future business) along the way. Actually, it's started to dawn on some banks that they've been wrong to ignore the market all these years; the more enlightened ones are trying to play "catch up" so they can capture some of the future business. In the meantime, these SMEs have spent the past few decades scrambling for funding because the Street has been unwilling to do its part. The same is true with the agricultural sector, certain "high quality" emerging market countries, and so forth—no money when needed. Of course, when a lack of capital is deemed to be at the heart of larger socioeconomic problems, regulators and politicians have to step in and remind the Street that it's going to do its part. So legislation like the Community Reinvestment Act, which requires banks to lend a certain amount to communities, is a way of making the Street cough up a little cash where it's needed.

WRONG PRICE

Sometimes the Street prices the capital wrong. It sells bonds or syndicates loans with spreads that are too low for the risks involved, or it sells equities at prices that are too high for projected earnings; or it sells bonds and loans with spreads that are too wide, and equities with prices that are too low. Okay, pricing isn't an exact science. It isn't easy trying to figure out exactly where things should trade primary and secondary because there are lots of moving parts: the past and prospective financial condition of the issuing client, the overall state of the financial markets, the size of the competing deal pipeline, the way the hedge markets are trading, the appetite of the institutional investor base, the mind-set of retail investors, and so forth. Lots of things can influence pricing, so no one can criticize a bank for missing the bond by a few basis points, or the share of stock by a few cents (or even dollars). That's all close enough. We're talking about the times when the bank misses the target by a mile or two: when the bond spread is off by a few dozen basis points or the stock price by more than few dollars. And we're also talking about the fact that mispricing happens pretty frequently.

Why does capital get mispriced? Usually because a bank is misreading the markets (stumbling), or trying to please the client or investors (doing the wrong thing). Again, if the stumbling happens occasionally, no one's going to get too upset. If it happens regularly, then there's incompetence or internal breakdown involved: a Street underwriter better know how to price its deals properly most of the time, or it shouldn't be in the business. If the mispricing is happening for reasons other than stumbling—such as trying to win more business, pleasing preferred customers at the expense of others—then serious control and ethical issues may be involved. And how does a bank manage to misprice deals? It may misread the financial strength and prospects of the borrower/issuer, it may not really understand what it'll take to get investors to bite, it may want the business so badly it'll undercut the competition on purpose, or it may have bad internal controls, like "rubber stamp" commitment/lending committees that will approve any deal (at whatever price the syndicate managers come up with).

Let's divide the problem into underpricing and overpricing because each scenario affects different parties. If stocks are *underpriced* (i.e., the issue price is lower than the actual worth of the firm), then the company loses because it gets less proceeds than it was expecting. If it wants more proceeds then it'll have to issue more shares and dilute. If bonds or loans are *underpriced* (i.e., the spread is lower than it should be given its level of creditworthiness) then the bond investor or lender loses, because it gets less interest than it should for the risk being taken. If stocks are *overpriced* (i.e., the issue price is higher than it should be), the primary market investor loses because the shares will probably trade down after launch. If bonds or loans are *overpriced* (i.e., the spread is higher than it should be), then the company loses because it's paying more for its cost of debt capital than it should given its creditworthiness. That's four ways to get it wrong. Let's think about some of these scenarios in terms of real life.

Investment grade loans, as an example, are often priced too low—sometimes way too low—meaning the company wins (lower cost of capital) but the investor/lender loses (skewed risk/return profile). Consider that in late 2002 AT&T, still an investment grade credit, inked a $4 billion bank loan at 37.5 basis points over Treasuries. And where was the credit default swap market trading AT&T's debt? 475 over. That's a pretty chunky difference. Or consider AAA-rated General Electric, which was trading at T+12 in the debt markets and T+85 in the default swap market. Still pretty chunky. We could cite other examples, but most tell a similar story. In fact, as credit default spreads widened steadily in 2001 and 2002, loan spreads remained remarkably stable. The pricing of loans by a bank and its syndicate members can thus be radically different from the pricing suggested by broader market forces (forces that have no particular axe or agenda, and may therefore be a more accurate reflection of reality).

Why is this happening? A bank may be stumbling, but that would be quite a stumble. More likely it's doing the wrong thing. Maybe, just maybe, a bank is trying to win other business, and using the investment grade loan as a loss leader. Going the pure loss leader route (i.e., discounting one product in *hopes* of winning higher-margin business) is legal but often foolish. Explicitly attaching the loan to some other piece of business—a game known as tying—is illegal for banks (though not necessarily for securities firms, which may own banks these days). Under the Bank Holding Company Act of 1970 a bank isn't allowed to give a client a favorable price on capital in exchange for more lucrative business (e.g., an equity underwriting, an M&A transaction); we'll return to tying later in the book. So the bank shouldn't be offering AT&T or General Electric a favorable spread on the syndicated loan in exchange for the juicy deal that's coming up next month—that would be illegal. In fact, the greater the potential for future business, the lower the loan spread, though no one will ever put that in writing. How else can we account for such huge discrepancies between the primary and secondary spreads? It isn't all supply and demand forces, or misreading of the market. Banks set the spread on the loan, and market forces set the spread in the credit default swap market, so you figure out what's going on. The trouble with underpricing a loan (or any other debt instrument) is that the lead bank often gets stuck with a big wedge of the paper; it may be really tough to syndicate AT&T at +37.5 when the market wants +475. So the bank wears most of the loan until it can cajole its friends down the block to take some, or it may write down the value of its piece (only if it marks its loan book to market, though), or it may buy a credit default swap to protect against some catastrophe, and then just wait until it wins the M&A mandate. But the risk/reward profile is out of balance on an absolute basis, and across time: the piece of the risky loan that the lead bank keeps stays on its book for several years, until it matures. The M&A fee gets booked this quarter and then it's gone. So the client company wins by getting cheap funding, the bank's shareholders lose by subsidizing the event—and they really lose if the M&A mandate never materializes. Remember, banks have underpriced lots of debt deals over the years; every major bank has gotten stuck with way too much paper at some point (and some have gotten stuck on a regular basis). In a best-case scenario the markets bail them out over time, so the P&L fallout is negligible. In a more realistic scenario they have to widen out the spreads to get things moving, taking a P&L hit in the process. And in a disaster scenario they take big write-offs as the borrower/issuer defaults. Getting it wrong is risky.

Sometimes, of course, debt gets overpriced: bonds and loans are launched at spreads that are much wider than they should be, meaning higher interest payments for the borrowers. These mispricings usually get corrected pretty quickly because once the deals are launched and investors find discrepancies, they buy up the "cheap" paper in the secondary market and draw the launch spreads in where they belong. That doesn't help the borrower, of course, because it's stuck with an obligation that has to be serviced for a period of perhaps several years. In fact, if it's really upset with the spread it might even go so far as to refinance in order to bring interest payments back where they belong. While debt can get overpriced if market conditions are dicey and banks want to play it safe (e.g., making sure they can clear the decks of all paper by offering a spread that's wider than normal), sometimes banks misprice it for the reasons we've already indicated: they've got problems of their own or they get sloppy. Needless to say, there have been many instances of this over the years (you are almost guaranteed to find one or more examples in each weekly issue of the *International Financing Review*).

Pricing of IPOs and equity add-ons is a real conundrum for most banks, because two opposing forces are at work. Pricing a deal high (more than the shares are worth) means the company gets more proceeds with fewer shares issued (less dilution) and the underwriting bank gets greater dollar value of fees (e.g., 7 percent of a $100 million issue instead of 7 percent of a $90 million issue). But if it is overpriced, investors get hurt once trading starts: shares will immediately fall to the perceived equilibrium price (unless the underwriters are putting up their capital to support the price, which may happen for a while, but not too long). So investors buying at the allocated price lose and the optics are bad for the company. But pricing it low (less than the share is really worth) has disadvantages, too: the company gets less proceeds, meaning it has to issue more shares and suffer more dilution to get the desired proceeds, and the underwriting bank gets less dollar value fees. However, investors buying in at the issue price get a quick pop, and can flip their shares for an immediate profit (insiders can't, as they are subject to a 180-day lockup rule . . . thank heavens for that). The optics are better for the company because shares trade up instead of down, but the banks underwriting the deal look bad, like they can't figure out where to value the shares. There are different cycles of this problem, but most equity mispricing falls on the side of underpricing. That's unfortunate, because raising equity (whether as an add-on or an IPO) ought to benefit the issuing company. A bank raises capital for a company—not investors—so it has a duty to get deals priced as properly as possible; if a deal is underpriced and it trades up, the differential is going straight into the pockets of investors rather than the corporate coffers—and that's a significant breach.

So where does a bank price the deal? It really depends on the market cycle and the specific goal the bank is trying to achieve: is it hoping to please the company with less dilution, or would it prefer to make the company pay less in fees and have the shares rally in the aftermarket? Or would it rather give the company more up-front proceeds but make it pay more in fees and risk a down trade in the secondary market? And, does it want to give preferred clients a "freebie" by pricing low enough to ensure a strong market showing and instant profit (e.g., hot equity allocations to preferred customers, aka illegal spinning, which we'll get to later in the book)? In fact, during the latter part of the 1990s and into the millennium (before markets corrected), many equity deals were underpriced, sometimes severely. That meant issuing companies left money on the table, investors receiving the allocations got rich very quickly, and the banks looked silly (and sometimes even criminal).

Leaving money on the table through underpricing isn't particularly new. The SEC has found at least four major phases of this behavior since the Great Crash: 1959–1962, when "glamour stocks' (especially electronics) were all the rage; 1967–1971, the "go-go" years (or the "great garbage market" as Richard Jenrette, cofounder of DLJ, called it) when there was lots of action in conglomerates, computers, computer leasing, electronics, and fast-food chains (and after which the SEC and National Association of Securities Dealers [NASD] clamped down on the Street's blatant schemes to reduce supply and stimulate demand, in order to cool off the "shooters" [soaring stocks]); 1979–1983, when the focus was on technology, robotics, computers, and medical products; and 1998–2000 when dot coms and TMT ruled the roost. In fact, the Street's most significant mispricings happened during the last bubble, when underpricings moved from the 5–20 percent range common in previous hot streaks to 50–100 percent and more. And the dollar magnitudes were large by virtue of the underpricing percentage rather than large issue size. So although Allstate left $163 million behind when it converted from a mutual to a stock company in 1993, the deal was underpriced by only 8 percent—the fact that it was 68.5 million shares in size contributed to the large dollar underpricing. Not so during the dot com bubble. In most cases issue sizes were relatively small and the price discrepancies large, suggesting that other forces were at work (i.e., bankers got it spectacularly wrong, or they were more interested in spinning). Apart from the IPOs of United Parcel Service and Goldman Sachs (which were underpriced by $1.6 billion and $960 million, respectively), the rest of the top underpricings were all tech stocks with smaller issue size and bigger margins: Corvis left behind $1.54 billion, Palm $1.3 billion, Sycamore $1.09 billion, Akamai $1.07 billion, Aligent $970 million, AT&T Wireless $948 million, VA Linux $920 million, Free Markets $835 million, and so on.[3]

Mispricing the IPOs

Street banks face a conflict on how to price new equity issues—particularly IPOs, which lack prior trading history. Price the IPO too high and the company will be happy (more proceeds, less dilution), the bank will be happy (more fees), but the investors will be mad (sharp downtrade and a loss). Price the IPO too low and the company will get upset (less proceeds, more dilution), the bank will be unhappy (less fees, unless it's doing some spinning on the side), but the investors will be happy (nice short-term gains). What's a bank to do?

Well, banks should be pricing deals with the corporate issuer in mind: that is, to maximize the capital funds flowing to the issuer. As it happens, though, they tend to underprice them. And when markets are really pumped up, the new issue pipeline fully loaded, and investors all chomping at the bit (probably put into a frenzied state by overeager brokers and salespeople), then they like to seriously underprice them. The average first-day return over the past 20 years has migrated from a low of 3.6 percent (pretty attractive one-day return, but pretty close to the mark, on average, for a decidedly imprecise science) to 71.7 percent in 1999 and 56.1 percent in 2000—the peak TMT bubble years. The small new-issue discounts that had been the norm grew into huge discounts. So lucky investors in 1999 received a one-day bonanza of 72 percent: they put up $1,000 at breakfast and got back $1,720 before dinner (less commissions, of course—a broker's got to live); or, they put up $100,000 and got $172,000; or, if they were preferred executive customers (like CEOs of companies ready to award corporate finance mandates), they put up $1 million and got back $1.72 million (and maybe a break on the commissions, too). That was serious money. The flip side, of course, is that lots of issuing companies left a great deal of money on the table and were forced to dilute just to get back what the bankers failed to deliver. So the issuing company and its shareholders were effectively subsidizing the underwriting bank's investors. That doesn't seem quite right, but it happened (happens?) frequently. Consider the case of Gadzoox; CSFB launched the deal at $21 and watched it trade to $74 at the end of the first day, meaning the company left $180 million on the table (and happy "preferred" clients made $180 million). Or MP3.com, which was issued at $28 and traded up to $63 within hours, for a $250 million difference. The list of *one-day* pops goes on and on: VA Linux up 697 percent, theglobe.com 606 percent, Foundry Networks 525 percent, Webmethods 507 percent, Freemarkets 483 percent, and so on. Can you imagine being a lucky investor putting $100,000 into VA Linux at market open, and cashing out almost $700,000 at the closing bell? Or can you imagine being one of the unhappy VA Linux executives who saw all that money left on the table?

During the early 1990s, when the markets were a bit calmer and more orderly, pricing seems to have been more precise (and, dare we say, honest): in 1990, for instance, companies tapping the U.S. IPO market left a total of $300 million on the table. From 1991 to 1995 they left behind between $1.5 billion and $4 billion per year: a bit worse, but maybe acceptable, since more companies were coming to market. Then things really started sliding: in 1996 bankers underpriced deals to the tune of $6.4 billion (lucky investors), and by 1999, when the dot com revolution was in full swing and bankers were granting favored executive clients hot shares in exchange for future corporate business, they underpriced by an astounding $35.2 billion. Things weren't much better in 2000, as companies left behind $26.7 billion.[4] When the market finally imploded and new issues dried up, mispricing receded to the $2 billion level. So during the two peak years of the TMT boom, Wall Street bankers decided it would be better to leave $62 billion out of the corporate coffers and deliver that value to preferred investors. Of course, when the bankers underpriced deals they left lots of fees on the table. But they weren't worried because they got dollars back when those happy CEOs start handing out more fee-rich mandates.

What about those who say that deals occurring during one of the frothy periods aren't actually underpriced, but are realistically priced—and the fact that they trade up so sharply in the aftermarket is just evidence of speculative demand, not bank error (i.e., blame the investors, not the bank underwriters)? That seems not to hold much water, for at least two reasons: not all of the underpricings occur in the same "hot" industry (they are often found in other industries as well, including those that haven't been the direct focus of speculative fever), and more than a few of the underpriced deals show staying power—prices remain buyout for months and months (even longer), not just for a few days or weeks. Of course, if there is any speculative fever creating unrealistic and unsustainable demand for some of the issues, we've got banks to thank for that, too: hyping stocks, creating artificial demand, and pumping out overly optimistic research, all in order to get investors to pony up more money and boost prices; but we'll get to all of that later in the book.

Broken Toys

Etoys, the now-defunct Internet toy retailer, had a shot at stardom a la eBay and Amazon—or so it believed. It worked hard to come up with a good plan and platform, a novel idea that no one had tapped into, and it did: selling toys via the Internet. And why not? Amazon had done it with books, eBay had done it with everyone's unwanted loot, so why shouldn't eToys do it with GI Joes and Barbies? As early as 1996 it got some of Silicon Valley's brightest venture capitalists—Idealab, Sequoia, Highland—to back the business plan and concept, and give it seed money to flesh out the strategy and platform. And for a time during 1998 and 1999, things looked pretty bright for eToys (during the holiday season of 1999 it did more toy sales than Amazon or Toys-R-Us online).

Then came the IPO. After three years on the venture capital lifeline, eToys' management felt it was time to cut the cord, so they hooked up with bankers from Goldman for an IPO. By March 1999 things were looking promising, and Goldman gave the thumbs-up. Remember, this was right in the middle of the TMT hot patch, the eToys concept had proved itself through a few selling seasons and, even though it wasn't yet profitable (none of the business-to-consumer platforms were), the company had a recognizable name, good traffic, good strategy, and a good management team. So why not price the deal on the high side and get the company a little extra working capital?

Nope. Goldman priced it low: $20/share, 13 million shares, raising $166 million for the company. That doesn't sound bad, except that the stock traded up to $85 at the end of the first day—meaning eToys left $470 million on the table. That's an awful lot of jack for a company that's trying to make a go of it and needs every last nickel to succeed. And you only have one shot at the IPO; every subsequent capital issue is dilutive. Unfortunately for eToys the $85 level wasn't a one-day wonder: the price remained buoyant for months and months, meaning that Goldman really got it wrong. From that point on, things went downhill for the firm. The company struggled through 2000 as the TMT bubble burst; revenues dropped and cash became tight (and, of course, it didn't have that $470 million, which it really could have used). In early 2001 it couldn't hang on any longer and filed for bankruptcy. KBToys, a brick-and-mortar operation (that eventually went under in late 2003), bought $40 million of eToys' inventory, the domain name, and some additional intellectual property, and that was that.

Or was it? In 2003 the rump of what was once eToys (EBCI Inc., trading on the pink sheets at a penny a share) decided to sue Goldman on several fronts: deliberately underpricing the IPO (claiming that by doing so the firm suffered financial distress that led ultimately to its failure, failing to disclose that "material portions" of the IPO were going to preferred client accounts (not just Goldman's, but also Merrill's and Robertson Stephens', who were on board as comanagers) and soliciting and receiving excessive and undisclosed commissions in exchange for IPO allocations and secondary market orders (these constitute spinning and laddering, two no-nos we'll see later). Though there have been many instances of investors suing badly damaged or failed dot coms and their underwriters (to wit, actions against Priceline.com, Expedia.com, Goto.com, Garden.com, Boo.com, MVP.com), this action represented the first instance of a failed company suing its own underwriter over mispricing. And maybe the company is right: $470 million is a lot of money.

───────

The lesson in all of this is that even though the Street is supposed to raise debt and equity capital for issuing clients—as needed, and on good terms—it sometimes can't, won't, doesn't. And, when it does, it may well get the price wrong—charging too much or too little, accidentally or on purpose. It's especially troublesome when it misprices for the wrong reasons: not only does the issuing client wind up paying more for capital or leave dollars behind, it shows that the banks have some ethical problems. The capital-raising function is too important to allow such failures to go unchecked.

Chapter 4

BAD CORPORATE ADVICE

Wall Street firms routinely give their corporate clients advice on a wide range of deals and strategies. The biggest banks are like counselors, trying to guide CEOs, CFOs, and institutional investment managers down the path to prosperity by recommending deals and strategies that can help them generate more revenues or investment income; some are even designed to let them gain additional market share and outpace competitors.

Though corporate advice can take lots of different forms we'll tackle it from two broad angles: corporate finance advice, meaning M&A, tax-driven structures, and off–balance sheet transactions, and investment advice, like structured asset plays based on leverage, derivatives, and other risky things. Both are extremely important for companies and other institutional players if they are to progress in a highly competitive business environment. Unfortunately, things don't always work out as planned. Banks often hand out bad corporate finance advice and questionable (sometimes dangerous) investment advice. Let's take a look.

BAD CORPORATE FINANCE ADVICE

Corporate finance is big business on the Street because, like the equity IPOs and add-ons we talked about in the last chapter, the fees are big—sometimes very big. It's little wonder, then, that most of the top players devote significant time and effort to developing, expanding, and honing their corporate finance skills and getting their teams to come up with ideas for companies from a whole range of industries. Transactions like mergers, acquisitions, divestitures, spin-offs, carve-outs, recapitalizations, LBOs, and tax/regulatory arbitrages all feature in Wall Street's institutional business arsenal. Some of these deals are smart and really do increase the worth of client companies. A wise acquisition, a well-timed spin-off, or a tax-efficient (and legally sound) financing vehicle can help a company generate value for shareholders (which, if corporate governance means anything, is still an overarching goal of directors and executives). The best part is that everyone walks away happy: the company has the deal that it likes, the bank earns fees, and shareholders of both organizations feel like they've come out ahead.

However, as with other aspects of Wall Street's business, some of these deals don't work out as planned. Some of them are questionable, others ill-conceived or poorly executed, and a few even illegal—not exactly what a company wants to discover when it's paying tens of millions in fees to its supposedly clever bankers. But it happens. Indeed, no less an authority than Lazard banker Felix Rohatyn has noted that "[t]here has always been the temptation to urge a deal on a client, because if it doesn't do the deal, you don't get a fee. . . . I've seen lots of bad deals. I've seen a lot of deals where people got overenthusiastic, paid too much, or bought the wrong company."[1] And he should know.

M&A

Bad M&A advice comes in different forms and can inflict varying degrees of financial damage. For instance, a bank may help a company develop unwise strategies, like purchasing a beleaguered (and deeply troubled) competitor, expanding into unfamiliar territory, or buying another firm because that's what competitors are doing. Or it may let its client overpay on a transaction or chase a "megadeal" solely for the sake of publicity and market share (and not for sound strategic/financial reasons). Even though bankers have a fiduciary duty to guide their clients in the right direction they sometimes fail to do so because, as Mr. Rohatyn says, they really want to earn those fees.

So many questionable M&A deals have been arranged over the years that the list seems almost endless. Though bad transactions go back many decades, they became really noticeable during the 1960s when the "conglomerate movement" was in full swing (more on this below). And they've become even more apparent in the modern era because the pool of companies is much larger and the pressure to do deals far greater. Let's consider a very small sampling: does anyone really think that Asea Brown Boveri (ABB) should have bought asbestos-laden Combustion Engineering (CE) for $1.6 billion when CE already had $4 billion of litigation swirling around it? Shouldn't the bankers have advised ABB's management not to do the deal? Well, they should have, because ABB was ultimately forced to put CE into bankruptcy to avoid further liability. Or perhaps AT&T's bankers shouldn't have let it pay $43.5 billion for MediaOne in 1999, or Compaq's bankers should have advised against the purchase of Digital, Novell's bankers should have scotched the acquisition of WordPerfect, IBM of Lotus, WorldCom of CompuServe? Maybe Conseco's bankers shouldn't have let the company pay $7 billion—an 86 percent premium—for GreenTree Financial, a company with so many problems that it propelled the combined firm into default? What did any of these firms get from its M&A adventures? Nothing good: depressed profits (sometimes even worse), lagging equity returns, slowing market share growth, integration problems. All of these deals (and lots and lots of others) look pretty lousy in retrospect. They spawned many losers— except the banks, who earned big fees (and sometimes the selling shareholders, who received big takeout premiums on their shares because the acquirer's inept bankers allowed overpayment).

Sometimes bankers advise a client to buy a firm that is unrelated to the company's strategy, just to get a deal done—part of creating a "diversified conglomerate." They make the case for "strategic revenue diversification" and "cross industry synergies" which, unfortunately, don't usually amount to much. The conglomerate movement has actually been active for years. Goldman was one of the first banks on Wall Street to create a dedicated M&A unit to focus on acquisition opportunities for conglomerates, and others soon followed suit. In the 1960s bankers told Standard Oil to buy into the office machinery business and Mobil Oil to get into department stores. (Both firms ultimately abandoned their noncore businesses at a loss.) They advised International Telephone and Telegraph (ITT, founded in 1920) to expand into hospitality, fertilizer, care rental, auto parts, food, and a grab bag of other things. Results: more than a hundred mergers between 1960 and 1969, good fees for the banks, bad returns for ITT shareholders. Wilson, the sporting goods company, was urged to get into meatpacking and pharmaceuticals, Litton into computers, ships, conveyor belts, and food, Textronic into zippers, snowmobiles, helicopters, and ball bearings, Gulf and Western into auto parts, zinc, sugar, cigars, and entertainment. Many other sprawling conglomerates were created during the key period of 1966–1969; in fact, 20 of the 200 largest companies in the United States were diversified conglomerates, created with considerable help from the Street's M&A wizards (and funded by Street-supplied loans and convertible bonds). These are just a few examples of diversified acquisitions promoted by bankers that went nowhere and added no particular value. Investors eventually figured out that it was far more efficient for them, and not companies, to construct diversified portfolios of assets, so they sold their conglomerate shares; in many cases share prices lagged the market so badly that bankers had to be called back in for the "deconsolidation" phase, dismantling what they (or the bankers down the block) had created in the first place. More fees, more expenses—good for the Street's shareholders (for a change), but bad for the company's shareholders (and maybe bad for the Street's reputation).

Bankers periodically urge their clients to mimic their competitors by playing the "me, too" game—which can be an enormously expensive, and sometimes unwise, strategy. We've got plenty of examples here, too: in media, where a number of firms tried to create questionable, and generally flawed, content/distribution convergence platforms (e.g., AOL/Time Warner, Vivendi/Universal/NBC, Disney/Cap Cities, KirchMedia/Pro Sat 1); in networking, lots of firms purchased competitors in order to expand quickly and race to lay more (ultimately dark) fiber (e.g., Global Crossing/Frontier, JDS Uniphase/SDL); in banking, banks tried to create "critical mass" by becoming larger (though not necessarily better, or more profitable) (e.g., Bank One/First Chicago NBD, J.P. Morgan Chase/Bank One, Wells Fargo/First Interstate, First Union/CoreStates, Wachovia/First Union, Bank of America/FleetBoston); and so on. Wall Street bankers were right in the thick of things, pushing and promoting all the way.

Sometimes the Street helps push transactions for their marquee value. What's more impressive than a blockbuster deal between two corporate monsters? For the banks the incentives are considerable: they look like clever rainmakers (for a while, at any rate), and they earn enormous fees. Never mind if the mergers or acquisitions aren't always what they're cracked up to be—or, indeed, fail utterly to match predeal hype. For instance, there's R.J. Reynolds (RJR)/Nabisco, the acrimonious $25 billion LBO of 1988 that pitted an investor/management group (banked by Lehman) against buyout experts Kohlberg Kravis Roberts (banked by Morgan Stanley, Merrill, Drexel, and Wasserstein Perella). It was the marquee deal of the decade, and it put $20 billion of debt on RJR's balance sheet (with a challenging $3 billion in annual interest payments); it also caused existing RJR bonds to get downgraded to junk (obliterating $1 billion of market value for the unlucky investors who happened to be holding the paper), and led to thousands of employee layoffs—but yielded no especial economic benefit. It did, however, spin $1 billion of fees for the bankers (and lawyers, accountants, and others). The same has happened with some of the other blockbuster deals of recent years: AOL/Time Warner ($166 billion), Pfizer/Warner Lambert ($94 billion), Daimler/Chrysler ($39 billion), SBC Communications/Ameritech ($56 billion)—they all traded down well after being concluded, and they all suffered from serious integration, cost, and strategy problems. Actually, 17 of 21 of the largest multibillion-dollar megamergers arranged between 1995 and 2001 were bad trades for shareholders of the acquiring companies, who watched the value of their investments slip below their peer groups, often dramatically.

A brief interlude: when M&A bankers are advising a company's directors on whether to proceed with a deal they are usually asked to prepare a "fairness opinion"; this indicates whether the transaction is reasonably valued, so that directors can then determine whether the deal is in the best interests of shareholders. That sounds like a good thing: the experts should be able to value something and tell those that are less expert whether it's too high, a bargain, or just about right. Unfortunately, bankers often say that deals are fairly priced when they're wildly overpriced, meaning that their clients overpay. This is a serious and frequent problem, but one that everyone seems to blithely ignore. Companies want to do deals (or think they do), and bankers want to get the deals done (often at any price, because the higher the price, the bigger the fees—a conflict of interest). Though every deal is supposed to be accompanied by a fairness opinion built atop in-depth due diligence and a thorough crunching of the numbers, bankers routinely botch it up. Sometimes they get the numbers wrong because they are too optimistic in assuming postacquisition synergies, revenue growth, cost cutting, financial leverage; sometimes they get it wrong because they don't understand that companies are fluid and can change their stripes postdeal; sometimes they get it wrong because they are outsiders and don't understand the real nuances of the businesses they're advising on; sometimes they get it wrong because they sense management wants to do a deal, and, well, they are there to please management; and, sometimes they get it wrong because they just want to line their own pockets. Bankers will argue that valuation is not an exact science, so there has to be some allowance for error. True enough. But not that much room for error and not that frequently. Perhaps if fairness opinions were put together by independent parties rather than bankers eager to close a deal there would be less conflict of interest and the numbers would be a little less squishy; but independent opinions are still the exception, not the rule.

Let's return. It's pretty easy to see when an acquirer has ended up overpaying—when some of those fairness opinions aren't close to the mark. Just look at the acquirer's stock price one or two years after the transaction and see if it's better or worse than (a) the preacquisition price, (b) the competitive peer group, and (c) the market at large. That usually tells the story. Again, we can look at lots of examples here. A survey of M&A deals arranged between 1995–2001 (including the record period of 1998–2000, when deals worth $4 trillion were inked), indicates that 61 percent of transactions destroyed shareholder wealth.[2] One year after deal completion more than three hundred acquiring companies were trading below their peers, and even two years later 80 percent of transactions were still underwater. Not exactly compelling evidence for doing M&A deals—certainly not those at the wrong price. Consider these: Healtheon-WebMD bought Medical Manager for $3 billion (a 48 percent premium) in 2000; 12 months later the company was trading 150 percent below its peers. Daimler bought Chrysler for $39 billion (54 percent premium) in 1998 and was trading 30 percent below the auto group a year later. Starwood bought ITT for $9.5 billion (98 percent premium) in 1998 and was trading 65 percent below its peers a year later. Tyco/CIT illustrates the corporate finance life cycle in its entirety: Tyco bought CIT Financial for $9.2 billion in 2001 and resold it via an IPO in 2003 for $4.6 billion after writing off $4.5 billion of goodwill. Maybe the original purchase price was a tad high? (Similar overpayments and share underperformance were apparent in deals like Kana/Silknet, Dillard/Mercantile Stores, Office Depot/Viking Office, JDS Uniphase/SDL, Clear Channel/AMFM, Dupont/Pioneer, Cendant/GreenTree, AOL/Time Warner, Vivendi/Universal, ad nauseam.) We hate to be too repetitive, but we are actually repeating to make a specific point: overpayment happens time and again, and that is largely the fault of Street bankers who often fail to come up with the correct valuations or aren't dissuading management when the premiums are too high.[3] We can't even argue that the selling companies' bankers are brilliant, advising management to hold out for higher prices, because they usually aren't the ones initiating the deal—more often they're just reacting to it.

AOL + Time Warner + Investment Bankers = Value?

The merger of AOL and Time Warner stands as one of the most dubious M&A deals of all time (never mind that *Mergers and Acquisitions* magazine called it the 2001 "Deal of the Year"). By virtually every measure it's been a bad trade for everyone—except the investment bankers, who collected big fees for their work in advising the two companies to get together, at virtually any cost. The bankers: Citi, Merrill, and Goldman for AOL, and Morgan Stanley and Wasserstein Perella for Time Warner.

The $166 billion merger, the largest in U.S. corporate history, was negotiated and concluded in January 2001 at the top of the market, with AOL buying up Time Warner at a $60 billion premium. Two years later, with the stock trading at $15, the combined market value of the company had fallen to $67 billion, less than half the proforma value of the deal when it was first announced. Not quite what the acquiring shareholder wants to see. By all accounts AOL started off by significantly overpaying for Time Warner (presumably on the advice of its bankers, who actually provide this kind of advice for a living). Then it was unable to create the distribution/content synergies that formed the basis of the merger. Add in internecine politics, organizational chaos, and bursting of the TMT bubble, and you have a recipe for disaster.

The deal basically became a merger of two big brand names rather than a corporate integration (never mind *M&A*'s effusive comments during the "Deal of the Year" award: "Rarely does a merger or acquisition embody the major elements of a new age in the development of global business as the combination of the corporate giants that create AOL Time Warner." Oops). After the deal was concluded there was lots of stumbling, including uncertainty about how to create a competitive advantage to expand enterprise value, poor organizational integration, and so forth. And there was considerable financial pressure: executives had to rush to figure out which assets to sell in order to pay down a heavy debt load and keep the company from entering a downward spiral. The effective failure of the merger took its toll on the executive ranks of the firm, particularly among former AOL-ers. Three of the four top executives departed (chairman, CEO, and co-COO) and no former senior AOL executives were left within the combined management team. Sometime thereafter management decided to drop the AOL name from the corporate moniker, feeling it added too much baggage and was hurting broader marketing efforts—again, not exactly what one might expect to see at the conclusion of the largest M&A deal in the U.S. market. This, of course, just crystallized what many in the firm already knew: the deal was a bad apple from the start, certainly at a price of $166 billion.

Let's be clear: AOL and Time Warner executives who made the deal happen bear responsibility (as do the board directors and shareholders who approved the deal). Without their participation the ill-fated marriage wouldn't have come about. But the bankers blew it—especially the AOL bankers who, in counseling AOL directors and executives and giving their fairness opinions, probably said that a $60 billion premium was okay. Events have proved otherwise. The job of investment bankers is, of course, to help find good M&A opportunities for their clients or, when presented with something that's been cooked up in-house, rip it apart, figure out where it makes sense, where it falls down, and what the premium should really be. The job of the investment banker is not to urge the company to make a foolish decision at any cost. Yet that mind-set exists, particularly when marquee deals are involved. Anything running into tens of billions of dollars means very fat fees, so the pressure to get it done is tremendous. What investment banker is going to tell the senior corporate executives not to chase the overpriced megadeal? Well, the diligent, prudent, and smart investment banker should be doing just that. The game should be about creating value for the merging companies, it shouldn't be about doing a deal at any price, just to generate fees and bonus dollars.

—————————

Of course, bankers occasionally do the reverse: they trash a deal if they think management doesn't want to do it. Even if it's properly priced and would be in the best interest of the shareholders, they simply go along with whatever directors and executives want to do (one small example of many: Wasserstein Perella, in supporting publisher Macmillan's management against an unwanted advance, declared that offers of $64, then $73, and then $80 per share, were completely inadequate, even though the bank had valued Macmillan at $63–$68).

It's not all the bankers' fault, of course. The client company's executives and directors, signing off on these deals, have to step up to the plate, too. If they don't agree to press ahead with a deal brought to them by Wall Street, it's no go. So they are culpable as well. But most of the deals start with those creative, and fee-hungry, bankers (as Robert Rubin, former head of Goldman and the U.S. Treasury, has rightly noted: "The merger wave, without regard to the question of whether it is good for society, comes out of Wall Street").[4] Wall Street pushes deals: good ones, but lots of bad ones, too.

SPEs, Window Dressing and Tax Deals

Some of the Street's bad corporate advice comes from more obtuse and opaque sources, like offshore special purpose entities (SPEs), off–balance sheet deals, related-party transactions, window dressing, and tax plays. Though much of this business is legitimate (even though it can look pretty suspicious) some of it is wrong—or, worse, illegal. For instance, banks periodically advise their corporate clients to create and deal through SPEs, offshore subsidiaries that are located in sunny, tax-friendly jurisdictions. SPEs are useful because they attract good tax treatment and aren't the most obvious and transparent things to understand; they take things off the radar screen. It doesn't mean that they house anything illegal or that the companies sponsoring them are doing anything untoward—just that no one has to answer a lot of questions about what's going on (and they're usually referenced only in little footnotes in the financial statements that no one bothers to read). Banks sometimes advise clients to use SPEs to arrange structured financings (like securitizations and loans) or monetize the value of assets. In most instances these are fine (if a little convoluted and hard to decipher), but occasionally they run afoul of the letter or spirit of the law. It's tough for outside stakeholders to know what's going on, and sometimes things do get out of hand, as we've seen in some of the games played by companies like Adelphia, Tyco, Enron, Parmalat, and others.

———

Yosemite and Mahonia: To Lend or Not to Lend?

Enron became one of the largest bankruptcies in U.S. corporate history when it flamed out in December 2001. The Number 7 Fortune 500 company came crashing down to earth as its web of deceit unwound; though it took a bit of time for the forensic specialists to figure it all out, the picture that finally emerged was ugly: self-dealing, conflicts of interest, falsification of financial statements, collapse of internal controls, ineffective auditing, lying, cheating. Anything that could have been manipulated was manipulated. And, yes, Wall Street was right there, doing some things it shouldn't have done. Did the banks directly contribute to Enron's collapse? Probably not. Some of Enron's top officials seem to have been doing just fine destroying the company on their own (while lots of the directors were snoozing in the hot Texas sun). Should they have been more forthright and diligent in considering and explaining what they were doing with the company? Certainly. Should they have pulled back on what they were doing once it became clear that things were suspicious? Absolutely. But they didn't and wound up creating an even bigger mess. Though we'll consider more of the Street's dealings with Enron in chapter 6, let's introduce the topic by looking at Yosemite and Mahonia, two SPEs that were used to dress the company up.

Yosemite and Mahonia were SPEs that actively dealt with Enron in what are known as prepaid swaps (or prepays). Starting in 1992, Yosemite (aka Citibank) and Mahonia (aka J.P. Morgan) became very large lenders to Enron through prepays. There was certainly nothing wrong with lending to Enron (at least in the early, precrisis days), and many financial institutions did just that. The difference was that the lending that Yosemite and Mahonia did through the prepays was not actually classified as lending, but as "price risk management activities" because it was arranged through off–balance sheet swap contracts. That meant Enron's balance sheet reflected a lot less leverage than it should have, and its cash flow statement showed "operating cash flows" rather than "financing cash flows"—both of which helped disguise the company's real financial position. In fact, between 1997 and 2001 prepays were the single largest source of cash into Enron (in 1997 alone Citi did 60 prepays, accounting for 76 percent of Enron's cash flow). Despite the large volume of deals, most people outside the banks didn't even really know about them.

So how did these deals work? Let's look at Yosemite. Citibank created Yosemite expressly for Enron so that capital markets investors (rather than

Citibank) could fund the company's prepay activities (Citi, it seems, already had lots of credit exposure to Enron). Investors bought bonds issued by Yosemite, which passed the proceeds on to a Citi-controlled entity in the Caymans called Delta. Delta passed dollars on to Enron. Concurrently, oil, gas, or some other commodity flowed in the other direction: from Enron to Delta, Delta to Citi. Sometime later (either months or years) Enron passed the dollars to Citi, which passed them back to Delta, which passed them back to Yosemite, which returned them to investors (the oil went in the opposite direction so that it wound up with Enron again). If you cancel out the commodity element of the transaction you are left with a loan to Enron. Mahonia deals worked in the same way. While technically legal, the cash flows were always characterized as off–balance sheet transactions rather than the loans that they actually were.

Perhaps the worst part is that Citibank and J.P. Morgan knew that these deals were loans but never bothered to tell anyone. The internal e-mail evidence says it all. From J.P. Morgan: "The transaction provides a mechanism for Enron to . . . replace long-term debt with a trade payable" and "Enron loves these deals as they are able to hide funded debt from their equity analysts because they . . . book it as deferred rev[enues] or . . . bury it in their trading liabilities" and "They are understood to be disguised loans and approved as such." Or from Citibank's Capital Markets Approval Committee: "Although the deal is effectively a loan, the form of the transaction would allow the customer to reflect it as a liability from price risk management activities on their . . . balance sheet" and "[the deals are] simply manipulating cash flows."[5] (Come on, guys.) Why did the banks do it? To keep the machine going, to win new business, to keep the fees coming in. Citi earned $188 million from Enron between 1997 and 2001, Chase and Morgan $96 million. That's real money, and a powerful incentive to keep on doing what needs to be done.

In fairness, Citi and J.P. were not alone. They were the biggest, with more than $8 billion in "hidden loans" (Citi at $5 billion, including $2.4 billion via Yosemite and the rest via Jethro, Nixon, Roosevelt, Truman, and other entities, J.P. at $3.5 billion), but FleetBoston, CSFB, Barclays, Canadian Imperial Bank of Commerce (CIBC), and Deutsche were there, too. (Let's also note that they came up with other variations on the SPE theme, too, like Bacchus and Sundance, two Citi-sponsored SPEs that Enron used to inflate the value of its pulp and paper business, Nighthawk and Nahanni, two Citi-sponsored minority interest window-dressing SPEs, Braveheart, a CIBC-sponsored SPE that the company used to pump up revenues from a deal with Blockbuster, and so on. And the banks didn't just arrange these deals for Enron, they did similar things with other companies, like Pacific Gas and Electric, Duke, Phillips, Williams, El Paso, Mirant, Dynegy—so lots of other firms were playing the same silly game, thanks to accommodating bankers). Too bad these firms didn't call a spade a spade; it might have saved a bit of grief and caught some of the problems before Enron's Chapter 11 filing.

Of course, when things imploded, the Street (no, Street investors) had to pay up. Citi and J.P. Morgan agreed to pay more than $300 million to settle SEC and New York State charges related to "aiding and abetting" Enron in the manipulation of its financial statements through Mahonia and Yosemite (among other transactions); CIBC followed with an $80 million payment of its own. The banks initially tried to slither away, claiming that they shouldn't be responsible for how customers account for financial deals, but the authorities were having none of that. Manhattan District Attorney Robert Morgenthau indicated in his settlement speech that Citibank and J.P. Morgan knowingly helped the company disguise the full amount of its debt; he also said he wanted internal overhauls at both banks so that there would be no more "phony baloney"—and we all live in hope of seeing that day! A *Wall Street Journal* op-ed piece captured the essence of the whole affair very nicely: "It's no defense for the getaway driver to say he didn't know what those guys with the masks were doing at the teller window."[6]

On certain occasions banks help clients do discreet things to make their year-end financials look better through a process known as window-dressing. They arrange transactions that shift revenues or cash flows from one period to another, or change the composition of a portfolio, or reengineer some other aspect of corporate assets, liabilities, and contingencies so things look better than they are. The end goal is to help a client meet earnings, or show less leverage or more liquidity, all in order to keep the stock price buoyant. Japanese companies have historically been big window-dressers (which has meant big business for Japanese securities firms and the Street's largest houses). It's also popular with many U.S. companies and mutual funds, which like to look prim and proper for the quarterly snapshot. Some window-dressing is technically legal but ethically questionable, while some of it, like parking assets with a bank or in an unconsolidated SPE, is completely illegal (but let's save that for chapter 6). Any bank that's helping a client window-dress, even within the letter of the law, is helping alter or obfuscate, all for the sake of some fees.

The Street has also learned that it can advise corporate clients to do things with their businesses to minimize (or avoid, or, dare we say, evade) tax liabilities, often through offshore SPEs. Companies do, after all, want to lessen their tax bites, and banks have found lots of clever ways to help them out. Sometimes, though, the Street pushes the edge of the envelope and draws the ire of the Internal Revenue Service (IRS). But banks are willing to take the risk because of the fees: the Street has discovered that arranging complex structured transactions that move taxable income to "other places" can be very lucrative; some tax deals entitle bankers to fees of 20–40 percent of taxes "saved," so that's up to $4 million for a $10 million tax structure, $40 million for a $100 million structure. Powerful motivation. Unfortunately for the banks, the IRS has caught on to lots of these schemes and disallowed many (although that just means that the Street will have to dissect the tax code from another angle and cook up some other clever ways of spinning money).

Playing "Catch-Me-If-You-Can" with the IRS

Tax trades have historically been big, if discreet, business on Wall Street, and the most aggressive banks have done everything possible to stay ahead of the IRS in sheltering income for their clients. Of course, tax minimization is a legitimate goal, and some areas of the tax code are, indeed, "gray," subject to interpretation. Wall Street has used the shades of gray as a way of squeezing every nickel out of a client's tax bill. The IRS has always been one or two steps behind, trying frantically to catch up: in 1986 it disallowed lots of the simple tax-driven limited partnership shelters that were in vogue during the 1970s and early 1980s—many of them created by lawyers and accountants, rather than the Street. By the time the 1990s rolled around bankers were heavily involved, adding in a layer of structural complexity that made the shelters much more difficult to detect—meaning the IRS lost more ground, which it didn't start to regain till 1997, when Congress passed some "antishelter" legislation (which doesn't spell the end of clever corporate tax trades, of course—they'll just appear in some other fashion).

The 1990s generation of "catch-me-if-you-can" deals took lots of different structural forms, but most of them centered on creating paper losses in shell companies and applying the losses to real capital gains, thus allowing client companies to reduce their tax liabilities. But the shell companies usually existed only to generate losses for tax purposes and the courts eventually disallowed their use. Once the smoke and mirrors vanished it became pretty clear that firms were simply trying to pay the IRS less than they were meant to be paying—meaning individual taxpayers were footing the bill for the misadventures. Some economists have estimated that up to $30 billion in tax revenue may have been lost through these arrangements.

Let's consider a few examples: in April 1997 Bankers Trust created a new tax shelter for Enron, "Project Steele" (or maybe the bank misspelled it, and actually meant Project Steal), intended to shelter the company from taxes (naturally, the term sheet had the usual legal disclaimers, noting that the deal would be nullified if any law enacted by the IRS required the transaction to be registered as a shelter). Through Steele, Bankers Trust transferred underwater mortgage-backed securities to an offshore SPE known as ECT Investing Partners, which was jointly owned by the bank and Enron. Since ECT was jointly owned, both claimed a share in the deduction arising from the losses on the securities (Enron claimed $78 million, and the bank took its share and $11 million in fees. Not bad). Unfortunately for Bankers Trust and Enron (and lots of others), the congressional antishelter bill passed in August 1997 required Street firms to start disclosing their tax shelter structures, including vehicles like ECT/Steele; that would put them up for review by the IRS and possibly reverse tax loss applications if they were found to be in violation of tax law. Never mind, Bankers Trust contacted Washington, D.C., law firm Akin Gump and, for a fee of $1 million, asked it to "opine" on the validity of the Steele structure. The lawyers helpfully noted that the "newly added provisions relating to corporate tax shelters should not be applicable." In fact, the deal and its supporting legal opinion were eventually the subject of much ridicule, and Steele was disallowed (one company can't buy another just to get its deductions); in a last-gasp attempt Enron and Bankers Trust tried to claim that ECT should be legal because it served a legitimate purpose—to "obtain financial income" for Enron. Nice try, but no go.

This bank wasn't alone, of course. Lots of others played the same game, including Merrill Lynch, Bear Stearns, and Deutsche Bank (lawyers and accounting firms were well represented, too). In fact, Merrill has had its share of ink in the press as a result of tax deals it created in the late 1980s and early 1990s for blue chips like Allied Signal, Wyeth (then known as American Home Products), Honeywell International, Brunswick Corporation, Schering Plough, Colgate-Palmolive. Each deal was unique, but based on the same premise as Project Steele: generating capital losses on paper to offset capital gains embedded in real corporate operations. The Wyeth deal was a bit convoluted and generated several years' worth of legal fireworks: in exchange for $7 million in fees, Merrill advised Wyeth to set up an offshore partnership (Boca Investerings) to generate paper losses for the U.S. businesses; the gains in the Netherlands Antilles' sub would generate nice tax benefits. This scheme continued for several years, till the IRS began reviewing its raison d'etre. Since Boca's sole mission in life was to reap tax benefits, the IRS instructed Wyeth to pay $226 million in back taxes, plus fines and interest. Wyeth protested and went to court; the judge ruled against the IRS in October 2001 and ordered the company be refunded. The saga continued when the IRS took the case to the U.S. Appeals Court, which overturned the previous ruling—meaning Wyeth became liable, once again, for underpayment of $226 million. End of the line. In fact, the presiding judge noted that the Boca operation established by Merrill and Wyeth was just "a sham." Several of Merrill's other clients lost out on their appeals and had to fork over back taxes and penalties as well. And Merrill settled up, too, paying the IRS fines for promoting the shelters.

This incarnation of corporate tax advice appears to have run its course. But wait till the next round, because there's always a next round. (Speaking of which, a few big banks were skewered in 2003 for sheltering hundreds of millions of dollars by creating registered investment companies that paid tax-free or tax-advantaged dividends: the banks transferred loans and other assets into their investment companies, which used the interest income to pay out dividends—in California there are no taxes on dividends flowing between a parent and sub; in New York, only 40 percent of the income is taxed. A total of $17 billion was transferred, lots of taxes saved. Till they got caught.)

———————

Even when banks do naughty things, like helping out a client with a questionable SPE financing or a tax dodge, they generally emerge with slightly dented reputations and checkbooks, but nothing worse. It's very difficult for regulators to nail banks on fraud charges—meaning lessons are not necessarily learned, and behaviors are repeated. If regulators want to prove fraud (as they apparently considered when they caught Merrill, Citi, and J.P. Morgan doing things like prepays, wash trades, and asset parking) they have to demonstrate, at a minimum, proof of "reckless disregard for the truth." More likely it will have to show that a bank had "actual knowledge" of a client's intent to deceive, and that's actually pretty tough to do. The end result? Fines, some wrist slapping, the usual no-contest pleas, and that's it—till the next one.

The bottom line is that Wall Street doles out good corporate advice intended to enhance enterprise value—but it also hands out very bad advice that does just the opposite. Whether the advice given is wrong or illegal, client companies and bank investors generally wind up losing.

BAD INVESTMENT ADVICE

Institutional investors—mutual funds, pension funds, hedge funds, trust departments, companies, non-profit organizations—are huge players on the Street. Even before May Day 1975 and the elimination of fixed commissions (which squeezed revenue margins from the retail business) big institutions have been the main draw. The first mutual fund was created in 1924, and the industry grew steadily to become a mainstay of the financial scene by the 1960s. Pension funds were introduced in the 1930s and 1940s. These fund companies, along with hedge funds, international companies, and state/municipal authorities, absorb a lot of the Street's primary offerings and routinely buy and sell in the secondary market. They are big users of all kinds of products, mechanisms and techniques, including derivatives, leveraged structures, indexing, portfolio optimization, and so on. But for all of their importance, institutional investors are often on the short end of the stick; the Street's shortcomings become clear when we look at some of the rotten investment advice it gives the big clients.

Before we dig in, we should note that there are different kinds of institutional investors. Some are very sophisticated and have a good understanding of risks, portfolio management, leverage, and derivatives. It doesn't mean they get it right all the time, but they have fundamental knowledge of what it's all about; they can price some reasonably complicated structures on their own and can usually manage risks by themselves. This sector includes hedge funds and very large, well-established pension and investment funds. Then comes a group that is a bit less sharp: active enough in the financial markets to know how to think about different strategies but not skilled enough to price a structured note or a complicated swap without help—meaning it's at the mercy of the Street. This group includes mutual funds, insurance companies, and multinational corporations with fairly active treasury centers. Then we have the "widows and orphans" set that doesn't really get any of this at all. They have lots of cash but don't know what to do with it. They don't know a present value from a future value, a callable bond from a putable bond, a collateralized mortgage obligation (CMO, a pool of mortgage-backed securities) from a collateralized loan obligation (CLO, a pool of corporate loans). That means they are prime targets for getting ripped off by some of the Street's less savory characters. This group includes municipalities, nonprofit organizations, endowment funds, and small companies without any financial/treasury management expertise. So these three broad classes of investors are the main focus of the Street's institutional pitches.

The Street is always looking for new institutional clients to sell things to. They come up with some ideas, pitch them to a whole bunch of current or prospective clients, get one to bite, offer the same to the client's competitors (who may follow suit once they hear their archrivals have done the same deal), and so on, and so forth, till entire sectors are involved in the same kinds of deals (usually speculative, of course). These "hot client sectors" become the dumping ground for whatever products the Street has cooked up. That can last a few months to a few years, depending on how toxic the underlying investments are and how well the markets are behaving. And when things go bad, as they in-variably do, all the institutional clients with the same trade get hit at the same time. The Street has actually followed this pattern for decades: in the 1820s banks urged investors to buy shares in fraudulent or speculative canal compa-nies, and in the 1840s and 1850s shares in mismanaged railroad companies. In the 1920s, industrial companies (as well as small investors) were lured into buy-ing leveraged investment trusts sponsored by J.P. Morgan, Goldman Sachs, and Dillon Read; the trusts were usually nothing more than giant, leveraged ponzi schemes that ended up collapsing. Goldman created one of the most abusive schemes, Goldman Sachs Trust Corporation, a high-flying pyramid fund that owned the Shenandoah Trust and the Blue Ridge Trust, among others. The leverage and pyramid structure didn't fare well in the 1929 crash, so everything came undone. When the share price of the fund collapsed from \$326 to \$2, causing \$300 million of losses for forty thousand institutional and retail in-vestors, the bank was hit with a spate of lawsuits that depleted its capital and sul-lied its reputation for years. Similar pyramids existed well into the 1960s, burning corporate investors on a fairly regular basis.

Fast-forward to the modern era of finance: in the 1980s the S&L industry, fresh from deregulation courtesy of the disastrous Garn–St. Germain bill, had a voracious appetite for anything turbocharged that the Street could come up with, including junk bonds (10 percent of S&L assets eventually found their way into junk), CMOs and mortgage derivatives, funky swaps, and LBO syndica-tions; much of this was funded by Street-supplied brokered deposits. In the late 1980s and early 1990s, Japanese *tokkin* funds, insurance companies, and indus-trial companies happily played the *zaitech* financial engineering game on the back of the Street's creativity in new issue arbitrage, stripped convertibles, eq-uity derivatives, and historical rate rollovers. In the early to mid-1990s, domes-tic and international companies and municipal/state funds in search of extra yield followed the Street's advice and piled into CMOs, derivatives, and struc-tured notes (many of them based on leveraged interest rates and emerging market currencies). In the late 1990s, hedge funds put on big carry trades, volatility strategies, convertibility risks, and superleveraged structures; in the millennium everyone got into index and single stock volatility. The Street was there during each episode, trying to stuff as much as possible into institutional portfolios. Unfortunately, market dislocations during each one of these invest-ment cycles caused massive investors losses. But never mind, the banks always find other clients to chase after.

So what kind of advice are the banks giving? What, exactly, are the Street's salespeople pitching? It ranges from the vanilla to the exotic, from the safe to the toxic, from the unleveraged to the superleveraged. Sometimes institutional salespeople (those charged with courting potential clients, building relationships, and closing deals) sell things that are pretty benign and boring: they advise clients to buy stocks or bonds for the long term or put on low-risk arbitrage trades (e.g., maybe an unleveraged convergence of on- and off-the-run Treasury spreads). Sometimes they pitch things that are a bit riskier, but still comprehensible even to relatively unsophisticated clients: they get clients to buy a foreign currency bond in dollars and leave the currency unhedged (meaning gains or losses from at least two sources), or buy options on stocks or bonds or indexes (meaning a little leverage works its way into the program), or CLO residuals or subordinated CMO tranches. And sometimes they sell things that are very risky (and which should be reserved for those who aren't faint of heart and can take some hits without fear of collapsing): they get institutions to buy juiced-up structured notes (with complicated coupons, nasty payoff profiles, and multiples of leverage), sell naked options on volatile references, and buy or sell exotic options with very complex payout formulas (e.g., a cubed power option on the implied volatility of the Financial Times Stock Exchange 100 index with an outside barrier on the price of 30-year sterling gilts, "quantoed" into Japanese yen. Don't ask). The latter category of risky instruments should be directed primarily at a handful of very sharp players who know what they're doing and can afford potentially large losses (even so, transactions should be accompanied by proper risk disclosure, downside scenario analyses, high-level clients authorizations, caveat emptors, regular revaluations, and periodic tear-up prices). But sometimes risky instruments are sold to those who don't really get it, because the aggressive Wall Streeters want to make a buck. And if a nonprofit organization in Des Moines agrees to buy some of the toxic waste, do you think a Wall Streeter is going to tell it not to? Probably not, as events have shown. In fact, the salesperson will make it pretty easy for the client. To put all of this into perspective let's divide our discussion of bad institutional investment advice into leverage, derivatives, and other dangerous creatures.

Leverage

"Leverage" is the Street's term for borrowing. It comes in lots of different forms, from standard things like loans, bonds, and repurchase (repo) agreement (short-term collateralized borrowings), to more subtle things like structured notes with coupons/payout formulas and embedded options that are automatically leveraged. No matter what form it takes, leverage has the effect of magnifying gains and losses. If you buy a $100 bond for $100, and the price of the bond rises to $101, you've made 1 percent. If you borrow $50 of the $100 needed to buy the bond, then that $1 price increase means a 2 percent return (forget about the borrowing costs). And if you borrow $99 of the $100, then you've made 100 percent: you put up $1 and made $1. Or you put up $1 million and made $1 million, you put up $10 million and made $10 million. Sounds enticing! Of course, if the price drops by $1, you've lost 100 percent. And if it drops by $10, you've lost 1000 percent. You put up $1 and lost $10. Too bad. You put up $10 million and lost $100 million. Big trouble. That's the magic of leverage, and it finds its way into lots of the Street's investment strategies, because the more leverage (and possible gains/losses), the more the bank can earn on the trade, and that's still the name of the game.

The Street's institutional salespeople routinely sell investment deals with leverage. The big game of the 1990s (and one which still exists, though in more discreet form) was to embed the leverage in structured notes, bonds with a nice wrapper on the outside (e.g., a AAA-rated issuer) but some fairly bizarre stuff on the inside, such as payoff coupons incorporating fantastic amounts of leverage: 5, 10, 15, 100 times—meaning big gains when things went right and big losses when things went wrong (some structured note coupons were based on exotic derivatives, which we'll consider later in the chapter). During the early to mid-1990s the Street found structured notes were a convenient way to give institutional clients (and some retail clients, as well) market action in ways that were palatable to the clients' stakeholders (e.g., investors, regulators). The advent of shelf registration in the late 1980s via SEC Rule 415 meant an issuer could sell securities "off the shelf" on very short notice, and the passage of Rule 144A in 1990 made it easier for private placements to be arranged and traded. Both were perfect kindling for the structured note fire. For instance, if a pension fund was restricted through its operating mandate to investing in AA- or AAA-rated paper, the clever Wall Streeters would just call up an issuer with a AA or AAA rating (there was a lot of World Bank, Freddie Mac, Fannie Mae, Sallie Mae, and General Electric paper out there for a while), ask if they could issue some notes on their behalf (maybe for a fee or a break on the funding cost), and then incorporate some exotic little coupon that didn't pay investors LIBOR or Treasuries plus a spread, but LIBOR minus a spread, or three times LIBOR minus a spread, or LIBOR squared, or five times five-year Treasuries minus two-year Treasuries, or things of that sort. They sold that note to the pension fund as a AA or AAA security (which it was, from a credit perspective, as the issuer had a low probability of default); never mind that the interest and/or principal on the note could be completely obliterated with a wrong turn in interest rates (or equity prices, or emerging market currencies, or other assets, because notes were linked to lots of exciting market references). The fund was adhering to the letter, if not the spirit, of its investment mandate, the issuer got some cheap funding, and the bank got some nice fees from the fund. Everybody won, so more deals got printed: $20 billion, $30 billion and $50 billion per year. It all seemed unstoppable. Until rates rose (or equities fell, or currencies devalued) and all of the leverage stuffed into the payoff formulas caused clients to lose 20 percent, 50 percent, or 100 percent of their principal. Then the fireworks started: our irate pension fund threatened action against the bank, the issuer got upset because even though it didn't do anything wrong its name got dragged through the mud with the latest Wall Street fiasco, and the bank wound up assuaging both of them: some quiet restitution (to the fund) and a 5 basis point break on the next funding deal (for the issuer). Guess who paid? The bank's investors. The really egregious leveraged structured note business faded but it still exists, sometimes in forms that aren't quite as obvious (leverage has, and always will have, a happy home on Wall Street).

It's not all structured notes, of course. There are plenty of investors who are urged by persuasive salespeople to get into the pure leverage play by borrowing in the repurchase agreement (repo) market. The effects are the same, of course: bigger gains when things are going well, bigger losses when they aren't. Again, there are lots of examples of clients getting burned: Orange County is the king of leverage gone bad, but there are many others, like West Virginia's Consolidated Investment Fund, which lost $300 million of its $1.2 billion in assets by betting on long maturity securities that were leveraged up through repos. The state's investment managers, apparently acting under the guidance of various Street dealers, were expecting a drop in rates and were very exposed to the reverse scenario which, of course, came to pass. Rates rose, the portfolio managers sold securities to meet margin calls on the repos, state investors in the fund panicked and bailed out, and a spiral followed, until 25 percent of the value of the fund had eroded. Then West Virginia sued Merrill, Salomon, Goldman, and Morgan Stanley, claiming that the large losses were the direct result of inappropriate strategies based on an excess of leverage. Merrill, Salomon, and Goldman decided to settle out of court (coughing up $28 million); only Stanley decided to play hardball. It was an unpleasant experience for everyone (and the banks probably aren't too welcome in West Virginia).

For the big players who understand the downside of leverage, there's no real problem—it's a free country, let them punt away. For the rest of them— the sitting ducks waiting to be picked off—it's a huge problem. And history shows that Wall Street doesn't always explain the downside as thoroughly as it should. It doesn't always tell its clients that they could lose $100 million on the

$10 million investment if the bond price falls by $10. For municipalities, unsophisticated companies, nonprofit organizations, and others that are relatively clueless (and susceptible to the charms of persuasive institutional salespeople), such a loss can be ruinous.

The Ways of Wall Street: Orange County's $21 Billion Punt

Orange County, a prosperous and important region of Southern California, has secured its place in financial history by being the site of the largest-ever municipal trading loss. To set the scene we first introduce Robert Citron, the treasurer of the county and the investment manager of the Orange County Investment Pool (OCIP). Over the course of 22 years, Citron built a solid record as a capable investment manager who was routinely able to outperform the market and return attractive yields to Orange County investors (e.g., school districts, water council, towns, and so on); OCIP's long-term average yield was 9.4 percent versus 8.4 percent for other state funds. For two decades everyone in the county was happy with Citron and OCIP.

We now move to 1994 and remind ourselves that there is no free lunch. If Citron was doing so well with OCIP—if he was regularly earning more than the average of other funds, and a great deal more than the risk-free rate—then he was obviously taking some kind of risk. There is no above-market return available without taking risk: Wall Street's sharks will always make sure this holds true, because they swim around and snap up any arbitrage opportunities that exist—if they appear, they might last seconds or minutes, maybe days. Not months or years, and certainly not 22 years. Citron was taking risk, whether or not the good citizens of Orange County knew it. What kind of risk? Interest rate risk, as it happens: mostly to the direction of rates (betting against higher rates), but also on the shape of the curve (betting against a flattening). No credit risk, no currency risk, no commodity risk, just interest rate risk—but lots of it. Citron built his whole investment strategy on the belief that rates would continue the downward march that had been in place throughout the latter 1980s and early 1990s, and positioned OCIP accordingly. Falling rates and a steep curve, more money to OCIP. Rising rates and a flat curve, well . . .

Enter Wall Street. Citron, with the help some friendly institutional salespeople and bankers, didn't just take the $7.5 billion OCIP had on hand in 1993 and buy a bunch of Treasury bonds; he leveraged the $7.5 billion several times. That is, he borrowed against the portfolio and bought more bonds, then used those bonds as collateral to finance the purchase of even more bonds. And he bought structured notes that already had leverage baked in (like inverse floaters: securities that pay more as rates fall and pay much less as rates rise). The county even issued its own short-term notes so that it could invest in 20-year inverse floaters. So, on the surface OCIP may have looked like a $7.5 billion fund, but in reality Merrill, CSFB, Stanley, Nomura, and a few others helped the county jack the fund up to the equivalent of $21 billion. That's how Citron made above-average returns, and that's why he looked like a hero—until Alan Greenspan started a series of rate increases in February 1994. That was the beginning of the end for Citron and OCIP, and the start of some massive headaches for all of the Street banks that had sold Citron structured notes and given him repo financing. But Citron and others ignored the dislocation at first—OCIP was a "hold to maturity" fund, so if it didn't have to liquidate securities it would sustain only paper losses; if rates retreated, all would be well once again. But that works only if you've got enough cash to cover obligations as they come due. As it happens, OCIP didn't have enough cash. (It's worth remembering, also, that OCIP wasn't a marked-to-market vehicle; as a municipal investment fund it didn't have to reflect its unrealized profits and losses on a daily basis, the way Wall Street banks do—so outsiders had no clue as to how much money was actually going down the tubes).

As interest rates rose steadily through 1994, OCIP started bleeding more profusely. By September 1994 the cash market value of the fund was down several hundred millions of dollars, and by November 1994 fund officials were trying to persuade Wall Street banks not to pull the plug on the repo financing (i.e., not to sell the Treasuries to repay the loans). Though there had been steady chatter throughout the third and fourth quarters of 1994 within the county regarding potential problems in the fund, Citron and his colleagues didn't drop the bomb till December 1—when they finally announced to the public that OCIP had sustained paper losses of $1.5 billion. The $1 trillion municipal bond market, worried that there might be other such counties out there, immediately took it on the chin, losing 1 point almost instantly—$10 billion total. As panic set in, J.P. Morgan took a look at the unencumbered structured note portfolio and offered to buy it for $4.4 billion (that was a $100 million profit to OCIP based on where they were valued, but almost certainly a lowball bid as it seemed that Citron didn't know how to value structured products and the banks weren't telling him how). The county declined the offer, forced Citron to resign, and tried to figure out whether to reorganize or declare bankruptcy. Everything collapsed shortly thereafter: with little cash left to pay interest or redeem notes that had been put to the county, the banks circled around the portfolio. In the first week of December Nomura noted OCIP was in technical default on $5 million of bonds, CSFB demanded repayment of $1.25 billion of repos, and a run on the fund started. (The whole timing was a bit unfortunate, as it coincided with Mexico's devaluation of the peso, which burned lots of other leveraged players, including companies and banks—so everyone was already in a bad mood.) All the repo lenders, save Merrill, liquidated their collateral, crystallizing losses in the fund. Orange County had no choice but to file for bankruptcy.

Years of good performance (because of leverage) were blown away by eight months of rate increases (because of leverage): no free lunch. After the collateral liquidation some $5 billion of underwater leveraged structured notes that hadn't been repoed remained untouched, along with the remainder of the Treasury portfolio. Over the course of the next six weeks Salomon arranged the sale of $7.5 billion securities—$4.7 billion flowed back to the county, and the rest went to creditors. The total loss came in at $1.7 billion: $360 million from fixed rate notes, $620 million from inverse floaters, and $620 million plus from repos. Of course, all the Monday-morning quarterbacks were quick to point out that the securities were liquidated at the worst possible moment: by the end of 1994 the Fed was done raising rates, and if OCIP had been liquid enough to hold the portfolio, $1 billion of the loss would have come back. If only . . .

Citron was certainly to blame for the fiasco, as the courts eventually decided; though he claimed he was "unsophisticated" and was being led around by Wall Street, no one much believed the babe-in-the-woods defense. He pleaded guilty to six felony counts related to making misleading statements in selling securities, falsifying accounting records, and redirecting investment funds (not for losing the $1.7 billion). But the banks were to blame, too. Without Wall Street on hand to cram the latest (overpriced) structured note down OCIP's gullet or supply all of the repo leverage, the damage would not have been as great. CSFB had $2.6 billion of repo out to the county, Merrill $2.1 billion, Morgan Stanley $1.6 billion, Nomura somewhat less. Merrill's star salesman, Michael Stamenson, sold OCIP $2.8 billion of inverse floaters over the years and kept pushing the bank to do more repo, more leveraged business. (To be sure, some within Merrill wanted to cut OCIP off and repeatedly warned the county about the danger of its exposures; some bank officials begrudgingly offered to repurchase some of OCIP's structured notes in early 1994—but the objections and proposals came to naught and business just chugged along because it was very profitable: in 1993 and 1994 alone, Merrill earned $100 million in underwriting fees and trading commissions from the county). Merrill also seems to have taken the country for a ride on some of the notes it sold, charging far more than they were worth. For instance, just one month before OCIP's bankruptcy, the bank underwrote a $600 million structured note issue (under a Sallie Mae wrapper) and sold the whole pile to OCIP at 100.628. The next day the bonds were valued via financial information services at 96.89. Sure, Merrill's got to make a spread, but 4 points on $600 million sounds like an awful lot. Merrill was also sloppy in other areas: when the bank led a bond issue for the county in July 1994 it said proceeds would go to a "leveraged pool" but made no reference to the unrealized losses that were already mounting—bad disclosure. If a large unrealized loss isn't a material disclosure item, then what is?

The banks weren't really at risk to the county's credit performance: everything they had done or sold had been collateralized or sold outright. OCIP investors/pool participants, however, were at risk—in fact, school districts, fire-houses, and other municipal entities that had invested with Citron lost real dollars. But the banks were at risk to client suitability. In January 1995 Orange County sued Merrill for $2.4 billion, claiming the firm had "wantonly and callously" sold the county risky securities in violation of state and federal laws. The county claimed ultra vires, saying that it was acting out of its legal scope and that the trans-actions were unsuitable (the same claim was used by the City of San Jose in a case against Merrill; the city lost millions on asset-based securities that Stamenson os-tensibly said were "absolutely safe" and "couldn't lose money." Merrill settled that one out of court). County bondholders also sued Merrill and Citron for false dis-closure in the July 1994 bond prospectus, and separate suits were filed against No-mura and CSFB for their role in granting excessive amounts of leverage. All of the banks initially denied any wrongdoing, but then changed their minds, and settled out of court: Merrill paid $437 million, Morgan Stanley $70 million, CSFB $52 million, Nomura $48 million. Leverage can hurt everyone, it seems.

Derivatives and Other Dangerous Creatures

Derivatives are the lifeblood of Wall Street's risk and investment efforts. These instruments, in whatever form they take (e.g., futures, options, swaps, forwards, and lots of exotic variations thereon, plus structured notes with embedded de-rivatives) let banks hedge their own risks and make trading profits. Just as im-portant, they let banks create clever risk-management solutions and investment ideas for clients. Of course, derivatives can be opaque, complex, and difficult to value, which means they are perfect for the banks—lots of gray areas to swim around in, sometimes to good effect, and sometimes not. The fact that these fi-nancial instruments have existed off the balance sheet for the past two decades has not been helpful in promoting transparency; the chance to get swaps and options on the balance sheet was defeated in 1985 and remained unchanged till the passage of some accounting rules (Financial Account Standards [FAS] 133) in the millennium—during that time period no one really knew what was out there, as evidenced by all of the horror shows that appeared (and even FAS 133 isn't too helpful when trying to decipher what's going on). The most complex structures, whether standalone or part of a structured note package, can be exceptionally difficult to price and manage. In fact, they can be so complicated that even the banks that put them together can stumble on occasion. So you can imagine what happens to the poor institutional investors on the other end (to wit, George Soros, megafund manager testifying in 1994 before the House Banking Committee, noted, "There are so many . . . [derivatives] and some of them are so esoteric, that the risks involved may not be properly understood by even the most sophisticated of investors").

Derivatives have become something of a dirty word over the past few years, particularly for those outside the financial industry who don't quite understand what they do, why they exist, why they're needed, or how they can cause so much destruction. Of course, things can get a bit sensationalized on the evening news when an Orange County or Enron or Procter & Gamble suffer some derivative-related explosions. They even make the evening business news when someone as respected as Warren Buffett calls them "weapons of mass destruction." But the bottom line is that derivatives are a fantastic innovation and extremely useful in helping the financial system transfer risks more appropriately (even Mr. Greenspan says so pretty regularly). In reality, the problems have more to do with the way banks structure and market derivatives than with the instruments themselves (unless we happen to see a systemic dislocation, in which case Mr. Buffett is almost certainly right on the money). Knocking on the door of an unsophisticated client and giving it the latest high-powered derivative is like going up to a teenager with a newly minted license and giving her the keys to a souped-up, turbocharged 350-horsepower sports car. The derivative, like the sports car, has its place, but it's not with the novice. Lots of the bad derivative-related investment advice that has appeared in recent years has come from aggressive Wall Streeters giving relatively naïve clients access to products and strategies that are wholly inappropriate (e.g., too risky), not really explaining up front what could go wrong, and then failing to disclose what trades are really worth on an ongoing basis. All of this spells trouble.

═══════════

Bankers Trust, Part I: Procter & Gamble's Gamble

Procter & Gamble (P&G), renowned maker of consumer goods, must rue the day when it started talking to the derivative sales representatives at the friendly bank on the corner, Bankers Trust. Because what started out as a rather silly and misguided effort to lower corporate funding costs morphed into a huge speculative play that spawned very large losses. We go back to late 1992 when the bank's sales force, try as it might, was having little luck getting P&G to bite on any derivative deals. After much persistence, though, it managed to interest the company in a small spec transaction on the Mexican peso (quite why P&G was punting pesos is not too clear). Throughout 1993 the bank pitched more deals, to no avail—until October 1993, when its salesman Kevin Hudson offered P&G a "superior alternative" through which it could earn "an enhanced coupon" with risk levels that the company was comfortable with. P&G's treasury apparently felt that Hudson's structure could help lower the firm's funding costs by 40 basis points (bp), to a level equal to commercial paper (CP) rates – 40 bp: that was its funding bogey (though why it chose to pay large fees and gamble in order to achieve its target funding is still something of a mystery).

In the event, P&G entered into a few deals with the bank in late 1993 that were intended to lower funding, initially to a very enticing CP – 75 bp (but only if rates remained stable or declined). The company first booked something called a leveraged constant maturity Treasury (CMT) 5-year/30-year swap ($200 million total) based on a rather convoluted formula: for the first six months P&G received a fixed rate and paid CP – 75 bp (simple enough), but for the remaining 4 1/2 years, it paid CP – 75 bp + (98.5 x [5-year CMT yield]/5.78 percent – 30-year Treasury price)/100. Meaning the whole thing was a leveraged bet, mostly on the general level of U.S. rates, but also on the 5/30 spread. Lots of leverage, too: about 17x to start (so the $200 million face value was really equal to a risk position of $3.4 billion) and, depending on curve movements, as much as 30x ($6 billion). The deal was not really about lowering funding costs, but speculating. Of course, if P&G got it right, it would lower its costs, but if it didn't it would lose. Big. It lost. Big. (An aside: P&G also booked a $100 million leveraged deutsche mark/dollar play a few months later, which eventually blew up).

It's now February 1994, and the Fed tightens rates by 25 bp—the first of several rate increases for the year, spelling big trouble for P&G. As rates kept rising, P&G's treasury started panicking and asked Bankers Trust for tear-up prices on chunks of the deals. When it became pretty clear that rates were only going to rise further, the treasury team should have closed everything down; but they feared the impact the mounting losses would have on quarterly earnings and were counting on a reversal. (There's an important lesson here: never hope, expect, or pray that the market will bail you out of a position, because it probably won't happen—better to take the pain rather than let it get worse). It finally closed out the 5/30 swap in $50 million pieces during March and April at spreads of CP+1055 bp to CP+1412 bp (just a tad higher than the company's funding bogey); that cost the firm $141 million. It also closed down the deutsche mark swap at a loss of $54 million. Total tab: $195 million. Then it went to court, claiming that Bankers Trust had cost the firm $160 million in excess interest costs (the CEO accepted only the first $35 million of losses, since that was the last time the firm had received trade valuations from the bank). It later came to light that BT didn't really provide any scenario analysis or regular updates, and actually lied about the early values of the swaps. As early as February 1994 P&G was down $38 million, but had no clue. To be sure, P&G wasn't asking about the value, but the bank wasn't telling. In the end, the two reached an out-of-court settlement and the bank (no, its shareholders) ate most of the loss.

P&G was silly to do a trade like this if it was really trying to lower funding costs. It was obviously in way over its head and naïve about the deal and the way things work. But, at the end of the day, a review of more than sixty-five hundred audiotapes from the Bankers Trust trading floor made very clear that the bank was taking the client for a ride. Hudson admitted on some calls that P&G had no idea just how leveraged the position was and didn't know how to value it: "They would never be able to know how much money was taken out of that . . . [n]ever, no way . . . That's the beauty of BT [Bankers Trust]." Not quite what you want to hear from a fiduciary you are trying to do honest business with.

Bankers Trust, Part II: Greeting Cards and Leveraged Swaps

Let's take a peek at Gibson Greetings, another Bankers Trust client that got caught up in the same maelstrom. Back in late 1991 Gibson (which makes greeting cards) entered into two $30 million interest-rate swaps with the bank: it received 7.12 percent over five years and paid 5.91 percent over two years. So for the first two years the company was to receive a low rate. Just six months later the bank offered to close Gibson out of the trades at a $260,000 profit, and the company agreed. Unfortunately, the swaps were worth at least twice that amount, meaning the bank: (a) made some extra money from Gibson and (b) proved what it already suspected: that Gibson couldn't value its own positions. That set the stage for bigger and more complicated trades—ones in which Bankers Trust could pump up the leverage (and fees/spreads) and tell the company whatever it felt like telling it regarding risk, valuations, and profits (so much for client relationships and any notion of fiduciary responsibility or ethical conduct). Subsequent deals were increasingly exotic, like one where Gibson received 5.5 percent fixed and paid the bank LIBOR squared divided by 6 percent: it was essentially a spec bet on rates, and Gibson would be in good shape if rates stayed low (which they didn't, of course). In another, a spread lock swap, Gibson paid the bank an off-the run Treasury rate plus a spread lock and received the midmarket swap rate plus an on-the-run Treasury rate: Gibson was basically taking a two-year leveraged view on swap spreads and Treasury yields. In yet another deal, a Treasury-linked swap, Gibson received the lesser of $30 million or ($30 million x 1—[103 x two-year Treasury yield/ 4.88 percent]—30-year Treasury price)/100). In this gem, principal repayment was determined through a 21 times' leveraging of Treasury rates (plus a side bet on the price of 30-year Treasuries just to spice things up). There were other deals, similarly esoteric and risky: a ratio swap, a periodic floor, more spread locks, some knock-out calls, a time swap—and various restructurings of all of these as the Fed kept raising rates and Gibson kept losing. In fact, the company picked the worst time to engage in leveraged speculation in U.S. interest rates on the downside, and it's not too clear what Gibson was doing or why it was doing it. To make matters worse, during the two years in question Gibson didn't even know the true value of its positions and was routinely misled by the bank (in some cases Bankers Trust underestimated the company's losses by up to 60 percent). Again, Gibson needs to take a little responsibility for all of this. If it couldn't value the trades, why was it doing them? And why didn't it tell its own shareholders what was going on (e.g., in its 1993 annual report, the sum total of its disclosure to investors regarding these little bombs amounted to "$96m notional [face value] of swaps." Not very helpful. In fact, the company didn't come clean with more information until the news started getting bad).

Bankers Trust earned $13 million from Gibson on the trades before everything blew up. Gibson, for its part, lost $27 million on its package of swaps and options (the company's core operations had only made $50 million total over the previous five years, so this was quite a chunk). After it shut everything down, the company sued the bank for $23 million plus $50 million of punitive damages. The two finally settled out of court, with Bankers Trust releasing Gibson from $14 million of payments.

The bank didn't treat P&G, Gibson, or its other derivative clients properly, didn't have controls over periodic client disclosure, and generally seemed to encourage a "cowboy" mentality in its sales reps. And the bank ultimately paid the price for its lack of control and poor behavior: it damaged its reputation so severely that few could trust the bank (even senior management changes didn't help much). The market pummeled the stock and kept it down as it became clear that the bank didn't have much of a franchise: it was pretty much all about questionable, high-margin business—which was all but gone. Clients decamped, key employees left, and the balance of the bank's business became lackluster. The next chapter in the bank's saga involved some trading hits during the Russian crisis of

1998 and a subsequent sale to Deutsche. Bankers Trust's "glory days" ended in disgrace and absorption.

Of course, these trades happened a few years ago, and clients now have access to tools that can help them value their positions. But today's deals can be even more complicated, and they are still driven by the banks and their prices, so what they say tends to go. If a bank knows a client can't value its positions very accurately, and it can get the client to speculate, then there's room for abuse. It has happened regularly since derivatives were created, and there is nothing on the horizon to suggest that the behavior will change.

────────────

Since OTC derivatives hit the financial mainstream in the 1980s, the Street has always featured certain houses that have been at the leading edge of clever derivative-based investment ideas. The leadership tends to change every few years as institutions run aground or encounter troubles with clients or their own trading books, or decide to "refocus" their efforts away from risky derivative trading to more mundane things (for a while, at any rate). During the mid- to late 1980s it was Citi, in the late 1980s and early 1990s it was Bankers Trust (now part of the Deutsche combine), in the mid-1990s it was CSFB (via its CS Financial Products subsidiary, which eventually got into trouble with Japanese regulators for obfuscation and obstruction, lost its banking license, and got folded into the main CSFB unit), then it was J.P. Morgan Chase, and so on. The leader of the moment often sets the tone for the rest of the industry. Once the leading bank comes up with a smart (and often risky and profitable) derivative structure, it gets a few clients to trade (usually by putting in a little first-year teaser, like a higher coupon on a structured note or a juiced-up rate on a swap), and makes a bit of green. Competing banks get hold of the term sheet, reverse engineer the deal, and then pitch it to their own clients. As competition heats up, profit margins compress (meaning the banks probably aren't getting paid enough for the risk they're taking, a problem we address in chapter 7), so new variations are introduced—anything to try to get clients to bite. Then a market dislocation sweeps through the system and flattens all firms holding the same risky trades; that might spawn a few lawsuits, and force the banks to take hits in "making the clients whole." The cycle was especially evident in the mid-1990s, but it continues through the millennium.

While much of the Street's corporate derivative business operates on a pretty even keel, it certainly hasn't been trouble free. Lots of institutional clients have had problems with derivatives, failing to obtain the hedge or speculative results they were expecting; in some instances they appear to have been utterly clueless about what they were doing. More than a few companies have succumbed to bad advice and intense pressure from institutional salespeople and entered into inappropriate transactions, sometimes without getting the right risk disclosure and valuations. In some instances those suffering losses take legal action against the arranging bank(s). And some who get burned but decide not to take action against their advisors (blaming themselves for what might have been bad internal decision making) swear off derivatives entirely. The list of wounded parties runs into the hundreds, so we include only a small sampling to illustrate the point: in 1994 Caterpillar lost $83 million on caps and swaptions, and Dell lost $30 million on leveraged interest-rate swaps; in 1995 French state tobacco company Seita lost $80 million on a series of currency swaps and options (and sued Salomon); in 2000 Asia Pulp and Paper lost $220 million on several currency swaps; they are joined by others such as Procter & Gamble, Gibson Greetings, Air Products, Sandoz, Federated Paper Board, many Japanese, Korea, Chinese, Thai, and Indonesian companies (some that took action against J.P. Morgan, Deutsche, and UBS), and a large number of municipalities and nonprofit organizations. Risky derivatives aren't necessarily bad, but they aren't always appropriate for nonfinancial institutions—yet the Street often pushes clients to deal.

J.P. Morgan's Adventures in Korea

Before its merger with Chase, J.P. Morgan was a powerhouse in derivatives, particularly structured transactions (after its merger it became even more powerful, as Chase was a huge player in its own right, especially in the liquid derivative markets). And like several other Street houses, J.P. sought to capitalize on (and sometimes create) offshore demand for speculative trades. Despite all of the lessons from Bankers Trust's misadventures with Procter & Gamble, Gibson, and other companies, J.P. decided to continue selling relatively unsophisticated clients high-risk derivative instruments, meaning lots of leverage on volatile (or potentially volatile) market references. In early 1997 J.P.'s derivative sales team started pitching some very risky trades to a number of Korean firms (one insurance company, one securities firm, three investment companies [and three banks, as guarantors]).

These trades—dubbed "promax" for profit maximization (whether this promax was intended to benefit the clients or J.P. Morgan isn't entirely clear)—were essentially speculative deals on Japanese yen, Thai baht, and Indonesian rupiah. But they all started when clients said they needed access to cheaper funding. Borrowing in Korean won was costing them 7 percent, but borrowing in yen was only 2 percent. However, there were fears that the won would weaken against the yen, which could theoretically boost borrowing costs if not properly managed. So the J.P. Morgan gurus came up with a "synthetic yen loan hedged with baht." Somehow they made it seem that, because the baht was pegged to a basket comprised of dollars, deutsche marks, and yen, there was enough of a link to provide a yen hedge. Unfortunately, if baht weakened, the client would lose. To add a little zest, the bank urged clients to use proceeds from the synthetic loan to invest in rupiah-linked notes. They would earn 30 percent in dollars as long as baht and rupiah remained relatively stable. Thirty percent is a lot of juice, which a firm doesn't usually get without taking some risk. But there doesn't seem to have been too much discussion on the risk angle—about what would happen if baht and rupiah fell out of bed, about how bad it could actually get. Sure, baht and rupiah had been stable for the past 20 years, but there had been a huge buildup of speculative capital in both Thailand and Indonesia during the early to mid-1990s, and balancing capital flows, asset prices, and reserves was becoming more challenging. Remember, the Mexican peso had been stable for many years—and then December 1994 came along, the Bank of Mexico devalued (for many of the same reasons), and everyone got clobbered. But memories are short. The clients were apparently convinced that this was the right thing to do. Maybe they focused a bit too much on the 30 percent dollar returns and not enough on the downside; and maybe J.P. Morgan did, too. So, everyone signed the deals and it was off to the races.

Let's see how one of the transactions, for SK Securities, worked: J.P. Morgan and SK first executed the synthetic yen loan hedged with baht, which gave SK cheap funds. Then the two established a Labuan-based SPE called Advanced Investment. J.P. Morgan used its Frome legal vehicle in the Channel Islands to raise funds, which it invested in Advanced. SK and its partners chipped in sums from the synthetic yen funding, and Advanced used the combined proceeds to buy a one-year rupiah note, underwritten by J.P. Morgan. At maturity of the whole deal SK would earn $1.5 million if everything remained stable, but would lose if things started falling apart; indeed, the baht component of the trade was highly leveraged, requiring SK to pay the bank five times the percentage decline on $50 million of face value. So, if baht fell 2 percent SK would owe Morgan $5 million. None of the promax deals had any cap on losses, meaning real red ink if things turned ugly. And they turned ugly. By the time the first five promax deals had been booked in early 1997, baht was already looking a bit shaky. One week after the last two deals were booked (June 1997), the Bank of Thailand threw in the towel and stopped defending the currency. The initial devaluation produced a $50 million loss for SK; by September, with baht down 48 percent, SK was $120 million in the hole. In fact, by the fourth quarter of 1997 the clients were down a total of $757 million ($500 million from baht, the rest from rupiah, which had also delinked), so J.P. Morgan's management decided to stop all credit extension in Korea.

By early 1998, the bank had a pile of unsecured credit exposure and was trying to persuade its clients to make good on monies owed; if it couldn't, it would have to report sharply lower earnings. It wasn't too persuasive: two banks paid up on some of the losses, but the rest felt they had been wronged and chose to fight: they started a series of lawsuits in Seoul and New York, claiming the trades were unsuitable and the bank had breached its fiduciary duties by not adequately explaining the risks. Housing and Commercial Bank of Seoul, a guarantor on three of the trades, was outraged, calling the deals "casino trades." J.P. Morgan countersued, claiming that everything was aboveboard and properly documented (but it also set aside $500 million in reserves in 1999 to cover the losses, just in case). Ultimately, the bank wound up eating most of the losses, which was unpleasant for J.P. Morgan's investors, but not bad compared to the fact that one of the clients, Shinsegi Investment Trust, went bankrupt and another, Hannan Investment Trust, came under such severe financial stress that is was forced to sell out to a competitor—all because of some highly speculative derivatives.

Throughout the dénouement, J.P. Morgan argued that it had valid contracts with its clients, so the trades were good, legitimate, and fair. Legally, maybe. Ethically, who knows? Would a client really knowingly sign up for a trade that could put them down $120 million with a 50 percent currency movement? And it's not clear what folks at J.P. Morgan understood, either: would a bank really want to put itself in a situation where it had to knock on a client's door and ask for $120 million (all for a few million in fees)? Or tell shareholders that it had to take a $120 million pop in the quarterly financials because it didn't realize that the trade could generate so much unsecured credit risk? Or $757 million? The job of the Wall Street firm is to guide clients, and to take some extra responsibility when it's clear that they are unsophisticated (forget the fact that they might be greedy, because that's not really the point). It's far better to tell them in plain terms that losses could be $100 million or $1 billion if particular scenarios were to happen (because those scenarios tend to happen) and make sure that everyone within each client organization—from the board down to senior executives—acknowledges the downside, in writing. It's far better to cap out the losses so that no one walks away too disappointed. It's far better to go the extra mile, especially on risky deals.

———————

Derivatives aren't the only things in the eye of the storm; other instruments, like CMOs, can turn out to be just as risky. CMOs are just pools of mortgage-backed securities (MBS) except that Wall Street, in its creativity, found a way several years ago to convert some of those pools into high-powered, high-risk packages by carving up the underlying MBS cash flows into different forms, sequences, and amounts. The real heyday of CMO exotics was in the late 1980s and early 1990s, when Kidder, Merrill, Bear, Salomon, and others put together very exotic tranches that reacted in different ways to movements in interest rates (CMOs of the late 1990s and millennium have reappeared in more benign form—which is not to say that the dangerous stuff won't return, of course). Lots of the riskiest CMO tranches—things like companion bonds, superfloaters, and sticky jump z-bonds (no kidding), were sold to fairly unsophisticated and unsuspecting institutional customers as "mortgage investments." Hardly. Many securities were leveraged, volatile and illiquid, and they often reacted unpredictably to mortgage prepayment rates—meaning that as soon as rates started moving investors could get hurt badly. One of the dangers of esoteric products like customized CMO tranches is that there is no liquidity and no price except the Street's price. So if investors want to get out of a position that's heading south, they're at the mercy of the Street, meaning even more losses. In fact, institutions like Glaxo, Capital Corporate Federal Credit Union, and Postipankki, among others, found out during the 1990s just how dangerous CMOs could be—all lost heavily. One major fund, Askin Capital, went under in a matter of days, blowing through $600 million of capital invested in CMO sludge; when Askin missed some repo margin calls, the Street liquidated all of the toxic CMOs held as collateral and the fund disappeared. And they were so dangerous that Kidder Peabody, the market leader of the time, basically came undone by holding too much risky paper when rates rose (if they couldn't get it right, how could investors?). Though the bank had General Electric's balance sheet behind it, the losses it suffered on a big inventory of unsold CMOs (coming at about the same time as the Jett zero coupon fiasco, next chapter) led General Electric's management to dismantle the bank and put it to rest. Although the market for really exotic CMOs derailed by the mid-1990s, it is by no means dead and gone. In fact, it's alive and well (if slightly tamer) in the millennium; of course it's hard to predict whether sticky jump z's will ever return, but if it's not z's, rest assured it'll be something—maybe the CMO equivalent of the corporate credit market (collateralized bond or loan obligations [CBOs, CLOs]) or something else with a very sharp edge.

Again, there is nothing wrong with advising clients of risky investment opportunities, including those that are best done through derivatives or CMOs or CBOs or any other instrument. Every institutional client has the right to decide what is, or is not, appropriate for its own portfolio or business. So, it's perfectly fine when investment banks put together risky investments for sophisticated players, who must then determine whether they understand what's going on and whether they are in compliance with internal and external rules. It is, however, wrong for Wall Streeters to (a) be less than candid about what it's going to cost a client when the investment structure they've arranged goes sour, (b) pitch things that are wholly inappropriate for a certain segment of the institutional population, and (c) rip their clients off. Most of the Street's houses have been guilty of these behaviors in recent years (and some continue to be): the stories of traders at CSFB and Bankers Trust expressing great joy whenever they took advantage of a client are well known, and the pitching of "inappropriate" deals by the likes of Merrill, Goldman, Morgan Stanley, and others are a matter of court records. They should all know better.

In fairness, the clients should know better, too. They should know better than to open the door to salespeople with turbocharged products that are inconsistent with their operating mandates. Maybe Mattel should be making toys, not speculating (and getting hammered) on Mexican peso derivatives to the tune of $20 million; Yakult Honsha should be making yogurt and milk drinks, not losing hundreds of millions of dollars on Nikkei-linked structured notes; Glaxo should be making pharmaceuticals, not losing $140 million in CMOs. The same is true for all the other corporates that have lost big: Air Products, Sandoz, TPI Polene, Sinar Mas Group, and on and on and on. And the same goes for municipalities and nonprofits: Hammersmith and Fulham and other local authorities in the United Kingdom should be managing municipal affairs, not getting killed on sterling interest-rate swaps. The Wisconsin Investment Board should be managing the state's pension assets and finances safely, not losing $95 million on speculative currency and interest-rate swaps; the same goes for San Diego County, City of Auburn, Louisiana State Pension, City Colleges of Chicago, the Baptist Association of America, Odessa Junior College, and a whole load of state pension funds that have lost piles of money on risky things.

Belgium: Land of Chocolates, Lace, and Power Knockouts

Belgium is a charming and attractive country, boasting picturesque cities like Bruges and Antwerp, famous historical sites like Waterloo and the home of the artist Rubens, delicious chocolates and fine, handcrafted laces. Back in the mid-1990s it was also home to some rather enormous currency losses, courtesy of the clever derivative marketers at Merrill Lynch. While currency losses are interesting, and large currency losses even more so, what makes this case especially notable is that the losses were caused by exotic and dangerous derivatives: power knockouts—very risky options that expose the seller to an exponential liability that only disappears if a certain price level is reached. Not the sort of thing you'd expect a government treasury department to be dabbling in.

The story goes like this: between 1989 and 1993 the Merrill team convinced Belgium to sell it some power knockouts: Merrill paid some large amount of premium for these options, putting the country on the hook for an exponential payout if the options moved in-the-money. Power option sellers can make some good premium income while the options remain out-of-the-money, but all hell breaks loose if they start moving in the money. In fact, every exponential tick can be painful to watch. So to take away some of the potential pain, Merrill was kind enough to build in some knockout levels, extinguishing the country's obligations once particular currency values were breached. Phew. Through these trades, Belgium was effectively taking naked positions on the U.S. dollar strengthening against the deutsche mark and Swiss franc. It sounds pretty speculative, but maybe the Belgian officials were comforted by the knockouts, which would let them extinguish any accumulated liability and hang on to the juicy premium income. As it happened, the dollar started weakening. And it kept on weakening to the point that Belgium's reported unrealized losses reached $1.2 billion—a staggering sum, probably well in excess of anything the Belgian treasury officials ever thought could happen. And so the dollar kept weakening, to within a hair of some of the knockouts—but not quite. Then it started strengthening a bit, leading Belgium away from the life-saving barriers and leaving it with big losses. Toward the end of 1993, as the dollar rallied a bit, unrealized losses declined to $500 million or so—still a chunk of change for the treasury. When it became clear that the options weren't going to knock out, the country finally threw in the towel, unwinding the trades and taking a hit of "undisclosed size." And then it had a go at Merrill, accusing the bank of putting the country in a bad situation with the exotic derivatives and misrepresenting the risks of the trade (i.e., forcing it to take much more risk than it should have). For the next two years Belgium demanded restitution, reportedly asking the bank for $300 million. Merrill held firm (for a while) and then apparently got tired of dealing with the issue, so it wrote the Belgians a check for $100 million. The two parties signed a confidentiality agreement that barred them from talking about the deal and settlement, so many of the gory details will remain buried for eternity.

Another instance of poor Street advice, this time given to a sovereign. Again, there's no doubt that the Belgian officials have to bear some responsibility for agreeing to put on such risky derivative trades; it's hard to know what they were thinking. But what was Merrill thinking? It was the bank's trade idea (we can be pretty sure that a bunch of Belgian treasury guys sitting in the Brussels town square sipping coffee didn't come up with the idea of selling power knockouts to Merrill) and it should have known better than to put a country into a speculative situation in which it could lose $1.2 billion of taxpayer money.

━━━━━━━━━━━━━━━━

Sometimes, of course, the clients get so irate about all of the bad investment advice they've been given that they decide to tackle the banks head on in court. For some it can be a worthwhile strategy, because banks often seem willing to agree to some settlement (as discreetly as possible, of course). And remember: a bank that agrees to an out-of-court settlement—anything involving the writing of a check to the aggrieved client—has something to hide, no matter what the press releases say. The fact that there have been so many actions against, and settlements by, Wall Street tells us something isn't right with the investment advice that's been given to the institutional sector. The operating guideline for any Wall Street bank should be that the institutional client, no matter how sophisticated, seemingly sophisticated, or completely unsophisticated, should be handled with kid gloves. But that guideline doesn't always exist (or maybe it exists for a while in the aftermath of a problem, and gets discarded after everyone moves on to other things)—so wholly unsuitable investment strategies/products are still sold to clients who are pretty clueless.

Chapter 5

BAD PERSONAL FINANCIAL ADVICE

The Street's advice isn't just limited to Fortune 500 companies, middle market players, or whole countries, it reaches down to the grass roots. Most of the big players—Merrill Lynch, Morgan Stanley (through the Dean Witter folks), Citibank (via the old Smith Barney), UBS (Paine Webber), CSFB (DLJ), Wachovia (Prudential), plus big direct mutual fund companies—have legions of brokers (sorry, financial consultants) that blanket the country in search of willing customers (or customers, at any rate). Even firms that have more of an institutional tilt, like Goldman, Lehman, Bear Stearns, and Deutsche, are plugged into the high end of the retail market. They realize the importance of being able to pump securities and other financial products out to the masses, and generate trading commission or asset management fees from the millions of folks requiring financial help.

Even though the percentage volume of retail business flowing through the exchanges has declined steadily since the 1960s, the absolute dollar amount has increased dramatically. In addition, the amount of business that is funneled through mutual funds has marked a steady increase for the past three decades. Private clients purchase lots of shares and mutual funds (50 percent of outstandings), as well as government, municipal, and corporate bonds; they are also big users of 401(k)s, IRAs, annuities, company-sponsored savings and investment plans, and bank/money market accounts. The amount banks can charge retail for trade execution (commissions) and account/asset management (fees) is proportionally larger than what they can earn from institutions. If banks have the mechanisms to deliver service efficiently and keep costs down, and can keep persuading customers to bring in assets and trade, they can do very, very nicely from the private client sector. So retail is big business for the Street's major firms. It's also pretty important business for thousands of tiny registered broker-dealers, many of whom operate with the thinnest sliver of capital (and not always the best of intentions); there are more than five thousand of these little shops scattered around the country, so it's definitely buyer beware.

Though the private client business is important to the Street, it can create extra aggravation for banks, because the man and woman on Main Street have to be handled with kid gloves: these aren't professional investors with big balance sheets and deep pockets who are strong enough to take a few body blows. These are individuals who can be financially ruined by the misdeeds of Street brokers, meaning they have to be treated with care. None of this is particularly new, of course. The retail investor has been the subject of abuse since the 1920s, though the absolute number of private clients was still relatively small back then (between 4 million and 5 million). By the late 1960s, however, with a growing base of clients (30 million), a larger number of bucket shop brokers in operation, a big backlog in securities settlements (e.g., a whopping $4 billion of unaccounted securities in 1968), and a frothy market with lots of speculative opportunities, problems became larger and appeared more frequently. In fact, by 1970 there was enough funny business going on with little broker-dealers to prompt regulators to mandate the creation of the Securities Investor Protection Corporation (SIPC), an insurance fund to protect retail investors from brokers who hit the wall (a good thing, too, since more than 120 brokers failed or had to be rescued in 1970–1971). It also put in a few other regulations to give small investors a little extra protection, and has had to freshen them up regularly ever since as new abuses come to light.

In fact, many things can go wrong between Wall Street and Main Street, but we'll focus on two broad areas: risky investments and bad behavior (we'll save our review of breach of trust and fiduciary problems for the next chapter). The two are related, but different: risky things center on selling investments that are legitimate but inappropriate (or "unsuitable," as arbitrators say) for Mom and Pop (better, perhaps, for some offshore hedge fund that loves a dangerous punt). Bad behavior is doing the wrong thing, like not telling Mom and Pop the whole truth, pushing them to do things through uncomfortable, high-pressure tactics, deliberately steering them toward something that they don't need or that is more expensive, or stiffing them by giving all the good deals to the institutional clients. Sometimes risky things and bad behavior come together to create a real dog's breakfast. Either way, when things go wrong they often wind up in front of an arbitration panel or in some hushed closed-door settlement. It if gets to arbitration the panel might well side with Mom and Pop—because they are often right, and the Street's brokers are often wrong. But going through arbitration takes awhile, so Mom and Pop suffer till there's a settlement. Interestingly, Wall Street has protected itself from individual lawsuits in the court system by including arbitration clauses in account opening forms. So if the client signs the form, any future dispute is going to be arbitrated, not adjudicated; that's much better for the Street, as it's quiet and there's no public disclosure of the events (meaning no press or publicity that could tarnish the all-important reputation). In fact, most people are unaware of the depth of some of the problems precisely because there is no press. Lawsuits generally only come into play when there's a class-action movement—then lots of aggrieved investors band together and take action against the brokerage as a corporate entity (there's usually a lot more airplay, too).

Retail clients. So important, yet so often mistreated.

BROKERS SELL

Before digging into risky things and bad behavior we need to talk about brokers (sorry, financial consultants; no, let's stick with brokers, because that's really what most of them still are). There are two issues here that can affect behavior: pay for production, and the agency role.

Brokers are salespeople, and salespeople have to sell in order to survive (brokers have to be licensed, of course, but getting a license isn't difficult). When salespeople are selling something they're usually just interested in completing the sale—not necessarily in making sure that what they're selling is good, right, or appropriate. So things can break down. There is, of course, a fundamental conflict in retail brokerage: pay for production. Brokers get paid based on what they produce, so the more they produce, the more they get paid. Each trade they execute for a client generates commissions, fees, spreads, or markups, which together lead to gross production, and gross production links to a broker payout: the higher the production, the higher the percentage payout. So the broker may get 40 percent of the first $100,000 of gross production, 50 percent of the next $200,000, and so forth. Not surprisingly, risky investments have higher commissions, fees, or spreads, and that helps boost production. That means brokers have more incentives to put Mom and Pop into a very risky, illiquid limited partnership or a private placement (with wide spreads/large commissions/great payouts) than into a Treasury bond or commercial paper (with tight spreads/small commissions/low payouts)—even though the limited partnership or private placement may be wholly inappropriate for a risk-averse Mom or Pop with very little room for capital erosion.

Then we've got the agency issue. Although we commonly think that brokers work for their clients, giving them the best possible advice and doing the right thing, they actually don't—brokers aren't fiduciaries of the clients, they are agents of their firms. Under securities regulations, those who offer advice and charge a flat fee are supposed to register as investment advisors, and, in so doing, they become fiduciaries. This means they have to put the clients' interests first, take the clients' side at all times, disclose any potential conflicts of interest, indicate how much of a markup is taken on trades, and so forth. Not so with brokers. Even though they may walk and talk just like advisors, their main duty is to their employers, and their main task is to generate business (e.g., trades, accounts, assets under management) so that the firm can earn commissions/fees and they can get paid nice bonuses. Their duty is to the firm, first, and the client, second. Sure, most of them are interested in nurturing client relationships. If they can't keep their clients happy, they aren't going to deepen the business relationship—which means they won't do more trades, increase their production, or earn bigger bonuses. But when the rubber hits the road, they are still agents of the firm. All of this matters because the client may not always be getting the full picture, the best treatment, or the most beneficial advice. When some questionable advice is floating around, clients need to be very careful, because the broker has no legal duty to act in their best interests. That said, brokers are still supposed to recommend suitable investments for clients, meaning they have to make some basic effort to understand the client's risk/investment profile, goals and financial status, and then make proper recommendations; the exchanges, wearing their self-regulatory organization (SRO) hats, have said as much (e.g., NASD Rule 2310 and NYSE Rule 405—the gist in both cases is that, before pitching an investment, the broker has to know about the client and make sure that the investment is suitable). But a look at the list of arbitration cases suggests that there's lots of unsuitable advice being doled out (and think of all those that aren't in arbitration—the ones involving clients who are too shy or embarrassed to come forward).

Once you realize that a broker is paid according to his or her production and that a broker's primary allegiance is to the firm, it's not hard to see how things can go wrong.

The Secret World of Funds, Part I: On the Edge

Mutual funds—those sponsored by independent companies and those offered by the major banks—are extremely popular with retail investors: 95 million Moms and Pops own mutual funds, and they command a 50 percent share of the $7 trillion market (up from 10 percent of a $1 trillion market in 1980). But fair warning to all the Moms and Pops (and, of course, other relatively unsophisticated investors, like nonprofits): funds move in mysterious ways and, despite being regulated, don't always do the right thing. In fact, much of what they do, and how they do it, remains secretive. Investors looking for answers on what funds are up to often have to search long and hard—and still won't come away with all the information they need. (And, remember, these are the onshore, registered, publicly traded funds, not the unregulated, offshore hedge funds—just forget about those guys, they operate in a world that is exceptionally murky, which is one reason that small investors usually aren't allowed to give them any of their money to play with).

Funds are so popular because they take the active management of portfolios of stocks and bonds out of the hands of Moms and Pops and put it where it belongs: with the pros. That makes lots of sense, because professional investment managers are probably going to get it right more often than the little guys. But make no mistake, they take their pound of flesh, sometimes have pretty lousy performance, and sometimes operate right on the edge (they occasionally sail right over the edge, but let's wait till chapter 6 for that). In fact, the entire character of the industry has changed in recent decades: funds have slowly evolved from fiduciary organizations to big marketing machines, meaning management of the business and priorities are different than they once were. And clients can suffer as a result. Let's see how.

Some fund managers trade heavily on a short-term basis, turning over portfolios many times each year (e.g., one study has found that one in four funds had turnover rates high enough to indicate improper amounts of trading activity; another study shows that portfolio turnover averages have gone from 15 percent [once every six years] in the 1950s, to 110 percent [once every 11 months] in the millennium). That's bad for investors because they wind up footing the bill for the extra trading commissions payable to Street brokers. Some fund managers position their own personal accounts before they go out and buy or sell something in size for the funds they are managing (aka scalping); that gives them a little additional personal income. Some portfolio managers are into "portfolio pumping," buying big blocks of existing holdings before quarter-end reporting periods to boost asset values—a form of expensive, short-term window dressing. Some fund companies give big clients (e.g., prime institutional investors) preferential treatment over the average Joe: after-hours trading, market timing, and so on (more on this one later). Some fund companies don't really talk about the risks they're running in their operations. They gloss over any detail related to the riskiness of what they're doing, how they actually cope with risk, what they do when things go sour, and what kinds of exit strategies they employ when they get hit by a wave of simultaneous redemptions (and they don't usually talk about how they manage to wedge derivatives and structured notes into their portfolios, sometimes in breach of the spirit of their investment mandates). Many mutual funds are focused on marketing, talking about the returns they've generated over the past x months or x years (they often calibrate performance discussion to reflect the slice of time in which things worked out well; some, like Van Kampen, Dreyfus, and Legg Mason have been busted for what regulators term "false advertising"). When a particular fund isn't doing so well (a so-called clunker fund) it sometimes gets quietly absorbed into another, better-performing fund; that helps the fund company's overall performance statistics. And many funds have structural governance problems. With rare exception (e.g., Vanguard), each fund in a family of funds operates as a separate company that contracts services (such as investment management and execution) to the fund advisor; that means the board of directors of each fund company is largely in the dark when it comes to strategic and management matters—each board has access to information but little authority to act, which, as we'll see, has been the source of significant problems.

Some fund companies charge very high fees/commissions and try to bury the nature of the fees in creative language in order to confuse (e.g., distribution fee, management fee, deferred sales load, exit fee). Many are less than forthright about their expenses and how portfolio managers are compensated (in fact, most folks don't have a clue how much portfolio managers earn, and how much of their compensation is tied to meeting short-term performance bogeys—both of which can have a considerable influence on behavior). Funds get to charge "12(b)1 fees"—which help them to defray the costs associated with starting new funds (a practice that regulators have questioned for years but failed to resolve). And funds routinely pay the brokerage industry "soft-dollar" commissions for a variety of services and fees for being on the selected brokerage sales lists—and both get charged back to investors (the precise amounts are unknown, but some estimates place soft dollars at $1 billion a year and brokerage selected list fees at $1.5 billion a year). Depending on the metrics and population of funds one uses, the industry had between $35 billion and $70 billion of annual costs during the early years of the millennium; lots of these costs, equal to an average of one-half to more than 1 percentage point per year per fund, are passed on to investors (and despite the fact that economies of scale exist, the costs seem to be sticky—rarely, if ever, declining).

In truth, the average Mom or Pop doesn't really know what's going on, what he or she is paying for; expenses are often high, transparency is low. No, not all funds are into churning, obfuscation, scalping, or false advertising, and lots of portfolio managers and fund companies try to do the right thing. But some don't, preferring to live in the shadows. So, for Moms and Pops it's back to caveat emptor.

RISKY THINGS

Sometimes Wall Street tries to get its retail clients to buy investments that are very risky. There's nothing wrong with risk, of course. Contrary to popular belief, risk is not all bad; it's not a monster lurking in the dark, waiting to get some innocent Mom or Pop. Risk that is priced right (i.e., that carries the right return) can be a good thing. Actually, if no one took any risk (financial or otherwise), where would we be? Probably not nearly as advanced economically and financially, because risk capital fuels the engines of growth. But not everyone can afford to take risk, to put his or her money on the line. Individuals can, of course, take risks commensurate with their wealth and earnings, age, family status, and retirement horizon. But they usually can't afford to take very much risk. Because when they do, it often ends badly: they lose more than they can afford to lose and suffer financial distress; they may have to sell their houses or liquidate their college/retirement funds, or even borrow just to get even again. That's a slippery slope.

Even though brokers can (and do) sell their clients fairly low-risk and mundane investments, like blue-chip stocks, municipal bonds, Treasuries, and conservative mutual funds, and try to keep things pretty well diversified, some brokers do just the opposite, pushing things with the most juice (regardless of whether they're appropriate for the client's financial situation/goals). That means selling them investments like speculative technology stocks, junk bonds, emerging market bonds, CMOs, risk-laden mutual funds, and spicy structured notes (i.e., those with leverage, or exposure to the Argentine peso, Russian stock market, or Turkish bond yields—all under the guise of a AA or AAA agency issuer so things look attractive). It also means putting them into concentrated positions in securities, which is usually big trouble. A diversified portfolio may not have the same peaks as a single position, but it won't have the nasty dips, either; Moms and Pops need to avoid any situation where they might lose a vital slice of capital. And it may also mean getting them to leverage their portfolios through margin, or having them write some naked call options (even in a bull market) or naked puts (even in a bear market). A prudent broker will prevent risk-averse clients from engaging in any of these activities. But since the strategies generate big commissions, and since commissions mean bonus dollars, you can see what's going to happen.

Wall Street should know better, because they've been caught many times selling things that are too dangerous for the average client. A broker pitches Mom and Pop something with too much risk, it blows up during a market dislocation, they complain to the broker (and to the broker's manager and the manager's manager), write some letters to the regulators, threaten action, and end up in arbitration. There they receive some restitution, the broker (and the broker's employer) gets slapped on the wrist and pays some tiny fines, and the cycle repeats: time and again, client after client, cycle after cycle. And all because Street brokers are trying to flog risky investments so that they can generate more commissions and larger production, and earn bigger bonuses. They forget that the bank (and the bank's investors) loses when things go sour: it loses the client relationship (meaning future commissions), it loses money to penalties, and to some extent it loses its good name. It seems like a bad trade, yet it happens all the time.

There are so many examples of this misbehavior that we could fill thousands of pages. It's simpler, perhaps, to pick a few representative examples that provide a flavor for what goes on, and note that we can multiply these by tens of thousands (and more) to start approaching what's happened with private clients over the past few years alone (those so inclined can check out the websites of the SEC, NYSE, or NASD detailing violations and arbitrations, or the pending/concluded class-action lawsuits filed against brokerage firms, for additional fodder. It makes for somewhat gory, and depressing, reading). So here we go: in 1997 and 1998 Morgan Stanley lost several cases related to the sale of risky investments to its private clients; some were based on CMOs, and others related to emerging market currencies (through PERLS structured notes, which combined derivatives, risky underlying indexes, and fixed income notes to produce some very hot potatoes). The arbitration panels found they were simply too risky for the average investor. In November 2000 the NASD charged Morgan Stanley with violating antifraud provisions of securities rules by understating the risk of $2.1 billion of closed-end bond funds sold between 1993 and 1997 (by Dean Witter, before it became part of Stanley); thirty thousand retail investors lost $65 million because they bought something that was far riskier than they should have been buying. Bank of America (then in its NationsBank incarnation) got caught, too: the bank's broker-dealer affiliate sold investors a trust that paid 1 percent over 10-year Treasuries by investing 40 percent of its assets in inverse floaters (risky little things that sales managers often forgot to tell their clients about). When rates rose, the trusts lost a third of their value, and irate investors screamed—loudly. The SEC censured both the bank and its affiliate for "improper sales practices" that "culminated in unsuitable purchases by investors." In the mid-1990s a number of banks and investment managers cobbled together high-yielding funds for their private client investors, but sometimes forgot to mention that the extra yield came from taking risk (via leverage, derivatives); many funds blew up, customers complained, and the sponsoring banks had to swoop in and top things up (using shareholders' money, of course): Paine Webber had to pump in an extra $268 million to bail out its fund investors, Bank of America $68 million, First Boston $40 million, Merrill $20 million, and Piper Jaffray and Alliance millions as well.

Prudential's LPs

Prudential Financial (nee Prudential Securities, nee Prudential Bache, a sub of Prudential Insurance) has had a few misadventures in its life, being caught on various occasions for questionable sales practices, failing to properly oversee sales of mutual funds, wrongly selling more expensive funds to boost commissions, and other no-nos. The brokerage's worst failure, however, came from its limited partnership (LP) program, which probably seemed a gold mine when it was first created but became a nightmare for the firm and its retail investors. The problems date back to the early 1980s when Prudential Bache brokers began selling clients stakes in LPs that invested in a host of assets, including residential and commercial real estate, oil and gas development projects, and so on. The brokers pushed these because they received very handsome commissions—far more than they would on standard stock and bond trades.

Lots of the LPs were risky—loaded with credit risk, market risk, tax risk, legal risk, liquidity risk—but were sold by Prudential's brokers as entirely suitable for all kinds of retail investors, including retirees on fixed incomes. In fact, lots of investors were told they were getting low-risk investments with solid returns, a practical impossibility. But how were they to know, since that's how the brokers were pitching it? For a period of about seven years Prudential's brokers happily peddled completely inappropriate investments to more than three hundred thousand personal investors by misrepresenting the risks involved, lying about potential "guaranteed" returns—anything, in fact, that would lead to more sales commissions. The brokers were so slick that they managed to sell seven hundred toxic LPs—$8 billion worth—to the unsuspecting masses.

The worst of Prudential's LPs, based on real estate and energy, became almost worthless toward the end of the 1980s when tax laws changed and stripped away some of the benefits previously accorded to real estate, and as the energy sector became mired in problems of its own. LP prices collapsed and investors watched their capital evaporate. Perhaps worse was the fact that Prudential's management knew at an early stage that the LPs were souring, but kept on printing new ones for its hungry brokers to sell; it eventually came to light that management inflated payouts on some money-losing LPs in the mid-1980s by distributing borrowed funds, but kept on creating new deals until the end of the decade.

In 1993, after lots of complaints and a series of investigations into what Prudential and its army of brokers were doing, federal prosecutors charged the firm with fraud. Prudential was accused of all sorts of transgressions, including lack of proper disclosure, misrepresentation of risks/returns and liquidity, and misvaluation of investments. In an unusual move, prosecutors agreed not to press charges for three years if Prudential would establish a restitution fund and cooperate with ongoing aspects of a criminal investigation. Prudential cooperated and avoided a criminal indictment. The client restitution fund eventually topped $1 billion, and the firm restructured management and controls, but its reputation suffered (just as the pocketbooks of clients suffered, even after the restitution fund was created). Unfortunately, Prudential didn't learn from this rather horrific experience, at it was routinely hauled in on new charges (e.g., in 1999 it had to pay $20 million in fines related to deceptive sales practices, in 2001 it paid more fines for deceptive annuity sales, in 2003 it got caught forging annuity sales and market timing/late trading mutual funds). Some people (firms) never learn.

———————

A few more, to fill in the picture: in mid-2003 the courts awarded a family $1.8 million in damages because a Merrill Lynch broker didn't help it diversify a $57 million concentrated position in HALO Corporation stock acquired through the sale of the family business to HALO. HALO subsequently went south, and the family's fortunes with it. As if that weren't enough, the Merrill broker had encouraged the family to day trade actively—and it did, losing piles of money. Sounds like really bad advice: hold a concentrated position in an illiquid stock, and day trade whatever other assets you have. Then there's the 59-year-old teacher with $359,000 in retirement savings in an A.G. Edwards account who was advised to put her money into 15 superaggressive growth funds, in disregard of her needs or risk tolerance levels; she lost $200,000, more than half of her savings. Or a case in which Merrill had to pay a family $1.5 million in damages when the broker failed to do the basics of financial management, like diversify the family's concentrated position in Ariba, or arrange a collar to hedge the position, or give proper tax advice on a mortgage. Or the early retiree who was advised by his Merrill broker to take $325,000 out of his 401(k) (which was invested in an 8 percent bond fund) and put it into broadband and Internet stocks. Even though the client said he wanted no risk, the broker bought the high flyers, they plummeted, and the client lost a piece of his nest egg. He's not alone: millions of investors collectively lost billions of dollars as their brokers put them into overpriced stocks at the peak (sometimes based on the false/bad advice of research analysts, sometimes through aggressive sales pitches like "you're missing the boat, you're stupid if you don't buy this dot com *now* because its going to triple in value by next month," and so on). Olde Discount was forced to pay $7 million in fines to settle SEC charges that it created, and permitted to exist, an environment in which brokers routinely put clients into ill-suited investments, pushed margin down their throats, traded account assets without permission, and falsified records. Brokers regularly sold clients risky securities that Olde already had in inventory, whether or not they were suitable. In another case, a broker at a firm with an online trading platform let a client buy and sell more than $4 million of securities over a three-month period with only $12,000 on deposit in the account; the trading generated lots of losses for the client, lots of commissions for the broker.

The list goes on and on; many thousands of cases go before arbitration panels every year. Indeed, most firms with a significant retail presence, including Merrill, CSFB, Morgan Stanley, Citibank, and UBS, have been involved in arbitration and settlement on scores of these. Arbitrators have shown considerable sympathy for all the Moms and Pops who have seen their brokerage accounts, 401(k)s, IRAs, and savings accounts pulverized during financial dislocations. For instance, arbitrators sided pretty heavily with retail investors during the 1987 crash, the 1994 CMO collapse, and the 1997 Asian crisis because some of the advice given by brokers was unsuitable. They also favored clients hurt by the TMT collapse, holding many Wall Street firms accountable for recommending too much speculative, concentrated risk or for touting stocks through puffed-up research.

What about situations in which a client wants to buy something that is especially risky and wholly unsuitable, like a 10 times leveraged Turkish lira note? What if the client really, really wants that note? Surely that can't be the broker's problem? Actually, it can. Though it seems brokers are responsible only when they come up with some totally unsuitable investment, some arbitration panels have said that brokers have a duty to protect clients from themselves. But let's get real. How many brokers are going to turn away a client's order for the Turkish lira note—the one with the big spread? Not very many. They'll take their chances that it won't blow up, or that the client won't complain if it does.

━━━━━━━━

Bad Advice = Arbitration and Class-Action Lawsuits

Banks are probably wishing the technology boom had never come along because, even though they made lots of dollars on fees from IPOs, debt issues, and M&A deals, all of that is now gone, baked into past earnings and part of Wall Street history. But the arbitration cases and class-action lawsuits that it spawned linger on—and they aren't going away anytime soon. With $6 trillion of market value sucked out of investors' pockets from 2000 to 2003 (maybe half of that from Moms and Pops), lots of those who got burned are in a fighting mood.

Regulations require brokers to recommend suitable investments for their retail clients. There is some wiggle room related to the term "suitable," but it's pretty clear that a concentrated position in a dot com trading at 150 times expected 2010 revenues (not earnings) is probably not suitable for a retiree on a fixed income or a family building up a college fund for the kids. Neither is pushing volatile stocks on margin, or urging lots of day trading (10, 15, 30 trades a day), or a host of other high-risk spec strategies. But during the feeding frenzy at the turn of the millennium that's exactly what happened, and millions of investors got burned. Of course, many retail investors have rightly taken responsibility for their own imprudent actions. Lots of Moms and Pops recognize that they got greedy and have only themselves (and not their brokers) to blame. Win some, lose some, and they lost. So even though they may have been financially wounded, they aren't looking for scapegoats; they're just trying to rebuild their balance sheets (and maybe they'll remember not to be so foolish when the next speculative bubble comes along).

But many brokers gave their clients poor advice, and lots of these cases have gone to arbitration. Between 1994 and 2001 the NASD averaged between five thousand and six thousand arbitration cases every year. In 2002 that had figure climbed to seventy-seven hundred, and in 2003 to more than eleven thousand. Lots of them were related to "suitability": in 2002 alone the NASD noted that more than twenty-six hundred cases were filed on the grounds of "unsuitability," a 73 percent jump versus 2001. NYSE's own complaints doubled as well. (The NASD and NYSE figures exclude class-action lawsuits, which have grown in tandem.) And the same trends were evident in the mutual fund sector: in 2001, 543 cases went to arbitration, in 2002 that number jumped to 1,249, and in 2003 an estimated 1,800; again, most of the complaints centered on unsuitability. Though not all cases filed with the arbitrators go against the Street, retail clients generally are given a reasonably sympathetic ear and a greater likelihood of a payoff in arbitration (helped, no doubt, by the revelation of Wall Street's conflicted research, which is a topic of chapter 6).

Sometimes banks get slapped with class-action lawsuits because of their bad behavior. Hundreds, even thousands, of investors get together and lodge a suit against a bank (as a corporate entity) that has engaged in some malfeasance. Since lawyers and courts are involved, the proceedings can take a long time and the outcomes can vary widely. Not surprisingly, the TMT boom and some of the abuses it engendered have been a significant source of class-action activity. For instance, in 2002 the Street coughed up $2.1 billion in securities litigation settlements, an average of $20 million per case (up 40 percent from the average of 1996 to 2000); during the first half of 2003 the banks paid out another $1.5 billion, an average of $25 million per case. In one of the broadest actions, 55 banks were charged with manipulation of 309 IPO stocks during the late 1990s. Plaintiffs accused the banks of participating in a "coherent scheme by underwriters, issuers and officers to defraud the investing public." Allegations centered on unjust profiteering through misleading statements (designed to artificially inflate IPO prices), kick-backs of business, and prearranged aftermarket share purchases. This case appears to be indicative of what's likely to happen between Wall Street and the court system over the next few years—and beyond, if things like those mentioned here continue to happen. (Fortunately, judges are being the fair-minded arbiters we expect them to be and have thrown out class-action cases filed by retail speculators who made the wrong bets; to wit, a New York federal judge dismissed claims against Merrill, Goldman, and Stanley because the plaintiffs knew what they were doing in their investments, and were apparently trying to ride the wave of Wall Street settlements).

So Street firms (no, their investors) have paid out steadily on arbitration and class actions and are still facing potentially large tabs: not just adverse judgments or settlements, but also legal fees and wasted resources. In fact, some banks have already set up their "rainy day funds": through 2003, Citibank funded $1.3 billion for legal claims, J.P. Morgan Chase $900 million, and CSFB $450 million. Prudence, or an admission of guilt?

The important question is whether Wall Street brokers actually know that they're putting their clients into risky securities and just not telling them, or whether they haven't got a clue and are just reading blindly off some manuscript prepared by the research department, with little bite-size bullet points on what to say during the dinner-hour phone pitch. It's hard to know which problem is more serious. If brokers don't know what they're selling, then they should be selling something nonlethal, like vacuum cleaners or magazine subscriptions; banks should be called on the carpet (no pun) for letting unqualified people jeopardize the financial well-being of people who can't afford to be taken for a ride (in fact, there are regulations that say brokers must know all about the investments they're selling, but these are often flouted. How many brokers are going to read semi-undecipherable 200-page prospectuses on investments when they could be out playing golf with clients?). On the other hand, if they really do know they're selling clients risky investments (i.e., they know exactly how toxic the "attractive investment opportunities" are) but don't want to tell them for fear of scaring them off and losing commissions, then that's very frightening. Now we have a situation where brokers are scouring the land trying to take advantage of unsuspecting widows and orphans who haven't got a clue.

Squeezing the Little Guy

There are lots of little ways the average investor gets squeezed by the Street: payment for order flow, margin, and proprietary products, to name but three. All three are legitimate, but banks push them very aggressively for one primary reason: because they come out big winners—sometimes at the expense of the little guys. Let's take a look:

In the past, if a broker was associated with a brokerage house that wasn't a market-maker quoting two-way prices in a particular issue of securities, he or she had to get three outside prices and deal with the best one; that would give the underlying client the best execution price. In addition, the broker wasn't allowed to share in the spread when a trade was executed through an authorized market-maker. Now, however, the broker can take advantage of payment for order flow: it simply directs client trades to a market-maker (any one it chooses), the market-maker gets the business, makes money on the bid-offer spread, and then pays the broker a portion of the profits. It sounds like a kickback. Ethics aside, maybe it would be okay if the client was guaranteed best-price execution, but it's not: though the client is supposed to get the best bid or offer under this arrangement, the "requirement" is pretty soft, and often just ignored. The broker just channels the order to the market-maker it has the best relationship with, or the one that'll give it the biggest cut of the bid-offer spread—meaning the client loses if the market-maker's price isn't the best one available (and if a broker works for a firm with an internal market-maker, e.g., Merrill/Herzog, Goldman/Spear Leeds Kellogg, Schwab/Schwab Capital Markets, the firm as a whole gets to keep the entire profit, again regardless of whether it's the best price in town). Though the move to decimalization has reduced the profitability of this activity, it's still alive and kicking.

Margin is another little scheme: brokers often push clients to borrow against their portfolios to buy more securities. While margin is a good idea for the right investors and the right situations, it's often just used as another money spinner (and not because it's an appropriate strategy for a particular client) because brokers make money on three fronts: commissions on the original purchase of securities, commissions on the purchase of additional securities bought on margin, and interest charges on the margin loan being extended for the purchase. If margin is appropriate for the client and fits in with the client's strategy, great. But if it's not, then the client loses again. Brokers often sign their clients up for margin when they open accounts, regardless of whether it's appropriate—that makes it easier to push them into margin trades later on.

Proprietary products are a third way of squeezing Mom and Pop. Most large banks have product development squads that are responsible for manufacturing in-house investments to sell to their clients, like funds, trusts, LPs, structured notes, and so on. The rationale is good: by creating proprietary products, banks can generate commissions and management fees, and can keep the business in-house rather than watching it migrate to a competitor that already has a full complement of nifty products. In order to make sure the in-house products are successful, banks often give their brokers added incentives (i.e., bigger payouts) to push them out the door. Once again, advice to the retail clients may be biased in favor of the latest proprietary product the bank has created or some of the "oldy moldy" ones it's trying to get rid of—never mind that they may be totally inappropriate or that a much more suitable match can be made through a competitor's product. If a proprietary product is good and suitable and the best thing for the client (or a pretty close proxy), fantastic. But if it's not, and the intent is just to print more proprietary business, then the little guy gets squeezed again.

BAD BEHAVIOR

Some of the Street's bad advice comes from bad behavior, aka doing the wrong thing. Bad behavior doesn't have to relate to a risky thing; it can be about anything. Bad behavior can straddle the line of the ethical and unethical, it can cross squarely into the unethical, and it can go straight to the illegal. It comes in lots of flavors: churning accounts and encouraging overtrading, telling little (or big) lies, using nasty sales tactics, showing favoritism, and so on. The aim in all cases seems to be to earn more money (for the individual broker, the regional office, the entire firm), and the end result is usually a private client (or two, or a thousand) who gets taken to the cleaners. And bank investors often wind up holding some of the bag—client restitution, regulatory fines, loss of business.

Churning, Unauthorized Trading, and Selling Away

We know that the retail business is largely commission driven. Some firms are moving toward the annual asset-management fee scheme, in which clients pay a flat fee based on assets in the account and then get discounted, or free, trades (not that the annual fee is a great deal, of course, because the fees are usually pretty steep). But lots of folks still have accounts that are based on commissions per trade. This, as we've said, means the Street's incentives are skewed: brokers have every motivation to do what's necessary to earn more commissions, boost production, and win a place at the Chairman's Club annual golf gala in Palm Beach. In addition to getting clients to buy risky things with larger commissions, brokers can also maximize payouts through churning—unnecessary trading in an account with the sole aim of generating commissions (it doesn't only happen with retail investors, of course, but the results are usually much more damaging). Churning has been going on for decades, sometimes with very unhappy results for clients and brokers (e.g., some Street brokers—Pickard and Co., Gregory and Co., and McDonnell and Co.—got busted for taking liberties with client accounts during the market bubble of the late 1960s and were eventually shut down). Churning still happens pretty frequently, a lot more than is commonly known or reported—especially in discretionary accounts. There's no hard-and-fast rule that indicates it's actually occurring (because everything depends on a client's specific circumstances), but regulators and arbitration panels seem to have honed in on account turnover of two to five times per year as evidence that something fishy is going on (account turnover is just the market value of all trades divided by the average equity in the account; so $2 million of trades on an average equity balance of $400,000 means account turnover of 5x—lots of brokerage commissions).

Unauthorized trading of client assets is another example of bad behavior. Again, it's not confined to the retail sector, but the proportional impact is typically much greater. In order for a broker to have discretion over a client's account—that is, to execute trades on behalf of the client—the client has to give the broker specific authority. Sometimes the broker executes trades before the approval is in hand. Or sometimes the broker trades outside the specific discretion granted (e.g., the issue price and time limits that are often part of the discretionary agreement). In either case, the trading is unauthorized. If the client is paying attention and catches the bad trades, the bank has to reverse them (and make the account whole for any losses, plus commissions paid). This kind of unauthorized trading happens pretty regularly; arbitration panels spend lots of time reconstructing documentation, trade tickets, time stamps, and phone calls to see who authorized what, who did what, to whom, when, and why.

And sometimes brokers sell unsuspecting customers things that don't come from the bank or brokerage firm where they work, but from some other shop. It's called "selling away," and the regulators forbid it, but it still happens. So a broker at a bank might put her client into a toxic LP arranged by a dodgy bucket shop, and the bucket shop gives the broker a kickback. If the LP blows up, the client may not have recourse to the broker's bank (even though banks are supposed to have controls in place to stop this activity), so the injured client may have to bear the loss.

Lies, Nasty Cold Calls, Favoritism

Sometimes a broker says things that just shouldn't be said. It's tempting for a broker trying to sell a client an investment in XYZ to say that it's a "sure thing" or a "guaranteed winner," or that XYZ "can't lose" or "can't go down." So tempting, in fact, that it's a common pitch for brokers at some firms (especially the smaller ones, which may not go through the time and expense of training their brokers in the fine art of selling investments). Saying any of these things is, of course, illegal; a broker isn't allowed to promise anything about the prospects for an investment, but it happens quite frequently.

And then there are the very aggressive sales tactics that some brokers use. (Here, though, arbitration panels and courts distinguish between "puffery" and "pressure": sales tactics that involve puffery, like "this bond looks pretty attractive" are okay, but those that involve pressure, like "you have to buy this bond now," are not.) Remember: brokers have to produce so much in commissions on a continuous basis or risk being reassigned, demoted, or fired. If they can't hit particular commission targets, the client account may be handed to someone else in the office, and the broker has to start from scratch (in the meantime the poor client gets shuttled from one broker to the next—that's a great way to build relationships and show the customer respect). So, they try every trick in the book: calling at inconvenient hours, giving the illegal "you must act now" hard sales pitch, browbeating meek investors into doing something that's ill advised. In fact, this has been such a problem over the years that regulators have had to impose rules on cold calling (e.g., a broker has to identify himself/herself, state the purpose of the call, call at reasonable hours, and so on). But are regulators really checking up on all those cold calls? Probably not. It's exceptional for aggressive brokers to get caught on this because it's so tough to police.

Bad behavior also appears in other forms, like favoritism. For instance, the Street routinely stiffs its retail clients when it comes to new issue allocations. These are the hot new deals appearing regularly during the bull market (and very, very regularly during the expanding part of a bubble); everyone wants them, because it usually means easy money. If Mom and Pop get an allocation of 100 shares of the new ABC IPO, which is priced (or significantly under-priced, if you recall our discussion in chapter 3) at $10 and trades up to $20 at the end of the first day, they've just doubled their money. Wow. But Mom and Pop don't get any ABC, because all of the shares are going to preferred institutional customers who will write additional big-ticket trades with the bank, and the influential corporate executives who might be willing to give the bank some M&A or new issue business in the future as a sort of quid pro quo (spinning, which we'll see in the next chapter). So, the new issue allocation process is decidedly biased against the average retail customer. To add insult to injury, the brokers may start hyping the new issue to retail clients in the aftermarket once it's decidedly overpriced—and fill the orders just as the first wave of selling by lucky preferred customers hits. The only time a private client may actually get in the door is when a bank illegally charges inflated commissions for the "privilege" of an allocation; but we'll save that one for the next chapter, because it's a good example of breach of trust.

In some cases brokers say they'll do something for the client and don't it at all. They may promise a break on commissions or a tighter price or access to a new issue, all in order to win some current piece of business, and then forget all about it. At that point the client has very little recourse: he or she can try to chase after the broker through the broker's manager and demand satisfaction, but that usually doesn't lead anywhere—more likely the client will just have to drop the whole thing. Sometimes the entire industry tells the client base it'll do something and then "forgets" to do it. For instance, in 2003 the NASD caught more than six hundred banks and brokers in a scheme in which they promised to deliver break point discounts to about a third of the country's 95 million mutual fund investors but somehow failed to. Though regulators usually investigate these kinds of cases one at a time, they discovered that dozens of firms had neglected to cough up the discounts. When they suspected it might be even more widespread, they did an en masse investigation that netted hundreds of firms. At the heart of the issue was the rebate of fund commissions to investors purchasing certain kinds of fund shares: the mutual fund industry created the rules requiring investors to be rebated, the brokers agreed to go along with the plan, and then "forgot." So the NASD ordered the guilty parties to pay discounts and back interest to clients "expeditiously."

Warning Signs

How does the average retail client know if he or she is getting some bad advice, buying something that's too risky, or being led down the garden path? Short of a pool of red ink in the account (a nasty, expost reality) it's not always easy to tell, but a look at past disasters suggests there are some warning signs to watch out for.

- The broker never returns calls to answer questions regarding account activity or security valuations. That's never a good sign for someone in the client service business.
- The broker is overly enthusiastic about an investment, calling all the time, sending information by FedEx, e-mailing the latest research. It's probably an ugly dog of an investment that the bank is trying to get rid of, and the bank is probably paying its brokers double sales credits to move it out the door. It could be very risky.
- The broker can't explain the risks of an investment and can't clearly articulate the doomsday scenario. The coupon or yield or payout formula may not be standard or decipherable by anyone of average intelligence. The prospectus might contain words like "leverage," "principal is not protected," "reset," "Argentina," "Indonesia," "negative convexity," "deathlock," "illiquid," "volatile," "limited partnership," "private placement," and so on. It could be very, very risky.
- The broker can't explain whether a fund is charging a commission or not (a load versus a no-load). Some apparent "no-loads" are really loads—they may not have any up-front charges, but they may have annual charges or back-end charges.
- The bank is double dipping—slapping multiple charges on an account, like an annual wealth management fee and individual transaction commissions. This is overkill, just a way of ripping off the client.
- The broker recommends the wrong type of fee and account structure, e.g., the high commission and low annual fee structure for the active trading client, the high annual fee and low commission structure for the infrequent trading client. And it doesn't tell the client about all the other alternatives that are available.
- The broker urges lots of day trading, margin, and options. This means lots of commissions for the broker, lots of risk for the client.
- The broker uses words that are off limits (i.e., illegal) when pitching to make everything seem okay: "guaranteed," "a winner," "a sure thing," "I own some of this myself, and so do my folks," "no risk," "no problems," "I'm only showing this to my best clients."

Beware.

Abusing private clients by selling risky things or misbehaving seems to come from lack of client respect and lack of control. If a bank's management (at any level: branch office, regional office, national office, headquarters) doesn't care enough to make sure that the army of brokers is doing the right thing, communicating the right message, and selling the right investments—rather than just trying to earn commissions and fees in any way possible—then the army is going to do the wrong thing, communicate the wrong message, and sell the wrong securities. The tone at the top matters, and if the tone favors pulling a fast one on Mom and Pop so that all of those commission and revenue targets are met each quarter, then that's what's going to happen. Or maybe it's lack of control. Maybe the leaders back at headquarters or in the national sales office don't know what their brokers are doing. Maybe they don't know what they're pitching or how they're pitching it; maybe they don't know what kind of promises their brokers are making (you know, "Don't worry, Mrs. Jones. This [leveraged Russian rouble note/150 P/E Internet stock/CMO residual/energy limited partnership] is just perfect for you, and it'll be a nice supplement to your fixed monthly pension income. It'll give you a nice return, and you won't lose sleep at night. And if you ever want to get out of it, I'm sure we'll be able to arrange something. Guaranteed"). Retail problems are compounded by the fact that wayward brokers tend to escape unscathed, so there's no particular incentive for them to behave properly. Some Street firms might even choose to view the transgressions of their brokers as a cost of doing business. They'll get slapped on the wrist by regulators, pay a small amount in fines, give the client some restitution, and move right along, knowing that only a small fraction of the abuses that have actually been perpetrated have found their way to the arbitration panel (the rest disappear, as Moms and Pops are often too afraid or embarrassed to chase after their bank when something has gone awry). And since most of what happens is behind the scenes (e.g., a private arbitration rather than a public lawsuit), everything is very quiet: no publicity, no bruising of the reputation. So, even though the rules and regulations say the marketplace isn't caveat emptor, Moms and Pops still have to watch out.

Stanley's Family of Funds

Mutual funds are an important business for Wall Street's brokers, and they have all kinds of incentives to sell as many fund shares as they can. A bank generally wants to sell its own branded funds—those developed and managed in house, and then sold through its own sales force—because they generate more income: annual fees for the actual management of the fund, and commissions from sales to the private client community. Why should Merrill try to sell Fidelity or Morgan Stanley funds, or why should Morgan Stanley sell Vanguard or Citi funds, and lose out on the extra income? But, the argument goes, if Merrill or Stanley don't sell the Fidelity or Vanguard funds, their clients may not get the most appropriate investment. If the client should be investing in a New York municipal bond fund or an Asian equity growth fund and the bank doesn't offer either, it might be tempted to push the client into its Connecticut municipal bond fund (wrong) or its Latin equity growth fund (wrong), so that it can retain more fees and not give competitors any of the client's business. Regulators caught on to this scheme a few years ago and made banks offer third-party funds, which has helped somewhat (but not totally, as we'll see). Separately, they also came up with different kinds of mutual fund shares with different fee structures so that investors could buy the ones most suited to their financial circumstances: "A" shares have up-front fees but lower annual and back-end charges; "B" shares have no up-front fees but higher annual and back-end fees; and "C" shares have no front- or back-end fees but higher annual charges. Depending on an investor's tax situation, investment horizon, and liquidity position one of these three may be better than others. Regulations require brokers to take account of their clients' best interests by putting them into the right class.

All this is by way of background for Morgan Stanley's brush with the law. Morgan Stanley is a big mutual fund player, through its own in-house funds as well as those it picked up when it bought asset manager Van Kampen Merritt. Like other banks, it wants to sell its private clients the largest possible amount of family funds, and it wants to maximize the commissions it earns. Since 1998 it has been aggressive in doing both to the point of drawing complaints, lawsuits, and regulatory charges from the SEC, NASD and state securities regulators. In 2003 the bank was charged with bad mutual fund sales practices, and the head of its retail division was accused of supervisory violations. It seems Stanley brokers recommended inappropriate share classes to their clients in order to earn more commissions for the bank: too many sales of B fund shares and not enough information to clients about other investment alternatives (A and C shares). B shares look nice on the surface because clients face no up-front commissions, but they carry higher annual expenses and a deferred sales charge starting at 6 percent if shares are sold within eight years—and are definitely not the best alternative for every investor. Ninety percent of Stanley's funds were sold as B shares. The firm was also charged with violating antifraud provisions for paying brokers extra sums for selling internal funds and 14 "preferred partner" funds and failing to disclose to investors the existence of such "inducements" (between 1998 and 2003 at least 50 percent of Stanley's client fund sales were based on family funds and preferred funds—a much higher percentage than other banks). What kinds of inducements? Between 1999 and 2002 the bank held 29 sales contests in which brokers selling the most in-house funds (or the greatest proportion of in-house funds versus external funds) got free dollars to help them with their marketing and received extra noncash compensation (vacations, entertainment tickets, and so on). Branch managers received more pay when their brokers sold Stanley or Van Kampen funds (because regulations regarding cash compensation, oddly enough, don't cover branch managers). There was a little egg on the face, too: during an autumn 2002 contest to see who could sell the most in-house funds and capture $100,000 in "prizes," the associate director of the Northeast region sent around an e-mail announcing the contest, the target sales levels, and the prizes and added, for good measure, "Please DO NOT put anything in writing via E-mail or fax on the promotional part of your current campaign."[1] Which, of course, wound up on the front page of most major newspapers. Oops. The bottom line is that Stanley brokers earned more by selling in-house funds (and partner funds) and by selling B shares instead of A or C shares—meaning Stanley customers may not always have gotten the most suitable investments and may not have always been served properly. The bank finally pleaded no-contest to the charges, paid the SEC $50 million in fines (and paid NASD a few dollars as well) and agreed to reform its ways. The SEC, for its part, went off to examine similar practices at 15 other firms.

If banks and their legions of brokers have been busy promoting the latest conglomerate (or dot com, optical networker, energy trader, new media platform, wireless outfit, chip maker, software designer, or e-commerce consultant) through bad research (overly ambitious earnings targets and valuations, super-rosy profit outlooks) and aggressive tactics, they are going to lose when the bubble bursts. They'll be challenged by irate clients who lose pots of money when all of those 100 P/E stocks come crashing down to earth, and they'll lose valuable commission income for one or two or three quarters/years as Moms and Pops sit on the sidelines, licking their wounds and cursing their brokers. If they dip their toes in the water at all it'll probably be in the form of some cheaper no-load mutual funds or some market-tracking instrument (e.g., a basket or index-linked security or exchange traded fund), not the higher-margin single stock trades or expensive, full-fee funds. When retail investors got badly burned in 1987, it took the Street 17 quarters to get back to previous volumes. After Wall Street hyped TMT stocks and then watched them collapse, retail trading volumes declined by 70 percent and remained stagnant for almost three years. And since the retail arms of most banks are burdened with fairly high costs, two things usually happen: Street investors get poor returns on their capital, and lots of brokers get fired. Part of the boom-and-bust cycle—one of the Street's own making. It's not just stocks, of course: the same happens with lots of other assets, including leveraged emerging market notes, real estate investment trusts, currency funds, and so on. The Street talks up the asset and everyone piles in, then the market dynamics shift, prices fall, everyone piles out, and they have lots of losses for their tax returns.

Regardless of the root causes, there are usually lots of unhappy people left in the wake of the latest wave of bad advice. No, not all banks are guilty of abusing their private clients, and in some cases a few bad apples try to spoil the whole bunch. There are tens of thousands of good, diligent brokers out there who really are trying to do the right thing. But the Street's track record shows that it has real problems in dealing with Mom and Pop.

Chapter 6

BREACHING TRUST

We now turn to the last of Wall Street's client-facing roles: acting as trusted advisor and fiduciary. In some ways this may be the most important of all, because Wall Street is about trust. The business that gets done is based on acts of good faith, of banks doing the right thing for clients, looking after their best interests, and protecting them from things that can go wrong. At least it's supposed to be. It doesn't always work out that way, as we'll see.

First, let's go to the dictionary (in this case *Webster's New World,* Second Concise Edition), for a quick review:

trust: n. [ON. *traust*]

1. (a) firm belief in the honesty, reliability, etc. of another (b) the one trusted
2. confident expectation, hope, etc.
3. (a) the fact of having confidence placed in one (b) the responsibility resulting from this
4. care; custody
5. something entrusted to one; charge.

While we've got the dictionary out, let's also note:

fi-du-ci-ar-y: adj. [L. fiducia, trust < fidere: see FAITH]

1. designating or of one who holds something in trust for another
2. held in trust
3. valuable only because of public confidence.

These are important concepts. When clients—whether institutional or retail—look to the Street for a relationship, they expect it to be based on confidence, honesty, reliability, care, and safe custody. They are entrusting their financial assets, financial safekeeping, and financial future to Wall Street, and must therefore have confidence that they will be treated properly, and that the assets they convey to the Street will be safe. This generally works out okay; many Wall Streeters try to do the right thing: they give the right advice, they make sure the securities are safe, they don't buy something risky for the client if the client says, "no risk, please." They don't let personal or professional conflicts of interest stand in the way of their responsibilities, and they do their very best when it comes to evaluating deals and performing due diligence. They don't engage in fraudulent behavior and don't help dishonest clients with their dishonesty. But some Wall Streeters don't follow any of these rules. They take advantage of the trust and confidence of their clients for personal gain. They violate rules of ethical conduct and behave improperly; some ignore fiduciary duties and even commit fraud. Sometimes it's just a few bad apples that spoil things, occasionally it's a few bushels of bad apples, and every so often it's the whole orchard.

What happens if institutional and retail clients can't have faith and confidence in Wall Street? As we've said, many are entrusting their financial livelihoods, performance, and future to the actions of bankers, and if these are jeopardized, prejudiced, or threatened, lots of people lose. Disappointed or mistreated clients will go from Bank A, which has breached principles of trust, to Bank B in hopes of being treated better (they may also bring some legal action against A if warranted). But if Bank B winds up acting in the same way, they'll have to find other ways of taking care of their financial needs, perhaps by disintermediating some of the Street's functions (e.g., some companies issue commercial paper and bonds directly to investors, some use their own internal "investment bankers" to scout out and arrange acquisitions, individuals turn to electronic trading and DIY financial planning platforms to handle their needs). So it's in Wall Street's best interests to manage fiduciary responsibilities in an *undoubted* manner. Everything must be aboveboard—technically, certainly, but also overtly. The mere appearance of conflict or wrongdoing has to be seen as unacceptable because appearances matter. (Remember *Webster's*: "valuable only because of public confidence.") Whether the responsibilities are legal (e.g., the bank acting as agent of a client, under the express guidance and instructions of that client) or simply ethical (e.g., the bank as "moral creature" under obligation to be diligent in discharging its duties), the bank must fulfill the role properly. If it doesn't, it loses money (lost revenues, fines, or worse, depending on the problem or infraction) and, more important, it damages its reputation. Word gets around when someone on the Street has been pulling a fast one on the clients or shirking responsibilities. And at the end of the day, the Street is still about the human element. Capital is important, of course, because it helps business get done—no capital, no seat at the poker table. But without the human dimension—reputation, ethics, skills, intelligence, and integrity—it's all over. So one would think that protecting intangibles like trust and goodwill by making sure the fiduciary role is performed to a T would be a matter of course. Unfortunately, it's not. There have been many instances of Wall Street breaching the trust of its clients: violating regulations (like breaking through Chinese walls, front running, spinning, and the like), engaging in obvious conflicts of interest, failing to perform proper due diligence or protect customer funds, and so forth. In fact, trust is often a sacrificial lamb when bankers are trying to get business done.

Burn, Baby, Burn

Seventeen investment banks made the headlines in April 2000 when they agreed to pay $140 million in fines to settle charges that they had defrauded the federal and state governments by overpricing securities in what has become known as the "yield burning" case. It was the usual suspects (Merrill, Lehman, Morgan Stanley, Goldman, CSFB, pre-Citi Salomon, pre-UBS Paine Webber and Dillon Read, Deutsche) and some smaller shops (Lazard, Dain Rauscher, Hough, Piper Jaffray, Prudential, Raymond James, Bradford, Wheat First, A.G. Edwards, Southwest Securities, pre-CoreStates Meridian)—so Wall Street was well represented in yet another failure.

The saga dates back to 1995 when Michel Lissack, a managing director at Salomon, emerged as a whistleblower, filing a lawsuit against most of the firms noted above under the False Claims Act (and later also under securities and IRS liability breaches). That led to many months of investigative work by regulators, after which it became clear that Wall Street firms had been hard at work since the early 1990s defrauding the governments by adding in large price markups when issuing municipal bonds.

The game worked like this: when interest rates start falling, municipalities find it advantageous to refinance their debt (just as a homeowner might refinance a mortgage); this "advance refunding process" lets them lower their interest costs and save a bit on the budget. Proceeds that they raise go to an escrow portfolio that invests in U.S. Treasury bonds, which produces enough cash flow to service the municipal obligations. But in order not to encourage limitless borrowing at a low rate and investment at a slightly higher rate (i.e., just leveraging up the municipal balance sheet to capture the spread), the yield on the escrowed U.S. Treasuries cannot be more than the yield on the new municipal bonds. If it is, any excess profits go straight to the federal government. So, the return on the U.S. Treasury securities municipalities purchase with their tax-advantaged investment proceeds is capped. It's all very sensible: municipalities can raise only enough new money to pay down old, higher-cost debt, and not to speculate on interest rates.

Enter Wall Street. In order to circumvent this little technical hurdle, the banks, all active underwriters of municipal securities, took the opportunity to add in large price markups to the U.S. Treasuries that municipalities purchased for their escrow accounts. By marking the bonds up, the banks artificially depressed (or "burned") the yield (recall the inverse relationship between price and yield) and pocketed the profits—screwing the federal government out of the excess profit it was due. A number of individual municipalities were also cheated through overcharges—including the Commonwealth of Massachusetts (losing when Goldman over-charged the state on a 1993 refunding), State of Kentucky (overcharged by Lazard on a 1992 deal), and so on. So Wall Street decided that it was okay to rip off the federal, state, and municipal governments—meaning taxpayers. And they probably would have kept doing it had they not got caught by one of their own.

VIOLATING REGULATIONS

Wall Street has to abide by lots of rules and regulations so that clients, investors, creditors, and even taxpayers are properly protected. Firms that stick to the rules gain the trust of their stakeholders—especially clients, who like to know that the Street firm that they're dealing with is doing things the right way, not cutting corners or skating on thin ice. Those who don't play by the rules put trust in jeopardy and end up losing (but only if they get caught; we're not too sure how many don't get caught, but it's probably safe to say that quite a few escape scot-free). At a minimum, any bank that runs afoul of the rules puts its clients in danger and tarnishes its reputation. With that kind of downside, it's still amazing to see how often rules are violated by individuals, teams, and whole firms.

Chinese Walls

No, a Chinese wall isn't a residential construction technique from the Middle Kingdom, it's an invisible barrier meant to separate certain groups working within a bank. It's common for bankers in contact with institutional clients (particularly those that are issuing securities or doing some kind of corporate finance work) to be privy to sensitive nonpublic information, the kind of information that an unscrupulous character (firm) might try to use to make a quick buck. So the invisible barrier is meant to keep bankers, traders, and researchers from sharing information on a client, what it's doing (or planning to do), what its nonpublic financial position looks like, and so forth. The theory goes that if the wall is working, those who need to know about the confidential goodies will know about them, and those who don't, won't.

The Chinese wall on Wall Street is not a grand, well-built, ten-foot brick-and-mortar architectural wonder—it's actually an ugly, crumbling, two-foot mound with lots of missing bricks. The hard truth is that information often crosses the wall, meaning those that shouldn't be in possession of nonpublic facts on a client actually are. This is unacceptable because it's an ethical violation, but it's even worse when it turns into a legal infraction—when those in possession of sensitive information try to use it for professional or personal gain. So we see researchers regularly talking to bankers, bankers talking to traders, traders talking to everyone else—and you can bet that no one's talking about the weather or the ball game. They're all talking about the fact that Company XYZ is due to announce something major (a setback, expansion, lawsuit, acquisition) that will rock the markets and affect the pricing on the upcoming convertible bond issue. Let's see, how should we position the trading book? What should we tell (or not tell) our investing clients? What can we do in our personal accounts (no, our spouses', or sisters', or cousins' offshore Cayman trust accounts)?

Chinese walls are good in theory but virtually impossible to police in practice. Communications are free and easy, and it's tough to stop people from talking. Sure, there are some rules in place that are intended to protect against abuses—bringing a research analyst "over the wall" when the bankers are getting close to a new issue (e.g., giving him/her details on the deal and going into a research blackout period), or requiring companies to adhere to Regulation FD (Fair Disclosure, meaning whatever a company tells research analysts it must tell the rest of the world), but these can't do the job on their own. More often it demands internal leadership and control—and sometimes these are lacking. Clients and investors shouldn't assume that just because the wall is supposed to exist, it's working as it should.

Front Running, Collusion, Insider Trading, Improper Trading, Fraud

The Street has to follow certain rules when it comes to trading so that clients are properly protected: rules related to front running, interpositioning, collusion, and noncompetitive trading. It's all very technical, but it's important if clients are to have a fair shake. Since trading is a zero sum game, there's a loser for every winner, and without some basic rules, you know who's going to lose.

In simple terms, front running means getting ahead of a client trade in order to earn a few easy, risk-free dollars. It's a breach of the rules, and it's illegal. And it happens—in the listed markets (like the NYSE or the Chicago Mercantile Exchange [CME] or Chicago Board of Trade [CBOT]) and in the OTC markets (like any Wall Street trading desk), probably more often than we think or know. Front running can sometimes be detected in the listed markets because there's reasonable transparency—everything is duly recorded (though there's still no guarantee that all infractions will be caught, as events on exchanges have demonstrated over the years). It's tougher to spot in the OTC market, because very little information circulates publicly. For instance, a swap marketer gets a call from a client about doing a big trade, the marketer then passes the deal to the swap trader, who first fills an order for the prop book and then executes for the client. The client order is big enough to move the market a basis point or two, the bank's prop book makes a little risk-free money, and no one is the wiser. Or maybe a mutual fund portfolio manager plans to buy a huge block of Intel or Microsoft in a few days, then go on CNBC and tout the fund's performance record and its recent move into Intel or Microsoft—that'll give the position a bit of a run up and help the fund's performance before the quarter-end reporting period. Of course, the portfolio manager already has a big chunk of Intel or Microsoft in her personal account and will benefit from the price action—a little variation on the front-running theme known as scalping.

Listed exchanges also have to stick to other rules, like affirmative obligation, negative obligation, and interpositioning. Specialists making markets through an auction book have a duty to take one side of a public order if there's an imbalance between a buyer and seller (affirmative obligation) and stand out of the way when a buyer and seller can execute with one another directly (negative obligation). So if a buyer of shares comes into the market and a seller of shares already exists, the specialist can't stand in the way and become a seller for its own account (that would be interpositioning). Traders are also barred from collusion (which occurs when a few traders prearrange customer trades to squeeze out some extra dollars), and noncompetitive trading (which happens when a trader takes one side of a trade without exposing it to the market). And they can't penny jump; this happens when a specialist receives a limit order and a market order, and can decide whether to match the two or ignore the limit order and fill the market order—and, in so doing, limit the downside and leave open the upside. It goes like this: a market-maker gets two orders: a limit buy at

$10.10 and a market sell. It can match the two at $10.10 (which would be the right thing to do), or it can take care of the market sell by buying at $10.11 for its own account (that takes care of the market sell order but leaves the limit order unfilled). If the market trades down to $10.10 (or lower), the market-maker has a backstop in the form of an unfilled limit order, so the downside is limited. If the market goes up, the long position in the prop account looks better and better. All the market-maker has risked is a penny a share. And it's not just specialists or market-makers on exchanges that get caught up in trading manipulation: trading desks of Street firms get busted, too (e.g., seven Morgan Stanley equity derivative traders were suspended and fined for manipulating Nasdaq stocks in 1998). Again, front running, interpositioning, colluding, noncompetitive trading, penny jumping, and the like are breaches of fiduciary duty and/or violations of ethical conduct, informal rules, or formal regulations. And they happen all the time, to the disadvantage of customers.

Quarters and Eighths

For a good example of breach of trust, collusion, and corruption all rolled into one, we journey back to the mid-1990s and take a look at Nasdaq and the dealers who got caught in a multiyear scheme to keep quoted spreads wide, thus creating extra profits for themselves. The whole episode was an embarrassment for the exchange and the dealer community, but also for NASD, the self-regulatory arm of Nasdaq, which came out looking like a rather ineffective SRO.

Nasdaq, founded in 1971 as an alternate forum for companies that couldn't meet the NYSE's listing requirements, is a conglomeration of dealers. Unlike the Big Board, which operates as an auction market, Nasdaq puts dealers, as market-makers, in direct competition with one another over incoming orders. Market-makers have an obligation to quote a two-way market (i.e., bids and offers), which is how they make their money: buy on the bid (say $10) and sell on the offer (say $10 1/8) (now, of course, spreads are tighter because of decimalization).

All this is by way of background for the scandal that caught dozens of firms and hundreds of individuals doing the wrong thing. The scary part of the whole episode is that the regulators didn't catch on to this (or didn't want to?): it was actually brought to light by academics William Christie and Paul Schultz through a research article they published in the *Journal of Finance* (lucky for investors someone was watching). Specifically, they noticed that Nasdaq trading spreads in the late 1980s and early 1990s seemed to be much wider than might be expected given the exchange's growing level of volume and competition. After investigating the issue for some time, they discovered that traders routinely quoted their bid-offer spreads in "even eighth" increments rather than "odd eighths." That meant that, regardless of dealer competition, every trade had a guaranteed spread of one quarter—and not the 12.5 cents that might be expected in a highly competitive situation. By some estimates investors were paying an extra $2 billion in markups every year, a tidy sum for market-makers in on the scheme.

Following the initial findings, the SEC embarked on a two-year investigative mission before it managed to put all the pieces together (the NASD wasn't much of a help, as it refused to believe that there could be any collusion among exchange members). Federal regulators examined records, reviewed taped phone conversations, and interviewed dealers and eventually found that there was a great deal of monkey business going on at the exchange. Not only were many traders colluding by only quoting even eighths, many were also failing in other duties: harassing those who refused to go along with the price-fixing, refusing to honor prices they quoted (a direct violation of market-making rules), holding back limit orders within the spread, and so on. That led to a host of antitrust charges, civil lawsuits, and fines against 24 dealers, several dozen individuals, and the Nasdaq itself. Among those caught up in the scandal: Merrill, Salomon, Paine Webber, J.P. Morgan, plus a bunch of smaller houses. Over the next three years more charges and court actions circulated. In 1998 the parties finally resolved the issues through a two-pronged solution: a $1 billion settlement payment by the implicated parties (shareholders paying, of course) and reform of the obviously ineffective NASD and Nasdaq structure, including the addition of totally new management, creation of a new market surveillance subsidiary and new audit technology.

There are other forms of collusive activity, like rigging and cornering, in which brokers or bankers or entire firms get together to try to circumvent auction, sales, or trading rules to make some dollars. They might do so by trying to control a piece of a market, or security—the theory being that those who control the supply can control the price, and therefore earn outsize profits. It doesn't usually work, but that doesn't seem to stop some from trying. Lots of this dates back to the 1920s, when brokers reported "wash sales"—trades that hadn't occurred—in order to influence price and volume patterns. When that was banned they formed stock pools, syndicates that arranged their stock purchases and sales in a collusive manner in order to convey particular price information and get outsiders to buy (mostly) or sell (sometimes). They would arrange their price and volume trades so that things looked attractive on the ticker tape and outside investors would be lured into the action. When the pool had driven the market to a desired level (largely through self-perpetuating behavior reinforced by outsiders who were unaware of the scheme), they closed down their positions, split profits, and left unwitting investors holding the bag. Pool operations weren't strictly illegal back then (though NYSE officials routinely denied that any such activity existed and prohibited specialists from being involved in any such games [the specialists often led the pools under the names of friends or relatives anyway])—but gullible investors watching the tape got taken time and again. Different forms of this have carried on into the modern era.

Salomon's Treasury Auction Rigging

In the 1980s Salomon Brothers was the king of bond trading. Actually, it was the king of Wall Street, dominant in bond trading and underwriting, and very strong in investment banking and equities. As a result, it had plenty of swagger and pretty much did what it wanted to do. Salomon was a big risk-taker and had the brains and brawn to make lots of money at it. Sure, it made some bad calls, but more often than not it was right, earning hundreds of millions as a dealer and proprietary trader. The culture on the trading floor was aggressive, even cutthroat, and politics were rampant. Factions came in and out of power (depending on the state of the markets and the size of trading profits), so that at any time mortgages might have the upper hand, then government bonds, then corporates, then mortgages again. The bank also boasted an "arbitrage" group, created and led by John Meriwether. Meriwether, whom we'll see again in chapter 7 when we talk about LTCM, assembled a team of quantitative and trading specialists in 1977 to take advantage of market discrepancies within, and across, asset classes: on-the-run versus off-the-run Treasuries, bonds versus futures and, later, swaps versus corporates, bond volatility versus swaption volatility, and so on. By 1981 the little team (which was the first to feature a few Ph.D.s doing quantitative modeling) had made Salomon $100 million, one third of its profits. It grew stronger and more powerful over the years and was often a significant contributor to the bank's revenue stream (and a dominant user of its capital). In 1990 Meriwether persuaded CEO John Gutfreund to give the arbitrage group 15 percent of whatever it managed to earn. Gutfreund agreed, and the dawn of some unholy internal battles arrived. The compensation scheme netted some traders in the arb group $10 million to more than $20 million per year (including an eye-popping $23 million in 1990 for Larry Hilibrand, one of Meriwether's best arbitrage guys), and engendered an every-man-for-himself attitude. Bad blood soon flowed between arbitrage, mortgages, governments, and banking; the internal conflicts led to morale problems, politics, secrecy, and a breakdown in controls.

Which brings us up to the period of 1989 to 1991: the beginning of the end for Salomon as the dominant Wall Street force in trading, underwriting, and banking (a mantle that Merrill would assume for most of the 1990s). What happened? How did King Salomon lose its crown? Rigging Treasury bond auctions. Paul Mozer, head of Treasury bond trading, made no secret of the fact that he was upset by the amount of capital and risk capacity given to the arbitrage group and the size of the payouts that team members received. So what did he do? The only thing you can possibly do if you want to make some big money in a razor-thin market: corner some bonds. Starting in late 1989 Mozer decided he would try to control Treasury bond auctions and squeeze other dealers doing when-issued Treasury (WIT) arbitrage trades (i.e., selling WITs and buying them back after the auction); he reasoned that if he could squeeze the shorts, they would have to pay his price for the bonds they needed to cover their positions—meaning big dollars. So off he went. In May 1990 Mozer bid for more than 100 percent of a bond issue at an auction. That yielded a phone call from U.S. Treasury officials, who reminded Mozer about the long-standing "gentle-man's agreement": no bank should bid for more than 35 percent of an issue at any auction. But Mozer kept on going, bidding even more aggressively: 240 percent at the next one, which led to another reprimand (plus a formalization of the 35 percent rule that had once just been an understanding).

Not wanting to be deterred by a silly U.S. Treasury rule, at the next auction Mozer decided to submit a 35 percent bid for Salomon, plus 35 percent for each of various institutional clients (who hadn't authorized such bids). Salomon wound up with half the issue and some good profits in the short squeeze. To complete the cycle, Mozer created some false trades that passed the unauthorized client purchases over to Salomon. Unfortunately, one of the clients that Mozer had falsely used, S.G. Warburg, had actually submitted its own bid, pushing the bank over the 35 percent limit. Never mind, Mozer kept at it, auction after auction: more false client bids, more false internal trades, repeatedly throughout 1990 and into mid-1991. But no one around the bank seemed worried: even though most of Salomon's senior executives became aware of Mozer's infractions as early as February 1991, they did nothing about it for months. Only that summer did Gutfreund try to rein in Mozer with some additional controls. But by then it was too little, too late. When Gerald Corrigan, head of the New York Federal Reserve Bank, learned about the misbehaving in August 1991, he demanded senior management changes. Warren Buffett, a holder of $700 million of Salomon preferred stock since 1987, helped the bank reorganize. That led to some housekeeping: Gutfreund, charged by the SEC with failure to supervise, was forced to resign as CEO and was barred from being a CEO on Wall Street ever again (he eventually wound up as a senior relationship executive at a tiny shop, Unterberg Towbin). Meriwether, by then vice chairman and nominally responsible for all trading (including Mozer's), was also forced out; he served a three-month suspension from the securities business and eventually went on to even more spectacular peaks and valleys through LTCM. Mozer was fired, fined, and suspended. Various other senior managers were buried as well. The bank (no, the bank's investors) was forced to cough up $290 million in fines for the flagrant rigging violations. The damage to the bank's reputation was considerable, too. No longer was Salomon held in the same regard, and pieces of the bank seemed to dissolve from that point on. Though Buffett's credibility as an active player created stability and ensured liquidity, the bank's glory days were over. Salomon's tremendous momentum from the 1980s was gone—it would eventually merge with Smith Barney, and then fall into the arms of Citibank. A decade later, reflecting on the whole affair, Gutfreund continued to hold that the whole affair was no big deal: "It was a victimless crime, it was just other Wall Street firms that were hurt."[1] Wonderful.

———————

Insider trading is, of course, another big no-no that rears its ugly head from time to time: trading on nonpublic information is against the law, and some on the Street get caught every so often. From the late nineteenth century until the Great Crash, insiders at banks regularly took advantage of private information to generate profits for themselves and their firms. But the practice wasn't actually illegal until the passage of the Securities Exchange Act of 1934, and there were no criminal prosecutions from the 1940s through the 1960s as Congress hadn't yet made insider trading a crime. A few cases popped up during the late 1970s, but the biggest abuses didn't really start till the 1980s (fortunately, additional legislation passed in 1984 and 1988 made it easier to dole out penalties). Once M&A activity heated up, a lot more Wall Streeters got caught with their hands in the cookie jar. For instance, between 1982 and 1986 regulators acted on 79 cases; during the balance of the decade, they prosecuted dozens more, including some very high-profile ones involving bankers and risk arbitrage traders at Kidder Peabody, Goldman, Drexel, and a few other shops (some of those caught even got hauled away in handcuffs, which provided great footage for the evening news). In recent years instances of insider trading have declined somewhat through improved regulatory surveillance, which can track trading activity more accurately. It has also been aided by Regulation FD, which requires companies to make simultaneous disclosure of "market-moving" information to the public at large. So gone are the days when bank equity analysts, cozy with company management, got first dibs on sensitive, nonpublic information. The information arbitrage that banks once enjoyed has compressed a bit.

But let's not pretend all is well. Insider trading still happens, in stocks, bonds, and other financial assets subject to information barriers. For example, in 2003 Goldman coughed up $9.3 million to settle SEC charges that it traded on inside information related to the U.S. Treasury's decision to suspend issuance of 30-year bonds. It seems a consultant "in the know" told a Goldman economist, who told the trading desk, who positioned the book to profit when the market moved on the news. And it moved: the announcement sparked the largest one-day price shift in 14 years, and the lucky Goldman traders made $3.8 million of essentially risk-free profits. Goldman fell on the sword, of course. It stated in a press release in the aftermath that "the firm holds itself to the highest standards and any failure in this regard is a great embarrassment." Yes, indeed.

And sometimes the Street skirts the law by engaging in fraudulent business activities, kickbacks, and so on. For instance, during 1996 and 1997 CSFB's very aggressive derivatives unit, CS Financial Products (CSFP), lied to Japanese regulators about the kind and amount of business it was doing in Japan so that it could show less onshore revenue and therefore pay less tax; it also obstructed official investigations into the matter. Japanese regulators revoked the bank's license in 1999, while U.K. regulators fined the bank £4 million and sanctioned several senior executives. In 2003 it came to light that some mutual funds allowed clients to improperly trade fund shares after market close and take advantage of the timing of fund trades. Funds aren't supposed to allow trading in their shares after 4 P.M. close (so-called "late trading") because their net asset values (NAVs) are set to the close. Late trading lets a client take advantage of market-breaking news without having to wait to get filled at the next day's price—to the detriment of all other fund investors, and that's why it's illegal. And sometimes funds take advantage of differences between closing prices of overseas-traded stocks and the closing prices reflected in the fund's NAV (so-called "market timing"); trading events may not be reflected in the NAV, so market timers can buy or sell on the "stale" price and benefit from foreign movements the following day. The practice isn't actually illegal, but most funds say they don't do it—meaning if they do it, they're lying, again to the disadvantage of the vast majority of clients (more on all of this below). And one more: in 2003 the FBI concluded an 18-month sting operation that netted 47 traders working at a few bucket shops and some of the biggest foreign exchange dealers in the market: J.P. Morgan, UBS, Dresdner, and Societe Generale. It seems that the traders set up several schemes to defraud Moms and Pops of millions in assets, and book money losing trades for the banks and then share in profit kickbacks from customer trades booked through brokers.

The Secret World of Funds, Part II: Over The Edge

In 2003 New York Attorney General Eliot Spitzer caught a few of the Street's most powerful fund companies engaged in market timing and late trading. Spitzer announced that hedge fund Canary Investment had agreed to pay $40 million in fines after admitting to market timing and late trading in funds run by Bank of America, BankOne, Janus, and Strong. In exchange for the "preferential" treatment, Canary promised the companies more business (which was apparently good enough for one Janus executive, who said in an e-mail, "I have no interest in building a business around market timers, but at the same time I do not want to turn away $10-$20m"). For instance, Canary was allowed to trade $15 million in and out of Bank One's funds; Canary borrowed the $15 million from Bank One at a high interest rate, and Canary officials also considered making a "sticky asset" investment in a Bank One hedge fund. Quid pro quo.

Unfortunately, it was just the proverbial tip of the iceberg. Massachusetts Secretary William Galvin blew the lid on similar activities at Putnam; revelation of market timing and late trading, along with some ill-advised trading by the CEO, caused institutional investors and government accounts to yank $32 billion out of Putnam funds in less than two months (and led, ultimately, to the ouster of the company's CEO). Merrill, Loomis Sayles, Schwab, MFS, UBS, Pilgrim and Baxter, Bear, Citi's Smith Barney unit, and others all had to fire some of their folks when they found out they were involved in similar practices. And more: a portfolio manager at Alger let a hedge fund trade $50 million in and out of the market in exchange for a "capital contribution" to a new fund; three Prudential brokers evaded internal controls so that they could do illegal market timing trades; Alliance Capital set up market timing arrangements for preferred investors that placed capital in certain Alliance seed funds (an act that led to the ouster of the CEO); the chairman/CEO of Strong had to resign his post after he was reported to have personally engaged in market timing and late trading; and so on. In fact, the SEC ultimately discovered that 25 percent of brokerage firms allowed clients to place late orders and that 30 percent actively assisted some clients in improper trading. The boards of fund companies were completely asleep, missing out on all of the misbehavior; indeed, more than a few directors claimed they were kept in the dark about what was going on, which may well be true as a result of the dual fund company/fund adviser structure we mentioned in the last chapter. And, except for the folks at the New York Attorney General's office, regulators missed the boat, too. The head of the SEC's Boston office resigned when it became clear he had missed out on the whole scandal by ignoring the warnings of a whistleblower.

The revelations caught many off guard, because the mutual fund industry had generally avoided Street problems of the late 1990s and early millennium (and had even boasted as much, a fact that a few fund officials probably now regret). The discovery of the depth and breadth of the breaches within a sector that was once regarded as sterling came as a shock to many. As more gory details on the fund scandals came to light, Illinois Senator Peter Fitzgerald noted that the industry has "disintegrated into the world's largest skimming organization." Former SEC Commissioner Arthur Levitt observed "[T]his seems to be the most egregious violation of the public trust of any of the events of recent years. Investors may realize they can't trust the bond market or they can't trust a stock broker or analysts, but mutual funds have been havens of security and integrity."[2] Those implicated wound up using their shareholders' money to pay restoration costs and fines (and in some cases also agreed to cut fees): Janus coughed up $32 million for investors and another $225 million in regulating settlements, MFS $350 million, Alliance $600 million, Bank of America $675 million, and so on. Some after-the-fact clampdowns followed, such as a mandatory requirement to have a compliance officer within each fund company to monitor activities, absolutely no trading after 4 P.M., and so on; others, like a gradual move toward publishing fresh, real-time prices (rather than the stale, once-a-days that currently exist) will undoubtedly follow.

Aiding and Abetting

Sometimes banks do the wrong thing by helping clients engage in naughty behavior; when it happens, they are just as guilty as the party that's doing the wrong thing. A bank should be walking away from anything that's not right, not helping promote it; but the lure of business is strong, and some apparently feel it's okay to aid and abet if it leads to more business.

This breach can take different forms: knowingly engaging in illegal window-dressing transactions to change the appearance of a company's financials (this being somewhat distinct from the rotten, but legal, window dressing we touched on in chapter 4), or helping prop up some illegal trading activity by providing credit lines or other services. Such breaches have occurred many times over the years; the Street has been caught helping Japanese companies execute historical rate rollovers in the foreign exchange market, assisting U.S. energy companies in round-trip "wash" trades to inflate revenues, parking assets over financial reporting periods to make client financials look better, and so on. Some of the biggest companies in the world have been involved, such as Showa Shell, Kashima Oil, Nippon Steel, Enron, Codelco, Nippon Credit Bank,

Sumitomo Corporation, CMS Energy, Reliant Resources, and Freddie Mac, among many others. In each case Street banks have been involved, to some degree, with client misbehavior, and have actually made that misbehavior worse.

Parking the Nigerian Barges

Though Merrill Lynch is an active and astute player in lots of global markets and assets, it doesn't really know a lot about Nigeria or about barges—facts that it discovered the hard way in 2002. The story dates back to 1999. As Enron's executives were busy tending to their house of cards, puffing up revenues and hiding liabilities, they hit upon a unique idea involving some barges the company owned. Enron had developed the Lagos (Egbin) barge power project in the late 1990s in order to generate power in the Niger River delta—a legitimate and no doubt worthy endeavor. So as executives scrambled to meet revenue targets and perpetuate the financial fiction, they called up Merrill and asked if the bank would take the barges off of its hands for a while (a supposedly legitimate sale to an Asian investor group had fallen through). Even though Merrill didn't know much about barges or Nigeria and didn't do any due diligence on the deal, it did know that Enron was a good client, and so it said, "of course." The bank bought a $28 million interest in three barges, which gave Enron $12 million in profits before the critical year-end reporting deadline; Enron verbally promised to repurchase them within six months, at a premium. (By the way, the barges were sold to the bank through a troublesome Enron special purpose entity called LJM2. And guess what? Merrill and a bunch of its executives were investors in LJM2.) Sure enough, when the six months were up, Merrill got its money from Enron and returned the barges, earning a bit of profit and—most important—keeping its relationship with the company on solid ground. Enron eventually sold the barge interests to energy company AES in January 2001.

All of this barge business was basically another way for Enron to inflate its financial worth. Asset parking—selling and repurchasing an asset with no transfer of risk transfer, just to window-dress—is illegal. So why did Merrill do it? It appears that the bank didn't want to irritate any Enron executives and jeopardize future business (even though internal notes from a senior Merrill banker discussing the deal indicated quite clearly that knowledge of the downside was understood: "reputational risk, i.e., aid/abet Enron inc[ome] statement manipulation.") In fact, a senior Merrill executive told a congressional panel: "Discussions with Enron went along the lines initially of continuing to increase the business relationship. They needed us to do something in the business of these barges." So Merrill did the wrong thing for the wrong reasons. The SEC apparently thought so, too, and in 2002 filed charges against four senior Merrill executives—a senior investment banker, the head of energy investment banking, the head of investment banking, and the head of the bank's entire institutional business—accusing them of aiding and abetting Enron's manipulation of earnings through the barge transaction (and some energy wash trades). After a little internal discussion, Merrill fired the four, pleaded no contest, and paid the SEC $80 million in fines. So, the firm swapped $36 million of fees from all of its business with Enron for $80 million of fines and significant damage to its reputation.

Merrill's willingness to aid Enron in its window-dressing schemes put the firm under the scrutiny of regulators. In late 1999 Enron sold Merrill a physical call option on power, and Merrill sold Enron a mirror image (except that it had a financial, rather than physical, settlement). The trade was fairly neutral from a risk perspective, but it let Enron report an additional $50 million of income to meet its year-end targets. Enron agreed to pay the bank $17 million for the trade (two months after the reporting period it unwound the transaction, so the two agreed that a payment of $8.5 million was sufficient). Merrill clearly knew that the deal was all about playing games with the numbers; an e-mail from an investment banker working on the deal was discovered by the SEC: "We were clearly helping them make earnings for the quarter and the year (which had great value in the stock price, not to mention personal compensation)."[3] Merrill got busted for this one and a few others and paid millions in fines and booted some senior execs. Who knows what the bank was thinking—why would anyone help a company alter its financial appearance, sacrificing ethics and reputation for a few dollars? Merrill wasn't alone in the Enron affair, of course. We've already mentioned that Citi and J.P. arranged the prepaid swaps, which gave the company some disguised off-balance sheet funding; the two banks got skewered for their role in "enabling" Enron's fraudulent activities. And various others got tagged through the investigative reports prepared by bankruptcy examiner Neal Batson: Deutsche, CIBC, Barclays, Royal Bank of Scotland, Toronto Dominion, and CSFB were all found by the examiner to have aided Enron officers in breaching their fiduciary duties by participating in window dressings, SPE-related deals, or asset parking. Most of the banks were sued by directors of the "new Enron" for their roles in the company's collapse.

And sometimes window dressing works in the opposite way: disguising profits so that they can be pushed forward to the future. Freddie Mac did this to the tune of $5 billion in the late 1990s and early millennium, which led to the ouster of the CEO and a tightening up of controls. And guess who was there helping Freddie understate profits? Morgan Stanley and Citi, through innovative trading structures known as "J Deals" and "Coupon Trade up Giants," which were window-dressing marvels that generated accounting losses so that derivative gains could be hidden. There are many, many other examples of window dressing (and, of course, there are probably lots of other trades out there that haven't been discovered).

Mr. 5% and His Bankers

Sumitomo Corporation, a huge Japanese industrial company and a large player in the global metals market, built a considerable trading capability in the early 1980s under head trader Yasuo Hamanaka. Hamanaka became so successful that Sumitomo gained a reputation as one of the savviest and most powerful copper dealers in the world. As Hamanaka's influence grew, he became known as "Mr. 5%" for routinely being able to control 5 percent of the global copper market (trading primarily through the London Metal Exchange [LME], the world's largest forum for listed copper trading). Copper traders all over the world eagerly watched Hamanaka's activities and tried to piggyback whenever they could figure out what he was up to. And, by all accounts, Mr. 5% actually made Sumitomo some real money between 1991 and 1995. After that, though, any gains he reported came from manipulating the market and hiding losing trades. Since Hamanaka generated such good profits (on the surface, at least), his bosses let him occupy the trading spot for many years—allowing him to gain control over all front- and back-office duties, which simply let him perpetuate the fiction for a few more years.

The game finally ended when global copper prices weakened in early 1996 (years of copper oversupply overwhelmed demand). At that point Hamanaka, who had successfully manipulated copper prices for at least six years (and perhaps as many as ten), had a huge long position in physical and derivative copper and was getting hurt by sliding prices. As his attempts to drive up market prices became more obvious to regulators and auditors, Mr. 5% knew the end was in sight. In fact, management "promoted" him out of the copper trading department. Hedge funds and other speculators, recognizing that Hamanaka's "promotion" meant irregularities, quickly drove the price of copper down (pushing it from $2,700 to $2,000/ton in just four weeks). As the internal investigation unfolded it became apparent that by controlling trading and back-office processes (including various unauthorized and unreported accounts) and manipulating prices on the LME, Hamanaka was able to post fictional profits. Enter Wall Street. It seems that Mr. 5%'s bad deeds were aided, wittingly or unwittingly, by several large banks, which supplied Sumitomo with extremely generous credit lines to meet LME margins. Sumitomo initially declared $1.8 billion of losses from illegal trading—

equal to approximately 10 percent of its equity—and eventually upped the figure to $2.5 billion. To share some of the financial pain with the willing bankers, Sumitomo decided to sue J.P. Morgan Chase, Merrill Lynch, UBS and Credit Lyonnais in 1999 for $1.7 billion, claiming they knew, or should have known, about Hamanaka's illegal trades. After a little bit of objection and some proclamations of innocence, several banks (in an all too predictable manner) pulled out their checkbooks, and settled up out of court; Merrill Lynch paid Sumitomo $275 million, J.P. paid $125 million, and so on. That's how shareholders came to pay for "aiding and abetting" in the global copper market.

Tying, Reverse Tying, Spinning, and Laddering

The Street has lots of other ways of breaching trust, like tying, reverse tying, spinning, and laddering—a wonderful collection of quid pro quos. Let's start with tying, basically a form of coercion in which a bank gives a client a loan—at a razor-thin margin that is wholly inadequate for the risk being taken—if the client promises to send some other juicy business its way: an advisory assignment, an equity financing, maybe management of employee pension assets, anything with a nice margin. No incremental business, no loan—so the two deals are "tied" together. The Fed has defined product tying as any instance in which a bank "requires customers to purchase the tied product to obtain the desired product." As we noted earlier in the book it's illegal under the Bank Holding Company Act of 1970 if the bank has a commercial bank charter (like Citi, or J.P. Morgan, or Bank of America), and it's frowned upon if the bank is a securities firm operating a commercial banking subsidiary. (But if a commercial bank with a securities subsidiary is crafty enough, it might be able to get around the regulatory hurdles, though it's still got to watch out for Section 23B of the Federal Reserve Act, which forbids reducing the price of credit to benefit an investment banking affiliate). Regulations aside, when banks tie they are being unfair to their clients, and what they're doing seems little different from blackmail (e.g., "Pay me $10 million or I'll tell everyone your darkest secrets," versus "Pay me $10 million through your next convertible bond issue or I won't arrange this syndicated loan."). And if the banks get it wrong (i.e., they underprice loans to win other business, and the loans go sour), bank investors get stuck holding the bag (remember Global Crossing, Enron, WorldCom, Qwest—no tying was proved, but lots of cheap loans, incremental high-margin business for those arranging loans, more cheap loans and, finally, loan defaults. Even if all the activity was the result of "successful cross-selling" rather than tying, it was a bad, bad trade).

The two squads on Wall Street snipe at each other about all of this "tied" business: the investment banks say the commercial banks use their big balance sheets to offer cheap loans in order to attract high-margin business—the loss leader approach. The commercial banks say that lending alone isn't profitable enough (e.g., 0.1 percent fees on the credit facility, 4–7 percent on the good investment banking stuff) so they need to get some of the more lucrative business (quite how they persuade their clients to give them that additional business isn't discussed, of course). In practical terms, a bank like Bank of America says it isn't going to lend a company like Wal-Mart $2.25 billion again because it hasn't won (received? been given?) any of the company's other financial business. So we see commercial banks pitching for the high-margin deals by offering the low-margin loans, sometimes coming dangerously close to the fine line that separates cross-selling and tying; and we see the investment banks beefing up their balance sheets to try to compete with the commercial banks by offering loans (so they can preserve the profitable part of their franchise). Neither scheme is particularly good for shareholders. Of course it all might become moot as the banks morph into the European universal bank model, with all the big players doing all of the same business. Then it will just be a question of determining whether what they're doing is cross-selling or tying.

Tying is tough to prove, because no one is usually silly enough to put the quid pro quo in writing. Everything is done on a verbal basis (and sometimes a very oblique verbal basis), so there's rarely a smoking gun. But it happens, and regulators have caught some firms with their hands in the cookie jar. (By the way, even foreign banks run afoul of this in the United States; for instance, German bank WestLB had to pay $3 million because regulators found the bank granted loans to clients only if they gave the bank higher rankings in underwriting syndicates; someone at that bank made the unfortunate mistake of documenting this little requirement). In fact, a large number of U.S. corporate finance officers at major companies have cited increased pressure to give banks other business in exchange for vanilla credit services: no lucrative assignments, no loans. Nearly 60 percent of CFOs and treasurers at large U.S. companies believe pressure to award "additional business" has increased in the past few years.[4] More than 50 percent said they had credit denied or loan terms changed when they refused to give banks other assignments on a noncompetitive basis.

Banks also get involved in something known as reverse tying, in which they agree to use a customer's products and services in exchange for getting the customer's banking business. So rather than give Company X an underpriced loan in exchange for the juicy M&A assignment, Bank A buys some of Company X's products: X gets some additional business revenues, A gets the M&A mandate (and doesn't even have to bloat its balance sheet or skew its risk profile by granting an ill-advised loan). This one can be difficult to prove, because there's nothing wrong with having reciprocal relationships—the bank knows the company, the company knows the bank, so why shouldn't they do some mutual business? The question is whether the corporate business would occur in the absence of the banking business. Would A really buy some of X's widgets if there was no M&A mandate hanging in the balance? Think about this one: in April 2002 UBS launched a $125 million convertible bond issue for Documentum, earning a handsome $3.8 million in fees. One month later, UBS placed a $1.1 million order with Documentum for some its document-handling services; as it happens, it was the company's fifth largest order of the quarter, and helped it exceed analysts' earnings expectations. Coincidence or reverse tying? Would UBS really have purchased $1.1 million of Documentum services in May 2002 absent that convertible deal? All parties, of course, deny any funny business. Or this one: in early 2002 Morgan Stanley was selected to lead the IPO for consulting firm Accenture. Stanley executives told Accenture they would purchase $20 million of Accenture services in each of the next two years (compared with only $3 million per year prior to the IPO). What changed? Did Accenture's services suddenly get so much better that the bank absolutely had to have more, or did the bank suddenly discover that it desperately needed Accenture's services for some new projects? Or was it the IPO? (It's worth noting that when Stanley fell behind the target service levels, Accenture's CFO complained to the bank's executives—so there obviously wasn't too much in the way of raging demand for consulting.) Similar episodes have happened with Infosys and Goldman, Siebel and Bank of America, EDS and Bank of America. Whether or not there's any monkey business going on is hard to say; at a minimum, some disclosure on the reciprocity would be helpful, but it's rarely forthcoming. So everyone's left wondering.

Another Wall Street favorite that we've already alluded to, and which pops up when the markets are red hot and new equity issues are being printed at furious speed, is spinning (mostly with IPOs but also with highly coveted equity add-ons). We touched on this in chapter 3 as being a driver in some of the obvious equity underpricings that have occurred over the years. It's a three-act play that goes something like this: Act 1: A Wall Street bank, doing an IPO for the latest "company of the moment" (Co. ABC), gets its sales troops pumped up about the deal so they can create a buzz with their clients. That virtually guarantees that the IPO, however it is priced, will have a strong first-day showing. Act 2: The investment bankers call up some senior executives at client firm XYZ to pitch for their forthcoming M&A business. Before the meeting is over, the bankers let the executives know about the ABC IPO—and that they could probably get them all a few shares for their personal accounts. The XYZ executives, always interested in lining their own pockets, indicate that they would be very appreciative of a few crumbs from the IPO. Act 3: Equity syndicate managers running the ABC deal plan to underprice it dramatically: it should be priced at $20 but they'll launch it at $10—with all of the pent-up demand and some generous underpricing it'll shoot to the moon. Of course, they'll lose some IPO fees (making only half as much), but they'll make it up on secondary commissions. More important, they'll earn it back on the M&A fees from the XYZ mandate that they now expect to win. Oh, yes, ABC will leave money on the table, but who cares? The deal gets priced at $10 and, with some help from the investment bankers, the XYZ executives get a 200,000-share allocation (at $2 million). During the first trading day, demand drives the price up to $23 a share. The XYZ executives bail out for $4.6 million, a tidy $2.6 million profit for doing nothing. Next day they announce to the financial press that the investment bank has been awarded the new M&A mandate. Curtain falls. Applause. The winners: the executives at XYZ, who made virtually risk-free windfall profits, and the investment bankers, who won the M&A mandate (ensuring that they'll get bigger bonuses). The losers: ABC, who got the short end of the stick on the valuation and left lots of money on the table, and the investment bank's retail clients, who were stiffed on the IPO allocation and don't get to enjoy the same profit opportunities as the favored clients. The ultimate loser: the bank's shareholders, who will pay the fines and suffer loss of revenues and income once the bank's management gets caught by regulators for spinning.

It's no particular surprise that spinning has been a feature of Wall Street for many years. J.P. Morgan and other banks were spinning shares to New York politicians, friends, allies, and bank partners back in the teens and 1920s. In fact, some of the spinning related to a 1929 issue of Alleghany Trust led to the Pecora hearings, a public examination into the Street's less-than-fair business practices (in the Alleghany case, shares in the trust, which traded on a when-issued basis at $35, were given to "friends" of the Morgans at a launch price of $20 with a recommendation that they immediately sell at the when-issued price—guaranteed profits for the favored few). The hearings led ultimately to certain mild reforms, but the practice has continued for years. Spinning gets particularly bad when the markets are frothy and deals are underpriced, as in the three cycles that appeared in the 1950s to early 1970s. And we can point to more recent examples. For instance, ex-WorldCom CEO Bernie Ebbers earned $11.5 million in profits between 1996 and 2000 from various Citi IPOs; over the same time period the company gave Citi business that generated tens of millions in banking fees. Executives at Qwest and McLeod Telecom received similar largesse and used Citi for most of their banking work. In fact, the SEC discovered this was pretty prevalent during the bull run/bubble of the late 1990s and filed charges against a number of banks in 2002 and 2003. Expect class-action lawsuits for the next few years, and expect bank investors to lose more, again.

════════════

CSFB's Little Headache, Part I: Friends of Frank

During the TMT boom times Frank Quattrone, CSFB's head of technology banking, was deal maker par excellence. Even though he got paid buckets of money for his efforts, the elders at CSFB must have felt like they had the golden goose: Quattrone and his team were printing new tech IPO deals at breathtaking speed, and the fees were rolling in. When the team walked in the door in 1998, CSFB was number 19 in technology IPOs; just two years later it was number 1 in both tech IPOs and disclosed fees, thanks primarily to Quattrone. Though Quattrone cut his teeth at Morgan Stanley (where he did big deals like Cisco and Netscape) he jumped to Deutsche in 1996 and then left to join CSFB after then-CEO Allen Wheat promised him the moon (e.g., bigger profit sharing, direct control of research, greater ability to call his own shots). By 2000 he had racked up an impressive record, launching dozens of new issues and earning lots of money for CSFB (and himself).

It was during this heady period that the bank figured out a good way to attract even more business: do a little spinning for the top brass of Silicon Valley. The idea was that by giving executives access to the bank's hot IPOs, CSFB would be in the running for additional mandates from the grateful executives. So CSFB's Technology Private Client Services group—the team that serviced all of the Valley's hot shots—was allocated 2–4 percent of all tech IPOs. It then placed the shares in one of 300+ special "Friends of Frank" accounts (as they were dubbed) to the benefit of specific corporate executives and venture capitalists who were promising leads for future underwritings (i.e., executives senior enough to call the shots on awarding future banking business to CSFB or venture capitalists with enough clout to steer promising IPO candidates to the bank—all contrary to rules against gratuities and unfair trade practices). The executives (including some at Phone.com, iPrint, El Sitio, Dell, Interwoven, etc.) deposited funds in the special accounts but typically left no specific instructions on what to do with the shares—the CSFB brokers were given full discretion. Then, several days after an IPO was launched, the CSFB brokers sold shares in the Friends accounts at handsome premiums, leaving lots of senior executives with fat checkbooks and big smiles. Let's figure that between July

1998 and December 2000—the peak period for technology underwritings—CSFB's deals gained a total of $10 billion of market value within five days of launch. Allocations of 2–4 percent to the "Friends" suggest five-day windfalls of $200 million to $400 million (and maybe even more). So the bank's preferred executive clients enjoyed this gravy, while the rest of the retail account base that put in for allocations, but received none, got stiffed. These practices eventually came to light, putting the bank and its executives in hot water. CSFB ultimately wrote regulators a big check for this and other funny business (but let's save the rest for later).

Spinning isn't the only breach of trust on new issues: there's also a game called laddering, in which investors get shares in a new issue only if they agree to buy more shares after the launch of the deal. Wall Street argues that these little conversations (you know, "how much would you pay in the aftermarket for more shares if you had some of the new issue shares?") are just part of the book building process: the banks need this kind of information to know how to price the deal (not that they know how to price deals, as we've already shown). But regulators have said that soliciting aftermarket orders while marketing a new issue is illegal because it artificially stimulates demand (this goes back to rules imposed during the second flagrant episode of stock market bubble abuses, in the 1960s). Despite regulations, laddering still seems to pop up frequently, especially when the markets are hot. For example, the SEC began investigating J.P. Morgan, Morgan Stanley, Goldman, and a number of others in the millennium for laddering practices during the tech boom (allegations of laddering also formed part of the class-action suit against 55 securities firms and 300+ IPOs we referenced earlier). And in a separate incident, J.P. Morgan agreed to pay $25 million to settle SEC charges related to nonequitable distribution of IPOs in 1999 and 2000 based on customer indications of how much they would pay for additional aftermarket shares.

A couple of banks have also tried out a little variation on the laddering theme by giving clients hot IPO shares but then "sharing" profits from the IPO by charging them higher than normal commissions on unrelated stock trades. On the surface, some of the parties involved seem to win: investors get some of the big IPO action (which they might otherwise not see) and they make some tidy profits—though not as much as if the bankers were playing fair. The banks get a kickback from investors in the form of higher commissions—good for bank revenues and broker sales credits (and year-end bonuses). But there are still lots of losers: those unwilling to play the game (who then get shut out of new issue allocations), and the underlying investing clients themselves (who are meant to be protected against kickback schemes). Let's look at a few examples from the real world. During the TMT bubble CSFB played this game aggressively, giving clients IPO allocations and then charging commissions on unrelated trades at an average of $3.15 a share instead of 6 cents a share. For instance, in one case a CSFB client received a $400,000 allocation of an IPO that rocketed to $3.2 million at the end of the first day, generating a $2.8 million profit; the client then bought 2 million shares of Compaq, paying $1 million more than it should have in commissions. So, CSFB had an extra $1 million in commissions, the client was still $1.8 million ahead of the game and everyone was happy (but, of course, it's just taking the client for a ride in a different car). This happened so many times that CSFB finally got caught, paid the SEC $100 million in fines, and disgorged profits to settle up on what the courts called a "pervasive scheme" to steal millions in customer profits. Robertson Stephens paid $28 million for the same type of client violations, J.P. Morgan (through activities in its Hambrecht & Quist subsidiary) paid $6 million, and a number of other banks paid hefty fines. During the announcement of all of these findings the SEC noted that banks "didn't observe the highest standards of commercial honor." An understatement.

Retail Infractions

Retail clients are protected from broker malfeasance and fiduciary breaches through a host of laws and regulations. At an individual level the marketplace is not supposed to be caveat emptor, which is a good thing for Moms and Pops (or else they would probably just get fleeced any time, all the time). For instance, blue sky laws, enforced by state securities boards/commissions, regulate the practices of brokers, honing in specifically on deceptive practices and fraud. The SEC also protects small investors through federal regulations, some embodied in the Securities Acts of 1933 and 1934. A U.S. Supreme Court decision handed down in 1987 said the acts are intended to "protect investors from predatory behavior by securities industry personnel." It also delegates authorities to SROs like the NASD and NYSE, and expects banks to enforce certain compliance standards. In fact, some of it works, and some of it doesn't.

Regulators try very hard to protect individuals against fraud by forbidding brokers from making untrue statements of material facts, omitting material information, or doing anything misleading. They've also come up with other special rules to keep everyone on the straight and narrow: no sharing of losses, no rebates or compensation for orders, no bunching of trades, no selling away, no circulating of rumors, no insider trading, no use of the words "promise" or "guarantee" in pitching investments, no churning, no overtrading, no unauthorized use of margin, no abuse of discretionary powers, and so forth. But there just aren't enough regulatory soldiers running around to enforce all the right behaviors. With tens of thousands of brokers dealing with millions of clients, how can a few hundred regulators possibly keep on top of things? Well, they can't, which is why a lot of the daily monitoring is delegated to SROs and individual banks. Unfortunately, some of the SRO oversight is a bit suspect, and some of the banks have pretty lousy controls. The end result? Many of the rules designed to protect Moms and Pops are ignored or violated because the risk of getting caught is usually pretty small. And even the "unlucky" ones that get busted face ineffective penalties—they would be laughable, except that it's not a laughing matter. The most a broker is likely to get is a small fine (e.g., a few thousand dollars) and a black mark against his/her name in the very, very, very fine print regulatory section of the *Wall Street Journal*. And that's about it. So it's no wonder there are so many breaches in the retail world.

And when a client tries to recover money lost through unsuitability or bad advice, the brokerage firm will try different tactics to weasel out of it: it'll claim the investor was sophisticated and knew what he/she was doing, or that the trade was unsolicited. Sometimes, if a client is well heeled, brokerage firms pull the "rich man's defense"—saying that because Mr. John Smith has a net worth of $1 million, or $10 million, or $100 million, he is obviously sophisticated and able to understand and bear risk, so he should bear the loss. Sometimes, believe it or not, they use the "you shouldn't have let me defraud you" defense (happily, most of these defenses don't work, but it doesn't stop some from trying). Any excuse so as not to pay out (and any, or all, of which may be untrue, as thousands of arbitration cases have demonstrated over the years). Whatever the specific circumstances of a rule violation, it's often off to arbitration and the "he said/she said" game, maybe a review of trade tickets and confirmations, a listen in on taped phone records—all the unpleasant things that do very little to engender client trust. Whatever the outcome, it leaves everyone feeling lousy.

IGNORING CONFLICTS OF INTEREST

The potential for conflict of interest is rife on Wall Street, and breaches appear frequently enough to tell us this is a real problem. Bankers (and sometimes whole banks) put themselves in situations where they are clearly conflicted: they try to win or earn or gain something that runs contrary to their job as trusted representatives, agents, or fiduciaries. When bankers morally or legally cross the boundary and no longer have client interests as their primary priority and responsibility, all kinds of reprehensible behavior can appear.

Drexel, King of Junk

Drexel, which started out as a second-tier Philadelphia firm and grew into a Wall Street power, showed the world how some innovation and hard work can lead to the creation of a truly useful financial mechanism. Unfortunately, it also showed the world how some unethical behavior and bad management can stop the whole show. The story of Mike Milken, marketer and trader of high-yield junk bonds, is by now well known. He was one of the first Wall Street figures of the modern era to gain public notoriety and thrust the whole industry squarely into the spotlight. The fact that he earned piles of money (based on a 1973 agreement that let him earn $1 for every $2 he made Drexel), almost single-handedly popularized the marketplace for junk debt, and then engaged in a series of illegal activities and wound up in jail is the stuff of movies. For a time much of the useful by-product of Drexel and Milken—securities issued by lower-rated companies that allowed access to much-needed investor capital—was overshadowed by greed and fraud. Junk bonds were tarred with the "Milken brush," and were criticized by many for a number of years. Only with the passage of a bit of time can we see more clearly that the problem was not with junk bonds, but with the way Milken, his associates, and his superiors originated, sold, and traded them, and how they managed the whole process.

Milken started his work at Drexel Harriman Ripley in 1969 and stuck with it through various successor incarnations, e.g., Drexel Firestone and, ultimately, Drexel Burnham Lambert. His early focus was on "out-of-favor" investments like real estate investment trusts, convertibles, preferreds, and, perhaps most important, fallen angels—investment grade bonds that had descended into the junk category. Milken analyzed default probabilities and returns on these securities and concluded that spreads were too wide given default experience (to be fair, some academics had already noted asynchronous risk/return characteristics as well—Milken just explored the matter in a practical light). Milken and Drexel didn't invent junk bonds, they simply realized that the securities represented a feasible way for lower-rated companies to raise capital; they also realized that investors holding diversified portfolios of junk would probably make out all right—taking more default risk, to be sure, but less than was apparent on the face of a pure credit rating (certainly when compared with the spreads that could be earned). This epiphany was the foundation of a decade-long effort that led Drexel to the forefront of junk origination and investment. Milken trundled off to California in 1978 to set up a West Coast shop for Drexel. This was the start of the bank's problems—decentralization, particularly when it involves a powerful figure, can be a recipe for disaster. During these early days Drexel started developing an investor base for junk bonds (e.g., Mass Mutual, Lord Abbett, Reliance Insurance, First Executive Life, American Financial Corporation, and others) that would supply capital. Then Drexel's bankers started calling on lower-rated companies, promising to deliver funds. The two sides were matched up, and Drexel took its fees. (Later on it didn't always match them up: it just promised the funding, took the bonds itself, and wore a lot more risk than it should have. More on this in a bit.) In 1978 Drexel became the number 1 underwriter of junk bonds, a crown it would wear till its downfall in 1990. Over the next decade it raised money for more than a thousand companies, including household names like MCI, CNN, and Chrysler.

The junk business of the early 1980s was active but benign: the bonds didn't yet have any negative connotation, and companies issued them mainly for growth (two-thirds of bonds were used for corporate expansion). By the mid- to late 1980s, though, they had acquired a negative patina and were increasingly criticized as contributing to the "greed is good" excesses of the period: the market had grown to $200 billion and had a cowboy mentality about it. During this critical period Drexel made a strategic decision to get involved in the "messy" part of the business, providing junk bond financing for hostile transactions and LBOs, and creating war chests for companies on the prowl. It also developed the "highly confident" letter, a loose underwriting commitment given to companies that were eager to buy up competitors and wanted to demonstrate funding availability (e.g., Icahn used a $1.5 billion highly confident letter in his run at Phillips Petroleum; many others did the same).

As things got more aggressive, Milken and some of his team started dancing on the wrong side of the law, violating their duties to issuers, investors, or both, and running afoul of securities regulations. Milken's "fused" role as originator, trader, and salesman of assets was contrary to Wall Street practice—the separation of roles exists to avoid conflicts of interest, access to inside information, valuation problems, and so on. Milken's infractions took lots of forms, some subtle, others more obvious. For instance, Milken pressured would-be issuers of bonds to buy securities of other issuers—refusing to raise capital unless they did what they were told ("buy these bonds that we issued for XYZ or we won't be able to issue a bond for you"—kind of like tying). Not quite how you'd expect a client to be treated, but something you can apparently do when your bank owns the market. He also firmly controlled junk bond prices, meaning that, for a time, the price he posted on his own portfolio of bonds was the only price that mattered (forget what the financial controllers might say). He could effectively value the bonds however he wanted, something that can't be done in a liquid and transparent market. And, of course, there were instances of insider trading, some of it very egregious. In fact, it was Milken's insider dealings with once-famous arbitrageur Ivan Boesky (who was convicted of insider dealing) that led to his downfall.

There were other actual or apparent conflicts of interest within the bank itself that would upset any client or outside investor. For instance, lots of Drexel executives invested in partnerships that bought up pieces of deals that the bank had underwritten. Though some of this may have been okay, the sheer number of partnerships that were developed over the years—more than five hundred—increased the opportunities for internal self-dealing and favoritism over outside clients. In fact, examinations later revealed that some of the partnerships received prices that were better than those given to outside clients and that front running occurred regularly. The fact that Drexel could underwrite a junk bond for an issuer on a primary basis, and could then retain or purchase the bond as dealer or a long-term proprietary investor and channel it to Drexel executives and employees as an investment was fraught with conflict.

Milken and other Drexel investment bankers also saddled the bank with lots of risk. There were many direct bought deals, and some of the highly confident letters eventually turned into bought deals as well—meaning Drexel owned the paper. As the market got frothier and the borrowers more marginal, it got harder and harder to place bonds. So Milken absorbed a pile onto Drexel's balance sheet, turning a supposedly fleet-of-foot investment bank into a semipermanent lender with a risky, illiquid, and bloated balance sheet. By the late 1980s the bank routinely carried billions worth of junk bonds, and funding the positions was increasingly difficult. While a typical Street bank with a liquid portfolio of Treasuries and high grade bonds can pledge them as collateral with only modest discounts to market value (e.g., less than 1 percent), Drexel faced discounts of 50 percent on its portfolio of junk bonds. It was thus extremely illiquid, a fact that became obvious when things started falling apart.

When regulators began investigating the bank in the late 1980s, they didn't like what they found: plenty of evidence of corrupt sales practices, insider trading, self-dealing, and conflicts of interest. Under the threat of criminal Racketeer Influenced and Corrupt Organizations charges (a near-certain death sentence) Drexel agreed to pay a $650 million fine and oust Milken and several of his associates. Milken himself was charged on 98 counts and pleaded guilty to six felonies (mostly minor ones, like some stock parking and tax evasion); he ultimately agreed to pay a $500 million fine and spent 22 months in prison. (The fine didn't exactly ruin him financially. He was allowed to keep a personal fortune estimated at $125 million, and his family preserved an additional $300 million to $400 million.) Drexel's punishment coincided with a downturn in the U.S. economy and a rise in corporate default rates (to record levels that wouldn't be seen again till 2001–2002). For a bank like Drexel, with stacks of unsold risky junk bonds on its balance sheet being financed at 50 percent discounts, the liquidity squeeze started getting more severe. Street banks started pulling back on their credit facilities, and falling junk bond prices—some the result of regulatory changes requiring S&Ls to sell their junk portfolios—triggered margin calls. Drexel got caught in a liquidity spiral and defaulted on $150 million in payments, which triggered other cross defaults and ended the game. Ultimately, the damage wrought by Milken's infractions, the riskiness and illiquidity of the balance sheet, and the regulatory fines and sanctions combined to bring the bank down. Though Milken and Drexel disappeared from the scene in February 1990, the junk bond market proved that it wasn't a one-man or one-firm show. The market went dead for a time in the early 1990s, more as a result of a high level of corporate defaults from economic dislocation than because Milken and Drexel were gone. It soon rebounded and appears to be a permanent fixture of Wall Street. Not so Milken and Drexel. They ignored client responsibilities and rules of prudent management, and it caught up with them.

———————

Conflicts can take lots of different forms: taking advantage of trust for personal aggrandizement, allowing "independent" research analysts to report to revenue-generating investment bankers, trading in personal accounts to the detriment of clients, exchanging favors with others to achieve a personal gain, failing to advise clients when a clear division of interests exists, and so on. Whenever the conflicts appear, the potential for abuse is front and center.

Conflicts are nothing new, of course. Back in the 1920s even the most powerful figures on the Street were engaged in funny business. For instance, the head of Chase Bank, Albert Wiggin, set up some personal accounts so that he could conduct bear raids on Chase's own stock. The CEO of the bank thus had every incentive to torpedo the bank's performance so that he could drive the stock down and profit in his personal account—and he did, to the tune of $4 million, and never got caught. At about the same time, the head of National City Bank, Charles Mitchell, set up personal holding companies to speculate in a number of stock pools using depositors' funds, another conflict.

We can also take a look at a few examples from more recent times (with our usual reminder that this is just a sampling). One of the biggest conflicts hitting the industry has come from structural problems within research and investment banking. Wall Street firms have research teams that are supposed to come up with good investment ideas on where investors should put their money. Analysts dissect all sorts of material and try to project where a company or market is heading: since there is an element of the "forward looking" in all of this, mistakes can creep into the process. Analysts are human, and they occasionally get it wrong. So instead of sell, they may say buy, or instead of bonds, they say stocks, or instead of yen, they say euro. That's okay: if the call has been made on the basis of hard work and reasonable interpretation of the facts, no one is going to beat up an analyst too hard (even when they get it spectacularly wrong, as when Mary Meeker, Internet analyst at Morgan Stanley, rated Priceline.com a "buy" after Stanley launched the company's IPO. The initial buy recommendation at $134 a share remained a buy at $80, a buy at $8 and a buy at $4. Just a bad call, that's all [but don't worry, Stanley made more than $90 million in fees from Priceline business]). The problems arise when there are deliberate attempts to mislead. Let's first note that research groups are cost centers. They don't generate direct revenues of their own, meaning they have to go around, hat in hand, looking for contributions (big contributions, too, because analysts tend to make good dollars). The logical place to turn for funding is investment banking, one of the groups that can theoretically derive direct or indirect benefit from research work—though only if the research says good things about the client company. Here, then, lies the conflict: creating value for the investment banking team so that they'll want to keep funding the research operation, but remaining true to the independent nature and quality of the analytical research work. It's a big conflict, one that became stunningly apparent during the boom of the late 1990s. Most of the big firms decided to use research as a marketing and deal-winning tool rather than an independent service for advising clients. Investment bankers—seeing cooperative souls that were willing to craft glowing client research reports—were suddenly eager to fund their research "friends"; everyone was happy (except the investing clients who got hurt). The conflicts centered on producing positive research reports regardless of the state of a company (e.g., Citi, Merrill), not downgrading ratings when they should have been downgraded (e.g., Citi, Merrill, UBS), and allowing bankers and clients to routinely receive and edit prepublication reports (e.g., Lehman, Merrill, UBS, CSFB). Even when retail brokers within the banks complained about the research bias/taint, their comments fell on deaf ears—the conflict just kept on deepening.

So the conflicted analysts on the Street changed their research views in order to help win business (and either line their own pockets through bigger bonuses or ensure job security). While they should have been making independent calls on the financial performance and prospects of companies in their sector, some (many?) were being overly bullish or creating fiction: rating lousy companies "strong buys" so that bankers could keep winning juicy mandates. There are all kinds of examples, but we've got room only for a few. We've got Citi telecom analyst Jack Grubman and Merrill Internet analyst Henry Blodget (whom we'll talk about later), who kept dodgy stocks rated as "buys" or "strong buys" so that their employers could win business. WorldCom, Winstar, and Focal Communications were some of Grubman's favorite picks even as they spiraled into bankruptcy (but by then Citi had already earned lots of fees from debt and equity deals). Blodget said he liked companies such as Internet Capital Group and Infospace, even though he said otherwise in private correspondence; no coincidence that Merrill did investment banking work for both of them. Then there's UBS analyst Howard Capek, who wrote in e-mails in late 1999 that HealthSouth was a "pig" and that "it was a mess," vowing "I would not own a share in the company." Yet he rated it a "strong buy" starting in early 2000 (as Pennsylvania Representative James Greenwood, Chairman of the House Energy and Commerce Subcommittee on Oversight and Investigations observed: "Clearly, Mr. Capek had an amazing change of heart. One day he said it's a dog and then he said it was a darling"[5]). For the next two years the "strong buy" remained unchanged, and UBS became the company's preferred banker (earning millions in fees on $2 billion of financings). But HealthSouth's stock price dropped steadily, and regulators eventually charged the company with massive, 15-year fraud related to a multi-billion dollar revenue overstatement. (Separately, UBS was investigated for tying, on the grounds that it may have prevented HealthSouth from working with other banks.) And there's Merrill analyst Phua Young, covering troubled conglomerate Tyco, who apparently wasn't sure if he had a duty of allegiance to Merrill's investors, Merrill's bankers, or Tyco. In fact, he got so confused that he was eventually fired by Merrill and charged by the NASD with preparing misleading research. In some rather bizarre e-mails, Young signed off as a "loyal Tyco employee" and stated, "I am paid indirectly by Tyco." He exchanged gifts with Tyco CEO Dennis Kozlowski (himself indicted on fraud). He wouldn't send his research out to investors till Tyco's CFO had reviewed and approved it. And he fed investors bad information. For instance, in a 2002 report he told investors that Tyco subsidiary CIT was worth $7 billion to $8 billion, but he noted in a separate e-mail to Tyco investor relations managers that "it wasn't worth anything near $8b" (it was eventually spun off for $4.6 billion). Young helped Merrill win four debt issues between 1999 and 2001 that generated $20 million in fees (and made several million for himself), but he sure didn't help investors out.

The Research Fiasco

In 2002 Wall Street was caught red-handed in a fiasco involving equity research—a startling display of the Street's failure on many fronts. This one had it all: conflicts of interest, mismanagement, lack of controls, lack of judgment, mistreatment of clients, regulatory violations, and lies. It wound up costing Street bank investors an initial $1.4 billion (plus amounts to be determined through future lawsuits), and further tarnished the reputations of most of the major players. When Eliot Spitzer, Attorney General for New York State, released his findings, street investors didn't take kindly to the news and dumped stock. Within a month, Merrill, Goldman, CSFB, Citi, Morgan Stanley, J.P. Morgan Chase, and others had each lost between $5 billion and $10 billion in market cap.

It went like this: for a period of at least several years, ten major Wall Street banks mismanaged their research functions in the pursuit of greater profits—putting dollars ahead of ethics, trust, or client considerations. Bank executives permitted (and sometimes openly encouraged) supposedly independent analysts to work closely with the bankers in pitching financing and M&A deals; they allowed analysts to be reviewed and paid by bankers (directly or indirectly); they allowed inaccurate, and sometimes fraudulent research to be prepared and distributed; they permitted bankers and client companies to "preview" research reports before publication; they let bankers bully analysts into maintaining buy recommendations when they weren't warranted. Research became a tool to hype and tout poor or mediocre stocks coming out of the pipeline (largely, though not exclusively, related to TMT, including many of those questionable dot com deals of the late 1990s we mentioned in chapter 3). Research was most certainly not a useful, objective analytical study of a company's prospects. (Of course, some of the companies were to blame, too. They were keen to have positive research floating around, especially in the months following an IPO or new issue; once the 180-day lockout period for executive shareholders passed, they could unload their shares at handsome, and sometimes artificially boosted, stock prices).

Some analysts were clearly under pressure from investment bankers not to publish bad reports or assign "hold" or "sell" recommendations. By mid-2000 this skewed behavior led to an industry-wide buy versus hold/sell ratio of 92:8 (and in some cases it was even more skewed; consider that Citi's research chief, John Hoffmann, reflected in his February 2001 notes that the firm had 1,177 stocks rated "buy," 1 rated "sell" and 1 rated "underperform"—a bit of an imbalance, even for a bull market). Bank executives were often aware of the practice, and some condoned it. E-mail traffic between two Goldman analysts appears to have been fairly typical, even as the market was selling off and TMT stocks were plunging: "Investment banking considerations have prevented me from making a change [to AT&T and WorldCom stocks]." Or, from CSFB: "Unwritten rules . . . I have learned to adapt to a set of rules that have been imposed by Tech Group [investment] banking so as to keep our corporate clients appeased. . . . [B]y following rules [I] have successfully managed not to annoy the company or banking."[6] In other cases, bullish reports were allowed to remain unchanged for up to six months, even as companies and sectors were deteriorating rapidly. The abuse of trust was formidable.

After the TMT meltdown, Spitzer and his crew started intensive investigations into the Street's research departments, gaining access to deal files, correspondence, and e-mails, and interviewing current and former analysts, bankers, and executives. The attorney general then started building his case. Among the laundry list of infractions and culpable parties:

- Fraudulent research [that's fraudulent, not erroneous or bad]: Merrill, Citibank, CSFB
- Unfair research: Bear, CSFB, Goldman, Lehman, Morgan Stanley, Piper Jaffray, Citibank, UBS—these firms were specifically charged with issuing "exaggerated" and "unwarranted" research reports
- Undisclosed payment/receipt of money for research: UBS, Piper Jaffray, Bear Stearns, J.P. Morgan Chase, Morgan Stanley
- Spinning: CSFB, Citibank

All ten banks were accused of allowing investment bankers to influence their research coverage.

With the writing very clearly on the wall, Merrill was first to step up to the plate and negotiate a settlement (May 2002); it agreed to pay $100 million and make internal reforms related to the organization and reporting of the research function, independent review of research prior to publication, and so forth. Merrill's arrangement served as the model for others who followed, and the end result was the $1.4 billion (non-tax-deductible) settlement. (In typical Wall Street fashion some of the ten banks started making noises about claiming portions of their settlement "losses" under their insurance policies—the regulators and courts quickly put a stop to that talk.) The agreement also called for separation of research and banking, provision of independent research at no cost to clients, and better disclosure of stock rankings (including the number of sells, specific performance of analysts, and so on).

The settlement didn't remove the specter of fraud charges or class-action lawsuits. That's good as far as abused investors are concerned because it leaves them with the possibility of trying to recover a bit more of what they've lost; the pact didn't materially help out any of the Moms and Pops who got hurt (bad news for bank investors). The first wave of NASD arbitration cases related to the misadventures of research analysts started in mid-2003, with 125 specific actions (some expect the number to build to more than four thousand over the years). Some banks started preparing for a few more shots, setting up reserves to handle the inevitable lawsuits and settlements. And guess who loses again? The bank investors. But the clients lose as well, because they've been the victims of a colossal breach of trust.

So will Wall Street learn from this episode? Will research finally turn the corner and become useful, or will it remain the bull market marketing tool it has been over the past few years? Will analysts actually put out "sell" recommendations, or will it be back to the same old game once the public eye shifts to some other problem and markets get back to full bull-market strength? Who knows? To be sure, all the CEOs lined up for their ceremonial sword-falling exercises, to wit Merrill's former CEO David Komansky said at the 2002 annual meeting, "We have failed to live up to the high standards that are our tradition, and I want to take this opportunity to publicly apologize to our clients, our shareholders and our employees."[7] Goldman CEO Hank Paulson told shareholders "With the benefit of hindsight it is clear we could have done better."[8] Former Citibank CEO Sandy Weill said "We are proud to be able to say that we acted decisively and honestly without waiting for regulators to order us to change"[9] (about 2 or 3 years after the fact). Is that good enough? Shouldn't Wall Street, in its role as a trusted fiduciary, avoid even getting to such a critical stage? Some, in fact, didn't quite get it, and got slapped around by the SEC and attorney general. Morgan Stanley's CEO Philip Purcell tried to downplay the effect of the whole episode on retail clients, drew the wrath of SEC Chairman William Donaldson, and was forced to apologize publicly. Merrill's new CEO Stan O'Neal wrote an op-ed piece in the *Wall Street Journal* noting the importance of risk-taking, and received a rather pointed response from Spitzer: "I saw an article in one major publication where one of the CEO's said this [settlement] is merely an effort to eliminate risk from the marketplace. Risk is inherent in the markets. We understand that and we thrive on it. What is not tolerated, however, is fraud. So, Mr. CEO . . . if I were you I would reflect. What your company did, and what we have alleged about your company, is that you committed fraud. . . . Because what you did was shuffle the risk to unknowing investors while earning your fees up front. That's not fair, that's not equitable and that's not the way markets should be run."[10] Ouch.

The research conflict also spawned other problems. For instance, to help boost the appearance of a number of questionable companies, some Wall Street firms paid other Wall Street firms to produce favorable research. The aim was to put more "buy" ratings on a given company out in the marketplace, making it easier for brokers to peddle the latest dot com wonder. It makes sense: if Bank XYZ is underwriting a deal, we expect them to come out with a "buy" rating (that's probably one of the reasons they won the mandate). But if a few palms are greased, and Banks ABC and DEF come out with "buys" (and they aren't involved in the new issue), doesn't that look good? An investor seeing three buys, including two "independent" ones, is going to be pretty eager to jump in, even in the aftermarket. Morgan Stanley, which called this "guaranteed economics for research," paid out $2.7 million in "research fees" to 25 securities firms providing research on 12 offerings (e.g., Veritas Software, Agile Software. E.piphany). When UBS didn't participate on a deal, it, too, produced research and received "special research checks" (e.g., Flextronics, Atmail). Five Wall Street firms got caught up in this little conflict, or what regulators have termed "under-the-table" payments. The firms claimed that they were acting under the instructions of their client issuing companies (e.g., Veritas gave Stanley underwriting and M&A business on condition it would arrange for research coverage). Whatever. In 2003 Morgan Stanley, UBS, J.P. Morgan Chase, Bear Stearns, and Piper Jaffray—all implicated and charged—pleaded no contest and paid their fines (Stanley had to pay an extra $1.65 million because it accidentally "overwrote" some sensitive e-mails the regulators were eager to read).

Analysts or Bankers?

At the height of the TMT bubble in the late 1990s, Wall Street analysts, especially those covering Internet, telecom, networking, and wireless companies, were demigods. They could do no wrong. They were everywhere, talking up the markets, promoting the latest high-flying dot com platform, jumping on planes with investment bankers to win deals. (Hmmm. . . .) They showed up on CNN and CNBC to talk about stellar corporate profits, earnings, P/Es, stock price targets, all to get investors to buy and help propel stock prices to the moon (and maybe win a few extra mandates for the home team in the process). Unfortunately, most of the rocketing companies that the analysts touted ended up coming back down to earth the hard way.

Investment bankers are supposed to be aggressive, pitch hard, outwit the competition, and win deals. That is what they get paid to do. Conversely, analysts are meant to produce independent, unbiased views of a company's prospects by ripping apart financial statements, grilling management, and generally being skeptical and contrarian. Analysts shouldn't look, talk, or walk like investment bankers, but some did. At Morgan Stanley some employees thought the firm's Internet analyst, Mary Meeker, was actually an investment banker; indeed, Meeker noted in her performance self-assessment that "my highest and best use is to help Morgan Stanley win the best Internet IPO mandates." (And here we thought the best use of the analyst was to independently analyze.) At Goldman, analyst Craig Kloner said in an e-mail that his goals for 2000 were: "#1, #2, #3: Get more investment banking revenue." At Bear, the head of research noted to his troops that "being a partner to banking is part of your job." And so on.

So analysts were mingling with bankers and masquerading as deal makers. It's been well reported that more than a few had significant conflicts of interest during the bull run of the 1990s, producing overly glowing (or misleading, or fraudulent) research reports in order to (a) help their employers win mandates, (b) get bigger bonuses, (c) keep their jobs. Bearish analysts were not welcome on Wall Street. There was no room for doubt, questioning, skepticism or sell recommendations during the final stretch of the market's ascent. Even when a sell appeared to be the only alternative, some banks chose to simply drop coverage. (Putting it all into perspective: in 1990, before researchers became so conflicted and the market was still in a bit of a bear mood, there were more sells than buys among the recommendations. By 1998, as conflicts deepened and the TMT boom hit its stride, the Street's analyst community had two-thirds of all stocks rated buys/strong buys, one-third holds, and only 1 percent sells. Banks that were heavily involved in deal making had even worse skews: 90 percent, 95 percent, even 99 percent buys or strong buys).

Though there were (are?) many conflicted analysts, perhaps no one symbolizes the problem more strikingly than Jack Grubman of Citibank (originally part of Salomon Smith Barney). Grubman, a telecom analyst, helped the bank win lots of debt and equity mandates between the start of telecom deregulation in 1996 and the sector's last gasp in 2001. Citi raised a stunning $190 billion of debt and equity for the telecom sector during that span, earning more than $1 billion in fees— thanks, in large part, to Grubman's efforts. Lots of what Grubman did while at Citi resembled what a banker might do (Grubman once stated that "what used to be a conflict [between research and banking] is now a synergy." Really?). In fact, the analyst was in deep with the top management of companies such as Qwest, Global Crossing, and WorldCom, building personal relationships, attending board meetings, and helping executives create strategies (all in effort to win coveted mandates for Citi)—even though he was supposed to be giving independent, unbiased research opinions on these companies. It's a bit difficult to see how that can actually occur when someone's pitching hard for deals, advising company management, and attending a company's meetings and parties. You can imagine the problems that can crop up, and there's plenty of evidence of a disconnect between the corporate performance of certain preferred clients and the published equity recommendations. For instance, Grubman kept WorldCom rated a buy during the company's long slide from $90 to $4. Not until the company was within spitting distance of a bankruptcy filing did he downgrade the stock to "neutral." That's bad luck, bad analysis, or a conflict. (U.S. Congressman Michael Capuano remarked of Grubman during the House investigation of WorldCom: "We have an independent analyst who is neither independent and apparently can't analyze.") Same thing with Winstar: just two months after Grubman publicly criticized other analysts for their bearish calls on the company, Winstar filed for bankruptcy. Same thing with Focal Communications: Grubman held the stock as a buy at the same time his e-mail correspondence referred to the company as a "pig." Same thing with McLeod USA: Grubman maintained a buy rating until the company filed for bankruptcy. It comes as no surprise that Citi earned lots of fees from WorldCom, Winstar, Focal and McLeod. Then there's AT&T: in November 1999 Grubman upgraded AT&T from neutral to buy after Citi's then-CEO Sandy Weill asked him to "take a fresh look at it." Shortly thereafter Citi was given a prominent role in the IPO of AT&T Wireless, the largest in U.S. history (for which the bank earned a princely sum of $63 million, but which it underpriced by nearly $950 million). Six months later Grubman downgraded the stock from buy to neutral. In January 2001 an e-mail from Grubman to a friend surfaced as part of regulatory investigations: "You know everyone thinks I upgraded AT&T to get the lead for [AT&T Wireless]. Nope. I used Sandy [Weill] to get my kids in 92nd Street Y pre-school (which is harder than Harvard) and Sandy needed [AT&T's CEO] Armstrong's vote on our board to nuke Reed [John Reed, co-CEO with Weill] in showdown. Once coast was clear for both of us . . . I went back to my normal negative self [on AT&T]. Armstrong never knew that we both played him like a fiddle."[11] Well, that's nice. Everyone, of course, denies any quid pro quo or conflict. You can connect the dots any way you want.

Even as the TMT boom was rapidly turning into a bust, Grubman kept promoting the sector's prospects, ignoring the excess capacity and overwhelming amount of leverage on TMT balance sheets, and still predicting that telecom services would double as a percentage of GDP within a decade. Again, when we look at the investment banking fees that Grubman helped Citi win over the years, it's little wonder that everything was a buy or strong buy and that the sector would remain robust for years: $69 million in fees from McLeod USA, $141 million from WorldCom, $84 million from Global Crossing, $34 million from Qwest. Do you think a bank's going to earn all of those fees when its analysts are rating the companies neutral or sell? No way.

When the jig was up and most of Grubman's "buys" had cratered, the investigations and charges came in thick and fast: NASD, SEC, and the New York attorney general filed charges against Grubman, and the lawsuits started. As Spitzer's investigations honed in on some of the questionable practices, Grubman left Citi, pleaded no contest to charges that he issued fraudulent research (e.g., Focal, Metromedia, Fiber) and misleading research (e.g., Level 3, RCN, Williams, Adelphia, XO), and agreed to pay $15 million in fines; he was banned for life from the securities business (but was still able to fall back on some of the $67 million he reportedly earned between 1999 and August 2002, plus $15 million of "forgivable loans" from Citi and some other goodies, like shares and options). But he's not done yet: he's named in more than seven hundred arbitration cases filed with the NASD.

Grubman wasn't alone, of course. Others walked the same fine banking/research lines, including Merrill's Henry Blodget, who covered Internet stocks and gained fame while at Oppenheimer for making a very bullish call on Amazon before anyone really knew what Amazon was all about. That established his reputation, and Merrill hired him for lots of dollars to be a research analyst covering the increasingly attractive Internet sector and helping the technology bankers do deals. Conflicts galore. Even when the Internet sector headed south, he remained bullish, keeping his "favored 15" loaded with companies he referred to in his e-mail correspondence as, variously, "powder keg," "dog," "crap," "toast," and "going lower." For instance, Internet Capital Group was in Blodget's top pick list as a "2"-rated stock (1 being strong buy, 5 being sell) even as his e-mail said "going to 5." InfoSpace, which he rated a 1, was a "piece of junk" in his e-mails. Of course, Blodget was willing to trash a company if Merrill didn't win a deal. For instance, prior to GoTo's IPO, Blodget prepared a research report based on company-supplied data and had GoTo's officers review and change the draft as they saw fit; he told the company that he was prepared to give it a strong rating. But he also prepared a negative report to be used in the event that CSFB, and not Merrill, won the IPO mandate. And when CSFB indeed won, he issued the negative report.

When the game was finally up, Blodget pleaded no contest to hyping Internet stocks during the bubble years, agreed to pay the NASD $4 million in penalties and was banned for life from the securities business (Merrill paid $10 million in fines related to these little hickies, plus a few extra dollars to assuage irate retail clients). Blodget, too, has some lawsuits to deal with, but Merrill gave him a $2 million goodbye peck (plus he's got all that money he made in his banking/research role, including a reported $12 million in 2001).

Once the conflicted analysts were exposed, the spotlight turned to their bosses: heads of research at the banks came under the regulatory microscope on a range of possible infractions, including misleading advertising, failure to supervise, and unfair dealings with customers. Some/many/most managers seem to have been aware of the tainted research but didn't do anything to stop it. The fact that they knew research was a tool to win business rather than honestly advise clients, and did nothing about it, is just another in a long series of fiduciary failures. Investigation also turned to the investment bankers and the kind of pressure they may have applied to researchers in order to win business. Where else this will ultimately lead is uncertain. What is not uncertain, however, is that millions of investors lost billions of dollars because analysts acted more like bankers, and no one stopped them.

———————

Of course, the Street's conflict-of-interest problems can take many other forms, like not disclosing existing commercial/investment relationships when other business is at stake, not being "unbiased" in the evaluation of a business opportunity, or not putting client interests ahead of profit opportunities. Let's look at a few examples of each one of these.

Sometimes banks don't tell everyone what they should about their existing business relationships, so outside stakeholders aren't totally sure whether there is some ulterior motive behind actions or dealings. Consider that in 2003 the SEC censured and fined Deutsche Bank $750,000 because it failed to disclose a conflict of interest in advising on the controversial Hewlett Packard/Compaq merger. The crux of the matter: Deutsche Asset Management (DAM), which had a big block of Hewlett shares, forgot to tell its clients that its big brother down the block, Deutsche Bank, had a significant banking relationship with Hewlett—and was, itself, voting client shares on the Hewlett deal. According to the regulators (and basic common sense) DAM had a duty to disclose Deutsche's work with Hewlett Packard to its investors (including the fact that Deutsche had just co-arranged a fresh $4 billion credit facility), but it didn't. Equally troubling is that Deutsche itself intervened in DAM's proxy voting process: DAM originally planned on voting 17 million shares against the deal, but once it found out about Deutsche's business relationship with Hewlett and got a few calls from the Deutsche folks, it switched its vote.

In other cases Street executives invest in funds or structures or vehicles that they're doing business for; quite how unbiased decisions can be made in such situations is a mystery, because any of those in a position of influence will do what they have to direct business to, and/or protect the value of, that relationship. For instance, various senior executives at Merrill, UBS, and Bear invested in the LTCM hedge fund (which we discuss in the next chapter); their employing firms did lots of business with the fund and, more important, participated in the fund's bailout. Of course, the executives argue, they were only trying to protect the broader markets at large, as the systemic implications of an LTCM collapse would have been tremendous. Of course. But they also saved their own capital by agreeing to the bailout, so the real motivations behind their actions are questionable. And remember Enron's Nigerian barges and the LJM2 SPE? Merrill, and some of Merrill's bankers, invested in Enron's fraud-laced LJM2 partnership and then helped arrange the barge parking trade (and some wash trades) to boost the SPEs income and Enron's stock price—an obvious conflict.

The list of examples goes on and on. In fact, some have noted that the Street's overall business model is one big conflict: how can a firm equitably serve its investing clients and its corporate clients at the same time? Whose interests does it really hold to be most important, and can proper protections really be built into the business structure so that neither party is prejudiced? Within this broad sector conflict, we can hone in micro conflicts, such as investment banking. For instance, if an investment bank finds an undervalued company that might be a suitable candidate for a corporate client, it can take the prospect to the client company, or it can keep it quiet and invest as principal through its merchant banking operation. Who gets the call, who wins, who adjudicates? Or LBOs: if a company wants to LBO itself, the bank can act as an adviser to the management group or to the investment group, or it can act as a principal by providing funding and retaining upside. It'll be holding all the cards, so it's bound to know which route puts it ahead—and that route may not always be the one that's best for the client. Conflict also pops up in other areas, like the payment for order flow scheme we mentioned in chapter 5. It's a legal practice, though one that many oppose as it breeds all kinds of problems: when a broker sends customer orders to specific market-makers or trading firms in exchange for a kickback, the broker's overriding aim is to maximize dollars in his/her own pocket, not necessarily provide best price execution for the client; that's clearly a conflict of interest.

Conflicts can come home to roost. Sometimes the Street can keep one or two steps ahead of regulators, lawyers, and irate clients, but in the end a little stumble means they get caught. Most Street firms have been hit with lawsuits and regulatory sanctions over the years—they've had to pay several billion collectively, and the prospect of coughing up several billion more over the next few years is very real.

CSFB's Little Headache, Part II: More Tech Troubles

We've already introduced CSFB's powerful technology banking presence and some of the problems the bank had with its Friends of Frank accounts. Let's continue with other aspects of the story.

Despite the fact that Frank Quattrone and CSFB ruled the technology league tables by 2000, lots of the deals the bank (and others, to be sure) underwrote during the TMT boom collapsed to nothing—in fact, more than 95 percent of Internet IPOs launched during the boom cycle were underwater by 2002, with more than 50 percent trading below $1. As stocks cratered and unhappy CSFB investors lined up to complain, threaten, or file grievances, a litany of deceit was tracked by regulators: conflicted and fraudulent research, spinning, laddering, commission rigging, and obstruction of justice. Though the SEC was initially reluctant to chase CSFB on all of these issues (because of the complexity in trying to prove fraud), it eventually enlisted the help of the Justice Department and proceeded. Months of investigations led to charges against the bank and, eventually, to Quattrone as head of technology banking. CSFB initially denied any problems or wrongdoing and even defended Quattrone (in May 2001 the bank, still under the direction of CEO Allen Wheat, released a statement saying that Quattrone was not involved in IPO allocations or research compensation, which was contrary to all available evidence). When former Morgan Stanley president John Mack was brought in to replace Wheat, he plotted out a course of action and decided to settle the SEC charges (including those related to spinning, supervision, and compensation of analysts by the technology banking group, and creation of fraudulent research (e.g., Digital Impact, Synopsys) and false research (e.g., Numercal Technolgies, NewPower, Winstar). Total cost: more than $300 million. After Quattrone failed to cooperate in the ongoing investigations, CSFB booted him out (invoking its policy of dismissal in the event employees don't cooperate with regulators). As he was leaving, regulators slapped him with criminal charges related to obstruction of justice (including the advice he allegedly gave to colleagues to destroy incriminating documents) and other infractions.

CSFB must have been relieved when it concluded the settlement with regulators: after more than three years with black clouds overhead, the bank could finally get on with things. Even Mack, once a staunch supporter of Quattrone (noting at one point that he had "complete confidence in [Quattrone's] integrity and ethics"),[12] admitted that legal wrangling related to the technology banking business had been a "huge distraction" and that competitors had taken advantage of CSFB's sullied reputation. And, though some of the dark clouds blew away with the bank's settlement and Quattrone's departure, CSFB still had to contend with more than a thousand lawsuits and significant damage to its reputation. In the end it was all about doing the wrong things in exchange for fees and league table credit.

BAD DUE DILIGENCE

One of the Street's most important fiduciary duties is to perform due diligence—the painful but necessary process of digging into a company's financial operations to figure out what's going on, and then disclosing findings. Due diligence is also used to develop fairness opinions which, as we've noted, are part of M&A deals. The due diligence process involves delving into the details of balance sheets and income statements, cash flows and off–balance sheet activities, verifying that what's being reported to the public or the bidders is accurate. Lots of the work gets done with the help of lawyers and accountants because it's technical, detailed, and tedious. But it's mandatory in many situations, meaning that the bankers had better not blow it. Because if they do, and the company issuing securities goes under or the M&A transaction falls apart, there will be hell to pay. Unfortunately, bankers do blow it. They get the due diligence exercise wrong because often they don't take it seriously, they are sloppy in their work, or they overlook important things. Bankers don't like doing due diligence—they would rather be out drumming up new business—so the process can suffer.

Banks have been caught on this before, in some cases becoming financially liable. It's nothing particularly new, of course: the Street has been messing up its "investigative" duties for many decades. Back in the 1920s, for instance, when leveraged investment trusts were all the rage, most houses were very eager to print deals to win new investing clients. So eager, in fact, that they ignored their due diligence responsibilities and sometimes ended up floating things that were rotten to the core. One example: reputable investment bank Lee, Higginson sold $250 million of shares in various companies controlled by several industrialists into a newly established investment fund, which it then sold to its clients. Unfortunately the bank forgot to investigate the companies that issued the shares going into the fund, and most turned out to be shams—something that a little investigation would have unearthed. All $250 million went down the tubes.

More recently bad due diligence has been evident in the commercial paper market, as point of legal fact. The bank that doesn't do proper investigation and lets an unsound issuer sell paper that subsequently defaults has breached a fiduciary duty and is financially liable. Goldman found out the hard way with Penn Central, one of the watershed legal cases regarding underwriters' liability. In 1969 and 1970 Goldman actively recommended and sold the troubled firm's commercial paper to investors, even though it hadn't done a thorough job of financial investigation. When Penn Central defaulted on $87 million of paper in 1970, the bank got slapped with 45 lawsuits and suffered a reputational hammering every bit as bad as on the one it experienced through the Goldman Sachs Trust Corporation pyramid scheme of 1929. The SEC rebuked the bank, noting "Goldman Sachs did not communicate this [adverse financial] information to its CP customers, nor did it undertake a thorough investigation of the company. If Goldman Sachs had heeded these warnings it would have learned that its condition was substantially worse than had been publicly reported." The bank was found guilty and had to repurchase the defaulted paper from investors at par plus accrued interest (which put a dent in partners' capital). Lehman experienced similar problems with BarChris, and other banks have suffered in recent times as well. A bank shouldn't be underwriting short-term securities for a firm that's wobbly, and the due diligence process is designed to help determine if it's wobbly. Unfortunately, due diligence doesn't apply in every market, just those that feature specific regulations. The Euro commercial paper market, for instance, has always been caveat emptor, so there's no due diligence process and no requirement for banks to do the right thing; that means that when issuers like Integrated Resources or Polly Peck blow up, investors can't come after the banks. Nice for the banks, tough luck for the investors.

Failed due diligence happens in other sectors, too. For instance, in one case Merrill advised HFS in its merger with Cendant and ostensibly did its premerger due diligence on Cendant; bankers apparently uncovered no problems. Bankers then performed due diligence when advising on the CUC/Cendant merger and apparently found no problems then, either. Then the bank did a structured convertible bond issue for Cendant, with a bit of due diligence before launch, and discovered no problems then, either. However, a short time after all of this activity regulators managed to turn up some large accounting holes at CUC which put Cendant into a tailspin and eventually forced a $3.2 billion investor settlement (largely through the efforts of CalPERS). Nice due diligence job: three times on the same company, but nothing uncovered. In early 2002 Merrill and Citi launched a $1 billion convertible issue for energy firm Williams after having completed due diligence. Well, maybe they weren't too diligent, as just two weeks later Williams announced a delay in the release of its fourth-quarter 2001 results and pointed out that it had found an extra $2.4 billion of liabilities; the bankers apparently missed all of that.

Enron, of course, is good hunting ground for bad due diligence. A number of banks that sold bonds or arranged loans for the company one to two months before it flamed out were sued by investors or other syndicate members who claimed that the banks (a) should have known that the company was in bad shape, (b) failed to do any reasonable degree of due diligence, (c) screwed up the disclosures. Surely, they argue, if the banks had done a proper amount of scrutiny, they would have seen that something, at that very late date, was not right. And they're probably correct. We're not suggesting that a bank-driven due diligence exercise would have uncovered all of Enron's problems, but some suspicious things would certainly have come to light (and let's be frank here: some of the banks served with papers on the due diligence failure, e.g., Citibank, J.P. Morgan, were in deep with Enron on the prepaid swaps and already knew that the company was massively understating its balance-sheet leverage). It's hard for plaintiffs to prove complicity by the defendants in Enron's downfall, but maybe not too hard to prove carelessness in basic due diligence and disclosure. One investor group, having lost $120 million on bonds underwritten two months before the meltdown, brought suit against Citi, Goldman, and Bank of America for failing in its due diligence, investor warnings, and disclosure duties. Separately, Unicredito Italiano, a syndicated loan participant on a loan deal, filed a suit against Citi and J.P. Morgan Chase on multiple conflicts of interest, failure to do due diligence when arranging a loan, and fraudulent misrepresentation in the disclosure (such as omitting the fact that, at the time the loan was being put together, Enron was already being investigated by the SEC). Either the banks knew what was going on during their investigations or they botched the process. Either way, it's a breakdown in the role. Of course, in hindsight everyone's a hero and can point to Citi and J.P. Morgan and say they should have caught all of the problems. No. The Enron executives involved in the obfuscation obviously had every intent to deceive and were able to keep lots of things well hidden. But certainly these institutions, involved as they were in other less savory aspects of the company's business, must have known that things were not 100 percent, and they should have taken extra care to be as thorough as possible in the due diligence exercise. That's what it's for.

In late 2003 CIBC World Markets (the investment banking arm of the Canadian bank, incorporating part of the old U.S. Oppenheimer operation) was told by the courts to reimburse three sophisticated institutional investors (Oaktree, Trust Company of the West, and Pacholder) $52 million for blowing the due diligence and disclosure on a $200 million bond issue underwritten for Renaissance Cosmetics in 1997. In particular, the judge found that CIBC's investment bankers were liable for intentional nondisclosure of material facts and misrepresentation when they underwrote the issue; some of the bankers' internal correspondence noted that Renaissance's sales projections, discussed during the due diligence process, were "padded" (a fact that proved true two years later, when the issuer filed for bankruptcy and liquidation). Despite suspicions on the matter, the bankers completed their due diligence without further delay, incorporated the erroneous data in the prospectus, and printed the bond—and watched the company default. Again the due diligence process was glossed over, and untrue disclosure was distributed to investors, all in order to do a deal and book some fees.

One more, for good measure: In January 2001 Merrill agreed to sell its energy trading business lock, stock, and barrel, to Allegheny Energy for $490 million; the deal closed two months later, in March. The head of the Merrill unit, Dan Gordon, was part of the deal and joined Allegheny as head of energy trading. Fast forward to April 2001, two weeks before Merrill was due to issue $667 million of stock for Allegheny. Officials at the bank (and the company) received a letter from a Canadian law firm indicating it had reason to believe that Gordon was involved in unscrupulous activities, possibly criminal fraud. Sounds like something that's worth investigating, right? So what did Merrill do in advance of the big stock deal? Nothing. It didn't investigate the matter, it didn't take up the law firm's offer to meet with them to review the details, it didn't expand the scope of its due diligence, and it didn't disclose the matter in the offering prospectus. It just launched the $667 million deal as planned (lots of fees, you know). Merrill had reason to believe an Allegheny employee was not being totally forthright and, as underwriter, had an obligation to do an independent investigation to confirm the accuracy of the prospectus. But it didn't. (However, it may have wished it had—if not for the benefit of the new issue investors, then for its own account: it later came to light that the criminal activity the lawyers were speaking of involved Gordon's re-routing of $43 million of Merrill's own money to a shell company; Gordon ultimately confessed to the fraud in late 2003.)

Black Holes and Due Diligence

In May 2001 Citibank and J.P. Morgan (as leads) and Deutsche, ABN Amro, and Bank of America (as co-leads) issued an $11 billion bond for WorldCom, the high-flying telecom wonder we visited in chapter 3. After a good roadshow during which the bankers touted all of WorldCom's best features, investors lapped up the bonds. Some of the proceeds from the issue were used to pay down existing bank loans (which had been granted, not coincidentally, by the two leads) and commercial paper (which released the banks from their backup line commitments). (Of course, paying down loans through the issuance of securities is perfectly fine if the issuer/borrower is in good shape and the banks have no reason to suspect otherwise; however, if the issuer/borrower is in bad shape and the banks know it, then they are displaying the same behavior that led to the passage of Glass-Steagall.) Just six months later there were growing rumors about fraud at WorldCom, and by early summer 2002 the company had filed for bankruptcy under the weight of its massive debt load and some $3.8 billion in fraudulent revenue overstatements; several months later, as WorldCom wound its way through bankruptcy reorganization proceedings, the account overstatement was increased to $11 billion. Specifically, between 1999 (two years before the bond issue) and mid-2002 (weeks before the Chapter 11 filing), company officials fabricated four hundred transactions that led to the fraudulent overstatement; at issue were fictitious revenues, reserve manipulations, deliberate misclassification of cost capitalization, and more. The books were being cooked even as the bankers were buzzing around the company doing due diligence for the monster bond deal; in fact, nearly $800 million of line costs had already been wrongfully transferred from operating expenses to capital expense as the due diligence team marched around WorldCom's hallways.

In the aftermath of WorldCom's bankruptcy filing, irate bondholders—including influential activist investors like the New York State Common Retirement Fund, the Florida State Board of Advisors, the State of Alaska, and CalPERS—sued the underwriters. The bondholders claimed that the banks failed to perform proper due diligence and sold the securities under "false pretenses" because they hadn't warned investors about the "black hole" in WorldCom's accounts—a black hole, they argue, that the bankers would have uncovered had they been a bit more careful about their due diligence. They also said the prospectus failed to disclose the fact that banks had preferentially allocated IPO shares to WorldCom executives in exchange for future underwriting business, and that investors were misled during roadshows by being told that the company had a conservative financing program and was targeting an "A" credit rating. Alaska went on record: "We hope to restore money to the State of Alaska's funds and send Wall Street a message that we will hold them accountable when they abandon honesty for profits."[13] Mighty CalPERS chimed in as well, saying: "Our interest is in getting some of our losses back, but also send the message to the underwriters of the world that they need to look under the rock before they sign their name to a bond deal. If we can't depend on the due diligence of the underwriters, how can we ever buy bonds? It's about rebuilding investor confidence."[14] When CalPERS et al.—which have had some success in corporate governance battles and fiduciary lawsuits, and are enormous bond investors—are saying things like that, the banks of the world might be wise to pay heed.

Of course, Citi and J.P. said that they weren't to blame—they relied on WorldCom's 2000 numbers when doing their prelaunch due diligence and couldn't have foreseen the fraud (which was one and a half years into its cycle at that point). J.P. Morgan officials said that fraud cannot be detected by "standard due diligence" (whatever standard due diligence happens to be; who knows, maybe if you want a better level of investigative service, you've got to sign up for "super due diligence"). Then what's the point of due diligence? Why spend the time, money, and effort to investigate a company prior to a transaction? Isn't the purpose of due diligence to thoroughly investigate what's going on and either confirm facts or uncover problems? Doesn't the issuance of $11 billion of bond—that's $11,000,000,000—that are going to a whole host of institutional and retail investors, warrant some extra work, some extra digging? In the end Citi decided to pony up $1.45 billion to make bond investors whole (they added another $1.2 billion to cover equity investors who got burned on the research problems we described earlier).

JEOPARDIZING CUSTOMER ASSETS

One of the Street's most important jobs is to safeguard institutional and retail customer assets and obey customer instructions: to make sure that assets are locked up tightly (metaphorically speaking, of course, in this age of scriptless securities), that they're valued correctly, monitored regularly, and can be accessed with ease; to make sure that securities that are meant to be bought and sold per the client's instructions are in fact bought and sold per those instructions—no more, no less. A customer has to feel warm and fuzzy about the safety of all those hard-earned assets and all of the activity going on in the account. Trust. Confidence.

Unfortunately, things often go wrong with customer accounts. Sometimes assets go missing—they just disappear. A client will look into the account and find that 1,000 shares of General Motors or 10,000 Treasury bonds just aren't there; or maybe that the whole account has been sucked dry. Other times bad, or unauthorized, trades appear in accounts. The client says sell the Brazilian bonds, and the broker buys more. The client says buy 10,000 IBM call options, and the broker sells 10,000 IBM put options. Or the client with a safe, non-discretionary account doesn't say anything, and the broker buys 50,000 shares of Amazon on margin and finances the purchase by selling 10,000 naked at-the-money puts on Oracle. Other times assets are misvalued. The account, worth $1 million last month, is only worth $500,000 this month because all the prices in the portfolio are off; or the $100 million par position in the BB-rated tranche of a CLO is now quoted at 85, for no apparent reason.

What causes these problems? How can Wall Street lose track of customer assets and the activity that happens in customer accounts? How can it let bad trades happen? How can it misprice positions? How can it fail to monitor what's going on? How can it put the client's assets in jeopardy?

Generally speaking, all these problems come down to operational error or fraud—it's just that simple (on the surface, at any rate). Let's look at operational errors first. Wall Street firms are big—lots of people, lots of accounts, lots of clients, and lots of transactions, meaning lots of volume. And much of what the Street does still involves the human touch. People get involved in different parts of the business by reviewing, signing, checking, faxing, copying, e-mailing—

meaning that mistakes are bound to happen. So if you combine volume with mistakes, you get lots of problems—or operational risk errors, as the Street calls them. Technology would undoubtedly help solve some of these problems (and the headaches that they cause), but real technology (i.e., a seamless platform, not just patchwork quilts) is expensive and time-consuming to implement. Concepts like "paperless transaction flow" and "straight-through-processing" are still very much theoretical, meaning that operational errors can generally be controlled (though not eliminated) only by inserting more layers of control: more audit checks, reconciliations, and reviews/sign-offs, meaning more people, time, effort, and costs. The whole machine slows down, and expenses start mounting. The support-to-producer ratio, a mark of Wall Street's efficiency—how many staffers it takes to support the activities of each revenue generator—rises from 1.1 or 1.2 to 1.7 or 1.8, which isn't good. And there's still no guarantee that the extra layers would be able to solve everything. But the downside is considerable: irate clients, to be sure, but also billions spent plugging the holes—holes which shouldn't even be there in the first place. By one estimate the Street collectively lost $7 billion in 1998–1999 on tens of thousands of operational risk errors involving institutional and retail accounts and internal processes.[15] And that estimate was based on tallying up only the publicly disclosed losses. The truth is that the Street probably loses multiples of that amount, but they're not telling. The bottom line, in any event, is a bunch of fuming clients, which does nothing to help the Street's reputation, and irate bank investors who wind up eating the losses because the firms aren't running particularly tight ships.

Things get worse when customers suffer losses through fraud. This happens when brokers decide to do whatever they feel like doing with client accounts, most likely hoping to generate more commissions and earn bigger bonuses (or maybe just walk off into the sunset with the client's assets). How they expect to get away with this over the long haul is a mystery, but some certainly try. Some rogue brokers rig internal systems and bypass controls and compliance officers so that they get hold of client statements, then doctor them up to reveal a perfectly normal picture—even as they are dipping into the accounts and enjoying a lavish lifestyle at the expense of Ma and Pa Jones, who are sitting in Peoria without a clue. Even though internal compliance checks are meant to stop this from happening, it still happens.

In the Boiler Room

Bucket shops and boiler rooms represent the sludge of Wall Street: fly-by-night operations that no one should associate with, as most exist solely to rip off unsuspecting retail clients. Even though regulators warn people not to deal with "no name" brokers with outrageously aggressive sales pitches, it's amazing how many folks actually wind up dealing with these shady outfits, and how frequently they end up losing money; the North American Securities Administration Association estimates several billion dollars are lost to boiler room fraud every year. Fundamentally, Moms and Pops want to trust their brokers, meaning that the most gullible hand over their assets and generally end up getting burned. Even when these boiler room operations are legitimate, they deal in the riskiest possible stuff, like volatile limited partnership units and microcap stocks for which there are basically no markets (they used to deal in penny stocks, but regulators tightened up some of the dealing rules so they headed one step below pennies, to microcaps). Some of the most infamous bucket shops of recent times include Hibbard and Brown, First Jersey, Stratton Oakmont, Sterling Foster, and A.R. Baron—names that more than a few clients wish they'd never heard of.

Boiler rooms operate on the thinnest sliver of equity and have no real premises or infrastructure. Getting a broker/dealer license is not, unfortunately, very hard to do: a little bit of capital, a few people who aren't currently suspended from the securities industry, some paperwork, application fees, and that's about it. What boiler rooms have aplenty are ultraaggressive salespeople: cold callers who pitch extremely hard to Moms and Pops, trying to get them to buy into highly speculative investments (often in violation of the nasty cold-call rules we mentioned in chapter 5). Most of their calls lead nowhere, but the few that do pan out give them a bit of business and buy them time till they've landed the next round of suckers. Many boiler rooms have been censured for abusive sales practices, management/securities licensing violations, fraud, and so forth; even when they get busted, though, Moms and Pops typically get little back, as the outfits have no financial assets of their own—just enough to pay next month's bills. The principals get slapped on the wrist, pay some nominal fines, and get suspended from the industry for a few months—then they come back, set up a new shop in some other basement, and see how many more unsuspecting clients can be scammed.

Though private clients are generally the ones that get hurt in these schemes, sometimes even the big boys get hooked. Bear Stearns, for instance, is a big clearer for small broker/dealers, meaning it clears trades on behalf of introducing brokers. During the 1990s it did a fair amount of clearing business for the likes of Sterling and Baron, two firms that went under at the end of the decade. Unfortunately for Bear, the head of its clearing operation was implicated in some of the schemes intended to defraud and was fined and suspended by regulators. Baron proved particularly damaging to the bank: the shop had stolen tens of millions of dollars from client accounts, leading disgruntled investors to take action against Bear—claiming that, as a clearing firm, it should have been aware of Baron's activities. In the end Bear pleaded no contest and wound up paying $38 million into an investor restitution fund. So retail clients (and clearing firms) have to remember that it's a bit dicey down in the basement.

━━━━━━━━━━

None of this is particularly new, of course. We can turn the clock back to 1938 and see Richard Whitney, a very prominent and reputable figure on the Street—the head of the R. Whitney and Co. brokerage, house broker to J.P. Morgan, and head of the NYSE—looting customer accounts, the New York Yacht Club, and even the NYSE's Gratuity Fund. The fraud was so scandalous that it brought down the entire Whitney brokerage firm and prompted the SEC to create new regulations to protect customer assets. In more recent times, some Merrill Lynch brokers operating in offices as varied as Las Vegas, Beverly Hills, and Singapore have taken clients to the tune of tens of millions of dollars; Lehman and S.G. Cowen had a rogue broker that bilked clients for $115 million over 15 years (more on this below). And UBS had to settle SEC charges that it failed to monitor a broker who robbed clients of tens of millions over 4 years. Unbeknownst to the clients, the broker illegally invested their funds on margin in small, speculative gold stocks, receiving kickbacks from the companies; UBS managers didn't monitor the broker's activities, the gold companies ultimately went south, the client funds evaporated, UBS got egg on its face (and emerged with a slightly lighter checkbook after making the clients whole and paying the SEC some fines), and the broker got thrown in jail. There are obviously many other instances of this kind of infraction, but most follow along similar lines. Naturally, if a broker overtrades an account in direct violation of client instructions, or a broker walks off with a suitcase full of client assets, the bank is going to have to step up and make things good. So lax controls, inability to keep a close eye on brokers, and/or failure to implement the right checks and balances mean the clients wind up paying with temporary aggravation and bank investors wind up paying with dollars.

━━━━━━━━━━

Oops . . . Rogue Broker

The folks at Lehman must rue the day they bought a bunch of branches from Cowen (now S.G. Cowen, part of the Societe Generale pack) in the mid-1990's because they got broker/manager Frank Gruttadauria as part of the deal. Cowen, for its part, must regret the day they hired Gruttadauria, because he turned out to be a very expensive broker. It seems that over a period of 15 years (dating back to the

1980s), Gruttadauria managed to deceive his private clients so thoroughly that he made off with $115 million of their hard-earned dollars. What did he actually do? You name it: falsification of client statements, lying to clients, improper use of client funds, fraud, and theft. He routinely told clients he bought and sold securities per their instructions when he had done nothing of the kind, and he changed client statements to reflect the fake activity. He then pocketed the money for his personal use. He redirected real account statements to Post Office boxes that he controlled (a practice that compliance teams are meant to prevent) and sent out false statements that reflected overstated account balances, inflated securities prices, and nonexistent securities holdings.

The dénouement was equally bizarre. After failing to show up for work one day, Lehman officials became a bit worried; they became more concerned when he remained missing for a whole month. Still, they didn't notice any particular problems or discrepancies in any of Gruttadauria's accounts; in fact, they never caught on to the deception at all—so much for controls and oversight. Gruttadauria actually brought the charade to an end: after deciding he couldn't carry on with the deception any longer, he sent a confession letter to company officials and regulators, and surrendered to the FBI. When the full extent of his deception became known, Lehman and Cowen officials expressed "shock and dismay." According to the NYSE, they shouldn't have been too shocked or too dismayed, as the exchange had found that Cowen branches had violated broker oversight rules as early as 1994 and had done nothing to fix the problems; Gruttadauria served as both broker and office manager and supervised the branch office compliance manager—clear conflicts of independence and organizational integrity, and pretty much guaranteed to lead to problems. Cowen and Lehman were criticized by the SEC for inadequate supervision—poor oversight, improper audits and controls, inadequate systems, insufficient procedures related to client correspondence, and flawed safeguards and reporting structures. Fundamentally, it is the responsibility of regulated broker-dealers to supervise their employees so they don't do anything untoward with client assets. Clearly, the two firms didn't. The SEC and NYSE extracted $7.5 million in fines from the two banks for failing to detect and prevent "the most egregious example of misconduct in the securities industry." Gruttadauria pleaded guilty to theft and securities, wire and bank fraud, and was sentenced to over four years in prison. And the clients who lost piles of money? Most were made whole, but some remained in limbo as they awaited more satisfactory offers from company officials.

All of these problems hurt clients, because they've got to spend time, money, and energy trying to resolve them. If a client is missing half of the securities in the account it can be tricky navigating the labyrinthine corridors of Wall Street trying to find them. The broker or institutional salesperson should be doing it, but he or she will probably just hand the task over to some operational assistant, who's got lots of other problems to resolve—and will get to the client's in a month or two. Lots of wasted time and effort. And if the problems are bigger, like some dispute about trades or values, then the whole thing can go on for what seems like an eternity, and eventually wind up in arbitration.

Plus ça Change . . .

Bad behavior—breach of trust, blowing fiduciary responsibilities, doing the wrong thing for the client—isn't new. Markets change, new products and players walk in the door, bankers come and go, but lots of the sloppiness stays the same. Everyone talks about cleaning up Wall Street, getting things fixed up, and keeping a closer watch on what the bankers, traders, salespeople and controllers are doing. But at the end of the day, the more things change, the more they stay the same. It's kind of interesting to dust off some of Wall Street's archives and take a look at what some of the Street's bright lights have noted over the years. They sound hauntingly similar to what leaders of the millennium are saying on CNBC and the *Wall Street Journal*. As we rewind to look at some of these observations, let's remember that the views are 30 and 40 years old.

"An area of special concern to me at Chase was ethics, and now I fear that the financial world is not doing very well these days. Unhappily, the vast sums of money, and accordingly high fees involved in the recent rush of M&A have created an atmosphere in which some of the financial community are acting like sharks in a feeding frenzy."[16]

—D. Rockefeller, former chairman, Chase Manhattan

"[Wall Street] hasn't always been managed with a dedication to integrity and a feeling of responsibility. If the downfall of Wall Street ever comes it will be because these aspects of integrity have been ignored. . . . The people who are in charge of the big organizations should be spending time thinking about how they can protect the system against those few rotten apples. . . . I wonder if enough is being done by the leaders."[17]

—J. Whitehead, former co-senior partner, Goldman Sachs

"The problems in regulation now have to do with a bunch of bad guys doing things. People are tempted by money, and there is an incredible amount of money in the sys-

tem, and there's a general attitude among the firms: 'Get the deal now and we'll worry about the repercussions later.'[18]

—J. Phelan, former chairman and CEO, NYSE

"People had pretty good manners and followed standard rules of behavior. That seems to be out the window today. Certainly we were always anxious to make money but today all sort of things are happening that are inexcusable, like greenmail, poison pills, golden parachutes—not to mention insider trading. I have some friends who tell me their branches are like factories now. They get new products to sell all the time and a lot of their salesmen don't even know what they're doing."[19]

—J. Loeb, former senior partner, Loeb Rhoades

"There is a danger nowadays, in young people in particular, in believing that banking is the art of making a quick profit and selling whatever product seems fashionable."[20]

—W. Guth, former chairman, Deutsche Bank

"Today it's all win or lose. And the thing that's ironic is that many times the people who win will wish they'd lost 2 years later, because they've bought bad business at crazy prices."[21]

—F. Rohatyn, former partner, Lazard Freres

What does all of this tell us? That it's been the same old story for the past 30+ years. The senior statesmen of Wall Street have seen these problems time and again and haven't done anything about them. In fact, they've let them grow worse—the place is bigger, the dollars are larger, the temptations greater. Bad behavior—the kind that destroys an outsider's trust in the Street—has been alive and kicking through the years.

With each breach of fiduciary duties, with each internal or regulatory investigation or client complaint that leads to one or more banks' being charged with some infraction, we have to wonder why banks have to be reminded that they are supposed to adhere to rules, do proper due diligence, take care of customer assets, behave with integrity, and demonstrate proper conduct. Kids have to be reminded to stick to the rules, behave nicely, and not lie, cheat, or steal because they don't know any better. But should well-paid professional bank executives have to be reminded?

Chapter 7

BAD RISK MANAGEMENT

At the start of the book we said that taking and managing risks is one of the Street's main jobs. That's what banks do—it's how they earn a living and pay the bills. GM makes cars, GE makes light bulbs and jet engines, Nokia makes phones, Morgan Stanley and Goldman and J.P. Morgan and all the others make risk capacity: they do it by trading different assets and markets, and by granting loans. Naturally, different Street banks have different approaches to risk. Some are big risk takers, swinging for the fences at every opportunity (meaning some strikeouts, along with the occasional long ball out of the park). In traded markets they take risks as principals or dealers, buying from one client and selling to another; until they've sold the risky positions they've bought, they reap the gains and suffer the losses. They also take risk directly: dedicated proprietary (prop) teams, using pieces of shareholders' capital (as it were Monopoly money), come up with clever ideas on how to take advantage of the markets to make some dollars. Banks like Goldman, Citi, J.P. Morgan, Morgan Stanley, Lehman, Deutsche, and UBS may fall in this category. Some firms are risk-takers of a different sort: they'll take a punt, but usually by concentrating on business that flows through the doors. So they'll act as dealers and take the residual risks that come from the client dealing role, but they don't necessarily have dedicated squads of prop traders betting the markets, and they don't usually throw a lot of capital behind the risk effort. Merrill, CSFB, and a few others may fit in here. And there are some banks that take a few risks, but not too willingly. They prefer to focus on customer business and discourage, minimize, or bar prop trading. Here we see some of the smaller firms and niche players, like A.G. Edwards, Schwab, Lazard, heavily focused on institutional M&A or retail customers rather than risk taking. The same scheme applies to lending and credit risk; some banks are big lenders and credit risk takers, others prefer a more modest level of involvement and exposure. So the Street has gradations of risk-iness among its own, and it's generally true that those taking a significant amount of risk run into problems every so often.

WHY TAKE RISKS?

The core of the banking business is based on risk taking, so banks generally have to take some degree of risk if they want to progress. Relying solely on fee-based advisory business or other nonrisk business (e.g., trust, custody, asset management), as some of the smaller or niche players do, means a lower absolute amount of revenues and potential problems when flows dry up. But banks often have other reasons for taking risk. Some, for instance, take risks to win business, while others do so to try (at least theoretically) to diversify revenues.

In Wall Street's very competitive world, putting up the balance sheet—risking the firm's capital—is a way of winning deals. By buying primary debt and equity deals, extending loans prior to a full syndication, funding bridge loans before a takeout in the capital markets, putting on client derivative trades before coming up with solid hedges, or ramping up a CBO, CLO, or CMO conduit before securitization, banks are using their resources to get business done. Those hoping to crack into the top tier (or keep their spots there) may find themselves putting more capital at risk than they might want, which is dangerous business and decidedly not for the faint of heart.

Those seeking to insulate against lower banking fees, a bad credit/lending cycle, or meager retail commissions sometimes turn to prop risk taking as a diversification strategy—and hope they get it right. It's a bit nerve-wracking if you've got pure prop traders carrying the firm for a few quarters, till other business picks up. A firm of ten thousand may rely on the brainpower of 10 or 15 sharp traders to earn hundreds of millions of dollars every quarter to keep the lights on and the computers humming. What if they get it wrong? What if they are betting a huge chunk of the firm's capital on a 25 basis point rate cut that has a 50 percent chance of happening? What if they can't spot the thunderheads forming over a heavily indebted emerging nation? What if they mis-price some enormously complex derivatives or huge block trades? Any of these can spell trouble. But when banks are operating in a bleak business environment with no pipeline or deal flow, and have already done what they can to squeeze out excess costs, the move to additional prop trading surfaces as one of the few alternatives. There is so much riding on this scenario that it's little wonder the stock prices of those known to be relying heavily on prop trading can get hit: investors don't want shares in a bank that has turned into a one-trick pony, so they sell (which is why some banks don't tell just how much prop risk they are taking or how much they are making or losing—they just lump any profits or losses in with other things so that things don't look too skewed). In fact, the turn toward trading when other business gets sluggish happens pretty regularly: in the late 1980s, in 1992–1993, in the early part of the millennium. In fact, during the post-TMT crash, when there was no deal flow to speak of on the Street (e.g., global M&A down nearly 70 percent between 2000 and 2003, IPOs down a whopping 90 percent), a number of banks jumped back into the risk business, quietly or with fanfare, depending on the image they were hoping to project (those trying to be a bit more forthright called it a "revenue diversification" strategy, those preferring stealth said nothing at all). Many houses added people and capital to the effort—CSFB, UBS, Deutsche, Credit Lyonnais, Merrill, Lehman; Stanley launched a special group to focus on prop fixed income opportunities, Goldman set up a low-profile group in London to trade across markets (somehow, though, "Goldman," "proprietary trading," and "low profile" just don't go together). Citi, which closed down the rump of the old Salomon arbitrage group in 1998, ramped up its pure prop currency, equity, and debt trading, too. J.P. Morgan, which has been in and out of prop trading for years, got back in during 2003 (even after closing down chunks of it in 2001 as it tried to calm investors after all those massive credit losses from Enron, TMT loans, and Argentina). Merrill, never known for being a big dedicated prop trader, set up a cross-markets group in 1995, shut it down in 1997 after losing some dollars, then started things up selectively in 2002. Of course, since it's difficult to know what's really going on, a good rule of thumb for all investors is to assume risk levels are on the rise whenever other business flows have dried up and costs have been trimmed; investors should be on guard because the banks are probably speculating again (even though most of them said they wouldn't, as they also said in the aftermath of the 1987 crash, the 1990 junk bond dislocation, the 1994 Fed increases, the 1998 crisis, and so on; memories are woefully short).

Why is risk taking so dangerous? Because it's hard to manage all of the moving parts properly, meaning there are lots of ways to screw up. More, in fact, than the person on Main Street knows (or will every know), because there are also a number of ways of making losses disappear (unless they are huge, in which case a bank usually has to come clean—or semiclean, as the actual losses are probably more like 2 x huge or 3 x huge, rather than just the huge reported in the quarterlies). Problems appear when firms take too much credit, market, or liquidity risk, when they make bad long-term equity investments or build deep relationships with clients that go sour. They can also crop up when banks can't measure the risks they've got or keep an operational handle on them. For all of the money banks can make in the risk business, they still leave an awful lot on the table. And it's generally true that after pretty successful runs in credit and market risk taking, lots of banks get sloppy or greedy and get burned; each market dislocation (e.g., 1990–1991, 1994, 1997, 1998, 2001) reveals just how badly the Street can stumble. But it's a cycle that is destined to be repeated many more times because the Street doesn't learn from its own extensive, and painful, history.

Before digging in deeper, let's reiterate what we said in chapter 5: risk is not a bad thing, even though it's sometimes seen as the root of all evil. People probably think risk is so nasty because it's usually presented to them in the context of a problem or loss. You'll only hear about the riskiness of derivatives or leverage on the evening news when somebody has suffered a large loss (maybe one that hurts the widows and orphans). The rest of the time the world goes marching along, oblivious to the fact that risk taking is a vital function, and risks are out there generating dollars for someone. The widows and orphans are often shielded from risk because someone else is willing to take it for them. Think of those risk bearers—banks, insurance companies—as so many bodyguards, ready to take the bullet if they have to (and getting paid if everything works out okay).

So risk is not inherently bad—as long as it's understood, priced correctly, and controlled. First of all, risk has to be understood. Before you get in your SUV to go on a journey, you want to make sure you know how to drive it and where you are trying to go—that seems sensible. Same for a bank: if it's going to take risk, the theory goes, it should know how much risk it can afford to take (how much it can stand to lose) and what kind of risk it should be taking. Second, risk can't be underpriced or overpriced. GM isn't going to sell a $50,000 SUV for $25,000, and a bank shouldn't be selling $5 million of risk for $2.5 million. If GM underprices its SUV it won't be long before it's in the poorhouse; the same goes for the bank. Of course, if they overprice, they get squeezed out of the market and lose business—so it's a fine line to walk. And third, risk has to be controlled. If you're not in control of the SUV when it's going 20 mph you'll wind up in a fender bender; if you can't control it when it's doing 100 mph, you're going over the cliff. Either way, it's an unhappy situation, and it happens because you can't keep the vehicle under control. The same thing applies with financial risks: a bank that can't control its mortgage-backed securities book, or emerging market loan portfolio, or long-dated exotic derivate operation is eventually going to suffer some big losses.

NOT UNDERSTANDING RISKS

If a bank doesn't understand its risks very well, it's eventually going to go down the wrong path, and it probably won't make it back onto the right track until it's taken some hits. Misunderstanding risks comes in various guises: trading (or originating) things that are far riskier than anyone believes, investing the firm's capital in things that are too unpredictable or which the bank just doesn't know enough about, and building up relationships with clients to the point that they are just too big or too complicated to be properly understood or managed. Let's look at each one.

Trading and Originating Risky Things

Banks deal in lots of things that are relatively benign, like government bonds, currencies, and stocks. That doesn't mean that they won't lose money trading them, because even simple, transparent, well-behaved risks have sharp edges. But it means that the downside is usually quantifiable, and the markets are liquid enough for everyone to get out when they need to. But banks also deal in some very risky stuff: products and instruments that have lots of downside, where the exposures can be tough to figure out, and where the profit margins may not be large enough to cover expected losses: things like long-dated and exotic derivatives, emerging market assets, junk bonds, bridge loans, mortgage-backed and collateralized debt residuals, and block trades. If a bank seems to be earning significant dollars from these businesses, look out because when things go the other way (and they eventually do) it can be painful. Even the experts aren't always that expert, because risky things can be hard to understand and value, and are prone to illiquidity and volatility, a potent mix that can create lots of red ink. It happens quite regularly because banks get overconfident in their ability to price, hedge and move particular instruments or don't fully understand how their exposures might react under stressed conditions. Or maybe the markets turn against them, or they create their own poor market conditions (e.g., stepping out of the liquidity flows till there is no more liquidity). Any or all of these can lead to mistakes in pricing. For example, Citi lost heavily in commercial real estate lending in the late 1980s because it wanted to be the premier banker to all the big developers and ignored proper credit discipline; it lent so recklessly that its $13 billion commercial property portfolio had a 43 percent nonperforming rate, putting the bank on the edge of collapse. Salomon and J.P. Morgan, two sophisticated risk-taking institutions, lost heavily on mortgage-backed securities in 1992 and

1993 ($250 million and $300 million, respectively), because they misread the market and got their pricing and hedges wrong; CSFB suffered the same problems in 2003, to the tune of some $100 million. Bank One, an active derivatives player (and now part of J.P. Morgan), lost $318 million in interest rate swaps and options in 1993 because it misvalued some positions and had more risk than it thought. Kidder Peabody, though damaged by the shenanigans of trader Joe Jett, came apart primarily because of its excessive presence in CMOs. During the 1980s and early 1990s, Kidder printed lots of superexotic CMOs. It managed a third of all new issues, had a very large secondary trading desk, and routinely held inventories of more than $10 billion (courtesy of parent GE's balance sheet). Then came the rising rates of 1994, the collapse of mortgage fund Askin (which Kidder had lent heavily to), troubles valuing and unwinding all the funky CMOs on hand, and lots of losses in the CMO book. GE finally threw in the towel: it brought in a new team to close down the CMO book, sold Kidder's branches to Paine Webber and got out of the banking business. UBS, once a powerhouse in equity derivatives, lost $420 million in 1997 because it misvalued lots of convertible bonds and European long-dated equity index volatility, and took too much risk by writing a lot of deep out-of-the-money put options on Japanese bank stocks (that plunged when Yamaichi Securities failed). So the experts aren't always right.

Let's take a look at a few of the Street's risky things, starting with long-dated derivatives—transactions with maturities out to 20, 30, or more years, where there is no market price, transparency, liquidity, or hedgeability. How does a bank know what value to put on such deals? Mark-to-model (or, as Warren Buffett says, mark-to-myth. Quite possibly). A bank says a 30-year sterling/dollar cross-currency swap on its book is worth $5 million because that's what the valuation model says. Well, maybe, maybe not. There's no curve out there, there are no references, no road maps, and no signs. So, maybe it's worth $5 million, maybe $10 million or maybe -$5 million. No one will know for sure till the swap comes into the liquid part of the market. Till then it is marked-to-model, meaning the position is valued and risk managed on the basis of a bunch of assumptions. The same is true with exotic derivatives—bizarre transactions, like a reverse knock-in on the Nikkei 225 with an outside one-touch barrier on Euribor, "quantoed" into dollars. It can be very tough to value such exotica because there are so many dimensions of risk to consider: delta, gamma, theta, rho, cross gamma, correlation, dividends, volatility, volatility of volatility, volatility skew, volatility smile. Any of these can be missed or mispriced, meaning there could be some nasty surprises when trades mature or are unwound, or value is otherwise crystallized.

Emerging market assets can also be risky business. Banks have to cope with sovereign uncertainties and event risks—things that are often unpredictable and don't follow the smooth, continuous price path that liquid market traders are used to. Things can jump, devalue, or explode very quickly, meaning there's often little chance for banks to rehedge or liquidate. It's happened many times over the years: sovereign events like deterioration, devaluation, moratorium, or default have led to massive credit and market losses (e.g., Latin America in the early- to mid-1980s, Mexico in 1994, Korea, Indonesia, Thailand in 1997, Russia in 1998, Brazil in 1999, Argentina in 2000, and so on). With each one of these dislocations, banks that are heavy players in emerging market loans, bonds, equities, currencies, and derivatives get burned. Virtually every major bank has lost big here—hundreds of millions per episode, and sometimes more.

Junk bonds fall into a similar category: they feature some of the same price gapping, illiquidity, and default characteristics, meaning they have the same potential for a quick and nasty loss. Think of poor Lehman back in 1989, when it was Shearson Lehman Hutton, a subsidiary of American Express. The bank decided that the time was ripe for a big punt in the junk market (the peak, as it happened). So, it ponied up $290 million for seven junk funds and $190 million for individual junk issuers with an average yield of 12 percent and funded the whole portfolio with 9 percent money, expecting to make 3 percent carry plus capital gains from anticipated spread tightening. It made a few dollars for a few months. But by early 1990 short-term rates had started rising, Drexel was coming undone, S&Ls were dumping their junk portfolios at the behest of regulators, and issuers were starting to default in droves (a whopping $40 billion of junk paper, 20 percent of the market, defaulted between 1990 and 1991). Everything about the trade went sour and, since it was big relative to the bank's capital, Lehman had to bail out—a $115 million loss, which American Express shareholders ate (a negative 24 percent return in six months, hardly a shining example of trading prowess, as Shearson Lehman CEO Peter Cohen found out when he was handed his walking papers). Stanley reportedly took some big hits in junk in 2000 and 2002 and others have suffered similar losses.

Over the years bridge loans have proven to be a very costly business for a number of banks. Bridges give companies temporary financing before the issuance of semipermanent or permanent funding: a bridge between a current and future financial position. Since these loans tend to be unsecured (though covenanted), and are often granted to weak credits waiting for junk bonds, they are loaded with credit default risk. That means they're extremely risky, and even though the fees and spreads are often pretty attractive, they don't always compensate for actual default experience. These deals first became popular during the 1980s when leverage was the order of the day and banks were competing aggressively for junk bond business (everyone, back then, wanted to steal Drexel's junk bond crown, and bridge loans were one way to try to do it). Some banks, like CSFB, Merrill, and DLJ, learned the hard way that bridge loans are tough to get right—all three lost hundreds of millions of dollars in their attempt to win junk bond mandates. First Boston got hit particularly hard, losing $1 billion on bridge loans in 1989, almost half of that from the infamous "burning bed" transaction: a $475 million bridge loan granted to Ohio Mattress (equal to 40 percent of the bank's equity) went so wrong that First Boston had to be bailed out by minority shareholder Credit Suisse, which led to the creation of the current incarnation of CSFB. CSFB and others pulled out of the business for a time, and then jumped back in during the late 1990s, when the next wave of bridge loans hit the shore. No surprise that a few more banks got hurt during the early part of the millennium as some of the TMT borrowers went down the tubes.

Block trading is another very treacherous business. Here a bank buys a big block of shares from a company or an institutional investor and then tries to place them, as quickly and quietly as possible, in the secondary market. In the late 1960s, as it became pretty clear that specialists couldn't handle the size of some of the increasingly large institutional orders and add-on tranches that were appearing, banks jumped in the fray by putting up their own capital. Of course, the bank takes all the risk of a downward move in the stock price between the time it buys the shares and the time it sells them; it may take minutes, hours, days, or—heaven forbid—longer. The harder the bank thinks it'll be to sell them, the bigger an up-front discount it'll demand from the company (or investor). So if the company wants to sell 1 million shares at $100 (raising $100 million) and the bank thinks it can blow out the shares quickly, it might buy them from the company at $99 ($99 million total) and then work like mad to sell them at that price. If it does, it keeps the difference. If the block is now 10 million shares at $100 (for $1 billion in proceeds), then it's obviously much harder to move them, so the bank might offer to buy the whole bunch at $97 (or $970 million). It might sell a slug quickly, and then dribble more out over the following weeks at an average price of $98, so it makes a bit of money. But, if it has trouble moving them, it'll have to keep cutting the price till it finds a market clearing level—maybe at $97 (breakeven), $96 (underwater), or lower (ouch). Since it can't usually hedge the position (that would just drive the position down in a self-fulfilling cycle), this is real risk business. Unfortunately, the competitive nature of Wall Street means the deals are often mispriced. The discounts can be far too small for the risks being taken, meaning the business is probably unprofitable; maybe it's breakeven, more likely it's a money loser. And when a bank does a big deal and gets stuck with it, you can bet the rest of the Street will known about it and move in to give it a little extra pain. There are plenty of examples of difficult block trades (without enough profit to offset losses). One of the biggest ever was the $13.2 billion block of British Petroleum shares taken down by Morgan Stanley, Goldman, Salomon, and Lehman in late 1987 as the United Kingdom was disposing of its 32 percent stake. Bad, post-crash market conditions and poor pricing meant the syndicate got stuck with a 20 percent chunk and $350 million in paper losses. The Bank of England, and then the Kuwait Investment Authority, had to bail the Street out. Then there's the big block Goldman and Deutsche did for Vivendi in 2002. The $3 billion buy and sell didn't go too smoothly and Goldman got stuck with $660 million and a 20 percent loss that came in at about $150 million. It's not a great business to be in, as the risk/return seems horribly skewed, yet the banks keep doing it. (They also do blind portfolio bids, in which they buy a whole portfolio of stocks on a no-name basis, with just some basic idea of the riskiness and concentrations. Same game.) Maybe all those block traders should remember some words from one of their own, Ace Greenberg, chairman and CEO of Bear Stearns: "Anybody who says they make money in block trading is, in my opinion, either joking or not telling the truth."[1] He ought to know. Billy Salomon, former head of Salomon, noted years ago that "we'll bid for almost anything and we take many baths."[2] True then, true now.

Residuals—aka asphalt, sludge, toxic waste—are the little bits of equity that remain after assets have been securitized into nice, highly rated packages. The actual kind of securitization doesn't matter—it might be pools of mortgages (MBS), or mortgage-backed securities (CMO), or credit card receivables (ABS), or loans (CLOs), or corporate bonds (CBOs)—the theory is the same: the residual carries the equity risk, meaning it's the first loss piece. Normally, that's okay. A bank buying (or retaining) a residual is basically holding an illiquid equity risk and, if it's done a proper job of analysis, has concluded that risk and reward are balanced and that the deal is worth a punt. If it wins, great; if it loses, too bad—that's what being a first loss piece is all about. Unfortunately, that's not how banks get into trouble with residuals. They blow up when they manufacture the securitizations (i.e., they assemble all of the CMOs, and CLOs, and ABS) sell off all the good pieces (i.e., the AAA, AA, A, BBB tranches) but get stuck with the residuals. Since residuals that aren't part of the lead order can be exceedingly difficult to sell, the bank just parks them away on its balance sheet and hopes it can get rid of them down the road. Now it's got a whole portfolio of toxic waste: the positions are illiquid, risky, and tough (often impossible) to hedge. One example: American Express started manufacturing CBOs for end-use clients in 1997, usually selling the rated tranches and residuals as a whole package. Then came the LTCM/Russia crisis. Markets got very shaky, but American Express kept putting together more CBOs. Only this time it couldn't sell the residuals or lower-rated tranches. So, what did it do? It kept on printing more deals and accumulating more toxic waste. Then the credit markets fell out of bed, and all of those residuals and BB-rated pieces started looking very, very ugly: $826 million ugly, to be exact, which is what the American Express shareholders had to foot.

These are only a few examples of risky things, because the Street deals in lots of other turbocharged products and strategies. Again, there's nothing inherently wrong in dealing in instruments or products with lots of risk. That's one of Wall Street's functions, and banks have to do it so that they can serve client needs, create risk transfer efficiencies, and make some money for their shareholders. The problem comes when the Street doesn't really understand the risks it's trading—when it has trouble valuing them, when it makes extreme assumptions, when it takes too much (willingly or unwillingly), when it fails to consider liquidity or event risks, or when it doesn't really take account of what will happen when everything heads south *at the same time* (e.g., CSFB in 1998 with Russia, LTCM, and hedge funds, J.P. Morgan in 2001–2002 with Enron, TMT loans, Argentina, venture capital, and prop trading, and so forth). When banks don't understand their tricky or concentrated risks thoroughly, they're almost bound to mishandle them, meaning a skewed risk/return profile; the Street stretches too far, to the point that it's virtually guaranteed to stumble.

Investing Badly

Sometimes the Street supplements its trading and client risks by taking on the time-honored "merchant banking" role. When London was the seat of banking power in the nineteenth century, the merchant banks pulled the commercial and financial strings; houses did acceptance and underwriting business, to be sure, but they were often at their most formidable when they invested their own capital in promising or speculative ventures. So, too, with banks of the modern era. The business centers on private equity (aka principal investing): putting up the firm's capital to invest in new or established companies that haven't gone public. Venture capitalists do lots of this business (most of it, in fact), but that hasn't stopped the major banks from setting up their own "private equity" groups to create and manage private equity funds (in which they also hold stakes).

Private equity can be lucrative if done right, but disastrous if done wrong. And the Street sometimes gets it very wrong. Banks that are dedicated to the business for the long haul and are extremely prudent and diligent in analyzing opportunities and allocating funds can do very well. They recognize that the business is risky and illiquid, with payout horizons of three, five, seven, or more years, rather than the usual one-day, one-month, or one-year mark-to-market mentality that characterizes trading business and the short- and medium-term horizons that characterize many credit facilities. It demands a skeptical eye and unwavering discipline. But some banks are sloppy and uncommitted, mostly interested in catching a piece of the latest hot trend— which often means buying in at the peak of the market and getting caught as things fall apart. This can include problems like overpaying for a stake, being overly optimistic about growth prospects, and not being totally sure if the exit strategy is viable. For instance, Merrill lost heavily on its private equity activities at the end of the 1980s takeover boom; by the time the default cycle of the early 1990s hit, Merrill Lynch Capital Partners (as the merchant banking unit was known) was losing hundreds of millions of dollars on ill-advised equity investments. It wrote off most of its portfolio and wound down the business. CSFB suffered similar problems during the same time period, and so did others. The process repeated itself, on a much larger scale, during the TMT boom. From the mid-1990s as the dot com and telecom growth phase began, to early 2001 when it all came to a screeching halt, most Street banks had private equity groups chasing after the same deals (and generally competing against funds set up by Silicon Valley's venture capitalists). Some transactions were profitable, some weren't; again, that's fair enough, and it's how the game is played. But those that really took it to an extreme during the tail end, such as J.P. Morgan and Wells Fargo, got badly burned. They took too much risk and accepted the prospect of mediocre returns so they could win deals; chasing deals by lowering returns below the threshold of expected loss (even when looking at portfolios of business) is almost guaranteed to generate a problem. So when the dot com bubble burst, the IPO market dried up (meaning no more takeouts for all of the private equity investments) and all of the potential third-party buyers for the incubated companies crept back into the forest, leaving banks with lots of worthless equity stakes on their books and no solid exit strategy, except the final frontier: write-offs. That translated into lots of red ink, closure of private equity groups (till the next boom, of course), and bank investors wondering what hit them (again). Unlike the Street's trading and credit risks, private equity investments are usually held in an investment account, and are not marked-to-market. They may be periodically revalued when there has been a "permanent" change in value, but the fact that no one sees P&L movements every day, week, month or quarter means they're off the radar screen. But when there's a permanent impairment, the banks have to mark down their books, and shareholders finally get to see huge losses from positions they didn't know much (or anything) about.

Dot Bomb

During the go-go years of the Internet boom, funding little dot coms was all the rage. Silicon Valley venture capitalists led the charge, raising private equity funds to invest in companies that were often little more than a few fresh faces, a couple of folks who could program in Java and C++, a general idea about a business line, and a cool name. That's part of capitalism and the entrepreneurial spirit: take a chance on a complete long shot, because you might end up with the next Netscape, Amazon, Google, Yahoo, or eBay, or new industries like electronic trading, online insurance, or centralized B2B procurement. There's nothing wrong with rolling the dice and funding some of these things. But, as with any hot thing, any speculative venture, any bubble, things get overdone. All of a sudden it's not just funding a few start-ups, it's funding lots of them; it's not just funding a few reasonably good but still half-baked ideas, it's funding things that are just stupid. All in order to grab a piece of a market that seemingly can only go higher and higher.

Enter Wall Street. Following the lead of the venture capitalists (and after dusting off their merchant banking/private equity business plans from the 1980s), a number of banks set up their own private equity funds so they could chase after many of the same dot com platforms (pure vapor, no hard assets). In true Wall Street fashion they did it in a big way: lots of money, lots of projects, lots of people, lots of flash and splash—all the while hoping for lots of profits. For a time some of the banks—J.P. Morgan, Citi, CSFB, Wells—made some money. Though it's hard to say whether the risks/returns were appropriately balanced, some of the early ventures (funded in 1995–1998) were pretty solid and enabled cash-out at good levels (some were busts, of course, but easily absorbed on a portfolio basis). However, most of the banks didn't know when to say "when." They just kept pushing the edge of the envelope, trying to best the venture capitalists at their own game by setting up their own incubators and accelerators, throwing more money at strange ideas, arranging IPOs for those who were not ready—basically, helping inflate the bubble. (Even when the private equity funding involved telecom/networking ventures with hard assets, banks sometimes lost their way by providing capital to firms with overvalued assets.) Some of the more aggressive banks were even hoping to translate their investments in dot coms to higher multiples for their own institutions; instead of trading at a 15x or 20x multiple of earnings (typical for a bank), they wanted the 50x or 100x multiples common of many of the dot coms: higher valuation, higher stock price, more money in the checkbooks. (Some even talked it up when the sun was shining, to wit, Chase's CFO [pre-J.P. merger]: "I really believe we have an education process to go through with our investor base and the analyst community to convey the extent of our investment in the new economy." Oops. Wonder what she said when the bank got tagged in dot coms' post-J.P. merger and a chunk of the operation got shut down?)

And we all know what happened next. By late 2000 it was becoming clear that the technology party was winding down. All of the IPOs and third-party sales vanished, meaning all of the clever banks (and venture capitalists, of course) that had provided the seed capital were stuck holding the bag. After a couple of years of reasonable gains the red ink started flowing in a big way; marking down investments reflecting "permanently impaired value" was an expensive proposition. Several big banks started writing off their Internet, media, and telecom investments, taking huge hits in the process. For instance, in 2001 J.P. Morgan, one of the biggest players (through private equity funds set up by both J.P. Morgan and Chase prior to their merger, as well as the LabMorgan incubator), wrote off more than $1.1 billion; the bank followed with $730 million of writedowns in 2002 and an announcement that "while we believe in the strategic importance of JP Morgan Partners to the firm, we are acting to reduce the impact of its earnings on the overall firm's results."[3] Translation: J.P. was throwing in the towel after getting burned on too many bad deals. It wasn't alone: Wells Fargo wrote off $1.1 billion in 2001 (plus a total of $280 million in 2000 and 2002); FleetBoston, a little less than $300 million; and so on. Street banks weren't the only ones who got caught up in the frenzy and got sandbagged when it came undone; lots of venture capitalists and technology companies were right in the thick of things, too. But the banks fared even worse because they lost on two fronts: write-offs of private equity positions and loss of fees from a dearth of technology IPOs.

Unfortunately, during the boom phase some banks didn't reserve for the rainy day; maybe in their euphoria they forgot that markets go down as well as up, and that exits don't always work out as planned. Whatever the reasons, some didn't have enough reserves, meaning large shocks to their balance sheets and income statements. It's not clear if investors really knew what hit them, but some probably didn't (e.g., earnings for J.P. Morgan in the third quarter of 2000 came in 30 percent below consensus expectations because of private equity/venture capital write-offs that no one was expecting. Similar things happened with other banks). As we've said, private equity is not a transparent business: it's buy and hold, with none of the real risk showing up in an obvious way and none of the accounting showing potential downside—until it's a harsh reality.

Building Risky Relationships

Paradoxically, building strong client relationships can sometimes add a bit of fuel to the risk management fire. On the surface, close client ties would seem to be a good thing. A bank should want to service its clients in the best way possible by offering a whole range of products and services. But there are still limits to this—regulatory limits and prudent limits. Get in too deep with a client through loans and other credit-sensitive transactions, clearing arrangements, corporate finance and tax advisory, structured transactions, research, due diligence, asset management, safe custody, and watch out. In the era of the universal bank—the financial supermarket with the big balance sheet and an army of originators and specialists offering any one client a host of choices—risk can accumulate rapidly, and client relationships can get exceedingly multidimensional and complex. That's all fine if things work out the way they're supposed to, but if they don't, things can get very ugly. Fortunately, the amount of credit, clearing, and custody business that a bank can do is partly capped by what regulators say; for instance, a bank can't lend more than a certain amount of its capital, directly or indirectly, to a given client. Unfortunately, there are ways of getting around this particular rule, and there are other business dealings that fall outside of the regulatory scope entirely—call them contingent exposures, risks that don't seem to be risks until a client starts falling apart.

The lure of building deep ties with a client is, of course, revenue. By becoming a company's "preferred provider," a bank likes to believe it has a better shot at some of the future banking business that will arise. Some of the relationships are built legitimately: offering value-added services at a fair price, executing efficiently, being responsive to requests, coming up with good ideas, and so forth. Sometimes when chasing the almighty dollar, however, banks try to build their relationships the wrong way. We've seen many instances of this already: creating false research to boost the client company's profile and share price, and spinning IPO shares to its executives. We've also noted the tying/reverse tying problem: exchanging underpriced loans for lucrative M&A or new issue business, or buying a client's services in exchange for banking deals. So building a relationship by doing the right kind and amount of business is like walking a financial tightrope. A slight misstep, and the results can be awful. Unfortunately, more than a few banks have had some slipups while walking the tightrope: building client relationships at almost any cost, until they are virtually guaranteed to see (if not always win) a wide range of financial mandates. But in getting to that stage, they intertwine themselves with a client so deeply that some element of their own fortunes rise and fall with the client's. Though these risky relationships don't necessarily have to deteriorate as a result of client default or distress, they often do, meaning the banks stumble by misreading the creditworthiness and the credit prospects of those they're involved with. Again, we don't have to look too far to see how some banks have mishandled client relationships, paying out in dollars and reputation when things didn't turn out as planned: Goldman Sachs and Robert Maxwell, CIBC and Olympia & York, pre-Citi Salomon and Development Finance Corporation, Citibank and WorldCom, Citibank and Enron, J.P. Morgan and Enron, Merrill and Enron, UBS and HealthSouth, Bank of America and WorldCom, CSFB and Russia, UBS and LTCM, and so on. Though prudent relationship management has to be a cornerstone of sound risk practices, it can be overlooked.

Dangerous Ties

Every so often a bank gets in so deep with a client that the relationship becomes extremely problematic. Relationships are important to nurture and build, but if a firm pursues them to excess then it had better hope it's backing the right horses. Because if it isn't, the losses can be significant. Three that know this all too well are Goldman, J.P. Morgan, and UBS.

For a time in the 1990s the names Goldman and Robert Maxwell were inexorably linked, much to the chagrin of the Goldman partners. Maxwell, who had assembled a media empire during the 1970s and 1980s, did not have a sterling business reputation, having been censured by the British government for inappropriate business dealings and criticized for failing in duties as a director (to wit, the authorities noted that Maxwell was "a person who cannot be relied upon to exercise proper stewardship of a publicly quoted company"). Nevertheless, Goldman proceeded to build a relationship with the tycoon. Dealings started off modestly: the bank's London office traded in Maxwell Communications Corp. (MCC) shares, it extended some secured loans to Maxwell, and did a few foreign exchange transactions. Over time, however, the relationship deepened: there was more share trading, and there were more loans and currency dealing. Indeed, by 1993 Goldman had become the leading market-maker in MCC stock and had extended $160 million in loans to Maxwell himself (collateralized by MCC shares). Then things went very wrong. In 1993 Maxwell committed suicide by throwing himself off his yacht. After his death, investigation into the company's books revealed a web of deceit, including widespread fraud, looting of company assets, illegal transfer of funds between public and privately held firms, and so on. Indeed, MCC pensioners were greeted with unwelcome news of a £400 million shortfall in the company's pension plan, courtesy of Robert Maxwell. As more bad news broke, Goldman's ties with Maxwell came into the spotlight; as the leading MCC market-maker and a heavy lender to Maxwell, the bank was accused of being in on schemes to defraud employees and investors. Shortly thereafter the bank was sued in U.S. courts on the basis that it had "conspired to defraud." The bank's partners vehemently denied any wrongdoing and tried to have the case dismissed, to no avail. Over the next two years Goldman suffered from a steady barrage of bad press. Goldman's name was so intimately linked with Maxwell's that it was impossible for the bank to distance itself from the mess. The media scrutiny damaged Goldman's reputation and business. Goldman was excluded from several prominent deals as a result of its Maxwell association, including the highly coveted third tranche flotation of British Telecom. By 1995, with the affair turning into an almost continuous distraction, the bank decided to bite the bullet, paying $250 million to settle the case; separately, it lost $62 million on loans and $29 million on currency deals. Most important, it lost a bit of its reputation. The old banker's rule, "Know thy client," would have served Goldman well in its dealings with Maxwell, a man with a record of questionable business dealings.

J.P. Morgan must regret the day it came across the name Enron. Perhaps more than any other Street firm, Morgan suffered an enormous amount of headaches and losses from what was once one of its key relationship accounts. Indeed, any fees that it earned from the defunct energy company were eclipsed dozens (hundreds?) of times by credit losses, trading losses, legal losses, and regulatory fines (and this excludes indirect costs from general aggravation and a bruised reputation). The bank had approximately $2.6 billion of secured and unsecured exposure out to the company when it went under. Apart from all of the troubles associated with Mahonia (which, as we noted in chapter 4, cost the bank $165 million in fines) the bank had to write off $400 million from surety cover that insurers refused to pay out on, and it took a $900 million charge for related litigation. It also wrote down the value of several hundred million of unsecured nonperforming loans, bring the total tab up around $2 billion. Separately, the bank drew the ire of others in the $1 trillion syndicated loan market who complained that Enron, just prior to going under, was instructed by J.P. Morgan officials to use a $500 million Morgan-led letter of credit facility (syndicated very broadly) to repay other Morgan debt arranged through a special purpose entity. (Some other syndicate members have declined to pursue the bank, as they are a little reluctant to irritate the largest [32 percent] syndicate player in the world.) The sum total of all of these charges and events took its toll on the bank's share price, which underperformed the peer group by nearly 40 percent (yes, the investor paid again). And as if to add insult to injury, the new executives of the reconstituted Enron filed lawsuits against J.P. Morgan (and several other banks) for bad financial advice, stating that J.P. and the others "bear substantial responsibility" as they were involved in schemes to manipulate, and were engaged in transactions that they knew were being used by the original Enron executives to misstate financials. So, even several years after the bankruptcy, J.P. Morgan still couldn't cut its ties to Enron.

UBS's problem relationship was with LTCM. We'll talk about LTCM later in the chapter, but suffice to say that some folks on Wall Street got badly burned when the hedge fund ran aground in 1998, perhaps none more than UBS, which got a bit too greedy when it came to potential business with the highflyers from Greenwich. Lots of the problems started when the bank wrote the LTCM partners an $800 million, seven-year option on their shares; UBS then bought fund shares to square its position (plus $266 million of extra shares for its own account or possible future repackaging). By all accounts, LTCM paid some $300 million for the option. UBS booked some $30 million to $50 million in profit and, unfortunately, decided to reinvest the balance in more LTCM shares. It's a bit hard to imagine what the folks at UBS were thinking when they put the whole package together. Sure, they flashed up to $50 million of profits on Day 1, but they seem to have ignored the possibility that the catastrophe scenario could occur: what would happen if LTCM went down? The bank would need to sell all of its shares, but it couldn't just blow them out in the marketplace as it was contractually constrained from doing so; the position was completely illiquid. The bank also extended credit to the fund, some uncollateralized, and even ignored its own credit policy standards in doing so, which apparently prohibited dealing with clients leveraged at more than 30:1; LTCM was already known to have more leverage than that (though not the full 250:1 or 300:1 that appeared in 1998), but bank executives charged ahead anyway. In fact, UBS's downside on an LTCM meltdown was estimated at more than $760 million (that's quite a tradeoff: maybe $50 million of P for perhaps $760 million of L). Senior UBS executives appear to have ignored the extent of possible problems even as LTCM started showing weakness in the summer of 1998. But they could ignore things only until September, when everything fell apart. When LTCM finally imploded, the bank was forced to write down its hedge shares, investments, and credit extensions, crystallizing a quarterly loss of $690 million—not far away from the catastrophe scenario. UBS investors picked up the tab of course, and they were probably a bit surprised to find out just how exposed the bank was to such a risky credit. The LTCM fiasco, coming on the heels of 1997's large equity derivative losses, left UBS on the ropes and the subject of a de facto friendly acquisition by smaller rival SBC (resulting in the "new and improved" UBS, which eventually went on to buy Paine Webber and the rump of Enron's energy trading business). A bunch of executives involved with the LTCM debacle were jettisoned in the aftermath of the merger, including the head of the bank, the COO, the chief risk officer, and the head of fixed income trading. Risky business for all.

MISPRICING RISK

Though it seems a bit odd, sometimes banks don't price their risk correctly. How can that be? Isn't it their business to know the price at which something should be bought, sold, issued, syndicated, or hedged? GM knows how to price its SUVs, GE its light bulbs and jet engines, and Nokia its phones. So why shouldn't Merrill and Lehman and Goldman and everyone else know where to price credit default swaps, or block trades, or long-dated FTSE options, or IPOs? For the same two reasons we've talked about before: accidental stumbling (they screw up) and doing the wrong thing (they deliberately misprice it to win business or fraudulently misprice it to come out ahead internally). Let's look at each of these generically, across any and all risks, remembering that financial risk comes in lots of different colors (e.g., credit, market [curve, direction, spread, volatility, basis, correlation], liquidity, sovereign, operational, model, legal, etc.) and that all of these can be—and, in practice, are—mispriced from time to time.

Sometimes banks get the pricing of risk wrong by accident. They don't really understand the characteristics or dynamics of the risk they have on their books, so they don't know how it's actually going to trade, how much other banks will bid to take it off their hands, how liquidity will affect value or where it can be hedged. This tends to happen when something is relatively new to the Street, when it's done in big size (liquidity considerations can overwhelm everything else), or when it's very complicated and no one has yet figured out all of the potentially dangerous nuances. For instance, when the Street first introduced interest-only (IO) and principal-only (PO) strips in the mid-1980s, they were so different from other instruments that some banks got the pricing wrong. The traders and researchers knew only generally, and not precisely, how the instruments would perform in up or down markets, because they had no firsthand experience—they had to wing it. And so they did, and some lost lots of dollars. For instance, Merrill dropped $377 million in 1987 mostly because Howie Rubin, a mortgage trader, stuffed some unauthorized tickets in the drawer, but also because the specific securities he was trading and then stuffing in the drawer (the PO stubs) were far riskier than anyone at Merrill realized. Sure, the researchers knew that the PO would get hurt if rates rose; but they had no real idea just how badly it could get hurt. Chemical Bank lost $30 million because it didn't know how to properly value its cap and swaption volatilities. When Bankers Trust put some of its clients into the exotic swaps we talked about in chapter 4, the trading floor tapes revealed that even the high-powered traders managing the risks, hedges, and valuations weren't entirely sure how to price them. In fact, traders routinely get burned when they roll out something new: CMO and CBO residuals, index amortizing rate swaps, volatility and variance swaps, commercial paper caps, barrier options, power options, and long-dated swaptions, among others, have all caused headaches (and pools of red ink) at major banks over the past few decades. Of course, banks have to be willing to lose money on a new product—they are innovators and risk takers, so that's part of the game. But maybe they shouldn't be *too* clever and try to do things that are *too* esoteric, and maybe they shouldn't do things that are *too* large until they've figured it all out.

Then there are instances when banks stumble because they wind up mis-pricing the liquidity of their books. They take on very large positions—much larger than they can probably bear—because they see opportunities to make money. The more risk they put on, the greater the concentrations, and the harder the hedging or unwinding. All the illiquidity they've injected into their books may not be properly reflected in the price. This doesn't usually relate to very large and deep markets, like on-the-run U.S. Treasuries or German bunds or U.K. gilts, where a bank can put on a sizable position and still manage to hedge or sell where it needs to (though it can happen if the positions are big enough: in 1994 Goldman lost $50 million on one big short-sterling position, and it lost a total of $800 million from its massive holdings of U.S. Treasuries and other instruments that were rocked by U.S. interest rate increases; Salomon, too, lost heavily on its huge positions in supposedly liquid instruments during the same period.) More often, it has to do with dicey corporate credits, emerging market risks, little-known arbitrage opportunities, carry trades, volatility plays, currency convertibility punts, long-dated structures, and so on—things where a bank can accumulate a fairly chunky position because of perceived profit opportunities, then wind up owning far more than would seem prudent because they haven't priced in the illiquidity; that means they can't back out or offload or hedge at a rational price. For instance, in the 1960s a number of mutual funds started buying up large blocks of "letter stock," unregistered securities that couldn't be traded (e.g., no liquidity) while in the registration process. Some funds bought big blocks of the stuff and decided to value the shares at the market value of the liquid, registered securities, rather than at cost, meaning that they failed to account for the complete absence of liquidity and were essentially overstating the value of the funds. When redemptions hit and they couldn't sell the letter stock to meet cash calls, they sustained large liquidity-induced losses. In 1986, when Goldman was trying to become an even bigger player in fixed income trading, it amassed a very large position in a single illiquid corporate bond, the position went sour, and it cost the bank $50 million. It's okay to lose $50 million as a prop trader, but maybe not on a single, illiquid position, and certainly not when the bank's total income is $360 million. In the early part of the millennium Goldman, CSFB, and a few others lost quite heavily in the long-dated sterling swaption market as they tried to cover short volatility positions built up through the sale of swaptions to the U.K. insurance sector. The banks learned that it's not easy trying to cover a short in a thin market: in a self-fulfilling market move, each purchase of a piece of the sterling volatility hedge raised the effective price for the balance of the hedge, meaning the losses got bigger and bigger with each attempt at additional hedging. Many Street banks (Stanley, CSFB, Goldman, Merrill, Citi, J.P., and others) saw good value in Mexican peso carry trades in 1994—they borrowed in cheap dollars, bought spot pesos with their dollars, sold pesos forward for dollars, used their pesos to invest in higher yielding Mexican peso assets, and captured the spread. Many thought it was free money, because the peso had been artificially stable for most of the previous two decades. So they printed the trade in big size because they were greedy (and, when they were full to the gills, they put together some of the structured notes we talked about earlier, and sold them to institutional clients like Mattel and the Wisconsin Investment Board, making some fees in the process). Then Mexico devalued and all those banks (and their clients) unwound their carry trades at huge losses. The positions were too big and the pricing too low to compensate for the risks. Of course, the red ink that flowed after the devaluation was not enough to deter the *same* Street banks from replicating the *same* carry trades in Thailand and Indonesia in 1995 and 1996 (they would have done the same in Malaysia and Korea but for currency controls); in 1997 the whole region devalued, and the banks (and their clients) got blown away again. Not to be deterred, the *same* banks went to the well for a third time in late 1997 and early 1998 on the *same* trade. Target: Russia. And, predictably, the red ink flowed again (in huge size) as Russia devalued in August 1998. Which brings us back to a point we made earlier: the Street just doesn't seem to learn from the lessons of the past.

Sometimes banks misprice the risk—either too low or too high—on purpose; this moves from stumbling to doing the wrong thing. When a bank deliberately prices its risk too low, it's hoping to earn it back somewhere else; this brings to mind the loss-leader approach we talked about earlier: offering something at a lower price in hope of winning something else with a better return or bigger fees. Remember those wildly mispriced investment grade loans for firms like GE and AT&T? They were almost certainly mispriced for a reason: to have a shot at winning more profitable business. Maybe that works if the firm can look at all of its businesses on a portfolio basis and it wins the juicy transaction (without tying, of course). But if it can't or doesn't, then it has a book of business that's misbalanced—the meager profitability of the transactions doesn't cover the expected losses. Again, maybe that's okay if it just relates to a single deal or client (as an exception), but it probably doesn't—it's usually part of a broader corporate strategy (e.g., have the loan desk subsidize the M&A team), so the portfolio could be chock-full of misbalanced positions.

In a few cases banks (or individual traders) deliberately and fraudulently fabricate prices that don't reflect the reality of their risk or the marketplace. This involves overvaluing positions and generally happens when there is a dearth of external pricing information and controllers can't independently verify the worth of a particular risk a trading desk might own (of course a bank can fraudulently undervalue its positions, but that isn't going to give it extra dollars unless they are short, so overvaluing seems to be more common). Things traded on exchanges have ready prices, and so do some things that are traded OTC (as long as they are vanilla, and fairly liquid). There's no problem then, as controllers can verify trader values against an external source. But anything else can be challenging. That's when Wall Street enters the mark-to-model realm—a twilight zone, a world of smoke and mirrors, guesses and assumptions; a world with room for unscrupulous traders to pull all kinds of shenanigans. If a price doesn't exist, then it has to be valued with a financial model. The model is going to be built around some assumptions that may or may not reflect reality. There is nothing inherently wrong with models, particularly those that are well established and time-tested, and which are built atop conservative assumptions and have some grounding in reality. The problems come when models are more esoteric and assumptions more extreme, when the risks are very complicated, when there's no good track record of performance, or when the controllers can't quite figure out what's going on (and they usually can't, as the financial mathematics tend to be quite intense). That's when the trouble starts: the trader(s) (and/or the quant researchers) come up with a model that doesn't really convey an accurate picture of the desk's risks or the value of its positions, or uses the wrong market inputs—meaning lots of wiggle room to push the P&L in the trader's favor, overstating revenues and understating risks. Here's one scenario: traders trade up a storm using their (flawed/questionable) models, seem to do well P&L-wise, and collect their bonuses; some might then go to another bank, leaving behind a ticking time bomb. Then the bomb explodes: when trades mature or enter the liquid part of the market, they have a market price, and if the market price is different from the model price, look out. Again, this isn't just theory; it has happened many times. In 1987 Bankers Trust found that the volatility quotes in its FX book were at least 25 percent too high, leading to an $80 million markdown (which executives took out of the compensation expense account in order not to miss profit targets; according to CEO Charlie Sanford: "What's the big deal . . . it's just an accounting thing."[4] Great). The same happened with NatWest (now part of Royal Bank of Scotland) in its deutsche mark and sterling bond options and swaptions book, Bank of Tokyo Mitsubishi in its bond options book, and various others. So quantitative valuations can be a problem, leading to trading losses/position writedowns. And Street banks generally lack the expertise at senior levels to police this effectively. Executives just don't get it. And how can they be expected to? They are managers, not mathematicians. Even someone as savvy as Robert Rubin—former head of Goldman, former U.S. Secretary of the Treasury, late of Citicorp—has said as much: "I think one of the problems on Wall Street today is that people in management positions don't have the quantitative framework to evaluate the worth that underlies the conclusions they're being presented with. I can't ask a quant person how he got his conclusion because when you start talking about his equations, they don't mean anything."[5] Look out.

What is the end result of all this stumbling and underpricing and overvaluation? Often it's a skewed risk profile, and a skewed risk profile means surprises when things go in the wrong direction. A bank that takes too much risk (e.g., market concentrations, illiquidity, credit portfolios ready to explode) is going to find out just how wrong things are priced or how hard it is to lighten up when it's forced to syndicate, cover, sell, or hedge risks quickly (as when there's a market dislocation and everyone's running for the same small exit at the same time). That's when the losses mount and powerful Wall Street trading houses, with their trading risk portfolios maxed out, look decidedly fallible. That's when the banking experts, with their books of huge, but rapidly souring, loans, look like amateurs. Citi, Drexel, Merrill, J.P., CSFB, Lehman, Goldman, Bear, Stanley, and most others have suffered significant losses from loan operations, trading desks, derivative books, and leveraged "hedge fund style" prop trades over the years. Again, there's nothing wrong with losing dollars in the risk business—that's part of banking. The issue is whether the losses are understood, explainable, justifiable, and expected, or whether they are the result of mistakes or fraud. Often it's the latter, meaning someone is going to have to pay: bank investors, certainly, even if the firms they've invested in are known to be big risk takers, because the banks sometimes forget to tell their shareholders they've ramped up (again). But in this situation, traders, bankers, risk managers, and controllers can lose their heads as well, as irate executives flex their muscle.

A Year to Forget

In 1993, two years after John Meriwether left Salomon (in the aftermath of the Treasury auction rigging scandal we discussed earlier), he put together LTCM, a dream team of quants and traders (and a couple of Nobel Prize winners for good measure) who raised lots of capital and started to play in the markets in a big way. Wall Street, of course, was there from Day 1: Merrill helped arrange the early capital raising efforts, UBS wrote the partners a big option on their shares, Bear Stearns signed up to provide clearing services, and virtually every major bank was either an investor in, or lender to, the fund (or both). LTCM had so much clout that it was able to negotiate very attractive repo borrowing terms, which gave it the ability to leverage up almost infinitely; since everyone on the Street saw lots of potential dollars from dealing with LTCM, they were very, very eager to provide good financing and business terms. Then it was off to the races.

Over the course of the next two years LTCM stuck primarily to its fixed income arbitrage expertise and generated exceptionally good returns for investors (43 percent and 41 percent, on $7 billion of capital). However, by 1997 it was getting tougher to find profitable opportunities, so the LTCM gurus started getting into equities (selling equity volatility, putting on equity risk arbitrage positions in more than 75 stocks), chasing increasingly esoteric (and illiquid) spreads (e.g., long-dated callable German bunds versus deutsche mark swaption volatility, Danish mortgages versus Danish government bonds, Italian treasury bills versus lira deposits, Russian carry trades), and putting on larger and larger positions. In fact, the fund was becoming extremely risky: lots of leverage, lots of concentrations, and lots of illiquidity. Indeed, in 1997 LTCM's managers returned $2.7 billion of capital to investors because they just couldn't find enough profitable investment opportunities. But they forgot to unwind positions by a commensurate amount, meaning leverage spiked even higher. Still, the Street was happy to keep doing business.

Then came mid-1998. The financial markets had grown increasingly fragile; 1997 had been bad, with the Asian crisis leveling lots of funds and hurting a number of banks and their clients. In July 1998, as Citi started unwinding some of the old Salomon arbitrage positions, LTCM had its first taste of reasonably large losses. Russia was looking shaky as well, and by August it became clear that the country could no longer sustain the value of the rouble. The central bank declared a domestic debt moratorium (freezing interest payments on local currency instruments) and devalued the rouble. This was the catalyst for much broader problems. Equity volatilities spiked up, high-grade corporate bond/loan markets shut down, convergence trades diverged, and liquidity in many assets evaporated. All of this spelled trouble for LTCM, which had invested heavily in lots of markets that were starting to crack. And because the Street was in bed with LTCM in a big way, that meant big troubles for the banks, too: many major banks were suffering big trading losses from prop positions in Russia, Russian carry trades, swap and credit spread convergence plays, short equity volatility positions, and credit extended to the hedge fund sector and other emerging market borrowers. By late August LTCM was already on the ropes, having lost $550 million from its strategies. By early September total losses had mounted to a staggering $2.5 billion (down 52 percent for the year) as flight to quality, divergence, and volatility remained in full force.

As the meltdown continued during September (including another -$500 million day for the fund on September 21), panic set in around the Street (and within the regulatory community). By late September, as the fund's liquidity pressures increased, Fed regulators dropped in to inspect LTCM's books and were shocked by the size of the positions they found. The Street had bent over backwards to give the fund leverage through financing and derivatives. Balance sheet leverage was on the high side at 30x (e.g., $125 billion of assets supported by $4 billion of equity), but off-balance sheet derivative notionals of $1 trillion meant leverage was more than 300x. The fund was too big to fail—any collapse of LTCM would have tremendous systemic implications for the rest of the Street. As regulators and banks came to realize this, a number of different groups put forth proposals to fund/bail out/acquire LTCM (e.g., one by Warren Buffett, one by AIG/Goldman Sachs, several by other bank consortia). They moved with speed and care, as they knew a single default within the LTCM portfolio would trigger a cross default and bring down the whole house of cards. Bear, as clearing firm, was threatening to pull the plug, so quick action was essential. After some back and forth, a 13-bank group arranged $3.6 billion of bailout financing in exchange for 90 percent of the fund, which they planned to unwind gradually through an oversight committee (so as not to rock the markets and cause further damage to their own books). There is little doubt that their actions helped stave off what might have been a crisis of epic proportions. But there is also little doubt that they were all acting in self-interest: this wasn't a public bailout, obviously, but a reorganization with creditors risking $3.6 billion of their shareholders' funds to avoid a catastrophe; the Street's risk exposures were so large that many players would have been severely damaged without the bailout. After a few more weeks of losses, markets stabilized and the fund started making back some money. By June 1999 the fund was up 14 percent, leverage was down, and the fund was able to repay investors $300 million and the bailout group $1 billion. The fund eventually repaid its obligations and was wound down in an orderly fashion.

Critics descended as soon as the dust settled. By any measure, the clever folks at LTCM blew it. They relied too heavily on their models, they ignored concentrations and illiquidity, they took advantage of all the leverage they could get, they drifted away from their core investment expertise. But Wall Street blew it as well. The banks were hungry for profits and lax in their risk-management practices. They gave LTCM the leverage—repos, derivatives, and credit lines—on completely irresponsible terms; they mispriced their risk just so that they could see some of LTCM's other business. They lent without good disclosure (contrary to standard credit operating procedures), they didn't take up-front collateral, and they relied too heavily on their own flawed models. In some instances they attempted to replicate LTCM's positions, injecting the same illiquidity into their own books. And, in some cases executives were conflicted: they were investors in LTCM, and they were front and center in helping with the bailout, thus protecting their own investments (to wit, Donald Marron/Paine Webber, David Komansky/Merrill, Sandy Weill/Citi, Merrill employees, Bear Stearns executives, and so on). The President's Working Group on Financial Markets blamed Wall Street for the risk failures: it criticized the amount of leverage the banks had provided the hedge fund community and the shortcomings in their own models, and recommended direct regulation of derivatives dealers (a recommendation that died a quick death).

Lots of banks got it all wrong in 1998—on LTCM, on Russia, and on the types of trades that had given LTCM and other hedge funds so much trouble (e.g., short equity volatility, swap spreads, and so on). Lots of banks lost on LTCM: UBS lost $690 million, the Bank of Italy $100 million, Credit Suisse $100 million, Dresdner Bank $145 million, Sumitomo Bank $100 million, and so on. And some got hit in other areas, too: CSFB reported losses of $1.3 billion in Russia, including nearly $640 million in rouble forwards purchased via the Moscow Interbank Currency Exchange (MICEX) to hedge their rouble exposure (lesson #1 of risk management: don't hedge a local currency exposure [like $/rouble] with a local counterparty [like MICEX], because when things blow, they're going down together); Citi lost $60 million on Russia and $300 million on arbitrage positions; Merrill lost $1.5

billion, mostly on corporate bonds and preferreds; Goldman reported prop trading losses of $650 million, across various markets; and so on. Whether all of these figures reflect the reality of actual losses is something that we'll never know: profits/subsidies from other trading books, and reversal of rainy-day reserves established one, two, or five years earlier to cover just such an event, means that the actual loss experience remains a mystery. Whatever the numbers, they were staggering, calling into doubt some of the Street's supposed risk prowess. Investors were sorely disappointed and bailed out of financial stocks in droves, lopping off big chunks of market capitalization; during September and October most major banks lost between 40 percent and 50 percent of their worth, and climbing out of that hole took most of them 12 to 18 months. The Street got too greedy, too concentrated, too conflicted, too illiquid, too model-driven. Everyone forgot the rules of prudent risk management that year.

NOT CONTROLLING RISK

Banks lose in the risk game when they don't control what they've got. This usually happens when they do a poor job defining how much risk they want to take, or they define it but don't stick to it. It can also happen when they fail to keep track of the risk they've put on or don't have the infrastructure to prevent unsavory acts from happening.

Banks that actively take risk have to figure out how much of their shareholders' money they want to bet when they're sitting at the poker table. They are obviously in business to take some amount of risk, but they'd better know beforehand what the magic number is. The foundation is understanding how much money might go down the drain when everything goes wrong at the same time. Without a clear understanding of the disaster scenario, a bank may be tempted to keep piling on risk or get involved with things that it doesn't understand, until it's got concentrations, illiquidity, and complexity—all of the things that can cause big losses. In the disciplined, well-run bank, the board and senior executives define a risk appetite and dole out risk capital very strictly; businesses have to justify their use of capital (making sure potential profits meet certain hurdles, the volatility of profits is well understood, and so on). But some banks ignore the process, or flout it when profit opportunities look juicy or clients want something done. Discipline goes out the window and the bank sets itself up to lose control. It happens from time to time—international banks in the early 1980s, Drexel in 1989–1990, Kidder in 1990–1991, Goldman in 1994, Merrill and CSFB in 1998, J.P. Morgan in 2001, and so forth—but you usually can't tell till the bank has lost lots of money. When they report that they're down a few hundred million in this market or with that credit, you can be pretty sure that they took more risk than they should have by making exceptions for "good clients" or "attractive market opportunities," or they just ignored the whole process. There's not much point in having a risk management framework to control risks if management is just going to ignore it and take the risks anyway.

Sometimes risk positions wind up being losers because of weak controls that let traders create fake prices or hide losing deals in desk drawers (actually, in error or suspense accounts that no one can find until the damage is done). Most banks have controls that are meant to stop evildoers from taking advantage of the system by booking false trades or coming up with bad prices that make them look more profitable than they are. But if there's a chink in the internal control armor and a bank has some dishonest characters on its desks trying to make a quick buck, then problems can appear. It might start when a trader has a few bad positions and tries to make up for them by booking unauthorized trades (maybe in excess of internal limits, or with clients that haven't been approved). Since trading out of a hole rarely seems to work, the damage actually multiplies, and the losses (and lies) grow larger. The hidden error account is suddenly burgeoning with bad trades that no one seems to know about. The bank is sitting on another ticking time bomb, one that eventually explodes and leaves behind an ugly scene: management appears to be out of control, internal controls are shown to have failed, staff members get demoralized, regulators get upset, and the bank investors get burned, again. Take the $377 million blowup at Merrill we mentioned earlier. Not only did the firm not understand the risk dimensions of the IO/PO strips it was trading, but it had weak controls surrounding the business—which Howie Rubin, as trader, exploited. It went something like this: Rubin bought $935 million of mortgage-backed securities and stripped them, selling the IOs to S&Ls and keeping the POs; that was within authorized limits, though it was still a big bet on rates going down (and not even the mortgage researchers knew just how sensitive the PO stub was). Then Rubin bought and stripped an additional $800 million without telling anyone. Same game: the IOs went to the S&Ls, but this time the POs went into the desk drawer because limits were already used up. Rates went up, somebody at Merrill finally found the PO in the desk drawer rather than the computer system, and all hell broke loose. The bank ate $377 million, and Rubin went to work at Bear Stearns. Merrill is not alone, of course; there are plenty of examples of spectacular control failures: Barings, where rogue trader Nick Leeson lost $1.4 billion from unauthorized Nikkei, Euroyen, and Japanese government bond positions; Allfirst, where FX trader John Rusnak lost nearly $700 million from unauthorized dollar/yen currency trades; Kidder Peabody, where strips trader Joe Jett lost more than $400m from phony Treasury strip activities; NatWest (RBS), where swaptions traders Kyriacos Papouis and Neil Dodgson lost $135 million through overvalued deutsche mark and sterling swaptions; Daiwa Bank, where rogue trader Toshihide Iguchi lost $1 billion from unauthorized Treasury bond/option trades via the New York branch; Chemical Bank, where trader Victor Gomez lost $70 million from unauthorized Mexican peso trades; National Australia Bank, where four traders lost A$360 million from unauthorized foreign exchange trades; and so forth. It makes you wonder about all the control failures that never make the press because they're only $10 million, $20 million, or $50 million in size: small enough to absorb into the machinery without anyone being the wiser. Who needs all that negative press, anyway?

Ghost in the Machine and the Phantom Profits

Kidder Peabody, a name with us no more, had a few shining moments during its lifetime. Shiny enough, in fact, that superpower GE actually bought the investment bank. That, as it happens, was one of the company's worst-ever acquisitions. Why? Because the bank was mismanaged, took too much risk, and had lousy controls. The combination (and a bit too much risk in the CMO market) generated big losses, forcing GE to sell the retail piece to Paine Webber and shut the rest of it down. RIP.

Let's rewind a bit. During the 1980s Kidder was a reasonable force in investment banking—even after investment banker Martin Siegel got busted for insider trading, it did pretty well in M&A. And as we've already mentioned, it was very prominent in CMOs. In fact, it was a prime mover and captured big chunks of the market (too many chunks, as it happens). And, for a few years, it was the king of the Treasury strip market—it was the biggest player in Treasury reconstitutions (re-assembling stripped Treasury coupons and principal stubs at a profit), besting such Treasury dealing powers as Salomon and Merrill. How did Kidder get to be so dominant in reconstitutions? A trader named Joe Jett, a management team that didn't really know what was going on, a host of weak controls, and an awful trading and settlement system. Together, a powerful combination that helped seal the bank's fate.

Jett joined Kidder to trade Treasuries in the early 1990s. By all accounts his early performance was unspectacular, and he bounced around between desks, eventually winding up on the Treasury reconstitutions desk in 1991, where he looked for opportunities to put together decomposed securities and sell them at a profit. To make money in recons you've got to be able to sell the recombined package to another party for more than the price of the individual pieces plus financing costs; so it's generally not a very profitable business, though the sharpest players can make some money. Lo and behold, Jett started making some pretty good money from his recons; and then he started making more, and more, and more. And, in 1993, after two years of reconstitutions, he made more than $100 million for the bank—and earned himself a $9 million bonus (he was even named Kidder's "Man of the Year"). But instead of giving out big bonuses and awards, Jett's managers should have been drilling in to see just how Jett was making so much money from what is a notoriously thin-margin business (just as Leeson's bosses at Barings should have been questioning how he was making so much money in index arbitrage). The accountants should have been delving into the P&L and questioning the size of Kidder's balance sheet. The auditors should have been looking at the internal controls surrounding the business. But no one did any of these.

How was Jett making all that green? Actually, he wasn't making any at all; he was just taking advantage of a flaw in Kidder's system (which, ironically, GE had once publicly hailed as a "leading-edge platform"). The problem was that the system couldn't handle reconstitutions, so trades had to be recorded as a notional purchase of strips and a notional sale of the reconstituted package; each strip was represented as a zero coupon bond that accrued interest. The accountants allowed a five-day settlement period in the system and recorded the strip purchases at the current day price, but the sale of the bond at the T+5 day price, meaning the sale value was higher than the purchase value. So the system was letting Jett lock in a "profit"—a phantom profit, actually, because it didn't really exist. But the profit was only temporary, lasting only until the end of the five-day settlement period, when everything evened out. Jett knew all of this, and he figured out how to take advantage of it: by increasing the volume of reconstitutions, the phantom profits would keep looking like profits: profits from old deals would be replaced by profits from new ones, and so on. It meant putting on ever-increasing positions and expanding Kidder's balance sheet, but that was the game. And, when the accountants changed the settlement period from five days to several weeks, the game became that much easier for Jett to play.

By early 1994, with P&L coming in at an average of nearly $10 million per month, the whole affair had gotten so large that someone over at GE (not Kidder, mind you) wondered why the bank had $42 billion of strips on the corporate balance sheet. When no good answers were forthcoming, GE ordered a sale of a big chunk of the portfolio—meaning Jett's whole strategy unraveled. When the auditors and accountants finally started poking around, they found a nightmare: instead of $348 million in reconstitution profits recorded between 1992 and 1994, the bank had actually sustained $83 million in losses, much of it coming from the purchase of strips at ever-increasing prices; in an ironic twist of fate, Jett's demand for strips was so large that the desk was forced to source them at top dollar from other dealers, meaning the recon operation was actually losing money as a result of its own activities—a $431 million swing in P&L. In the end Jett was fired and sued (he was acquitted of fraud charges but was forced to repay his bonuses), and various other executives who had failed to supervise were jettisoned (the bank itself was wound down after sustaining losses in CMOs). All because of a ghost in the machine and a trader who sought to take advantage of it.

Lax internal controls that allow problems to occur can appear in many different forms: human, technological, and organizational. For instance, a bank may have staff who can't keep up with aggressive and creative originators and traders. Some of what the Street does is pretty arcane and complicated, and it demands technical rigor. Accountants, auditors, risk managers, and controllers who lack the expertise to understand, question, and challenge can have the wool pulled over their eyes. It's tough for someone who isn't technically sharp to spot problems or ask the right questions, so those on the front lines who choose to exploit the shortcoming can do so with relative ease. Control officers might also let themselves get bullied. Let's face it, if a seven-figure trader is screaming and shouting at a $50,000-a-year accountant about the price of a trade or the present value of a complicated structure, who do you think is going to win the match? The accountant is going to slink back to the finance department, head hung low. Once that happens, it's all over: the trader can pretty much do what he or she wants, which is a recipe for trouble. The bank may also have policies that treat risks inconsistently (meaning internal arbitrage) or fail entirely to address a particular issue. You can bet that an astute trader inclined to do the wrong thing will find these discrepancies and holes and exploit them.

Sometimes a bank forgets to watch what it owns, not because risks are too complicated but because things "slip through the cracks": human error. For example, as trading volumes on exchanges increased throughout the 1960s, lots of brokerages had trouble figuring out what they owned, didn't own, or owed. There were literally billions in securities that weren't, or couldn't be, settled (i.e., fails-to-deliver, peaking at about $4 billion in 1969) that sunk a lot of brokerages (Pickard and Co. was one of the largest to go under, but more than a hundred smaller ones succumbed as well); others had to be forced into shotgun weddings (e.g., Carter, Berlind, Weill & Levitt bought Hayden Stone, Merrill bought Goodbody); and regulators even came close to shutting down venerable Lehman because it had more than $600 million in unreconciled stock account balances. All this chaos occurred because firms lost track of things when business volumes increased. Two decades later, firms were still losing track. In 1982, Chase's failure to keep up cost it hundreds of millions. It seems that Drysdale Securities, a small broker, was busy doing reverse repurchase agreements with the Street via Chase on a no-name basis (Drysdale faced Chase, Chase faced the Street); apparently someone at Chase forgot that open, no-name reverses still have to be monitored and limited. As soon as banks on the Street found out that Drysdale had on $4 billion of open reverses, they started squeezing the market. Drysdale eventually had to liquidate its positions at a loss of more than $300 million, which was well in excess of its capital. But the banks didn't look to Drysdale for the shortfall; they went straight to Chase, which was legally bound. Apparently some Chase officials were a bit surprised to find they had done $4 billion of deals with Drysdale. The bank was obliged to cough up $250 million (a few other banks were on the hook for the remaining $50 million). It's certainly not the only one to have forgotten to watch the pots cooking on the stove—most banks have similar stories, even in an era in which banks are supposed to be attuned to internal controls.

In some instances the controls aren't up to snuff because of technological inadequacies. Banks live and die on good data and technology, especially when they are trading in and out of lots of markets rapidly and dealing with a host of global counterparties. If they can't keep track of what they've bought, sold, shorted, or hedged (and with whom), then they're in big trouble. The only way they can realistically get a grip on business is through technology. All too often, though, the ability for traders to develop new products and print trades far outpaces available technical capabilities—meaning something's not going to get into the system properly, it'll get misvalued, or it'll just be forgotten, any of which can lead to problems. Most banks have gone through these breakdowns (and some still do), and it can cost them serious money. For instance, Salomon was effectively out of control from the mid-1980s to the early 1990s. It had big positions and risks, as we've seen, but little in the way of technical controls wrapped around them: it often didn't know exactly how large its exposures were and had considerable trouble valuing its derivatives; managers had difficulty understanding the firm's risk profile and didn't have a good handle on positions because technology was woefully inadequate. In fact, things got so bad that when the bank finally decided it had better overhaul its systems, it discovered a huge accumulation of unreconciled balances in its New York and London trading operations: $281 million accumulated between 1989 and 1993 which it had to write off. It's not the only one to have suffered from technological failures, of course; similar things have occurred at Merrill, Allfirst, Barings, Kidder, UBS, NatWest, J.P. Morgan, and others.

Control problems can also come from structural flaws: front-office producers may have control over back-office staffers, telling them what to do, say, and report. Even though revenue generators aren't supposed to have any influence over what the finance/operations staff is doing (e.g., confirming trade tickets, documenting legal terms, approving credit limits, revaluing trades, funding exchange margins and balance sheet positions, verifying prices externally) it still happens from time to time (e.g., Barings in 1995, UBS in 1997, Allfirst in 2001); back to the fox in the henhouse.

From Singapore to Baltimore

Every so often the Street demonstrates just how important it is to keep front- and back-office functions independent. When firms don't properly segregate the duties of producers and controllers, independent checks and balances go out the window—allowing those so inclined to take advantage of the situation, generally to very bad effect. Two who have experienced this problem firsthand, losing a collective $2 billion in the process, are Barings and Allfirst.

Barings, an old-line British merchant bank with strong corporate finance capabilities, started getting involved in the futures business in the 1980s, offering client trading services through offices in London, New York, Tokyo, and Singapore. By the early 1990s the bank's futures business was gathering momentum and becoming well regarded in the marketplace. Enter Nick Leeson, a futures settlement specialist at Barings London who was transferred to the bank's Singapore office to oversee futures settlements in Asia. For reasons that are still unclear, he was soon given the additional job of running the bank's futures brokerage on the floor of the Singapore International Monetary Exchange (SIMEX, now part of the Singapore Exchange). That meant Leeson was in charge of the front- and back-office functions of Barings Singapore. Let's take a step back to consider how a futures brokerage is supposed to work: a futures broker accepts customer orders and executes them on an exchange, posting margins on behalf of clients and charging fees. The broker monitors the positions as markets move and makes calls for, or returns, client margin. So when a futures brokerage business is running properly, it's going to be a low-risk, low-margin operation. Sometimes, of course, a clerk makes a mistake in executing a customer order, or a customer disputes a trade. Disputed trades and clerical errors usually get resolved and closed out very quickly. In fact, the process tends to work so smoothly that the business is regarded as very low risk.

Let's return to late 1992, when Leeson ended up with some error positions in the SIMEX Japanese Nikkei index futures contract. Instead of closing them out immediately, he moved them into an unauthorized, off-system "error account" (the now infamous "88888" account) so he could make back his losses by trading. Remember, Leeson had control over front-office trading and back-office settlements, so he could do what he wanted without question. Of course the scheme didn't work. Indeed, Leeson's positions and losses grew steadily: by the end of 1993 he had lost $37 million, by September 1994 the figure had grown to $87 million; losses continued escalating into early 1995.

Because Leeson was well regarded internally, he was routinely able to convince London headquarters to fund the SIMEX margins on his rapidly multiplying unauthorized positions. Through the latter part of 1994 he secured $225 million of margin funding, and between January and February 1995 a staggering $1.1 billion (equal to 1.7 times Barings' total capital)—all without a proper reconciliation of positions by head office or local controllers. Eventually, though, the positions, losses, and margin funding became too large to disguise. In early 1995, as a last ditch attempt to conceal his activities, Leeson sold a large number of straddles (put and call options with the same strike price) to raise money and alleviate the margin funding pressure. To make money in short straddles the markets have to be very tranquil. Unfortunately for Leeson, on January 17, 1995, a 7.2 Richter earthquake hit the City of Kobe. The Japanese stock market tumbled, destroying Leeson's last attempt at salvaging his fraudulent positions. As the market fell and volatility spiked over the following week, Leeson's straddles lost $100 million; several weeks later another steep drop in the Nikkei (and a rally in Japanese government bonds, in which Leeson also held positions) created an additional loss of $225 million. The jig was up. Leeson jumped into his car, drove to Malaysia, and was eventually arrested getting off an airplane in Frankfurt. Barings, meanwhile, had lost all credibility in the financial markets and couldn't survive independently. The Bank of England helped orchestrate a sale of the bank, which proved difficult because no one was able to figure out the potential liability of all the positions held in the "88888" account. Several bank consortia tried to grapple with the extent of Barings' liabilities but were unable to get comfortable and refused to fund the institution as a going concern. Dutch bank ING ultimately gained exclusive rights to bid on Barings and was able to quantify certain downside scenarios; following its analysis it bid £1 to assume all outstanding liabilities, and was awarded control. Once the dust settled the extent of the damage, and the value of Barings, became clearer: Barings' capital of $680 million was depleted by nearly $1.4 billion of losses, creating negative net worth of $650 million. ING injected an additional $370 million of capital, valuing the acquisition at $1 billion.

In the aftermath of this episode, it became very clear that controls, governance, and management oversight had all failed: Leeson had full authority over front- and back-office functions and could create financial fiction; the financial control, treasury, and risk people never queried Leeson's demands for margin or the source of Leeson's impressive "profits" ($85 million over two and a half years). All that profit should have set off alarm bells, as it was much more than can be earned in traditional futures execution business. Leeson eventually did some time in a Singaporean jail, and regulators sanctioned some of his bosses. Barings was completely absorbed with giant ING's operations and faded from the scene.

Allied Irish Bank, Ireland's largest commercial bank, entered the U.S. market in the mid-1980s by acquiring a mid-Atlantic bank that became known as Allfirst. Allfirst had a reasonable loan and deposit business in Maryland and neighboring states, and also featured a small foreign exchange trading operation. Things went along swimmingly until early 2002, when Allied's management dropped a Barings-like bomb: one of its Baltimore FX traders, John Rusnak, had manipulated internal controls over a five year period, toting up $691 million of losses in the process. It seems that the trader (who must have been as bad in FX trading as Leeson was in specing the Japanese equity markets) thought that the yen would strengthen against the dollar and repeatedly took dollar/yen forward FX positions that were well in excess of his authorized $2.5 million daily loss limit; when he began posting losses, rather than throw in the towel he covered up his errors by creating fictitious option trades.

During the five-year run, and especially toward the tail end, Rusnak's bets grew larger and his strategies more bizarre (e.g., he sold deep-in-the-money one day currency options and bought the same options expiring one month out, which left the bank flat but just delayed inevitable recognition of the bad positions). A few Wall Street dealers thought it curious that a small regional bank in Baltimore was becoming so active in FX—but most kept on dealing with the bank anyway. Apparently this news never made it to Dublin, and things carried on till Rusnak couldn't hide his losses any longer. He confessed his evil ways and the bank came clean, apologizing profusely to shareholders. Then came the inevitable postmortem, which revealed all kinds of internal control failures: poor risk management, ineffective auditors, antiquated risk management systems, failure to reconcile trades, use of the trader's own prices in valuing the positions, bullying of operational staff, and so on. Basically, everything that could go wrong in controlling a risky business went wrong. In the end Rusnak was carted off to jail, and Allied finally bailed out of the U.S. regional bank market by selling Allfirst to M&T Bank for $3 billion. But Wall Street wasn't out of the picture. In 2003, once all the dust settled, Allied sued Citibank and Bank of America on the grounds that they had helped Rusnak in his scheme by not requiring him to collateralize false trades (which would certainly have revealed his losses at an earlier date). Citibank and Bank of America proclaimed their innocence. FX turnover in the Baltimore market has returned to normal (almost nonexistent) levels.

———————————

Wall Street is typically portrayed as being very savvy about risk and risk management. The truth is that banks have more problems and suffer greater losses in this area than is commonly known. And we're not referring to normal losses that might be expected in the course of doing risky financial business—that's out of scope because banks are supposed to lose some money in risk dealings. We're talking about all of the losses that extend beyond that. Of course, good trading or origination in another part of the firm can cover some of the problems up; dipping into reserves and smoothing out the P&L can plug some of the holes (there are rules on how and when reserves are supposed to be used, but banks still manage to massage them enough to make bad things vanish). Only when the losses are really nasty might a bank be forced to confess that it has hit a bad patch. Even then, though, what a bank winds up revealing may only be a fraction of the loss that's really occurred.

Part II

WHY WALL STREET FAILS

Chapter 8

INTERNAL BREAKDOWN

We've spent several chapters talking about all the things that can, and do, go wrong on Wall Street. We've recounted some real-life examples of the Street's failure (with the niggling caveat that what's contained in these pages is just a small sampling), and we've noted that the problems often reach out to harm lots of different stakeholders. We've spoken broadly about the reasons for the losses: accidental stumbling and doing the wrong thing. Now it's now time to dig into the causes in more detail. We want to get to the heart of why the Street stumbles and why it does the wrong thing. What particular factors cause it to fail? Why does failure happen so often? Is it company specific, systemic, or both? By understanding something about these questions we can hone in on root causes and set the stage for a discussion, in Part III, of a possible cure. After all, we aren't interested in just observing problems, diagnosing them, and then moving on to something else; we'd like to think about solutions to help solve what's wrong.

But the matter at hand right now is diagnosis. Many of the Street's problems, as you've probably realized, are of its own making: they are *internal* to departments and firms, and to the people who staff them. However, since Wall Street doesn't operate in a vacuum, some of its problems are caused or exacerbated by *external* forces, those operating outside of individual firms. We'll take a look at internal causes in this chapter and external ones in the next one.

When considering all of the internal problems that lead to accidents, client abuse, misrepresentation, fraud, and other nastiness, we find three major reasons for the breakdowns: flawed governance, bad management, and poor skills/controls. Each one of these has a part in leading firms astray, and when all three are at work simultaneously the problems can get very serious, indeed.

BREAKDOWN #1: FLAWED GOVERNANCE

Governance is the fancy name given to the practice of looking after a firm's stakeholders. Lots of parties—investors, creditors, clients, suppliers, regulators, and even broad communities—have a vested interest in a firm's continued success, so rules, regulations, laws, and moral standards have been created over time to make sure that the firm does what it should to protect these stakeholders. That's very comforting when you've invested money in a company, or you've lent it some money, or you use its goods or services. You don't want to wonder whether your money is safe, you'll get your quarterly interest check on time, or the goods or services will be delivered as promised: there are mechanisms that take care of all of that. At least, that's the theory. In practice, governance breaks down pretty frequently, either because the framework hasn't been properly structured or aspects of the process go unheeded. Bad governance isn't unique to Wall Street, of course. It can (and does) hit companies in other industries. In fact, some of the biggest scandals that the Street has been caught up in over the years have come from bad corporate governance at client companies (e.g., Enron, WorldCom, Tyco). But since we're talking about the Street here, we're talking about bad governance within banks. Bad governance often leads the Street down the wrong path.

Good governance says that board directors should properly represent the interests of shareholders (directors are, after all, shareholders' agents), the interests of shareholders and executives should be properly aligned, directors and executives should be held accountable for their actions, clients should not be prejudiced or harmed in the pursuit of profits, and corporate operations should be managed prudently, with robust controls. It's not too hard to see how the Street might fail at these and end up stumbling or doing the wrong thing. Let's examine each one in a bit more detail.

First, directors may not properly represent shareholder interests. For instance, they may support bank management in a particular endeavor, even if it isn't in the best interests of investors (meaning they might be accused of breaching legal duties of care and loyalty, which say that directors must make informed decisions that further the interests of shareholders). That's happened a few times over the years: signing off on expensive acquisitions at huge premiums; approving huge expansions and hiring sprees that aren't well grounded in strategy; refusing to sell the bank to another firm, even when the acquisition premium being offered is extremely attractive and a sale certain to be advantageous to investors; refusing to replace executive leaders who have led the bank astray; and so on. Any of these problems can pop up if directors are conflicted, disengaged, or technically incapable, if they're too close to management, or if they're more interested in furthering their own positions.

Second, the interests of shareholders and executives may be misaligned. One of the best ways of getting everyone on the same page is to make sure that executives get paid handsomely when they return good value to share-holders: everyone wins when the stock price keeps climbing, so why not tie ex-ecutive compensation to the sustainable level of the stock price? That happens, sometimes. But too often executives get piles of money regardless of what happens to the stock price—meaning interests are misaligned. Even if banks are firing hundreds or thousands, or they're suffering from poor rev-enues, wrestling with big trading or credit losses or the latest Street scandal, paychecks are usually still pretty big. (Maybe the big dollars are a reward for "managing through a bad environment"?) It isn't hard to find evidence of a complete disconnect in pay for performance. It's happened throughout the ages, but started becoming more evident in the 1960s and grew steadily from that point on. Over the past three decades Wall Street pay has taken a sharp turn upward even though stock prices don't always follow suit. It has re-mained true through the millennium, even after nasty market dislocations, poor operating results, and flagrant misbehavior. Let's consider just one ex-ample: in 2002, when Street investors saw their shares get flattened as a result of poor business conditions (low trading volume, zero M&A and IPO fees) and big write-offs (from prop trading losses, soured loans, settlements), top managers still walked off with seven—and eight-figure bonus checks. The CEO and president of Merrill each got $14 million, the CEO of Goldman $12 million, the CEO of Bear $20 million, the CEO of Citi $18 million, the CEO of Stanley $11 million, the CEO of Lehman $12.5 million—even as they cut jobs, reported weak earnings and got caught up in some of the scandals we've talked about. And even though the head of J.P. Morgan had his pay reduced by $5 million because shareholders got a −37.5 percent return on invested capital, he still earned a pretty impressive $11.4 million (including a $5 mil-lion "merger" bonus for bringing J.P. and Chase together "successfully"). What kind of signal does all of this send? A bad one: even if the executives re-sponsible for creating shareholder value can't pull it off, they still line their own pockets. A winning situation for the executives, a losing proposition for the shareholders. And that's because governance isn't working as it should; the compensation committees of the boards of these banks roll over and dole out big prizes whatever the market conditions or firm-specific performance. (To be fair, there are some exceptions. Every so often a few executives decline their pay packages when they don't perform: the top two at Schwab got no

206 / THE FAILURE OF WALL STREET

bonuses in 2002 and gave back three years of options because they didn't meet earnings targets. Unfortunately, these cases represent the exceptions, not the rule.)

And, of course, handsome compensation isn't just limited to executives; it reaches down to senior producers—bankers, traders, salespeople, brokers—who are supposed to bring revenues in the door. These folks get paid lots of bucks, sometimes without regard for the quality of the business they bring in. While some of the compensation may be justifiable in a strange Wall Street way, most of it isn't—it's disconnected from the realities of sustainable value creation and misaligned with the amount and timing of any value being created. For instance, a prop trader who books lots of long-dated deals gets to present value the earnings of the trades that'll be on the books for many years: she gets paid today but leaves the bank with tail risk that'll last till the next decade. A banker who lands a bond deal for a client that subsequently goes bust still gets paid up front; the bond buyers, and maybe even the bank's investors, suffer the losses. A broker gets paid an up-front bonus to come across with a book of business, and is then paid out on the basis of gross production. This translates into a buyout of the last employer (i.e., no risk of economic loss in job jumping) and a heavy focus on selling risky things and promoting lots of trading volume. If things go sour and the client loses, the broker doesn't really suffer—he or she has been paid on the basis of business brought in, not client performance. It's worth noting that many Street firms grant a portion of compensation in the form of equity options, which is good as far as aligning interests. Some, though, hand them out like candy, meaning a very large transfer of wealth from investors to employees. Do you think the investors are aware of just how much of a wealth transfer is going on? Probably not (unless they're reading those tiny little footnotes in the 10-K filing), but they will be when the day comes for option expensing through the income statement. When the pay process is disconnected from other realities and interests, dollars are all that matter; earning those dollars through *any* means possible is a strategy some choose to follow, to the disadvantage of the stakeholders.

Third: accountability may disappear. Directors are accountable to shareholders, executives are accountable to directors: that helps protect the shareholders and their capital investment. So what happens when banks get caught with their hands in the cookie jar, suffer from trading losses from overexposure to a risk or market, get slapped with class action lawsuits over regulatory infractions, or write off the latest multibillion-dollar strategic expansion? Generally, nothing. Accountability disappears. No one at a senior level, it seems, is responsible for problems or losses (though many come out of the woodwork when it's time to take credit for successes). During ugly events, those leading to losses or writeoffs in the hundreds of millions, a few senior bankers or traders or risk managers may get handed up on platter to assuage whatever constituency is upset, but that's about it. Once in a blue moon a senior executive gets thrown to the wolves, but that's usually only after there have been repeated blowups and the press coverage gets too embarrassing. For instance, Allen Wheat, former CEO of CSFB, was eventually booted by the bank's directors, but not until he had guided the bank through several years of rather expensive mistakes: mega-losses in Russia in 1998, a huge brouhaha over guaranteed bonus pools, run-ins with regulators around the world, the technology banking problems mentioned in the past few chapters, and so forth. When someone senior gets shoved out the door, it's usually about containing bad press or calming some constituency; it's not about someone standing up to say, "I am accountable and should take responsibility by leaving." Heaven forbid. And directors? Forget it. The world can come crashing down around them, and they still keep their comfortable board positions. How many board members have been ousted over a bad showing on Wall Street? It's hard to think of any, even when huge "unexpected" losses appear within the risk appetite approved by the board, when supposed strategic decisions taken by directors turn out to be rotten eggs, when share values slide and stay depressed for years. What does all of this say? Basically, that directors and senior executives aren't accountable for problems, so if there's a screwup, it isn't their fault. And with that attitude, it's little wonder that the Street fails as often as it does. Manhattan District Attorney Robert Morgenthau, commenting on the Enron/Citibank/J.P. Morgan settlement, noted that "when you have institutions this big it's difficult to pinpoint responsibility." That's too bad. Or perhaps it's a brilliant tactic, making banks so large and diffuse and so adept at playing dodge ball and musical chairs, that no one in the executive suite or on the board can be held accountable. When the seniors refuse to take responsibility for the actions of their employees, business units, departments, or institutions, governance is badly flawed.

And what about the argument that it is individuals, rather than institutions or the Street as a whole, that are to blame for the failures we've discussed? What about the notion that we shouldn't condemn the whole industry for the actions of a few (or a dozen, hundred, maybe thousand) people? Perhaps there is some validity to the argument; a few bad apples shouldn't wind up spoiling the whole bushel, and certainly not the entire orchard. But there are limits to this point of view. Directors and executives have to be responsible for the actions of each individual and for creating an environment with proper controls. If an individual mistreats a client or misvalues a book, or performs due diligence poorly, then there is an implicit expectation that those in charge will fix the problem. But too often that doesn't seem to occur, so the problem gets larger, and the influence of the bad apple spreads. There are just too many instances in which problems were created not by just one or two individuals, but by entire teams, offices, and firms. Yes, Leeson was the one who did all the false trading that caused huge losses at Barings, but the executives and directors who failed to question his P&L (and blindly accepted that he could make so much money on a low-risk business), the treasury and finance departments that didn't question huge funding requirements for exchange margins, and the failed management and operational controls that permitted lack of segregation all mean that the failure was much larger than the individual. We can say the same about most of the other problems we've discussed in the book: Kidder's strips, Salomon's auction rigging, Lehman's rogue broker, Merrill's PO "ticket in the drawer" and Nigerian barges, Goldman's Treasury insider trading, the Street's research scandal, the yield burning, the mutual fund problem, and so on. So the argument that the individual is the primary or sole cause of the Street's failure is not defensible. The failures stem primarily from improper firmwide action, and that is driven, to a large degree, by lack of appropriate executive accountability.

Fourth, governance demands that clients, as stakeholders, be protected. Clients are the lifeblood of the Street's business, so directors and executives are going to make sure that clients are protected, right? Well, not always. We've already talked about different ways in which banks can abuse clients, so it's pretty clear that this aspect of governance falls down more frequently than we might expect. Corporate principles espousing the importance of the client— of "the client as king"—are sometimes questionable, even laughable. How else do we explain the large number of client-related problems, actions and challenges that have occurred so regularly? If the client were truly king, there simply wouldn't be such widespread challenges and complaints. All of the arbitrations, class-action lawsuits, no-contest payoffs, and regulatory fines and sanctions occur because the Street's directors and executives are not taking care of clients the way they should. If the Street cared about its investing clients, would it have permitted the sale of leveraged pyramid trusts, or commercial paper on the brink of default? Would it have allowed the research scandal to occur? Would it have prejudiced "normal" clients by giving hedge fund clients and senior corporate executives preferential treatment? Would it have sold risky partnerships to widows and orphans? Would it have put consumer goods and pharmaceutical companies into toxic derivatives? Would it have allowed market timing and late trading in funds? Would it have spun, laddered, tied, reverse tied, front-run, colluded, and interposed? Unlikely. Failing to properly protect client interests, a cornerstone of governance, leads the Street to do things it shouldn't do.

And, fifth, controls may be either absent or ineffective. Directors recognize that they have to have the right people, skills, and infrastructure in place to protect the integrity of a big banking operation: that helps make sure nothing slips through the cracks, and that all rules and regulations are followed to a T. Well, we know that banks often fall apart in this area, with major operational, client, and risk losses coming from bad controls. In fact, this is such a big reason for the Street's failure that we'll save it for later in the chapter. Suffice to say, for now, that the Street's control weaknesses are another element of botched governance.

BREAKDOWN #2: BAD MANAGEMENT

If flawed governance is the origin of certain problems, bad management is the mechanism that puts them in motion. Management guides the entire bank the wrong way and, like the battleship that takes miles and hours to turn around, there is little that can be done to halt the course quickly enough to avoid damage. What types of management mishaps contribute to the Street's failures? Doing business without a clear sense of direction, executing poorly, or trying to reverse strategies midstream. Executives wind up looking confused and tentative, and they send mixed signals, waste corporate resources, and exacerbate or accelerate many of the problems we've talked about.

No Strategic Focus

Executives, with the support and guidance of directors, are meant to create a corporate strategy that is clear, focused, and consistent with shareholder expectations. That's actually what they get paid to do. Unfortunately, bank executives often have trouble formulating that clear, focused, and consistent strategy (and they compound problems by having difficulties executing whatever plan they actually develop, which we'll save for later). Let's look at two common strategic problems that seem to have plagued bank executives over the years: trying to figure out what markets to serve and deliberately wanting to be all things to all people.

What Markets to Serve?

Some banks don't really know what they want to be: one day [month/quarter/year] they want to be a full-service bank, with strong capabilities in investment banking and commercial banking; then a pure investment bank, shunning commercial banking to focus on M&A and sales/trading; sometime later a global player, with branches and subsidiaries dotting key centers around the world; then, maybe, an asset management house with a big team of portfolio managers and a platform to capture retirement and savings assets. Or maybe they want to downshift a bit, becoming a niche bank or boutique; or maybe one with more of a wealth management/private banking focus; or maybe one specializing on fee-based trust, clearing, and custody services. Or . . . you get the point. Banks change their stripes, and sometimes pretty quickly, particularly when they are being driven by managers that are trying to get involved in the latest "hot thing." (Of course, by the time they get it all figured out they are probably catching the top of the market.) Even though strategy, by definition, is meant to be long term, lots of "quick strategic changes" seem to work their way into the process. Some might argue that Street firms have to remain flexible in order to respond to market opportunities—it's in their nature to be chameleons. Tell that to the confused shareholders, because they probably don't understand what businesses a bank is pursuing, favoring, buying, selling, abandoning—even though it has a bearing on the worth of their shares. Being flexible and adaptable is one thing, but redefining the character of an institution over a span of just a few quarters or years reflects too much flexibility.

In the 1970s, for instance, a number of firms (e.g., Manufacturers Hanover, First Interstate, Security Pacific, First Chicago) wanted to be involved in international banking and foreign exchange trading, so they set up Edge Act banking subsidiaries and International Banking Facilities, beefed up foreign branches and assets through growth or acquisition, and hung on till the emerging market debt crisis of the mid-1980s proved too painful. In the late 1980s and early 1990s, lots of commercial and investment banks (e.g., Security Pacific, Prudential Bache, Smith Barney, Merrill, DLJ, Shearson Lehman) wanted to be involved in junk and derivatives, so they again bought or grew. Then came the collapse of junk, insider trading scandals, bad equity investments, collapsed bridge loans, public fallout over greenmail and hostile deals, and derivatives bets gone bad; the exciting businesses weren't much fun anymore.

Starting in the mid-1990s various commercial banks, seeing that Glass-Steagall was crumbling around them, decided that it was time to be in investment banking. After all, things were hot: great-looking equity and bond deals, trading, M&A, so why not take the plunge? International banks, which thought U.S. investment banking business was just the ticket, joined them. So regional, money center, and international banks started buying securities firms: Bankers

Trust bought Alex Brown (Deutsche then bought Bankers), Citibank bought Salomon Smith Barney, J.P. Morgan Chase bought Hambrecht and Quist and Beacon Group, CIBC bought Oppenheimer, UBS bought Paine Webber, CSFB bought DLJ, Dresdner bought Wasserstein Perella, FleetBoston bought Robertson Stephens, US Bancorp bought Piper Jaffray, Bank of America bought Montgomery Securities, Wachovia bought Wheat First Butcher and Singer, Everen Capital and J.W. Genesis—every bank wanted a piece of the investment banking action, at almost any cost. Not necessarily because it was part of the corporate strategy or fit in with their corporate banking operations, but because it was the thing to do. Some of the banks rode a modest wave for a while (it's tough to crack the lock of the Big 3 or Big 5 when you're on outsider) and then came the Asia crisis, the LTCM/Russia crisis, the TMT meltdown, and lack of deal flow, and all of those brilliant "strategic acquisitions" didn't look so good anymore.

At about the same time, a number of investment banks decided that it was time to get into the asset management business. So, they barreled right in, lockstep, throwing some money at their own nascent platforms or, more likely, throwing lots of money to buy up existing firms. Merrill bought Hotchkis and Wiley and Mercury Asset Management, Morgan Stanley bought Van Kampen, Societe Generale bought TCW, Lehman bought Neuberger Berman, and so on. Whether or not these were good strategies is a bit unclear: most banks wound up buying at the top of the market and later suffered portfolio management defections and client departures. But because bank managers didn't always get it, they happily wrote checks: now they were banks with significant asset management capabilities.

The same thing happened with the international capital markets footprint. Throughout the 1990s it became all the rage for investment and commercial banks to set up offices and hire lots of staff in all the big (and not so big) financial centers of the world, especially "emerging" ones where the lure of privatization and new-issue business was strong (but the actual amount and quality of business a bit suspect). Because banks lacked the requisite expertise, they had to go out and hire or buy, and they did, often at the top of the market. They moved into very comfortable office space, first taking too little real estate and then, as they expanded, signing up for way too much (usually at the peak of the market, meaning more expenses and losses when trying to sublease). So Merrill, Goldman, Lehman, Morgan Stanley, J.P. Morgan, Deutsche, UBS, and others, trooped into places like China, Hong Kong, Korea, Thailand, Malaysia, Indonesia, India, Brazil, Mexico, Argentina, South Africa, Poland, and Russia to win the business. But bank executives forget that international expansion tends to be a bull market game: as soon as any one of the countries hits the rocks (and they invariably do, as they weave their way down the rocky path to industrialization), business evaporates. And that's what happened: with each market dislocation (e.g., Mexico 1994, Asia 1997, Russia 1998, Brazil 1999, Argentina 2000) banks, clients, and investors got burned, and the global footprint strategy looked a bit unwise.

Then it was time for a new strategy: catching the e-commerce wave and associated electronic trading craze by setting up online trading platforms (at a cost of hundreds of millions and more) and cannibalizing part of the existing business; this let banks keep up with the new kids on the block (so it was DLJ Direct, ML Online, MSDW Online versus Schwab, E-Trade, Ameritrade, Scottrade, TD Waterhouse). Unfortunately, things came to a grinding halt with the first big market downturn. And then another great strategic idea: catch the spreads on day trading and TMT order flow by paying top dollar to expand market-making capabilities or buy up some of the independent market-makers (Merrill bought Herzog Heine Geduld for about $1 billion, Goldman bought Spear Leads Kellogg for $6 billion [including a whopping $4 billion of soft, mushy, intangible goodwill]); then they got hit by the TMT meltdown and a move to decimalization and realized that the strategy wasn't too great after all.

All of these uncertain courses—trying to figure out what markets to really serve for the long haul—add up to strategic confusion and management indecision.

All Things to All People

For some, part of the strategic conundrum rests in the belief that, in the dog-eat-dog world of the twenty-first century, an institution has to be all things to all people if it is to survive: that only by being a financial supermarket can challenges be successfully fended off. Some have come to believe that the niche or focused players can't survive and will eventually have to broaden their scope or, more likely, sell out to the bigger houses, as has indeed been the case with Beacon (Chase), Hambrecht and Quist (Chase), Wasserstein Perella (Dresdner), Fleming (Chase), Schroders (Citi), Smith New Court (Merrill). All the little fish, no matter how good, supposedly will be snapped up by the behemoths. Banks that follow this line of thinking have to buy or grow business in many sectors and many locations; they have to expand into every little niche in order to be "the player" that everyone turns to. That's very expensive and complex, and not necessarily guaranteed to be a winning strategy. The megasupermarkets don't always get all the business—lots of shoppers prefer going to their little local deli or bodega, or to the market across town where they've shopped for years. Just because a bank can service retail and institutional clients across commercial banking, investment banking, asset management, and insurance in any location, at any time, doesn't mean it's going to win all the business. And if it isn't winning all the business, can it justify the costs, resources, and capital? Running offices and branches all over is expensive, as is developing and offering hundreds of products and services. And neither strategy guarantees that profitable business is being won. There are, of course, several examples of institutions that have opted for the "all things to all people" strategy: Merrill, Citi, Morgan Stanley, Deutsche, CSFB, UBS. Some aspects of the financial conglomerate strategy they follow are probably justifiable, though the economics may not be compelling. But lots of the great opportunities to cross-sell across geographic markets and products—the oft-cited synergies and cost advantages that can be obtained by doing it all under one roof—appear sometimes to be just so much hype. How many clients actually buy their insurance from the same place they make their paycheck deposits; how many actually do their online trading in the same place they get their home mortgage? How many multinationals using an investment bank for a targeted bond issue are using the same bank for trade credit, political risk insurance, custody operations, or management of the employee 401(k) plan? If the bank can't service the online retail trader, is it really going to lose a company's bond deal? If it can't handle the 401(k) program, is it going to lose the M&A transaction?

A few firms realize that the all-things-to-all-people paradigm isn't necessarily the way to go and have remained focused. But others haven't, and they have expanded, perhaps for the wrong reasons. Again, this doesn't mean a bank can't or shouldn't have a broad sweep of businesses. The issue is whether following this path is part of the strategy and the entire matter has been properly justified from a financial perspective, or whether it's just reaction to a "belief" or gut feeling, and then reverse engineering the justification. If it's the latter, there will be many upset investors wondering what's going on, again. And the proof is in the pudding: when some of the "all things" banks start dismantling their big networks, selling off subsidiaries, closing divisions, scaling back market-making operations, "refocusing" operations and reigning in, then you know they've fallen victim to the hype (more of this later in the chapter). But watch out for the day when they decide, for whatever reason, that it's time to be a supermarket again. As we already know, Wall Street doesn't really learn from its mistakes.

We can go on and on, but you get the point. Is trying to figure out what markets to serve by chasing the hottest thing, or insisting on being everything to everyone at any cost, really about strategic planning? Or is it a knee-jerk reaction to what the folks down the block are doing, the way the markets happen to be trading, or the services that a bank believes clients want (but doesn't know for sure)? Good times = expansion, bad times = reversal, regardless of what the strategy document says. Why do banks pay lots of money to get involved with a market that doesn't make sense for the firm's real long-term goals? Is it just to catch a few of the deal crumbs? Is it just to demonstrate a presence, to be able to offer products/services that may not be economically justifiable (using shareholders' capital very ineffectively in the process)? Bad strategic focus, which is what results when directors and executives fail to set the agenda and abide by it, leads directly to some of the Street's failures: pushing to win business at any cost to justify the expense of buying or building; taking too much risk to achieve the same "goal"; doing business in an area, product or market without requisite knowledge; operating without proper controls and skills; and so on. Each of these leads to the problems we've discussed in previous chapters.

Bad Execution

Creating strategy is the first step in the management process; executing a tactical plan to realize the strategic vision is the second. The Street sometimes has difficulty defining the strategic moves, and often compounds problems by executing its tactical battle plan poorly. How? It may overpay for acquisitions; it may decide to "buy," rather than win, business; it may fail to define or stick to a risk tolerance level; and it may not keep a lid on costs. Let's consider each one.

Overpaying

Overpaying for acquisitions seems to be a fairly common executive blunder. Since some Wall Street management teams can be a bit slow to react and really aren't market timers, they tend to buy what they think they need at the worst possible moment: fully valued deals at market tops. It seems odd that with all of the trading talent they employ they can't quite synchronize the timing of their purchases. It's also curious that with all those investment bankers on staff, they can't get decent fairness opinions on premiums they ought to be paying for acquisitions (then again, we already know that the bankers often miss the boat on valuations). So top of the market it is, paying stiff premiums to buy whatever management thinks is missing. Merrill bought storied investment manager Mercury Asset Management for $5.3 billion in 1997—a price that most at the time believed was rich and now know for certain was far too high, since the deal has brought more headaches than business (e.g., lawsuits, client defections, staff departures, political infighting, poor fund performance). Deutsche bought Bankers Trust (with its Alex Brown subsidiary) in 1998 for $9 billion and hasn't met its own internal targets for fee business or league tables. UBS bought Paine Webber for $11.5 billion in 2000 in what the UBS CEO called a "match made in heaven"; never mind that it happened at the precise peak of the market and, several years later, hasn't boosted the bank to the upper tier of Wall Street's elite (the U.S. business takes in about 5 percent of available fees, well below the bank's own internal target of 8 percent). CSFB bought DLJ for $13 billion in 2000 "to be a leader." Same issues: top of the market, big premium, poor to mediocre results, bad integration, bloated costs, and excessive overlap. So Deutsche, UBS, and CSFB spent a combined $33 billion for their U.S. properties and through the early years of the millennium squeezed out a combined 12 percent share of U.S. equity business (Goldman alone did 17 percent); they did even worse in M&A and bond issues. They aren't alone: Dresdner paid $1.6 billion for Wasserstein Perella in 2000 because officials also believed it was a "perfect match"; except that Allianz bought Dresdner and started making noises about getting out of investment banking, Bruce Wasserstein left for Lazard, and business soured—money down the drain. Same with Chase, which bought U.K. merchant bank Fleming in 2000 for an eye-popping $7.7 billion, and Citi, which acquired U.K. merchant bank Schroders in the same year for a less staggering, but still handsome, $2.1 billion (Citi didn't get the asset management arm like Chase did with Fleming). And both Merrill's purchase of Herzog and Goldman's of Spear Leads occurred at the peak of the TMT, day-trading, ECN bubble. Ouch. The common theme in these, and many others, is massive overpayment for assets and business that don't work out as planned. Only occasionally do executives get lucky and pay about the right price, or manage to take the business and do something good with it, as when Merrill bought Smith New Court for $840 million in 1995 and jump-started its equity trading business entirely, or when Morgan Stanley and Dean Witter got hitched.

Buying Business

Some of the Street's bad tactical execution centers on buying business. In their eagerness to win clients, scale the league tables, and become dominant global players, some firms are prepared to put money on the table. Not directly, of course, as that would be illegal, but the effect is pretty much the same: by underpricing a product, service or trade, by cutting a few fees or spreads, a bank wins the M&A, new issue, or asset management mandates. It prints the deal or arranges the transaction, jumps up in the league tables and gets some good press coverage. To some executives all this matters, because they follow the "business begets business" theory: by looking dominant, more business will surely come knocking on the door. The truth is that it may, but there's no guarantee.

Unfortunately, this strategy is a surefire way for a bank to earn less profit than it deserves and absorb more mispriced risk than it should. When management chooses to follow this tactical approach to business, there is one place where the bank won't rank well, and that's disclosed fees and profitability. Results of doing high-volume/low-priced business or undercutting profits just to print eventually gets told in figures on an income statement, where they will look anything but impressive. And buying business at the wrong price can mean getting stuck holding the bag, and lead to writedowns as the deal goes sour or the risk turns stale. In fact, some Street firms take league tables and account volume so seriously that they will print any and all business, regardless of margin. For instance, it's not uncommon for those in the top three or five of a given category to compete wildly for slightly better positions each quarter-end, often by slashing fees. In bond deals, for example, the rule of thumb is "a million a billion": some banks will eat a million of losses for each billion of league table business they can execute. So if a bank is about $3 billion shy of the number 3 spot in U.S. fixed income with two days till quarter end, it'll call up one of the agencies or frequent borrowers and offer to float $3 billion of short-term paper that'll push it right over the top. Total cost: a few million. Buying business means sacrificing revenues and taking too much risk—central reasons for the Street's failure in a key area like internal risk management.

Uncertain Risk Appetite

Another tactical execution mistake comes from an unexpected source: dealing with risk. You'll recall that Wall Street exists, in part, to take, repackage, transfer, and hedge risks. Indeed, that is what many Wall Streeters do for a living, directly or indirectly. Theoretically, we'd expect risk issues to be front and center at every risk-taking firm. But we already know that that's not the case. In the last chapter we talked about the fact that the Street regularly screws up when it comes to taking and managing risks. This means risk becomes an afterthought, something to react to rather than plan for. Bank managers often fail to clearly articulate a risk appetite, or they simply ignore anything that's been articulated when the prospects of winning businesses are on the rise.

Let's start with the first problem. Even though lots of banks have lost piles of money over the years in their lending and trading activities, not all of them have decided what they want to do in the risk business: how much risk, where, with whom, how big the losses should be allowed to get before capitulation, which risks are off limits, what types of exceptions should be allowed, and so on—the important, daily nuts and bolts of managing risk. Some or all of these issues may remain unanswered. For instance, prior to 1998, Merrill Lynch had a decent enough risk management process, but it was disconnected from the top layer of management. So although individual risk decisions and positions may have looked okay, there was little input from directors or executives on how much risk the firm should be taking. The executives were too busy drumming up business; let's face it, risk isn't the most thrilling topic, especially for business-minded folks who want to get out and generate revenues, open new offices, or meet with high-level client executives or finance ministers. So, exposures just built up incrementally, without being explicitly tied to the firm's capital resources, strategic plans, client initiatives, market priorities, or shareholder expectations. No one upstairs let on to how much money they thought the firm should be willing to lose in risky business, and no one downstairs—either business managers or risk managers—was doing much asking, especially when the markets seemed so strong. No one thought the unthinkable could happen, so no one was really paying attention to the pockets of risk that were sprouting up around the firm. And unfortunately, no one was really questioning how money was being made (and a bank generally isn't going to be earning good revenues without taking some amount of risk). All that changed when Merrill got clocked in 1998. The Russian crisis, LTCM, and nasty market conditions in other assets (especially corporate spread products) led to huge losses—much bigger than anyone had expected, again because the folks upstairs had assumed nothing bad could happen, didn't really have a firm grip on what risks the firm was taking, and didn't express a view on whether exposures were too large, too small, or just right; unfortunately, the risk teams let them proceed without waving large warning flags. The end result: directors and executives denied any knowledge that risks had become so large, shot the head of risk management, overhauled the risk function, and finally defined a risk appetite. It took losing more than $1 billion of shareholder dollars for the firm to actually sit down and decide what to do in a core banking function like risk taking. Similar events occurred at Goldman, only the bank's epiphany came in 1994 after it lost $800 million in proprietary fixed income trading. Others have gone through similar problems and after-the-fact revelations, but others haven't, meaning they are ripe for the picking next time another 1994 or 1998 rolls around.

In some other cases, banks do define risk tolerance levels—and know how much they want to put on the table in each market, with each client—but the process is primarily form over substance because executives just move the goalposts when it suits them. It goes like this: a bank, loaded to the gills with risk (i.e., it's right at its stated tolerance level), gets a chance to execute a risky deal, and management magically finds room to squeeze in the extra ticket. Then an all-important block trade materializes, so the bank submits a bid because it wants to be a player. After it wins the bid, it has to wear the extra risk—maybe for a few hours, maybe for a few days (never mind that the "official" risk tolerance has been exceeded). Later on, the bank has a chance to do a junk bond for a new client, but it's got to be a bought deal, not best efforts. Management acquiesces, wins the deal, but can't move or hedge the bonds, and so gets stuck with risk that is now well in excess of authorized levels. The next day a client comes to the bank with a blind portfolio bid and, well, you get the point. The definition of a risk appetite is a farce, because the bank's executives always seem to find an "exceptional reason" for doing each incremental piece of business that comes down the pike. Like a junkie, the bank doesn't know when to stop, and the end result is a severe overextension (overdose?). Then comes the market hiccup, and all of that risk—approved on an exceptional basis by top management to three or four times the stated tolerance—blows up. With this M.O., there's really no point in even defining a risk appetite—executives are just fooling investors. But it happens, and that's how banks get into trouble: Chemical, Chase, and Manufacturers Hanover in the early—to mid-1980s, Drexel in the late 1980s, Citi and Kidder in the early 1990s, Goldman in 1994, CSFB, UBS, Merrill, and others in 1998, J.P. Morgan in the early millennium. All provide good examples of how to not tactically manage risk exposures. Failing to define a risk appetite or ignoring what's been defined is a central cause of all the risk-related problems discussed in chapter 7.

Bloated Costs

One final area of execution problems: cost-control. Costs are a perpetual problem for many Street firms; they constantly wrestle with their expense levels, not just in the obvious big-ticket areas like head count/compensation and technology, but in all sorts of other accounts, like real estate and office space, travel and entertainment, consultants, and so on. Wall Streeters like to live large: nice office space, the latest computers, expensive hotels and flights—all very costly. And some banks operate inefficiently. They don't do things in the smartest ways, and the most common solution to coping with the inefficiencies is to throw some warm bodies on the problem (especially during bull markets); that means nonproducing head count can get out of whack—there are lots of bodies running around, but bodies that don't generate revenues (they support the revenue generators). That's a pure drain on corporate resources: expensive head count that's not producing. And then there are all the highly paid consultants that are brought on for specific studies and advice on how to refocus strategies, retool internal control processes, redesign systems architecture, and so on. They produce lots of slick presentations and documents that tend to say very little and are unlikely to be implemented, all at great expense. So in the main, the Street is very sloppy with its costs. And how does tactical cost mismanagement lead to Street failures? Stretching for revenues. If a bank can't bring more down to the bottom line by keeping expenses in check, it has to boost top-line revenues: it has to win the business. For some, this may mean winning business at any cost, by doing a few of the no-nos we've already talked about. It doesn't mean every bank suffering from a bloated expense base is going to stumble or do the wrong thing, but the lure is there: if a bank has to keep earnings (and the stock price) buoyant, maybe, just maybe, there's enough temptation to do a little stretching.

Mismanagement 101

Gruntal, another on the list of Wall Street's departed, stands as an example of everything that a firm shouldn't be. Though it was one of the Street's oldest brokerages, its modern-day reputation and activities overshadowed the firm's origins and pedigree. Gruntal will be remembered for all of the bad—mismanagement, customer fraud, destruction of value—and none of the good.

Though the firm led a prosperous, if quiet, life from its founding in the nineteenth century through most of the twentieth century, things started changing in 1974: from that point on Gruntal's activities became sloppy, then suspect, and ultimately criminal. Mismanagement was the order of the day, and the firm's reputation marked a steady decline, which even deep pockets couldn't reverse. Between 1974 and 1995, the key period of the brokerage's slide, sales practices were often deceptive, customers were routinely put into deals that were far too risky for them, and the firm became known for dealing in marginal stocks, speculative securities, and investments that sometimes went sour. Indeed, the brokerage's reputation as one of the Street's "questionable" houses was forged at this time, and customers with any savvy avoided the firm. In 1994 a number of Gruntal employees were caught up in a $14 million client fraud scandal and wound up behind bars.

After Gruntal went public, Home Insurance bought the firm, but remained a passive owner—probably the last thing Gruntal needed. In fact, Home Insurance had so many problems of its own that it didn't even watch over brokers' activities, which continued to straddle the line of good and bad, right and wrong. Home eventually sold its stake to a few foreign insurance companies that were seeking a U.S. foothold; Zurich Financial Services wound up with a controlling stake through some preferreds and one-third of the board seats. To try and improve things, Zurich Financial booted out the management team and hired Robert Rittereiser, former CEO at E.F. Hutton, to run the show. The company entrusted him with rebuilding the outfit for subsequent sale and gave him a powerful incentive: Zurich Financial would get the first $225 million of cash from any sale, and Rittereiser and his team would get a 60 percent cut of the balance. Unfortunately, the executive team was not up to the task: even during the roaring bull market of the latter 1990s, when most Street firms were coining money, Gruntal bled every single year. Little wonder, as the firm continued to mismanage its operations: clients filed a large number of complaints and arbitration actions (some centered on loading retirees up with TMT stocks that subsequently collapsed, pitching products very aggressively, churning accounts, and so on); the Westchester Synagogue filed a claim against the firm for putting it into derivatives that wound up costing $630,000; managers were charged by employees with race and sex discrimination; some branches lacked managers, in violation of securities laws; high-powered salespeople were recruited for seven-figure packages, even as the firm was losing money; management expanded into investment banking by spending $20 million to buy a boutique known as Hampshire Securities—which did little business; the firm contracted to take two times more office space than it needed, at a cost of $40 million; executives were routinely overpaid given their poor performance; ad nauseam. In short, management of the firm was shoddy.

Zurich Financial finally lost patience with Rittereiser's poor leadership and started shopping the firm around in 1999/2000—Aetna, FleetBoston, Pacific Life, and others all looked and ran the other way. The company finally agreed to a sale with Prudential Securities; the parties reached agreement on September 10, 2001, only to see the deal collapse with the terrorist tragedy of the following day. That spelled the end of the firm: Gruntal hobbled along till mid-2002 (having brought the firm's liquid assets from a 1995 peak of $200 million to near zero as a result of all of the poor management decisions); six hundred brokers and $15 billion of customer assets were transferred to regional broker Ryan Beck and the rest of the company was stuffed in a shell company that filed for bankruptcy a few months later, leaving behind more than 90 arbitration cases involving $150 million of client losses.

Time to Reverse

Just as problematic as creating a business without proper strategic focus is reversing that blurred focus when things get a bit difficult or the environment too hostile. Unlike companies in other industries, which typically create a product or enter a market for the long haul (e.g., Intel's making of microchips, GM's building of SUVs), banks can be fickle. As we've noted, they sometimes operate in a knee-jerk fashion, responding to perceived market opportunities too rapidly: building up, exiting, rebuilding, and reexiting, often over relatively short time spans. That's expensive and confusing. It demonstrates lack of commitment and makes management seem inept.

Much of the strategic reversal is driven by the state of the markets, bank stock prices, and the competition. If the markets are strong and a bank's stock buoyant, executives start feeling confident, maybe even cocky. They may see the bank down the block getting into the credit derivative business or opening an office in Beijing, so they do the same. Never mind that it's not part of the multiyear strategic plan or hasn't been resourced; never mind that no one in the bank has the right skills to run the business or that the revenue projections look soft. Wall Street is about responding to market opportunities, right? Twelve months later bad economic data pummel the markets, or the bank's stock price comes under pressure, or the supposed opportunity to win big in credit derivatives or Beijing hasn't materialized (after all, those revenue projections were soft). That means it's time to reverse course: shut down the desk, close down the office (maybe the competitor down the block has already done the same thing). It doesn't matter what clients say or what regulators think, just get out of Dodge, as quickly as possible. That's what happens when firms don't develop sensible strategic plans and stick to them.

There are lots of examples we can point to here, some building on the "strategic initiatives" we mentioned above. Citi acquired Salomon in 1997, shut down all of the prop arbitrage activities in 1998, then started them up again in the new millennium. Merrill was in the energy trading business in the late 1980s, exited in the early 1990s, reentered in the mid-1990s, exited two years later, got back in during the late 1990s, then sold the business to Allegheny Energy in 2002. Some of the brave commercial banks that decided to spend top dollar to get into the securities business in the late 1990s bailed out at the turn of the millennium: FleetBoston shut down Robertson Stephens in 2002 after it failed to find a buyer for the once-hot technology house, US Bancorp unwound its $730 million investment in Piper after new management decided the business was too "volatile." All of the big banks that spent lots of dollars developing e-trading platforms decided to pull the plug on migrating business to the electronic world when volumes dropped off in 2001 (mothballing more than a few half-finished products and platforms). Then, as things revived in 2003, some of them changed their minds again, rehiring and throwing more dollars at people and technology. Then there's the international arena: we've already said that banks get excited about being in a new market and a new country and building up a physical presence (with much fanfare, ribbon-cutting ceremonies, big speeches about "long-term commitment" to the city/country); they stay awhile, then pull up stakes when headquarters cuts costs or decides that the offices are no longer part of the strategy (i.e., can't find any business to do). Till the next cycle. We've seen it many times: banks entering, exiting, and then reentering and reexiting in Latin America, Asia, the Far East. Merrill, Morgan Stanley, Schwab, Bank of America, Lehman, CSFB, and many others have all been caught up in the reversals. Lack of a clear focus and lack of commitment do little to help the Street advance its cause.

Sometimes there are good reasons for getting into a market and then abandoning it. Perhaps the economics are no longer good, the regulations too constraining, local competition too stiff, or costs too high; or perhaps the business flow dries up sooner than expected. And maybe a firm has to have another shot at it once the landscape changes: the marketplace is dynamic, and Street firms have to be able to react. But it's not that dynamic. It doesn't change so often that a bank should be changing course on the same business line or initiative every few years (and it shouldn't be buying the highs and selling the lows— which it would avoid doing if it had a strategy and stuck with it). Again, it's expensive (rehiring all of these traders, originators, bankers, support folks, putting in the systems, and so on) and it's confusing (so, who thinks Merrill is in the energy business or has a Canadian presence, or whether Stanley is committed to Japan, or CSFB is the place to go for online trading?). The reversals are simply a reflection of bad management and contribute directly to the Street's failures by demonstrating poor client commitment, lack of expertise, and inability to provide proper services and capital. The expense associated with the "start and stop" approach puts financial pressure on operations; for some, this might again lead to a bit of stretching in other areas (e.g., taking too much ill-advised risk or trying to win other pieces of business through less savory means).

Merrill's Changing Spots

Merrill serves as an interesting example of a firm that has changed its spots frequently, reacting to market opportunities, paying top dollar for acquisitions, and then reversing course when there's market softness or executive change. In the early 1990s the bank decided to get serious about dealing with its problems (e.g., clamping down on excessive costs and writing off all the bad bridge loans and equity investments it had taken on during the late 1980s); it wanted to become the dominant "everything to everyone" player and embarked on a significant expansion spree; the bank spent billions of dollars to hire teams and acquire other firms so that it could have a strong capital markets presence, an even bigger retail network, and a meaningful footprint in other markets. It bought most of its targets at pretty full premiums as it attempted repeatedly to do what perhaps only two banks in the world—Citi and HSBC—have been able to do: appeal to the local clientele. It purchased Mercury Asset Management (United Kingdom), Smith New Court (United Kingdom), McIntosh Securities (Australia), the rump of bankrupt Yamaichi Securities (Japan), FG Inversiones (Spain), Hotchkis and Wiley (United States), Midland Walwyn (Canada), Herzog Heine Geduld (United States), and lots of smaller shops. Total cost for all the purchases: nearly $10 billion. It set up a broad electronic banking joint venture with HSBC, with platforms, infrastructure and services that were supposed to dot the world (at a price tag of $500 million each over four years). It established a joint venture with DSP to tap into the Indian market, took a majority stake in a Thai securities firm and created a significant international banking platform in Dublin. It opened offices, subsidiaries, and ventures throughout Latin America, Asia, Eastern Europe, Western Europe, the Middle East.

Unfortunately for Merrill (and its investors), much of this "strategic expansion" turned out to be a disappointment (Smith New Court, which gave it a dominant presence in European equities, stands out as one of the few bright spots). By the turn of the decade, Merrill's management had reversed course on virtually all of its strategic moves: it shut down, sold, or whacked back anything it could, basically undoing most of what had been built up in the 1990s: Midland sold, Yamaichi closed, the HSBC joint venture blown away, glitzy offices shut down. What it couldn't sell outright it tried to somehow meld into existing operations (probably being reminded, on a daily basis, of just how much it overpaid for the assets). Mercury, in particular, has proven to be a tough nut for the firm to crack: the "crown jewel of asset management," which cost $5.3 billion, didn't pan out as expected. Though the purchase was supposed to propel the firm into the asset management stratosphere (boosting funds under management from $500 billion to an estimated $1 trillion by 2002), reality has been quite different: by 2002 the combined Merrill/Mercury platform still had about $500 billion under management, half of the anticipated target. To be sure, a nasty market correction had something to do with missing the target by a million miles, but so did poor portfolio performance, internal culture clashes, departure of key personnel, client defections, and lawsuits (e.g., Unilever, Sainsbury, Co-operative Group, and others sued and were paid off by the bank in out-of-court settlements); non-U.S. assets under management declined steadily, lots of longtime accounts departed. So Merrill absorbed the Mercury branding and tried to cram the whole unit together and make the best of a bad situation.

Other parts of the international scene have also been tough for Merrill, maybe because deep down, the bank is still all about Main Street USA, just as Charlie Merrill had intended back in the 1940s. Lots of confusion. Consider, for instance, that the bank formed a partnership with Sun Hung Kai Securities in Hong Kong in 1985, pulled out in 1987, started rebuilding modestly in 1992–1993, ramped up heavily in 1995–1996, shut most things down post-1997, then started building up again at the turn of the millennium (think of all that hiring, firing, office-space leasing, subleasing, client confusion). Or Japan: the bank started its retail branch network in 1965 and had expanded to a dozen offices by the late 1980s; it shut most of its network down in 1992, then decided to restart it in 1996–1997 (buying dozens of Yamaichi's branches and hiring thousands of its brokers). But long-anticipated deregulation didn't result in a mass migration of Japanese Moms and Pops to U.S.-style investing and mutual funds, so the bank ate $150 million to $200 million of losses per year, for four years, and then closed down virtually all of the retail network in 2001—back to square 1. The same in Canada: during the 1980s Merrill built up a retail brokerage firm throughout the country to complement its capital markets business. It shut it down in 1990. It jumped back in 1998, paying C$1.3 billion for Canadian securities firm Midland Walwyn. It reversed itself in 2001, selling it to CIBC for C$650 million. Same in South Africa: it built up a capital markets operation in the mid-1990s through the Smith Borkum Hare platform that came with Smith New Court and expanded its retail capabilities at the same time; a few years later it shuttered most of it, selling off the retail piece to local interests. The same in Thailand: it took a majority stake in Phatra Securities in 1998 and sold it off in 2003. The same in Germany: the German private banking unit that Merrill created in the late 1990s went on the block in 2003 and was eventually picked up by UBS. The same happened in the United Kingdom and on the Continent, the same in Australia, the same in Ireland. Build up, close down, build up, close down—all very confusing and expensive. The back and forth hasn't been good for shareholders (who have had to foot the top-of-the-market purchase prices and exit costs) or clients (who, once again, see a firm enter, build up, indicate commitment, then withdraw). What's the strategy?

BREAKDOWN #3: POOR SKILLS AND CONTROLS

The Street's failures are also driven by a third breakdown: lack of proper skills and controls. We've already said that good governance (to say nothing of prudent behavior and common sense) demands that a bank running client and risk businesses have the right people in place. If it doesn't, all hell's going to break lose. And the same applies to controls. We've already touched on the subject a bit in the last few chapters: if a bank can't keep track of things operationally because it doesn't have the right knowledge base, framework, or infrastructure, then it's going to fail at specific tasks, meaning losses for the bank, its shareholders, and its customers.

Poor Skills

A good deal of what the Street does is pretty technical: arranging deals, pricing and selling securities, processing trades, managing risks, auditing internal processes. If things are technical and specialized, then you want technically competent and specialized people involved. Unfortunately, some banks don't have the right folks in the right spots: they hire or transfer those who are wholly unqualified into an area that demands a very specific skill set. Why? Maybe it's cheaper or easier, or the candidate is a friend of a friend who really needs a job; or maybe it's because the bank wants to find a home for a team player who has outlived his or her usefulness in a particular area (that's when a senior government bond trader becomes head of U.S. derivatives trading, or an investment banker moves to junk bond sales, or a regional CFO moves over to run global operations and settlements). The point is not why it happens, but that it does. And a bank that believes skills don't matter is standing on a very slippery slope. If it doesn't have the skills to sell Japanese government bonds, decompose and process multileg derivative transactions, or lend on a collateralized basis, then it shouldn't pretend that it does. Unfortunately, some banks ignore this fundamental concept and try to do things they can't, a process that is guaranteed to lead to mistakes and losses.

Step into almost any bank on Wall Street and you'll find financial controllers and auditors who don't understand the nature of the business they are meant to be "independently monitoring." Go to any trading desk and ask a few traders about what kind of credit risks they are exposed to, and you'll get some pretty unsatisfactory answers. Step over to the institutional sales desk and ask some salespeople what their secondary exit strategy is if the lead order for the big bond deal vanishes at the last minute. No clue. Walk over to the risk department and ask a few credit officers to tell you why a currency swap is riskier than an interest-rate swap. Blank stares. Ask the technologists what kind of pricing routines are being incorporated into the new technology platform. More blank stares. And so on. It's generally evident that not everyone has the skills to do the job they're supposed to do. What's the end result? Mistakes: things go awry when those responsible aren't qualified. Worse, when someone displays his ignorance about something, less scrupulous people can jump in and take advantage of the situation—and that contributes directly to the Street's failure. For instance, in the Kidder, Barings, Allfirst, and NatWest cases, fast-talking traders bamboozled internal auditors and financial controllers. In all cases the postmortems revealed that some of the auditors and accountants were too unqualified to spot problems. There are, unfortunately, other examples of the same problems that never make the press.

This doesn't mean everyone has to be knowledgeable about everything, and it certainly doesn't mean that folks can't be given the chance to learn. The point is that those in positions of authority must be conversant with the main issues (or at least know where to go for help); they can't wing it or fake it. And their bosses should be responsible and accountable, so that someone who knows what's going on is actually there to take charge if (when) things fall apart. But maybe it's just not possible to expect that in a firm with five thousand, or ten thousand, or fifty thousand people. In which case, the stakeholders had better pray that whoever's sitting in a sensitive chair doesn't blow it too badly.

Poor Controls

The Street also screws up internally when it tries to operate without the right controls. This problem is revealed repeatedly through control-induced losses so big that they make the evening news, as well as the insidious, slow bleeds that no one ever hears about: the ones that cost $1,000 or $10,000 each (rather than the Leeson—or Rusniak-esque half-billion or billion) but that happen every day—death by a thousand cuts, because the right controls aren't in place to keep silly mistakes from happening. These "operational errors" usually involve things like bad trade or wire instructions, delays in getting funds from point A to point B, losing track of securities or special trades because they can't be wedged into trading systems, missing something important in a confirmation or legal document, miscalculating corporate action details, and so forth. It's all mundane operational stuff that winds up costing the Street a minimum of several billion dollars per year (and probably more, but no one is really making any of the information public—it's a bit embarrassing).

Why does this happen? Because firms don't have the right structure or mechanisms to keep track of what they're doing (and they might compound the problem by throwing some relatively inexperienced folks into the mix). From a high-level perspective, breakdown occurs when controls don't allow for proper segregation of duties. There is no independence, meaning the revenue generators are doing all the back-office work as well: confirming trades, funding their own margin balances, reconciling their own payables and receivables, and verifying their own marks and valuations. This, as we've seen, has the potential of leading to spectacular problems a la Barings, Allfirst, Daiwa Bank, UBS, and Kidder. Separation of duties is such a fundamental control mechanism that it's amazing that anyone still has to talk about it in this day and age; but the fact that a major explosion occurs every few years suggests that not everyone on the Street has learned.

At a micro level, control failure can come from infrastructure problems related to the hardware, software, and machinery that drives the Street; it can also come from flawed control policies. Most banks live and die by two things: data and technology. Data are all the information needed to conduct business: execute and value trades, compute risks, hedge positions, allocate profits and losses, determine collateral and margin, move money around, and so forth. It's a complicated issue. There is so much information floating around, some good, some bad, some essential, and some useless, that if a bank can't manage its data flow and surround it with controls that ensure integrity, then it's going to be doing a lot of business on the basis of garbage data. Most banks have pretty serious data problems, which suggests that more than a few dollars are being lost through mistakes that are otherwise avoidable. The other element is technology. No one on Wall street tries to do anything without technology; the days of pen and paper are gone, which means that the entirety of any bank's technology has to be up to scratch if it's going to succeed. If the underlying hardware/code can't accommodate new business, trades, clients, communications, and data handling, then all sorts of control problems creep into the mix, meaning more wasted time and effort, and more losses. This kind of scenario is typical: a bank's technology platform can't handle a new product that a trading desk has created, so management is faced with two choices: forgo the business till the technology guys can accommodate the product, or allow business to proceed by putting it into a spreadsheet till someone can figure it all out. What do you think happens? Right. It's full steam ahead, and the trade winds up on a spreadsheet on some trader's machine. Then, knowing that one deal has been approved, the trader decides that it's okay to keep printing similar deals. The floodgates open up and the trader soon has an entire village of trades living off to the side—not attached to anything the firm does, not forming part of the daily P&L close, or the books and records reconciliation process, or any other control mechanism. Then a 1987, 1997, 1998, or 2001 comes along, and the village of trades gets flattened. The trader or controller rediscovers the remains, probably by accident, and has to acknowledge that, indeed, the bank has lost $1 million (or $10 million, or $100 million) because of control failures (i.e., "we forgot about the trades because they weren't on the main system"). Many banks have been through this scenario a few times and some will continue to, because business pressures routinely overwhelm control capabilities, despite what executives say (find a senior Wall Street executive who's going to say no to a $1 billion, ten-year exotic derivative with a prized client [with $25 million of profit baked in] just because the system can't handle a particular aspect of the trade). So, until data and technology and general control procedures can keep pace with hard-charging business initiatives built atop aggressive business budgets/targets, expect more control problems (with shareholders digging in to pay for each successive round of blowups).

Similar infrastructure problems can come from bad policies and procedures. Those that are inadequate in controlling aspects of the business are virtually guaranteed to lead to more headaches and losses—for banks and their clients. If a control policy doesn't exist or fails to properly address the risks of a business, including local characteristics or nuances that might make it unique, the practical result may be internal arbitrage or exploitation by traders, or execution mistakes in dealing with client-facing situations. In fact, major banks spend considerable time and effort trying to craft control policies (e.g., settlement procedures, collateral management processes, stale/illiquid inventory valuation, mark-to-model benchmarking) so that they can plug the gaps. But in a large institution doing lots of business, this can be difficult to achieve (particularly when new products are being introduced, and new client relationships established, on a continuous basis); without a great deal of diligence, control policies can quickly become outdated, ineffective, or irrelevant, weakening the control environment.

It's not hard to see how poor skills and controls can lead directly to failures, including avoidable operational and trading risk losses, mistreatment of clients, and internal fraud. In fact these breakdowns, along with flawed governance and bad management, lead directly to the Street's shortcomings. Sometimes flaws in the external environment can compound these internal problems, as we'll see in the following chapters; when this happens the results can be particularly ugly.

Chapter 9

EXTERNAL WEAKNESS

Wall Street's failures aren't caused solely by the actions of misguided directors and executives, overly aggressive traders and bankers, unscrupulous salespeople, conflicted researchers, or inexperienced control personnel. They are aided, knowingly or unknowingly, by what happens in the external environment. There's no passing the buck here, of course. The Street itself is primarily responsible for what it does, how it does it, how it fails, and the damage that it causes, and there can be no scapegoats or shifting of responsibility. But external forces are part of the system of checks and balances. Regulators and auditors, representing two of these checks, have to step up and take their share of the blame when things go awry. Though much of what they do is successful and useful, not all of it goes as planned. These groups can be weak links in the chain, contributing directly or indirectly to the Street's problems, and if they aren't held accountable for falling down on the job, then what's the point of having checks and balances and examining Wall Street's actions from the outside? Why bother regulating, reviewing, inspecting, or auditing banks and their personnel if the parties that are nominally responsible for this oversight aren't up to the task or, worse, botch it up? Why create rules or laws that are ineffective or ignored? Wouldn't it be better to save taxpayers and shareholders a bunch of money? Wouldn't it be better to remove the sometimes questionable "regulatory/independent auditor" imprimatur that shareholders and retail and institutional clients still rely on?

Regulators and auditors aren't the only ones that fail to scrutinize, control, or discipline from outside. Credit rating agencies, activist institutional investors, and squeaky wheel consumer defense groups have a role to play, too, and they sometimes mess it up. But for our discussion in this chapter we'll stick with the two main overseers, since they're the ones that everyone turns to when things go pear-shaped.

WEAKNESS #1: STUMBLING REGULATORS

Since Wall Street is so large and complex, it has to be regulated by a number of different bodies: the SEC, the CFTC, the Federal Reserve, the Office of the Comptroller of the Currency, and certain state agencies. Each of these groups has jurisdiction over specific areas and is responsible for reviewing and enforcing particular activities (though sometimes they try to horn in on one another's territory, as when state attorneys general take on some of the SEC's role in rooting out bad research or mutual fund sales and trading practices, or the SEC and CFTC slug it out over certain kinds of derivatives; these encroachments aren't necessarily bad because regulators, like anyone else, can get a little sleepy on the job). Regardless of the area they represent, regulators face a thankless task and deserve some gratitude for even trying to pull it off. Their jobs are enormously difficult. They try to succeed against all odds and generally seem to be doing the right thing; sometimes they get it right, and sometimes they don't, but even when they fail it's usually not for lack of trying.

Here's the general picture: regulators of banks, securities firms, brokers, and funds are government officials responsible for inspecting the activities and financial strength of individual institutions. When they can't do all of the daily monitoring, they delegate duties to SROs and individual firms (and their compliance/control functions)—which, as we've said, doesn't always work out as well as it should. Regulators get paid a decent government wage for their efforts, they get to work 9 to 5 and have good job security. Most have college degrees (even advanced ones), and some have general training in the financial industry, though for many, especially field examiners, financial review and enforcement is their first job.

That background sounds adequate until you consider the fact that regulators are charged with monitoring very complicated institutions that run complex activities through lots of onshore and offshore entities. They may not fully understand everything that's going on, they may not have access to all the information they require, and they may be misled by anyone who is inclined to mislead. They are dealing with individuals who often have little respect for the regulatory process. And they are woefully understaffed (e.g., in 2003 the SEC's Office of Compliance, Inspection and Examination had only five hundred investigators covering more than eight thousand mutual funds and seven thousand investment advisors; the agency's case load has increased by 80 percent over the past two decades, but its staff has grown less than 30 percent.) In this light, things seem a bit more challenging—maybe it's not really a surprise that they can't always be effective.

Unfortunately, the regulation process is plagued by shortcomings: inexperienced regulators are often assigned to inspection tasks, the review process can revert to "checking the boxes," and the status quo may go unchallenged and conflicts unchecked. If (when) something blows up, regulators may be the last on the scene, which doesn't help those who have been burned. All of this means the external review process can be ineffective, lowering the probability of helping the Street avoid failure; mistakes or bad behavior might not get caught till it's too late (if at all—think about what's probably out there, now, that no one has discovered). Let's take a closer look at these problems.

Too Green

Unfortunately, some of what regulators do is based on the efforts of junior examiners who haven't got a clue about Wall Street does or how it does it; many are just too inexperienced to dig into things that are substantive and potentially important. They often lack the practical understanding of how financial institutions and other intermediaries work, and where some of the real problems lie. And the fact that they are so junior means they can be misled by those seeking to mislead them. A fresh-out-of-college examiner querying a seasoned financial controller, trader, or risk manager about some apparent discrepancy can have the wool pulled over her eyes very quickly. Is she going to query, challenge, criticize, or probe incessantly? Probably not, because doing so takes confidence born of experience. Again, it's not her fault: she is almost certainly doing the best job possible given limited knowledge and experience (as are her colleagues). But relatively inexperienced folks can't add much value in protecting the Street's stakeholders. (An independent report by consulting firm McKinsey, covering the state of the SEC noted that the agency "lacks the institutional structure and experience needed to systematically identify risks.")[1]

Why are so many green folks making the rounds? Economics. As we've said, these are government jobs, meaning government pay scales and government budgeting. You can't attract experienced talent without paying up, and you can't pay up if you don't have taxpayer dollars to put on the table. It's an unfortunate, and commonplace, reality.

Checking the Boxes

Regulators fail when they are willing to accept form over substance, checklists over forensics. They walk away happy because the apple is shiny on the surface, never mind that it's rotten to the core. A typical regulatory inspection (conducted by a few junior examiners under the auspices of someone a bit more senior) goes like this: the juniors run around collecting trade tickets, credit files, P&L reports, and risk information and then try to piece certain things together. They may conduct a few interviews with control staffers, play a little game of "gotcha" on unimportant stuff (e.g., this ticket had the wrong time stamp on it, that credit file was missing last year's balance sheet . . . who cares?). Then they go off, write up a report (aka "deficiency letter") that basically says most things are okay (they have to throw in some "room for minor improvements" here and there, because they don't want it to seem as though a bank is perfect. We all know they aren't!); sometimes a bank gets cited for things that are a bit more serious, but that doesn't necessarily mean much. And, that's that. Till next year, or whenever the cycle brings them back around. Again, we can't really blame them: they are placed in a situation in which they simply can't effectively sniff out problems. They are almost doomed to failure the moment they step into the lobby of a bank, because they often focus on things that are irrelevant at the expense of things that are vitally important—things that may be detectable only to those with a great deal of experience and a thorough understanding of the business and the firms. Think about it this way: if a bank's internal auditors, who live and breathe the firm every day, day in and day out, often fail to spot problems, how on earth can those poor regulatory examiners, who swoop in for a week or two, find them? They can't, of course. So, there's probably not much value added in their activities, yet everyone feels warm and fuzzy when the examiners issue their inspection report with the word "passed" stamped on the cover.

This is all somewhat dangerous because lax regulatory scrutiny breeds false comfort. Constituents may believe everything is copasetic when they hear that Bank XYZ has just passed the annual regulatory examination or is in full compliance with leverage and capital rules, control recommendations, or margin guidelines. But in fact much of the information (though not all) that regulators demand, review, and approve falls into the "form over substance" category, meaning that the real protections that stakeholders need may not form part of the regulatory review program. For instance, a bank may confirm that it has separated its financial control unit from the derivatives trading desk so that valuations can be independently reviewed. Regulators are always happy to hear that, and will put a big check mark in the "passed" column. But the regulators can never know that the controller assigned to independently verify the values of the long-dated, exotic option book has been out of college for only two years, has been browbeaten into submission by a few traders, and routinely signs off on the marks they provide (and they, in turn, have misvalued the book by $50 million in their favor so they can earn bigger bonuses). Form over substance =

false comfort = beware. Some institutions have figured out that if they fulfill these basic "form over substance" regulatory requirements they can keep officials at bay and then pretty much do whatever they want to do (not that they would decide to do anything untoward or malevolent; they just don't want regulators hovering over them, watching their every move).

Of course, there are rare occasions when regulators (in whatever guise) step out of their molds and do things a bit differently. They don't focus on liquidity, capital adequacy, regulatory value-at-risk, and adherence to the minutiae of the Securities and Exchange Acts of 1933 and 1934; they go for broke. Acting on a hunch, a tip from a whistleblower, or a loose gathering of facts and complaints, they send in some seasoned investigators or lawyers to focus on an unexpected area, grab a bunch of files and e-mails that may indicate some wrongdoing, grill some of the senior folks about why they did things the way they did—and catch them misbehaving. That was the case with former District Attorney (and New York City mayor) Rudolph Giuliani prosecuting a bunch of investment bankers for insider trading scams in the late 1980s/early 1990s, Spitzer blowing the lid on Wall Street's research scandal and the no-no mutual fund trading practices in the millennium, Galvin and Massachusetts officials doing the same up in Boston. The end result: more substantive, meaningful and helpful efforts to keep Wall Street honest. But it's still the exception, not the rule.

The Status Quo Is Okay

Sometimes regulators fail to add value because they don't challenge the status quo. There's great comfort when things work they way they've always worked, and that's very true down on Wall Street. Although Wall Street is changing continually, regulations and compliance practices often remain unchanged. That means that if regulators see that banks aren't conforming 100 percent to the technical rules (or, indeed, that no rules exist to control certain activities), but no one seems to be complaining or getting hurt, they may just let things carry on. Why rock the boat?

We can see the practical manifestation of this in a number of areas. For instance, OTC derivatives, the financial contracts that we talked about in chapter 4, are useful when banks and customers know what's going on, and there's no funny business related to pricing, hedging, or valuations. But they can be lethal when they aren't properly controlled and scrutinized. OTC contracts are, of course, unregulated. The CFTC oversees the exchange-traded market; futures and options traded on the CME, CBOT, and other floors are under the eye of the regulators. Not so with the listed markets' spicy cousin. Why? Status quo.

OTC contracts haven't been regulated for the past three decades, so why start now? The market has grown to $87 trillion in notional value ($6.4 trillion in credit risk), and there haven't been any major catastrophes (indeed, the market has weathered a couple of nasty moments and come out fine), so what's the fuss (never mind that some clients have been badly burned)? There have been a few half-hearted attempts at regulation (e.g., in the mid-1980s and early 1990s) but all have been easily batted down, largely through the lobbying efforts of International Swaps and Derivatives Association (ISDA, Wall Street's derivative industry representative and a most effective lobbying force). And there have also been a few meager attempts to inject greater transparency into the derivatives marketplace, getting banks to disclose something meaningful about the risks they're running (because they are often quite substantial). Unfortunately, the regulatory efforts have yielded very little; bank discussion of OTC derivative risks in the quarterly and annual reports is just so much thin gruel. Warren Buffett has been good enough to remind all of us that derivatives are a tricky and far too opaque, business: "When [we] finish reading the long footnotes detailing the derivative activities of major banks, the only thing we understand is that we don't understand how much risk the institution is running."[2] If Buffett can't figure it out, maybe there's a lesson in it. So life marches on, because the status quo in OTC derivatives is okay.

Front running down on the floor of the NYSE (and AMEX and other exchanges?) is another example. We've noted in chapter 6 that when specialists put on a trade before executing a customers' transaction in order to profit from subsequent market movements, they are actually breaking the rules. But it still happens, all the time. Why? Because of regulatory status quo, along with wholly ineffective SRO oversight. Specialists have always done a bit of front running, it's how they make a little extra money to pay the bills and take on the risk they're supposed to take. It's just another one of Wall Street's "open secrets." In fact, the regulators don't seem to have beaten up on the exchange(s) too hard. In the early 1960s, late 1960s, early 1990s, and late 1990s, the SEC asked the NYSE to clean things up, but it has been slow to follow up or crack down (this is often the case until the public spotlight shines on the whole matter; then everyone seems to wake up, at least for awhile). We can rewind to 1963, when the SEC accused the NYSE of "tenderness rather than severity" in disciplining members involved in rule violations and infractions like front running. But what did the SEC do about it? Nothing, apparently, because 40 years later the same issues are plaguing the industry.

And then there's the Wall Street research problem we talked about earlier. At the risk of a little Monday morning quarterbacking, we have to wonder whether regulators shouldn't accept a bit of responsibility for the whole fiasco. They didn't exactly challenge any of the questionable conflicts/structural issues that were in play for a decade or more. Why? Bull market status quo. Markets were booming, the little guys were getting rich, the big guys were getting rich, the banks were getting rich—a nice, happy party, so why not let it keep going? Why crack down on research analysts playing on both sides of the fence? Why challenge the obviously conflicted reporting lines between banking and research? In fact, the structural conflicts between research and banking had existed for so many years they were taken as industry norm. (Of course when the New York Attorney General shook things up, the rest of the regulatory community jumped on the bandwagon and started screaming and shouting.)

There are many others instances of sticking with the status quo, like market timing of mutual funds and allowing fund companies to continue charging 12(b)1 marketing fees, issues that regulators have known about for a long time and/or have promised to fix but haven't. That's not effective regulation.

Conflicts

Sometimes regulators fail to do an effective job because they are conflicted. At a micro level this can be as simple as a junior examiner, who hopes one day to be a big Wall Street player, glossing over an issue or giving a better examination rating than warranted in order to please the bank and have a shot at a future job. When authorities don't prohibit regulators from moving to the Street (they don't), and the Street has no rules against hiring regulators (it doesn't), then the potential for conflict of interest is real. Conflicts can also exist at a macro level. The most obvious example is with the major exchanges, which operate as commercial entities with SRO arms. Let's take the NYSE as an example. The exchange is a commercial entity owned by its membership (the thirteen hundred seats that constitute the exchange) that makes markets in thousands of stocks. It has also been anointed with special regulatory powers, meaning it watches over its own every day, making sure that everyone behaves properly. That sounds like trouble in the making. How can the exchange, owned by the members, watch over the members who own it—without prejudice or bias? And until 2003, many of the board's directors came from Wall Street (of the 27 seats, 12 came from Wall Street), another conflict. And the board's compensation committee (the one that paid the then-head of the NYSE, Dick Grasso, more than $140 million) had Wall Street reps on it. Another conflict. So much for independence in the governance process. In fact, it took the Grasso pay explosion to get officials to act: ex-Citi chief John Reed, acting as temporary CEO of the

NYSE, overhauled aspects of the board by cutting the number of director seats by two-thirds and kicking off the industry reps (permanent CEO John Thain, late of Goldman, may continue the overhaul). The SRO structure, whether related to the NYSE or any other exchange, is a vestige of history, of course, which brings us back to the status quo. Status quo and conflict don't make for a very effective regulatory regime.

───────────

Watching The Specialists

Even as the NYSE tried to shake off all the bad PR related to its well-compensated (and ultimately deposed) CEO Dick Grasso, the exchange's regulatory arm (after considerable prodding from the SEC) started an investigation into improper trading practices within the specialist community on the floor, including the seven that handle about 95 percent of all business: Goldman, Sachs' SLK unit, LaBranche, Fleet Specialists, Bear Wagner (with Bear Stearns as a minority owner), Susquehanna, Van Der Moolen Specialists and Performance Specialists. The main issues centered on interpositioning and skimming in advance of customer execution. The whole affair came to light when two firms failed to pass the NYSE's surveillance audit, which opened up a Pandora's box. Of course, the NYSE's SRO arm was a bit slow on the uptake, so the SEC did a separate investigation and came up with some damaging material of its own.

As we said earlier in the book, specialists exist to provide an orderly market in their assigned stocks (e.g., Fleet is GE's specialist, SLK is AIG's, and so on) and do so by operating an auction book of bids and offers, and buying or selling from their own accounts when there is an imbalance (not always, of course: the specialists covering HealthSouth and Enron and Global Crossing must have been out on a coffee break when the stocks got pummeled through huge selling imbalances; lucky they didn't have to step in and buy up any of those shares as the companies were in free fall). They are hugely powerful, controlling 80 percent of trading volume in Big Board shares. But the specialist-based floor system has been criticized by many as arcane, a relic that protects the membership at the expense of the client—and one that can be (and is) abused. Calls for a move to electronic trading and execution, similar to the Nasdaq and electronic trading model, have grown louder in recent years, but the exchange membership has held firm. (The NYSE benefits, in part, from the SEC's "trade through" rule, which was created to make sure that investors trading on regional exchanges get the best national price. The NYSE generally has the best "immediate" quotes, but they are not fixed [as they are via electronic platforms], meaning NYSE specialists wind up getting 80 percent of the business and can still print at the price they choose [some have noted that the NYSE ignores better regional prices several thousand times per week]).

Even though specialists make money from commission-based buys and sells, they make their real money from proprietary dealing (a potential conflict of interest, because they have complete visibility to trading flows). One-third of all volume on the NYSE is driven by proprietary trading; that's not surprising, when we consider that the margins are enormously attractive, 30–60 percent. To make things fair, specialists are supposed to stick to some fundamental rules: as we've noted, interposition and negative obligation rules require specialists to stay out of the way if there are enough buyers and sellers (though they still have reasonable discretion in matching buy/sell orders and intervening as they see fit). They can't front run (trade ahead of customer orders), collude (prearrange trades) or penny jump (skim off the top).

Despite the potential for abuse in these areas, regulatory crackdown by the exchange itself has been negligible, perhaps because of the inherent conflict that exists in the dual SRO/exchange function. Stories abound regarding bad execution prices that are resolved only when specifically challenged, big price discrepancies, and problems getting orders filled in a timely fashion at the price expected. Or strange behavior, like no trades within a specialist's account for a while, then a flurry of volume and change in price when a customer order comes down, and then execution of the customer trade. Through it all, the NYSE's regulatory arm has been very slow to discipline. Even after the Oakwood scandal (involving fraudulent trading by a member firm), when the SEC asked the NYSE to shore up its regulatory process, things didn't move very quickly; the SEC reminded the exchange again, in 1999, of its shortcomings and, as we've said, was a catalyst in jump-starting the investigation into interpositioning. In fact, the NYSE hasn't been harsh with its own at all: it levied only $19 million in fines between 1997 and 2002 while the SEC doled out $480 million. In fact, the ineffectiveness of the NYSE's SRO arm became clearer when the SEC published its investigative report in late 2003. The report criticized the NYSE for failing to supervise the specialists, ignoring blatant rule violations for a period of up to three years (which affected 2 billion traded shares), and turning a blind eye to front running and interpositioning violations that cost investors $155 million. The report went on to note that the exchange's surveillance arm was overburdened and didn't have the right tools to engage in supervisory activities (to wit, between 2001 and 2002 the surveillance system spit out 640 alerts, while the SEC indicates that 8,000 should have been flagged). The SEC also noted the lack of self-imposed penalties and the ineffective nature of controls within specialist organizations. Several months after the investigation a number of specialists agreed to pay $240 million in fines for their infractions. But that misses the broader point: someone else ought to be watching the specialists.

———————

The NYSE isn't the only SRO, of course. Nasdaq, AMEX, and the regional stock exchanges operate in the same way and are prone to the same problems (remember the Nasdaq's little "even eighth" problem from chapter 5). The AMEX hasn't been shining bright when it comes to administering regulatory duties. In 2003 the SEC came down hard on the exchange, first for failing to regulate the activity of its members and then for lying to regulators to cover it up. It all goes back to September 2000 when AMEX agreed to improve its surveillance process because regulators had discovered that specialists were engaged in two-tier options pricing (basically a form of price fixing in which wide prices were posted on-screen while tighter prices were given to floor traders); specialists also systematically ignored orders from professional clients or executed them at poorer prices than those indicated. But AMEX didn't really do anything to solve the problems. In late 2001 the practice was still occurring (e.g., 60 percent of professional orders were executed versus 95 percent of customer orders, discriminatory pricing and order handling still took place, and so on). Complaints sent to the exchange's disciplinary committee were apparently ignored as a matter of course. Things got even worse when the AMEX reported to the SEC that three hundred violations had been referred to the committee for action over the period in question when only a handful had actually been forwarded. The same thing happened on the Chicago Stock Exchange: the SEC charged the regional forum with failing in its supervisory duties between 1998 and 2001 (the regulatory arm was unable to spot 37 instances of front running over 12 months, failed to provide quote information 76 times, and so on). All of these collapses reflect poorly on the SRO concept. The same structure exists in the futures and options sector, where exchanges have been granted SRO status by the CFTC and the National Futures Association; so, even though the CFTC watches over what they're doing, it gives them slack to enforce rules and regulations on a daily basis. The question is whether the exchanges have actually been given enough rope to hang themselves, just as the NYSE, Nasdaq, and AMEX have. The SRO structure, in the form existing through the early twenty-first century, is a conflicted arrangement that renders its oversight capabilities ineffective.

Closing the Barn Door

Sometimes regulators close the barn door after the horse is out in the pasture, which is not particularly helpful. The Street's problems (and, ultimately, failures) become larger because regulators aren't aware of problems, or they're too slow to react, or don't have enough resources to do the job—or all of the above. This means something has to explode before it attracts regulatory attention (or, as the McKinsey report on the SEC noted, "enforcement actions usually occur too late to prevent large market losses").[3] There are so many examples of this routine that it seems to be standard operating procedure rather than an occasional misstep; rarely are regulators ahead of the game, being proactive, anticipating and stopping problems before they become problems. To wit, clamping down on stock market margin requirements, insider trading, and due diligence *after* the Great Crash; coming down hard on the NYSE and brokerages in 1969 *after* fails-to-deliver reached $4 billion and more than a hundred brokers had hit the wall; imposing bank capital rules *after* widespread emerging market debt reschedulings in the 1980s; reconfiguring NASDs SRO process *after* the spread collusion affair of the early 1990s; tightening up on the issuance and sale of structured notes *after* retail and institutional investors got badly burned in the mid-1990s; warning about the deficiencies of market risk value-at-risk models *after* the 1998 crisis proved they were flawed; demanding a separation of research and banking *after* the touting, spinning, and fraudulent behavior had already inflicted heavy damage in the millennium; and so on.

Again, it's kind of hard to blame the regulators: they are stretched, dealing with too many crises at the same time, so how can anyone expect them to be proactive? But their inaction leaves another opening for Wall Street's misadventures: banks can ride a particular unethical or illegal gravy train for as long as it takes the regulators to get wise to what they're doing.

The message is clear: regulatory loopholes, shortcomings, and flaws mean that the Street isn't always protected from hurting itself or others. These gaps allow the Street's failures to proceed unchallenged from time to time. Perhaps the scariest result is the false comfort that is bred. Shareholders and clients may think that everything is proceeding fine under the watchful gaze of the regulatory police, who swoop in and eliminate evildoers at the first hint of trouble (or even before!). Experience suggests this is very unlikely.

WEAKNESS #2: STUMBLING AUDITORS

Let's now take a look at the external auditors to see how they contribute to some of the Street's problems. Auditors, mostly from the Big 4 (Deloitte and Touche, Ernst and Young, PricewaterhouseCoopers, and KPMG) are independent assessors of a company's financial position and controls. They are meant to audit— that is, review, inspect, examine, verify—what a company is doing. At the end of the process they come up with a statement that usually says everything is okay (you know, the annual statements are a fair representation of the financial position, everything conforms to generally accepted accounting principles, etc.—which, unfortunately, tells us not a great deal). When stakeholders see a clean audit opinion they are supposed to breathe easier and sleep better at night because they know that all those certified public accountants have scoured the books of client companies (including Wall Street banks) and determined everything is in good shape.

Producing the audit signoff and management letter for the annual report is only the visible face of what auditors do. Much of their job happens behind the scenes—things like verifying controls, policies, and procedures and checking models and valuations. Which brings to mind the possibility of technical inadequacies. And even though auditors audit, they also like to do extra consulting work for banks (for all companies, actually). Which brings to mind the potential for conflicts of interest. So let's take a look at how technical inadequacies and conflicts of interest cause the auditors to stumble—doing nothing to strengthen what's going on down on Wall Street.

Technical Inadequacies

We already know that Wall Street is a pretty complicated place. A lot of what happens there is technically demanding and requires a certain degree of skill, experience and maturity. That means that if you're an auditor auditing the place, you'd better have the same capabilities: you've got to know what you're doing, what to look for, how to ask the right questions, how to dig in and dissect, how to spot discrepancies, how to stand up to egocentric traders, how to remain firm till the real answers are forthcoming (kind of what regulators should be doing, but with more probing and greater aggression). Unfortunately, some auditors aren't up to the task. Of those who are—the seasoned vets of the audit world who can hold their own against any banker, trader, or risk manager working on the Street—most are partners, so stretched that they don't have time to get involved in investigative work and the search for faults.

So, what happens? Junior auditors are assigned the task of doing most (all) of the grunt work, digging, and snooping that happens during the first three quarters of the year (the last quarter and the first month of the new year are reserved for anything and everything related to the annual financial disclosure). The juniors buzz around businesspeople and control folks like little gadflies, asking for things—trade tickets, reports, files, reconciliations, breaks, fails—so that they can compile their work papers. And just like the bank examiners, they use little details from their data collection exercises to play "gotcha"; again, there may not be anything too meaningful in what they report because they miss things. And just like the regulators, they are devoted primarily to the box-checking exercises as proof that controls are working/not working, and have only the slimmest chance of picking up on something important that's gone awry or that someone is trying deliberately to hide. We don't need to look too far to see how the technical inadequacies of these folks contributed to some of the rather massive control failures and losses at places like Salomon, Kidder, Barings, Allfirst, UBS, and National Australia Bank to say nothing of all the smaller control failures that we never hear about (or the corporate audit failures at Enron, WorldCom, Tyco, HealthSouth, Global Crossing, Adelphia, Parmalat, which, fortunately, are out of scope). Traders/originators at these institutions perpetrated multiyear frauds, taking advantage of control and policy weaknesses to try to cover up losses or make money. Or they unknowingly committed multiyear errors because financial controls didn't prevent them from doing so. That means that during each annual audit inspection, the auditors blew it. They didn't detect problems early on, and probably managed to spot them later only because they were so big (how long can you hide a trading loss of $350 million, or $691 million, or $1.4 billion? How long can you miss a derivatives reconciliation error of $280 million?). The technical inadequacies of the auditors contributed to the problems—the external check and balance system failed to spot the very things it was supposed to spot. Not fair, the auditors will (and do) argue: if an individual, a team, or an entire firm is committed to defrauding the company and its investors by fabricating documentation, telling lies, and so on, there is very little that the auditor can do to detect it. That may be true in some cases. Smoking out someone intending to deceive is a tough job. But if that's always true, then auditors add very little value. Maybe the shareholders should save themselves the expense of audit fees? If the audit signoff says that a financial institution's annual statements are a fair reflection of its financial position and conforms to generally accepted accounting principles when there are hundreds of millions of dollars of losses percolating in some unknown or unreconciled account, what's the use?

Conflicts of Interest

Part of the audit stumble centers on conflicts of interest. Auditors are human, so they face the same temptations as everyone else: more assignments, more fees, more pay, and in some cases maybe even a job at a big Wall Street firm. In fact, the temptations and resulting conflicts are a serious matter, because they have the possibility of rendering whatever independent value the auditor delivers to stakeholders somewhat suspect. Let's consider a few of these conflicts: audit work versus consulting work, job rotation, and long-term relationships.

Auditors are supposed to audit; that's their job. Unfortunately, they also like to consult and give advice, and sometimes they like to market. In fact, they like to do anything that generates fees—a lot more fees than the traditional, boring audit business. During the 1990s the Big 5 (the Big 4 + Andersen, which got smoked in the Enron affair) figured out that they could generate more fees (and thus partnership income) by telling banks and companies how to restructure themselves, what strategies to pursue, how to shelter more income from taxes, how to implement new technology platforms to serve customers, and so on. It turns out that the new consulting and marketing franchises were very lucrative. So audit services became the loss leader, the ugly stepchild, rather than the premier, value-added service that the Big 5 (actually, the Big 8, before a few mergers) had built their reputations on. Everyone wanted to be a consultant, no one wanted to be an auditor. Audit was just a way in the door to pitch the latest management consulting project. As the consulting arms started prospering and expanding in the late 1990s, most decided to spin off (or were told to do so by regulators), so the audit arms started building up their own consulting units. But this time their efforts were focused on tax advice and SPEs/structured transactions, and most have done quite well at it. The conflict? One part of the audit organization is supposed to independently review the financial position and controls of the client firm. The other part is busy creating structures and pitching deals that will alter that position. And they both get paid fees for their work. So if an audit firm wants to keep the juicy consulting business in-house there is a chance that it will just roll over on its audit work—not questioning, challenging, or debating a firm's accounting position or control deficiencies as it should. Think about it: if the consulting unit comes up with a clever tax shelter that can save a bank $25 million a year in taxes, but the audit unit says that the shelter contravenes the spirit, if not the letter, of the tax code, who do you think is going to win the argument? The auditors will probably stand down, find some "technical" way of agreeing to the treatment, and the consulting unit will book $7 million or $10 million in fees. There's lots of money at stake. Lawmakers finally caught on to the conflict and tried to bake a few protections into the Sarbanes-Oxley Act of 2002 (a corporate governance reform act passed in the wake of Enron), but there are still so many ways to get around it that a genuine separation between audit and consulting duties doesn't exist.

Then there's the job rotation conflict. As we've said, lots of auditors don't actually want to be auditors. Many see it as a stepping-stone to bigger and better things, like doing something fun and lucrative on Wall Street: working on M&A deals or trading the markets is bound to be more fun than reconciling fails-to-deliver or trying to see if illiquid bond valuations are fair. So it's not too difficult to spot the potential for conflict. An auditor who wants to move onto the Street may ignore some important finding or avoid a confrontation with the primary contact at the bank—all in order to appear cooperative in the eyes of a prospective employer (just like the bank examiners). Most banks don't ban recruitment from their external auditors, so there's nothing to stop a little quid pro quo from happening.

And then there's the long-term relationship aspect that develops between an audit firm and a client bank. In most instances banks use the same auditor for many years: 10, 15, 20, or even more. That means the two get to know each other very well. They often share the same office space, auditors are regularly seen wandering the hallways of bank headquarters', external audit partners are included in many internal meetings, and so on. With such close ties it makes you wonder: are they always being as unbiased and independent as they should be? Not that they would choose to deliberately do anything wrong, but might they be a bit more "forgiving" here and there when interpreting generally accepted accounting principles or the tax code, for relationship's sake? Fifteen years of shared history is not to be taken lightly. More potential for conflict.

The bottom line is that the Street's failures probably can't be reduced, avoided, minimized, or prevented by simply relying on external forces. With rare exception regulators and auditors often aren't up to the task of uncovering problems and preventing bad behavior before damage is done. Again, they aren't to blame; they're doing the best they can (though they do get sleepy and lose focus and momentum from time to time). Both groups are stretched very thin and simply don't have the resources to throw at all the different problems discussed in this book. The only time regulators, in particular, appear to be somewhat more effective is when they step in to try and contain a dislocation from spreading through the system. When there's a major financial problem (often caused by all the leverage and risk-taking occurring on the Street) a few regulatory bodies quietly pull some strings behind the scenes and keep things in check. But when things calm down there is often little or no follow-through. After a little public chastisement and maybe some agreement to provide more information on this risk or be less aggressive on that front, everyone forgets what happened and moves on to business as usual. Which is at least one reason why these dislocations seem to happen with frightening predictability: there is simply no meaningful pressure to change.

Unfortunately, things will only get more complicated as the financial world continues expanding. As Wall Street presses into new markets and jurisdictions and comes to use e-commerce platforms in a more meaningful way, the regulatory web will grow more complex and the possibility of someone dropping the ball—of losing sight of what needs to be monitored, inspected, regulated— increases dramatically. Till the day when the regulatory and audit regimes are truly an effective force in policing the Street, stakeholders must follow our caveat emptor mantra: Don't assume that successful completion of a regulatory inspection or a clean audit report means everything is okay. There are probably still some unsightly things hidden under the covers.

Part III

OVERCOMING FAILURE

Chapter 10

GETTING THE HOUSE IN ORDER

We've talked about how and why Wall Street fails—the essence of destructive problems that have been around for a long time. That's all by way of background so that we can tackle the next part of the program: a cure. Rather than being cynical or despairing, which might be the easiest course in the face of so much bad news, we want to talk about how some of the problems might be resolved. We want to consider how Street firms can get their houses in order so that they can do good business more consistently, and so clients and shareholders don't have to bear the brunt of the missteps. To be sure, a single book can't hope to change firms that are accident-prone or intent on misbehaving or carrying on with the old ways of doing things. That would be a tall order, indeed! But if it can get a few folks on the Street to rethink how they do business so they can minimize the likelihood of more failure, then it's a small step in the right direction. Consistent with our split between internal and external problems, we divide our "prescription" for overcoming failure into things individual firms can do (our discussion in this chapter) and those that outside parties can do (next chapter).

There are a number of things that a Street firm—big or small, domestic or international, retail or institutional—can do to get its house in order; the same, of course, applies to other Street conduits, like fund companies and exchanges, but we'll focus our comments on the banking sector. The more enlightened ones already do some (though probably not all) of the things we describe below. Some firms follow them when the spirit moves them, but not

on a regular basis. Some profess to adhere to certain good behaviors or practices when they actually don't; they have deluded themselves, their clients, and
their shareholders into thinking that everything is working just fine. And some
don't do any of them at all. There is obviously room for improvement across
the board, as evidenced by all of the problems we've touched on.

There's no magic formula to the "housecleaning," but there are ten internal essentials that every Street firm should follow religiously to lower the
chances of accidental stumbling or doing the wrong thing. Of course a bank
can't just put the essentials in place as a rote exercise, as more of the familiar
"box checking" that leads to trouble in the first place. It has to follow the essentials with conviction and consistency, and it has to drive them from the top
down. If directors and executives are on board—*really* on board—then change
works its way down the food chain. If they aren't, then it's back to the status quo,
and more of the breakdowns described in the preceding chapters. Some of the
essentials demand an investment of money (in a few cases, considerable
amounts); *all* demand an investment of energy. Nothing is free, though the payback is likely to make the financial and human investments worthwhile.

Here, then, is a list of ten essentials every Street firm ought to be pursuing
in earnest.

Essential #1: Make sure the board is top-notch. Reform has to start with the board
of directors: directors are agents of shareholders and represent their interests.
And they better represent those interests properly because shareholders supply capital, and capital makes Wall Street run. This means the board has to be
top-notch: a firm has to have the right directors in place so that it can do the
right thing by shareholders and continue to tap into the all-important supply
of capital.

What do we mean by the right directors? Active, qualified, independent,
and accountable. If a bank gets directors with these traits (and there's no reason why it can't, but for some political hurdles), the board has a good chance
of being top-notch. And the top-notch board will insist on good governance; it
will look after the shareholders and ensure that capital keeps flowing, that executives are kept on the straight and narrow, and that the bank grows, improves,
and stays focused. It sounds simple in theory, and it should be in practice, because there are lots of folks out there who are qualified to be very good directors. It just takes breaking with the past and getting some of the ineffective,
golf-buddy directors swept out of the boardroom. Some of that responsibility
falls to investors: they've got a certain amount of ability to choose which directors to vote for and should take action (and we presume they would want to,

given the billions that they've lost over the years through poor decisions and bad behavior, some coming from director ignorance, ineptitude, or laziness). Though board nominating committees usually come up with candidates for directorships, activist investors ought to be scrutinizing the process and asking the hard questions: Is the proposed director the best one for the job? What are his/her qualifications? Is he or she technically capable? Energized? What potential conflicts of interest exist? What level of time commitment and energy is the director able to devote to the endeavor? And so on. Realigning a board is likely to take time, particularly in banks that have no limit on the number of years that a director can serve (though most stick to annual reelections, so if a director is really awful, as demonstrated by obvious conflicts, lack of participation at meetings, votes that seem to run contrary to shareholder interests, and so on, then investors can choose not to reelect the incumbent). But it's the only way to move forward, because if the board doesn't change, the firm doesn't change.

So, remember, the successful bank director has to be:

Active: Present at all board meetings, participating, contributing, and advancing the firm's interests. Not dozing or missing meetings (or just showing up to collect director's fees) and not so thinly stretched by other commitments that contributions are marginal.

Qualified: Technically capable, knowledgeable about finance, the Street, accounting, risk—things that actually matter to a bank. A few generalists are okay because they can inject a useful outside perspective, but a board that is too general is going to get tripped up by the first technical decision (important issues, too, like expanding into new businesses, taking more risk, or buying up a competitor).

Independent: No conflicts: there can be no quid pro quo, no consulting arrangements, no passing of business between a director and the firm; no approval of big executive compensation plans in exchange for a little under-the-table business; no rolling over for the CEO, no failing to question, challenge, and cajole in order to preserve personal ties with executives. The corporate world in general, and the Street as a subset, has proved time and again just how damaging conflicts of interest can be; if directors are conflicted they should clean up the conflicts or leave (and remember, it's not enough for directors to simply disclose the conflicts and carry on with business—the conflicts actually have to be eliminated).

Accountable: Standing up for decisions that are made, good or bad: no more running for the hills when things get ugly. Directors who aren't willing to take responsibility for decisions that they've made and strategies they've helped form add no value. That's when it becomes obvious that they are just occupying the seats for prestige, contacts, and fees, not to represent and advance the interests of shareholders. Directors have duties of care and loyalty, so they'd better discharge them properly.

Which failures that we've talked about in the book does this essential item help solve? Lots of them, actually: strategic flaws, business mistakes and reversals, executive compensation that's out of line with the realities of shareholder performance, ill-defined risk tolerance levels, internal conflicts of interest, and unethical behavior. The board sets the tone, provides the leadership qualities and creates the broad strategic moves: success in creating the right board puts a halt to problems stemming from ineffective management. And who's responsible for implementing this essential? The nominating committee of the board is the starting point, but it should be acting in close cooperation with activist institutional investors so that the very best directors can be identified.

Essential #2: Align everyone's interests. Wall Street is about making money: money for clients, investors, executives, and employees. That's great, and in keeping with the capitalist spirit that makes lots of what happens in the financial world successful. But it gets out of hand, and its one of the big reasons the Street fails. When bankers focus solely on dollars, things can go awry. Greed makes people do things they shouldn't do: abuse customers, lie to controllers and regulators, slip tickets in desk drawers, all in order to make more money for the firm and themselves. Never mind what happens to the client or the shareholder. It can be tough keeping that greed in check, but some attempt has to be made, and two solutions come to mind: alignment and rationality.

Alignment means making sure that everyone doing business is synchronized with everyone supplying the capital that lets business get done. Executives and employees should only be getting paid when they are creating long-term, sustainable value for investors. It is so fundamental, yet so often ignored. How do board compensation committees justify paying mega-bonuses to senior folks even as the bank's stock price drops and/or revenues flatten or dip? They argue benchmarking: Morgan Stanley is paying $x for this position or Goldman is paying $y for that position, so they have to pay $x or $y to keep up. And then they argue retention: if they don't pay someone six or seven or eight figures, they'll walk to Stanley or Goldman. It's time to let them walk. If the compensation committees of boards (which, by the way, had better be independent) can't make the hard decisions on what to pay executive management, then they've fallen victim to implicit blackmail and are perpetuating a self-fulfilling cycle that will never serve shareholder interests. And if executives can't make hard decisions about what to pay their senior people and the rank and file, then they've fallen victim to the same problem. The alignment criteria should be simple: when a bank's management is creating sustainable value for shareholders (not just short-term bursts in the stock price around year-end), they ought to get paid more. When they don't, they shouldn't. When business managers meet or exceed their budgets (real budgets, too, not internal hocus pocus or puffery), they should get paid more. When they don't, they shouldn't. Paying someone who has failed to deliver the goods $3 million instead of $6 million, or $5 million instead of $10 million, is not really a punishment. But if any of these folks want to walk after receiving a dose of reality, directors and executives should let them go. We would probably all be surprised by how many wouldn't leave, and how many qualified job applicants would appear to fill the vacancies left by those deciding to go. Boards, and then executives, have to align pay and stick to the process. Forget what the competitors down the block are doing.

And, yes, dare we say it: it's time to get aspects of the Street's compensation into the realm of the real world. Why? Because extreme compensation alters behavior—it's what makes some folks do the wrong thing. There's nothing wrong with paying some people a great deal of money if it can be justified in the grand scheme of what a bank does and the value that it's generating for clients and investors. If a team of traders or bankers single-handedly wins a great deal of good business for a bank in an otherwise down market cycle, it ought to be paid well (even very well). The same goes for a controller who solves an ugly problem that's been haunting the bank for years, or the broker who lands an important account. But it's wrong to pay out big packages just to retain someone. And it's wrong to pay someone hefty sums when they are doing big volume, but not good quality, business or they've created tail risk for the firm by committing it to things that could boomerang. Ultimately, Wall Streeters should be compensated on the quality of the business that they do: long-term, sustainable repeat business rather than one-shot deals, and steady fee-based private client flows rather than volume-based commission/ticket writing; compensation for deals that create a lot of potential profit (and risk) over three or five years should be linked to those time horizons, not today's present value. There are all sorts of rational metrics that can be employed that still allow for big bonus checks but don't skew incentives or warp behavior. Executives have to draw the line. Again, there is a risk that people will walk, but it's a risk that needs to be taken to break the cycle, inject some normalcy to Street pay scales, and remove some of the temptations that lead to bad behavior.

Which failures does this essential item help solve? At least two big ones: client mistreatment and conflicts of interest. If bankers aren't so intensely focused on printing business (of whatever quality) so that they can boost their bonusable production or revenues, then one of key reasons for taking advantage of clients disappears. And some of the conflicts that invariably pop up in the pursuit of business fade as well. If pay scales are redesigned through a mix of alignment and rationality then Wall Streeters still have incentives to produce, but not to gouge or mistreat. And who's responsible for implementation? The compensation committee of the board, senior executives and line managers; they all have to follow the same template.

Essential #3: Demand ethical behavior. Once again, an essential that seems obvious and simple, but is often ignored. The Street should be all about ethical behavior, because its business is based on intangibles like goodwill and reputation. The operating mantra shouldn't be figuring out how many ways to pull a fast one on the clients, but how they can be protected and be made to prosper. There have been far too many instances of senior management looking the other way when there's some kind of misbehavior. In some cases it's even worse: managers encourage staffers to abandon ethics in pursuit of revenues. We've seen it throughout the Street's history, from churning, wash sales, leveraged pyramid trusts, and fraud in the early days to derivatives scandals, biased/fraudulent research, spinning, laddering, and insider trading in more recent times. Each one of these incidents represents a collapse of basic ethical behavior within individuals, teams, business units, whole firms, and sometimes the entire industry.

This essential, perhaps more than any of the others we consider, has to be driven from the top. Directors and executives have to set the tone for the rest of the firm, because if they don't, no one else will care. Directors have to develop ethical standards and enforce them, making sure that basic ground rules regarding the treatment of individuals and clients are respected. Executives then have to do the same with their senior managers, and so on down the line, to the most junior (but still essential) clerk or administrative assistant. This is not about creating ethical principles that make for good public relations (following the all too familiar "3P" [print-post-pray] approach) but about believing, and then enforcing, them. If principles are violated in any way (as evidenced by client complaints, regulatory infractions, discovery of conflicts or mistreatment of employees or competitors) the violator gets one warning. A second violation should lead to firing. Is it naïve to think that the Street can demonstrate more ethical backbone? After all, it's a dog-eat-dog world, so banks have to do what they have to do to win, right? We don't happen to think it's naïve, and we don't believe Wall Street lacks the capacity for continuous ethical behavior—continuous, not occasional. Other industries seem to display a higher level of moral behavior, so why not Wall Street? The Street's not all that different. It just takes raising the bar a bit and sticking to it: drive it from the top down (all the time), and make examples of those who don't play by the rules.

Which failures does this essential item help solve? All of the ethical breakdowns we've seen throughout the years that lead to client damage and bruised reputations, all of the things that the Street does but shouldn't be doing, all of the things that give clients and investors chills when they read about them on the front page of the *Wall Street Journal*. And we already know there are quite a few. And who's responsible for implementation? As we've said, it all starts with the top folks.

Essential #4: Define a rational strategy, and stick with it. Banks need to decide what they are, what they do, and how they want to do it. They need to come up with strategies that make sense for their operations and client needs and are consistent with shareholder expectations. Most important, they need to stick to them. This means directors and executives have to create core plans that span several years, determine the real performance goals that will spell success or failure, and remain committed. Of course, there always has to be some flexibility to take advantage of opportunities as they arise or to adjust to different market conditions (good or bad) as they wash through the system. But there isn't room for wholesale shifts in strategy once plans are in motion—with hundreds of millions (if not several billions) of dollars already committed to making it so. That just means no one has thought about the strategy to begin with, and executives and directors aren't doing a good job of critiquing and challenging before signing on the dotted line. And it also means resources are being wasted and confused signals transmitted.

Strategy, by definition, is a medium- to long-term exercise. Some argue that Wall Street is too short term to play by those rules: markets move quickly, new competitive threats appear out of the blue, client demands and needs change, and so forth. Wrong. Wall Street has bull and bear markets and expansion and contraction phases, so the strategy that a bank develops should fit within the extremes of these cycles. That may mean more measured expansion or acquisition to start, accepting some below-market returns on capital during the trough, or doing less business than budgeted for 12 or 24 months until markets change or deregulation sets in. Strategy can't be about bull market planning, timing, and execution, and thinking it is is one of the Street's great mistakes.

Everyone is happy to plan for the bull, because it means jobs, resources, expansion, money, and bonuses. No one, it seems, is thinking about the bear in the same strategy session. But if strategy is going to be useful, and if it's going to make a bank look and act like it knows what it's doing, it's got to take account of the fact that things can get ugly for a while—and that during the ugly times not everything has to be shut down, reversed, brought back to headquarters (just as during the good times a firm doesn't have to get into every new market or hot product, or duplicate the template developed by competitors). It means that in plotting a strategy, directors and executives have to take account of all scenarios before they agree to proceed. Why spend billions on acquisitions when the market is strong, just to liquidate them when things go sour, then start anew when the sun is shining again? Why hire, then fire, then rehire, en masse? Cycles will continue to impact Wall Street, so shouldn't the ex-ante strategy reflect that?

In developing that strategy, a firm ought to be looking at realistic and sober scenarios, not the inflated, super-rosy picture that CFOs and controllers and business unit managers often prepare so that they can get proper resourcing to build empires. Directors and executives ought to be on the lookout for bull market expansion plans and cut things back down to size. Strategy should include a look at major sea changes—events that might forever change the way the Street does business—and make sure that thought is given to how the platform has to be adjusted to cope beforehand, not during or after the fact. And in developing a sustainable strategy, one that covers the bulls and the bears, directors and executives should think long and hard about the image they are projecting. What is more damaging to client relationships than a bank that indicates commitment, hires, gathers business and then closes down or pulls out when things slow down or get ugly? How long does it take to rebuild the trust and commitment? Years. All because the planning didn't take account of bad times. So the essential is to create a rational strategy that fits within the Street's cycles and stick with it—remain committed.

What failures does this essential item help solve? Several: wasted corporate (i.e., investor) resources associated with multiple starts and stops, reversals, expansions, and contractions; client confusion and irritation about whether the bank is in or out of a particular market or service; employee unease and aggravation related to the specter of job loss as the bank changes its mind again. The bank moves from being wasteful, confused, and noncommittal, and all of the negatives these flaws project, to acting decisively and efficiently. And who's responsible for implementation? It starts with directors, who should be setting broad strategy with input from executives. Then it's up to the executive team and its line management to execute the program—and that means sticking with it.

Essential #5: Define a risk appetite, and stick with it. As long as the firm's leaders are doing some defining, they should define a risk appetite. We know that a bank is in business to take risk: sometimes it does it very well, sometimes very poorly. In either case, it sometimes fails to decide exactly what kind of risky business it's doing or how much it wants to do. Whatever it winds up doing happens by default or accident rather than design, and that's not a wise approach to risk management. All of this goes hand in hand with strategy. A bank needs to decide what it really is: a prop risk taker, a client-flow trader, or an agency shop; an unsecured lender to emerging market borrowers and highly leveraged companies, or a secured lender to well-established firms. It doesn't really matter, as long as there is consensus among directors and executives, and decisions about risk appetite are properly communicated to investors and other stakeholders (e.g., regulators, rating agencies, equity analysts). No one wants to be surprised, and they shouldn't have to be: no one holding shares in risk-averse Bank ABC should read in the *Wall Street Journal* that 90 percent of last quarter's earnings came from big prop bets, because that's not what ABC is in business to do. It doesn't matter if ABC has made money trading—that isn't the bank's mandate (until directors, executives, and investors say it is). In fact, it is more comforting when a known risk-taking firm loses a great deal of money than when a no-risk firm like ABC makes lots of money: someone at ABC doesn't know what's going on, and that's scary.

It's simple enough to figure out what kind of risk to take and how much to take. It just requires a bit of discipline, some linkage with what the strategy folks are plotting (like how risk relates to the business the bank is doing or plans to do, so there's synchronicity), and the right financial and human resources. If the intent is to expand into international markets and build a local presence by taking local market risks, and everyone agrees with that concept and truly justifies the budgets and potential revenues, then the risk appetite should factor that in. But if the strategy says no international expansion and no local market risks, then the firm shouldn't find that it's holding positions in those risks. And if a firm has $x billion in capital and feels like it can support 10 percent of $x as its maximum loss under most conceivable disaster scenarios, then it shouldn't wind up with 50 percent of $x on its books. And if the bank says it really wants to be in long-dated interest rate derivatives to service the insurance and pension fund client base, then it had better have the right human and technological expertise to manage the risky positions that come from that business. A key part of the process means understanding the real financial implications of risk—not just how much might be lost if the sky falls or how much how much might be earned when the bull market is roaring but, once the wheels are in motion, precisely how money is actually being earned or lost, especially the former. Over the years banks have tended to ignore just how they make money. Everyone jumps on the losses and does the postmortems when things go wrong, but few, it seems, care to question how money is made. As long as dollars are flowing in and everyone's above budget, management just carries on, not necessarily questioning or understanding the source of profits. That spells trouble, because some of those profits may be coming from very risky activities that might ultimately change course or boomerang (sometimes they can even come from illegal activities). The $1 billion in profit that the bank booked over 12 months from credit spread tightening may turn into a $1 billion loss when the credit sector suddenly diverges; all that credit spread risk that made money is now losing money, but management is caught off guard because it didn't question how the billion was made in the first place. So ripping apart the P&L every day to see how money is being made and lost and how that ties back to the risks being taken is absolutely vital.

Defining a risk appetite is one part of the equation, sticking to it is another. That means no incremental risk, no "please, just a little more exposure, it's part of an important client trade." Of course there can be, and need to be, exceptions to the process. But exceptions should be just that—they should happen once in a blue moon, last only for a short while, and be properly supported and justified. When exceptions become the rule, or are permitted to inflate the bank's risk profile on a semipermanent basis, the risk management process is for naught. So, when directors and executives—being the accountable agents and managers they ought to be—define the nature and size of risks they want the bank to take (and tell the outside world all about them), they have to stick to the program. No changing course midstream without thought, consultation, and communication. When a firm decides that it wants to move from being an agency shop to a full-time prop trader or a blue chip lender to an aggressive leveraged finance lender, it has to do it the right way, and not through stealthy moves or incremental exceptions that catch everyone by surprise.

Which failures does this essential item help solve? The risk-related losses that have plagued the Street, especially in recent years. It doesn't mean banks won't lose money when it comes to trading or lending—of course they will, and they should. They exist to take risk, and risk means losing as well as winning. But it means no surprise losses, nothing that directors, executives, and shareholders couldn't have foreseen as a possibility. And when the surprises are removed—

when banks take the risks they should be taking, based on the right financial and human resources, and keep them under proper control—then everyone feels a whole lot better when losses actually happen. They are expected and can be accommodated within each bank's resources. No more incremental risks sprouting up, no more concentrations, no more sloppiness, just appropriate amounts of exposure at a proper price. And who's responsible for implementation? It starts with directors and executives, who have to define the risk appetite, and then moves down to divisional business leaders and risk managers, who make sure everything fits within the parameters that have been set out.

Essential #6: Remember the client. Even though we've said it before (and it should be very obvious), we'll say it again: Wall Street exists to service the client. It doesn't matter whether clients are retail or institutional, or whether the service involved is advice, custody, or capital raising, the Street has to remember that clients make it all possible. We've already seen many instances where clients get ripped off (and what we've covered is, unfortunately, just the tip of the iceberg). Banks give out bad advice, they put Moms and Pops and big companies into lousy investments and deals, and they lie, cheat, and steal. They let conflicts and double dealing take hold, and they do shoddy work. Some talk about the client being "king" and holding the client's interests above all else, but that seems a bit disingenuous: there's too much client debris scattered around for anyone to seriously believe that firms always put clients first.

Yet they should, because the Street still has to live by its reputation. Mistreating clients damages that reputation, and a damaged reputation drives away business; some firms have discovered that the hard way. Again, it's relatively simple to say "remember the client," and it shouldn't be all that difficult to practice for those who are serious about business. How? A bank's leaders should absolutely forbid any behavior that jeopardizes client interests and should swiftly penalize any violations. This means executives shouldn't tolerate conflicts of interest, abusive behavior, or inappropriate deals or advice just for the sake of commissions, fees, or league table credit. Moms and Pops should be handled with the utmost care by making sure brokers give them sound and appropriate counsel, not commission-driven advice. And they should forbid any loosening in standard operating procedures that might cause client problems: no more bad due diligence, no more unfair fairness opinions, and no more toxic derivatives that aren't properly explained and valued. Executives should enforce much stricter capital-raising procedures so issuers *and* investors win. New issues should be valued properly so that proceeds for the issuer are maximized, and allocations should be handled fairly so that all investors get a fair shot and aren't subject to ulterior motives like spinning or tying. Of course, mistakes will happen from time to time that will hurt the client; the markets are too large, the deals too complicated, the client rosters too extensive, and the firms too big to believe otherwise. So when something bad happens and puts clients in jeopardy, management ought to be forthright about the problems: it should come clean with the facts and solve the problems, not try to sweep things under the rug and hope they'll go away. Again, they have to enforce the practice by getting rid of all those who tamper with client interests.

Which failures does this essential item help solve? Basically, every instance of client wrongdoing and mistreatment cited in this book, and there have been many. Take the client's interests seriously and losses decline, arbitrations and class actions fade, and the skies are a bit bluer for everyone. And who's responsible for implementing this? Though the tone has to be set by the most senior executives at the firm, the daily management has to occur with the front-line, client-facing professionals: investment banking relationship managers, institutional salespeople, and brokers. It's up to them to treat the clients right.

Essential #7: Staff with the best. If any bank is to overcome its problems—whether client facing, risk taking, or control oriented—it has to have the right people with the right skills doing the right jobs. This means hiring or internally rotating the best possible folks. It costs more in the short term, to be sure: getting the top talent, in whatever discipline, is going to be far more expensive than settling for the B team. Over the medium term, however, it's worthwhile: pay a little more today and reap the returns over years to come. This applies across the board: top producers, who can generate quality, return business, and top controllers, who have the experience and maturity to run a tight ship. Indeed, as we stress overcoming internal failures, the importance of the internal control personnel cannot be underestimated; having in place the right risk managers, auditors, accountants, and lawyers can make a world of difference.

The process means making sure that the right skills and experiences are brought to bear in all of a bank's operations, so that those that are truly qualified are actually sitting in the critical seats: this means less chances for screwups. We've said that managers often try to find homes for those that have outlived their usefulness or who are friends of friends, or golf buddies, or sorority sisters. Giving someone who may be wholly unqualified responsibility for a critical job because of who they know, not what they know, is unwise. Of course the Street is all about networks, connections, and who knows who; there's nothing wrong with capitalizing on contacts to get in the door, get a promotion, or make an internal or external move, as long as the goods are there to back it up. The networking game is wrong when a bank ends up sacrificing the quality of the products or services it produces or the controls it relies on. When the golf buddy ends up running the swap desk or the sorority sister is running mega M&A deals when the most he or she has ever done is work as a financial controller or analyst, everyone loses. So it's all about getting people with the right skills and demeanor doing the critical jobs.

Part of the process is making sure that the good folks stick around. This means compensation packages have to be structured correctly: not irrationally, correctly. Every employee should be tied, in some way, to the long-term success of the firm. Not only does this work wonders for retention, but it brings us back to the alignment issue we mentioned above. Don't let people cash out after one, two, or five years; make them stay and create value for themselves and the shareholders. But it's more than compensation. Banks have to create a good environment and make people want to work for them. Some already do this reasonably well by projecting a strong image, making the working atmosphere friendly, giving junior staffers greater responsibilities, and so on. These are all beneficial "intangibles" that make employees want to be there. But a lot more banks (and other intermediaries) need to do the same thing. Proper compensation plus a good working environment make for happy workers, who won't necessarily be lured by the offer of bigger dollars from some firm down the block (and reinforce the temptation/conflict issue we've mentioned). Some, it seems, are actually willing to sacrifice a few dollars for a better experience. Maybe more can join them.

Which failures does this essential item help solve? It actually touches on all of them, because people are the essential ingredient on Wall Street. Professionals supply the skills to get things done, and it's up to them to decide how they're going to play it. If they want to do the right thing, the Street won't have the kinds of problems it's had. Bad advice, silly fairness opinions, churning, laddering, stupid risk decisions, poor control work, breach of fiduciary duties, and all of the client and investor losses these things cause decline. And who's responsible for implementation? Senior executives and every business unit manager or team leader who's in charge of hiring and managing people; they have the power to staff with the best talent and reject the cronyism that leads to mediocrity (or worse).

Essential #8: Demand independence. Independence = no conflicts. Prudent behavior can exist only when a bank is conflict free. If a Wall Streeter is not subject to the temptations offered up by a conflict, then there's a much higher probability that he or she will behave properly. That means conflicts, or potential conflicts, in whatever form they take, have to be excised; there should be no situation in which an employee or executive is torn between competing forces. The same applies, on a macro scale, to an entire firm.

It's pretty simple: those who are supposed to control, police, review, inspect, analyze, or audit can't come under the direct or indirect influence of those generating dollars. Time and experience have demonstrated that when this isn't the case, a bank is at real risk. So risk managers can't be paid by traders; financial controllers can't report up to business unit heads; equity analysts can't be paid by, or report through, investment bankers; settlement professionals can't be managed by business leaders; software programmers can't be compensated by those using their code to make money. If these arrangements exist, they have to be altered, immediately. The audit and compliance functions should make sure this occurs, initially and continuously. Similarly, the Chinese wall has to be shored up throughout the Street. The wall is useful and important in concept but, as we've noted, fails miserably in practice. It is vital for compliance officers to make sure researchers, bankers, and traders are not sharing information or communicating on sensitive matters. Research has to be insulated from banking pressures, and the nature of the bank's business relationship with a client firm has to be well disclosed by researchers. It is also important for banks to avoid any possibility (or appearance of) Glass-Steagall type conflicts, such as issuing securities for a troubled company and redirecting proceeds to pay down loans. In the same way, funds and other financial firms can't put themselves in a position such that internal business, reporting, or compensation conflicts can arise.

Those working on the Street can't have outside interests that put them in conflict with the firm or its clients. A banker, trader, broker, or analyst can't serve two masters faithfully, so any instance of conflict has to be eliminated. Again, not just disclosed, but eliminated. There shouldn't be any instances of employees investing in third-party vehicles or structures for which the firm is doing active business, as these will bias behavior. While most firms have "restricted lists" that prohibit trading in securities of any company for which the bank is issuing securities or arranging a corporate finance deal, some don't, or they allow exceptions, or don't have mechanisms to cover anything nonstandard (such as hedge funds or special purpose entities), or can't monitor compliance. Any of these shortcomings leaves open the possibility of abuse.

Of course, the independence requirement must extend beyond the individual, the department, and the firm: it has to apply to other bodies on the Street, like exchanges. Regulators need help discharging some of their oversight functions, to be sure. But the answer is not to embed that oversight within the entity that's generating business. How is that different from executives at Barings allowing an arbitrage trader to manage settlements and fund margin calls? How is it different from investment banking groups compensating research analysts? How is it different from Merrill bankers covering Enron investing in the Enron SPEs they were arranging naughty deals for? It's no different at all. Those who create profits can't police themselves without conflict, regardless of the supposed "structural independence." They can't do the job effectively, and they can't provide the confidence and security the investing public expects and deserves.

Which failures does this essential item help solve? Situations like flawed investment research, fraud-induced trading losses, and mistreatment of clients. Lack of independence has led to some of the biggest blowups on the Street over the years—a surprising fact if you think about it, because enforcing independence rules is relatively easy: correct reporting/compensation structure, disclosure of internal and external relationships, and some periodic audit checks can do wonders. It's just a question of discipline. And who's responsible? Again, it falls to senior executives and business leaders, with some special help from general counsel/compliance, who can set up the right structural process, and internal auditors, who can make sure the process remains true.

Essential #9: Spend wisely on technology. We've mentioned that the Street lives and dies by technology, and that gets truer every day as business gets more complicated, trades and deals get more intricate, client rosters grow, information travels more rapidly, and markets become more global. Good technology lets things happen the right way: trades can be processed more rapidly and securely, valuation and modeling becomes more accurate, vital risk and financial information gets tracked more precisely, and a firm operates more efficiently and confidently. With the right technology platform a bank can even lower its support staff and cut back on expenses. So it's easy to see why technology is so attractive. It's important and can produce a competitive edge—but it has to be created or purchased very carefully and wisely.

Technology is typically the number 2 expense item for most Street firms (behind compensation, of course). So there are lots of dollars at stake, literally billions at a large firm. Unfortunately, it's very easy to throw money at technology and still not get the right goods. The Street has a history of spending piles on hardware and software, on huge IT staffs (many favoring the "in-house development" over the "outsource purchase" for reasons of politics and job security), and on things that come in well above budget, well behind schedule and without the right functionality. It's a useless squandering of shareholders' money, just like putting on some bad trading or credit risk, in large size.

Managing technology spending and investment wisely starts with figuring out what's really needed tactically and strategically by tying back to strategy and risk, and taking account of business expansions and contractions. Then it's determining what it'll cost to get there (internal versus external), resourcing the task, and holding folks accountable for delivering. On budget, on time, no excuses; excuses should lead to massive pay cuts and/or firings, because experience shows that technology folks working at banks always have a drawer full of excuses. There are always lots of reasons why something can't be delivered (unless, of course, a few more dollars can be thrown at the "unforeseen problem"), and that should be unacceptable. And, remember, banks are banks, not technology firms—they ought to let technology firms do most of the heavy work. It's a bit odd when a bank of ten thousand has one thousand or two thousand heads dedicated to the technology effort. Something is clearly wrong, and that "something" is probably empire building, using technology as the lever. Microsoft and Intel don't seem to have thousands of bankers or treasury officials running around doing financial deals, because it's not their forte. The same applies here: let the experts develop the technology, with the right input from the Street. The bottom line is that a bank can't, and shouldn't, be afraid to spend dollars on what it needs in order to operate more securely and efficiently: properly managed, that investment will pay for itself in pretty short order. But it should be very afraid to spend dollars if it can't guide the process and get responsible parties to execute and deliver; then it's just more money down the tubes.

Which failures does this essential item help solve? Many of the control-related problems that have hit banks over the years: things like misvaluation of trades (accidental or otherwise), lack of risk transparency (e.g., "oops, we forgot we owned these bonds/stocks/whatever"), and all of the operational/settlement bleeding that costs fantastic sums of money (billions per year, minimum). Imagine clamping down on all that silly waste—the shareholders would be eternally grateful. And who's responsible for implementation? Senior executives, to be sure, but also an in-house technology expert—one, we might add, that has no vested interest in running a bloated IT staff and every interest in arriving at the right technology solution.

Essential #10: Kick out the violators. Those who don't play by the rules (whether it's these essentials or other ones, plus internal policies, regulatory requirements, and so on) have to be shown the door. Violation of ethics, mistreatment of clients, misguided strategy, squandering of shareholders' money, and conflicted behavior should all be regarded as unacceptable by those running the firm. There should be no room in a bank, or on the Street, for such misbehavior, because it breeds so many of the failures we've talked about. But too often violators go unpunished internally. And without punishment, there's no incentive to reform or improve, and the same old game keeps being played.

Management should have zero tolerance for those who breach written and unwritten rules of proper conduct. Naturally, there can be gradations of how to handle those who are doing the wrong thing (or constantly stumbling). It might start with some penalties and sanctions, like no promotion, no bonus, or maybe a demotion or a pay cut. But it must escalate quickly from there: second infraction, and it's out the door. And discipline has to be applied uniformly: no double standards, especially favorable treatment applied to superstar bankers, brokers, traders, and analysts who are generating lots of fees for the bank. Anyone who blows it must suffer the same penalties, or the process becomes a mockery. Unfortunately, it's still a mockery at many firms. Those who do the wrong thing often escape unscathed. So why bother reforming? It may be worth risking some naughty behavior because the upside is potentially large, the downside nil: a free call option given to every employee by the bank's shareholders, thank you very much. Unless discipline is taken seriously, the shareholders lose. Since this point is so important, we'll revisit it in the next chapter when we talk about external penalties.

Which failures does this essential item help solve? All of them. If that sounds all encompassing, it should, because bad apples who are allowed to hang around can do damage on virtually every front. They can even influence others, particularly when they escape unscathed from a tight squeeze. All of the things that have plagued the Street in the past will continue in the future unless those who have the wrong approach to business are given a proper dose of religion. A regular purging of those who don't want to play by internal or external rules would do a great deal to stem the instances of failure. And who's responsible for implementing this? Again, we start at the top and work our way down: directors and executives must display backbone in enforcing penalties and sanctions for rule breakers, and every manager in charge of a team must do the same—without exception.

Are these ten essentials by themselves going to change the face of Wall Street? No. That would be a bit naïve, and we're a little too experienced (or realistic, or jaded, though not cynical) for that. But we hope the essentials can get leadership and the rank and file to think about what they're doing it, why they're doing it, and how they're doing it; to think about whether the way they are approaching business is really fair or if it's all just about making a buck; to think about lengthening the time horizon of actions and thought from the next bonus season to one five or ten years from now, when good behavior and good business will have led to the creation of sustainable value that is multiples of what the next season will yield. If they have the same hope of seeing things on the Street get better, rather than worse, then these essentials might be a spark that lights the fire.

Chapter 11

SHORING UP
THE DEFENSES

Wall Street can't go it alone. It can do its utmost to implement the essentials we've just covered—and that obviously has to be the focus of any move in the right direction—but it can't expect to solve all of the problems by itself. The Street needs to turn outward and get a helping hand if it's going to crack down on the failures that have proved so troublesome. Regulators and auditors, as we've seen, are two key external bodies that can, at least theoretically, provide an extra level of scrutiny and direction through their rules, regulations, and guidelines. They can help Street firms minimize the accidents and misdeeds. But before they can be effective, they've got to get their own houses in order. There's no point in sending the warden to watch over the inmates if the warden is incapable, conflicted, or unwilling.

But if reform is to be truly effective it has to go beyond regulators and auditors. Because the difficulties plaguing the Street are so complex and far-reaching, other outside parties have to play a role, too. Bank investors and bank clients, for instance, have to be much more active in helping keep banks on the straight and narrow. They've got to be willing to act as the collective thorn in Wall Street's hide, agitating until proper resolution comes about. Indeed, we believe strongly that these stakeholders have a *duty* to be active in dealing with the Street and its failings; they need to be at the leading edge of a challenge to the status quo, because they ultimately suffer the most when the Street fails. For some this is, and will be, an uncomfortable role. It's a lot easier to sell a bank's shares or find a new firm to do business with than to kick, scream, and demand satisfaction. But those willing to take the bold actions will add enormous value to the reform process.

So to help the Street progress, external defenses have to be shored up; the pressure is on outsiders to improve things by actively promoting a number of external essentials. The balance of this chapter is devoted to seven such essentials.

Essential #1: Make sure regulators and auditors are very, very good. The regulatory and audit process can only be as good as the folks involved in regulating and auditing. If you put in weak, inexperienced, gullible, or clueless examiners or auditors, you'll get a substandard review process that doesn't add much value. Regulatory and audit functions can be useful when they're driven by people who know what's going on and what's important, who can stand up to ego-driven Wall Streeters, who can bring experience and a somewhat cynical eye to the process, and who know what rocks to look under or where to search for hidden bodies. This means getting the right folks in place—tough, experienced, control minded, conflict free, and knowledgeable. If the external examiners and auditors are going through the trouble of calling on Street firms to see whether they're playing by the rules, why not do it with the right people? Not only does it increase the chances of catching something truly meaningful, it sends a powerful message to the Street: no longer can banks try to fool the junior examiners or auditors—rather, banks on the Street are going up against ex-lawyers, bankers, or risk managers with many years of experience who mean business. That's just a little something extra to help keep the Street focused on the right thing.

Naturally, this approach costs money. The truth is that would-be regulators and auditors with the desired qualities are tough to find, because most are working on Wall Street, in law or consulting firms, or somewhere else where the pay is a bit better. So it's time for regulatory agencies and audit firms to pony up for talent—the Street's certainly been doing it for a long time. Though the dollars might be big, it's a worthwhile investment because there will be less time and money spent trying to "catch up" with what Wall Street is doing and more time getting ahead of potential problems. If regulators and auditors can spend a bit more money today and, in so doing, catch a few problems before they become megaproblems, then the extra expense is easily justified. To get some of the good wood on board, regulators just need to slap "special inspection levies" on the Street firms they are reviewing, and the audit firms just have to raise their fees a bit. That should take care of the economics. (And if pay for regulators blows through government pay scales, just make a new pay category expressly for financial regulators.)

Which failures does this essential help solve? Most of what we've talked about in the book: anything related to breach of rules (like spinning, laddering, and front running) would be solved with the right regulatory expertise. Anything related to internal control sloppiness (like operational, legal, and model risk losses) would be taken care of by having top-notch auditors on the case. Replace the juniors with the vets, and the frequency of rule violations, silly mistakes, and misbehaving is virtually guaranteed to decline. Will that eliminate all of the failures? Of course not. There will always be problems that slip through. But it will catch, prevent, or eliminate many, and that would represent significant progress. And who's responsible for implementation? The heads of regulatory agencies and the heads of audit firms: they have the power and re- sources to get top-quality personnel on board so that the inspection process adds more value.

Essential #2: Make the inspections meaningful. Regulators and auditors have to stop the rote box-checking they've been following for years and start digging in deep—very deep. The days of pro forma exams and audits based on surface- level scripted behaviors, questions, and reviews have to come to an end if the external process is going to keep the Street from damaging itself and its stake- holders. Examiners and auditors need to throw away the old model, hone in on known or suspected problem areas, set up camp, and start digging. They need to dig away until they find a problem or walk away truly satisfied that everything is functioning properly. If that takes many months, so be it—at least it'll be a more valuable exercise than the traditional SOP box checks. It's easy enough to prioritize things that need to be scrutinized: functions and processes that are client-facing, those involving the integrity of controls and independence, those that might lead to conflicts of interest, and those that involve new products, markets, or risks. Or maybe those that have been the source of complaints (as reflected through arbitration activity, threatened legal actions, internal whistle blowing, and so on) or the cause of internal losses (as demonstrated by opera- tional, trading, credit, or legal red ink). Any of these can be clues to potential flaws that run much deeper than might be apparent through a cursory 30,000- foot review. With clues in hand, examiners can start really delving into the is- sues, performing meaningful, value-added inspections that can benefit a whole community of stakeholders. As part of the inspection process, regulators ought to be playing nicely with one another. Everyone's on the same team, though it's not always evident when we see the heated turf battles and finger-pointing, e.g., the SEC versus the CFTC, the SEC versus state attorneys general. We expect conflicts on Wall Street, not in the regulatory community. So forget territorial disputes and regulatory politics, just share information and resources, coordi- nate activities, and get the job done. Or, dare we say it, scrap the whole thing and set up a single, consolidated superregulator a la U.K. Financial Services Authority: one team, one goal.

There's another beneficial by-product in doing the deep probe: fear. Banks don't like having outsiders snooping around their operations, grabbing books and records, files, e-mails and phone tapes. Still, when it happens they know that regulators and auditors can't hang around forever—maybe two or three weeks, and that's about it—so they can make everything look good and nice for that short period of time if they need to. Imagine if banks thought that they might get hit with an inspection lasting 6 months, 12 months, even 18 months. They'd have to be on good behavior for a long, long time—and if they've got something to hide, that's a tough act to pull off. So maybe they'd be a little bit more control-minded to begin with, a little more careful about how they manage their operations, controls, compliance, policies, procedures, backlogs, fails-to-deliver, reconcilations, and so forth. In fact, they might start being more diligent about business and control management in order to keep from looking sloppy in front of examiners because that could prolong a most unwelcome visit.

Which failures does this essential help solve? Lots of the problems generated by breach of rules and regulations, to be sure, but also those coming from a weak internal process: a very thorough inspection of how a bank conducts its business from an internal perspective is bound to yield all sorts of little (or big) problems related to treatment of reserves, position valuation, stale inventory management, risk reporting and control, client disclosures, client valuations, collateral management, and so on. These are all internal procedures that, if flawed, can lead to stumbling or worse. A real probe can help root out these weak points. And who's responsible for implementation? Again, it has to start with chief regulators and auditors, who have to set the overarching philosophy and approach to investigations. It then becomes the tactical responsibility of (seasoned, we hope!) professionals on the ground, the ones managing investigations from day to day.

Essential #3: Implement wiser regulation. Regulators have to impose new rules and require new behaviors from everyone playing in the game. They have to improve oversight through stronger regulation and more regulation, if necessary. Free-marketers shudder at the thought of the words "more" and "regulation" in the same sentence. We all should because more regulation on its own is definitely not the answer. But more *wise* regulation can be the answer. With enough thought, foresight, consultation and cooperation, officials can create a handful of new and effective ground rules that everyone has to follow—in that way clients, investors, creditors and others will *feel* protected and will *be* protected. One of these ground rules centers on transparency, or revealing what's really happening down on the Street; the other is about abandoning the status quo, or actually fixing what's broken.

• *Demand transparency.* Regulators have to require more transparency. Wall Street firms are powerful, leveraged, and volatile, so why not get better information about what they're doing and put the details out in the open? If banks want to participate in forming the rules of transparency and voluntarily adhering to them, then they should. But if they don't, regulators should still proceed with wiser transparency rules. What are some of these?

Make firms give everyone meaningful information about their business operations, quickly and accurately. That means a *true picture of earnings:* no massaging of revenues, no fiddling with valuations or reserves, no pumping nasty things into SPEs or non–marked-to-market investment accounts. Regulators should require a more complete picture of how monies are flowing in and out of earnings accounts. If a bank makes or loses $x from its activities, it should just say so—it shouldn't hide, obfuscate, or "manage," just state the result. Who cares what the equity analysts say when EPS come in above or below for a quarter—aren't directors and executives in this for the long haul? If they are, then they should forget about the earnings forecasts and expectations, forget about the P&L games, and just be forthright. It's time to decouple fictional quarterly earnings "management" from the realities of financial operations (of course this ought to apply to all publicly held companies, not just financial institutions, but that's out of our scope).

And make Street firms give everyone a *true picture of risks.* They are, after all, in the risk business, so it would be nice, particularly for those who have given them capital, to know what risks they're actually taking and how they're faring. There have been lots of halfhearted attempts at improving this over the years, most of them driven by big credit or trading losses, concerns about systemic stability or damage to clients. Something bad happens, regulators ask for more risk information, banks produce it for a while, no one finds it particularly useful because it's couched in such oblique terms that nothing is actually conveyed, and then it gets buried in unreadable form in the financial statement footnotes; regulators, clients, and investors forget about it, and it's back to the status quo till the next blowup. Regulators should have banks publish meaningful data on risk profile and trend (again with a stress on the word *meaningful,* because it's easy enough to produce a load of risk information that says absolutely nothing): real intelligence on credit risk, market risk, liquidity risk, operational risk, legal risk—anything that can cause damage—reported in a sensible manner, with enough detail to let stakeholders know what could happen if things get bad. Some detail is essential, because stakeholders need to understand just how much risk is really embedded in an operation; broad measures (like value-at-risk, asset/liability gaps, gross credit exposure by rating) don't say much of anything, or are subject to too much interpretation to make them useful. And the point-in-time risk data that are conveyed in quarterlies and annual reports are largely useless because banks routinely window-dress to make things look better for the onetime snapshot. Far better for regulators to have banks focus on intra- and interperiod trends, concentrations, and illiquid positions to see whether the institution is getting more or less risky. We're not talking about giving away all the secrets and disclosing all the specifics of risk positions; that could result in a competitive disadvantage. But there is a level of granularity that can be supplied that informs investors without prejudicing the bank's stance in a particular market.

And then make banks disclose the *nature of their business relationships* and any potential conflicts of interest that may exist. Where things are a bit complicated or sticky regarding clients, relationships, dollars, and possible conflicts, a bank should be on record regarding how it manages to avoid prejudicing others. This has to touch on all areas: banking, research, sales, investment in client deals, directorships. Stakeholders should know, without any doubt, if a bank has ties that might lead it to do the wrong thing (or at least be tempted). And when independence is not the operating guideline within a bank's own board of directors (or, heaven forbid, its compensation committee), then it should be fixed, quickly. A board cannot have a majority of nonindependent directors running the show, or conflicts of interest will almost certainly arise.

Some will argue that all of this transparency will lead to a competitive disadvantage. We disagree. Everyone on the Street is doing the same business already anyway—slightly different versions, gradations, and magnitudes, to be sure, but it's all essentially the same. This just makes them a little more honest about it. Does it matter to the competition if Bank ABC says that it made $100 million in index arbitrage or lost $50 million in trading crude oil and that it actually did? Does it matter to the competition if ABC says it has a position in euros that will cost it $75 million if the euro appreciates 2 percent and gain $50 million if it depreciates 1 percent? Does it matter to the competition that ABC has increased its risk positions in index arbitrage and crude oil and lowered its exposure in euro over the past quarter? Does it matter to the competition if ABC says its "unthinkable disaster" scenario could cost $500 million if events 1, 2, and 3 occur, and that this represents an increase of $100 million over the last quarter? Does it matter to the competition if ABC says that it has completed a technology outsourcing agreement with a company that it floated on the exchange last month? It makes no difference. But it might make a difference to ABC's investors, so why not tell them? The same transparency needs to exist in other parts of Wall Street, like mutual funds: fund companies need to provide real information on their performance, risks, targets, fees, and compensation, without fudging or hiding behind shadows. Maybe some of the openness will remove some of the bad temptations that arise from running businesses and risks.

• *If it's broken, fix it.* We've talked about the comfort of the regulatory status quo; inertia is a very powerful force, so unless something is atrociously wrong, the "same old, same old" grinds on, and that's bound to lead to future problems. We've seen what happens when broken things remain broken: front running, collusion, research scandals, laddering, B share sales, abusive derivative transactions, late trading—all because a recognized flaw has been allowed to remain in place. When things aren't working from a regulatory perspective, they should be fixed as a matter of priority.

Regulators should never be satisfied with the status quo; they have to actively step in and fix things that aren't working properly. Why should history be the deciding factor in how things work? It shouldn't, but that means making some very jarring changes, like overhauling the obviously broken self-policing activities of exchanges as SROs; revamping a specialist/market-making system that allows front running, interpositioning, and collusion; holding banks much more firmly accountable for due diligence and fairness opinions; requiring brokers to be paid on a noncommission basis; clamping down on the sale of high-risk OTC derivatives to unsophisticated clients; banning market timing and late trading in funds; and so forth. Wise regulations can protect stakeholders from being hurt without squelching business.

Again, some will say this just creates a competitive disadvantage and is burdensome and expensive, to boot. And again, we would respectfully disagree, because an environment that is safer, even if it means some extra (wise) regulation, is going to generate more business over the medium term. Ultimately, of course, regulators want to think about deregulation as the end game. Generally speaking, the modern financial system wants a free hand to do what it can to generate profits, and that's certainly the right goal; the Street has succeeded, in large measure, because it hasn't been overburdened with regulations. But sometimes they're necessary, because when things are a little too fast and loose, abuses occur. Some of these regulations are useful enough that they have become (and should remain) permanent fixtures of the system. In other cases they have been (and can be) abandoned once they've served their purpose: when the abuses are brought under control, and banks can demonstrate they have adopted a more prudent approach to business, then it's okay to get rid of regulations. The final goal should be lower barriers to entry and greater disintermediation, but only when some of the good behaviors promulgated through wiser regulations have taken root. This approach is nothing new: when investors bought too much stock on margin in the late 1920s and set themselves up for financial collapse with the onset of the Great Crash, the Fed was given the power to regulate stock market credit; that prudent rule remains in place today because it's still useful for clients and intermediaries. When post-Garn-St. Germain S&Ls were allowed to do too much speculating in risky instruments and got into deep trouble, they had to be reregulated, and they have to adhere to the same rules to this day—prudent rules, certainly as far as S&L clients and customers are concerned. When banks lent too much to emerging nations and got burned, they had to abide by minimum capital standards, something that they still must do (again, prudent). When banks were taking advantage of capital markets investors by issuing new securities to pay off bad loans, regulators had to step in with Glass-Steagall; when that seemed no longer to be a concern, it was abandoned (it took a few decades, of course, but the proper behavior generally seems to have taken hold).

The key to all of this is making regulation stick. It's easy enough to create rules that say banks (and exchanges and funds) can or cannot do certain things. But if banks don't believe in them or don't find them useful, they'll comply only because they are requirements, meaning the right behaviors won't be inculcated into the culture. If regulations are not part of the culture—if they're not part of the internal operating environment—then the process again reverts to meaningless box checking: doing something because regulators say so, not because it's useful for daily business management. If regulation is synchronized so that everyone benefits, then it won't become a bureaucratic artifice. When regulators can develop rules that banks also find meaningful and that still provide the desired stakeholder protections, they've got rules that will be followed as a matter of course—day in and day out, without fail. It's already happened in some cases, but much more is needed. For instance, when the Bank for International Settlements was designing some new credit risk capital models, it shifted away from its old methodology—a mandated formula that everyone had to follow, but one so far removed from reality that no one used it except national regulators—to a new approach centered on what banks actually use to manage their credit business. So after each national regulator blesses credit risk models developed by each individual bank, regulators and bankers find they're using the same tools to control and monitor credit risk. This is a wise application of regulation: rules that are designed to protect stakeholders that are driven by the banks themselves. We need to see more of this approach because it works.

Which failures does this essential item help solve? Many of the client abuse problems we've talked about, including those based on misrepresentation, conflict of interest, and even fraud; it also addresses many of the problems that catch bank investors off guard (e.g., the firm is taking more risk than anyone believed, it is operating with very weak controls, and so forth). And who's responsible for implementation? Regulators, but not in isolation. Whatever they seek to do in terms of wise regulation should be done on a consultative basis with the industry—experience has already demonstrated that it's far better to get buy-in from the institutions that are going to have to adhere to the rules.

Essential #4: Clamp down on conflicts. This external essential is very simple. In the last chapter we said no conflicts of interest for those working at banks (or within SROs), and in this chapter we repeat the message: no conflicts for regulators and auditors responsible for overseeing or reviewing banks. This means banks can't poach regulators or auditors who are covering them, and regulators or auditors who want to make a move to the other side have to go through a cooling-off period lasting at least several years.

That some people in oversight roles want to work on the Street is a good thing because it encourages "cross pollination" and a diffusion of the regulatory mind set throughout the financial industry. But it's clear that any move where a previous oversight relationship has existed presents a conflict. Unfortunately, even the appearance of such a situation can strip away client or investor comfort in the independent control process, meaning it has to be avoided at all costs. If you read in the newspaper that Bank XYZ has just hired, as its head risk auditor, the former head of the risk audit practice at XYZ's long-standing auditor, you're at least going to wonder how the candidate got the job, whether there has been any funny business, and whether the right level of trust can remain going forward. Why take the chance, why leave stakeholders wondering and, indeed, why put the auditors and regulators into a situation where they might be tempted to do something untoward?

So regulators and auditors, from the most junior to the most senior, can't be permitted to work for institutions that they are, or have been, responsible for examining. The potential conflicts and temptations that surface when the gamekeeper can turn poacher are considerable, meaning the gamekeeper either has to remain a gamekeeper forever, or cool off before joining the ranks of the poachers. It's really not more complicated than that; regulators and auditors must forbid their own from making a switch to the other team for two, three, or five years, and bank managers must agree not to hire any officials or auditors over the same time period. All temptations are removed, all possible conflicts are excised and another little loophole that can cause a slipup is closed; the regulatory and audit processes become that much tighter.

Which failures does this essential item help solve? Any weakness in internal controls, regulatory reporting, policy, or process that might be purposely "overlooked" by potential job jumpers and that might lead ultimately to client or proprietary losses. Even in less extreme situations it can remove the appearance of any questionable business and let stakeholders breathe a little bit easier. And who's responsible for implementation? Executive leaders on Wall Street and the heads of regulatory agencies and audit firms: they must agree among themselves on proper cooling off ground rules, and then get their compliance/enforcement functions to monitor adherence.

Essential #5: Punish the violators. Those who violate regulations need to be punished by external authorities. If this sounds like something from the last chapter, it's meant to, because it provides a second round of discipline to keep folks on the straight and narrow. Just as directors and executives have a duty to punish their own, regulators have a duty and obligation to punish firms in their jurisdictions that don't comply with the rules. Unfortunately we've seen that they often let the bad guys slither away with some nominal fine or sanction—meaning we're back to the paper tiger, but this time a regulatory paper tiger, which is even more dangerous because regulators are supposed to oversee, control, discipline, and provide a sense of security. A look at the Wall Street track record of the past few decades suggests that no one cares what the regulators see, do, or find, because nothing bad ever really happens. We've already seen that those who take advantage of Moms and Pops or pull a fast one on institutional clients face light penalties and thus have little reason to change their behavior. The only exceptions seem to involve instances of widespread, sometimes industry-wide misbehavior or fraud—even then, the hundreds of millions in fines meted out sometimes do little to alter behavior (for banks with deep pockets, fines of $50 million or $100 million or $200 million are pocket change). Smaller infractions go unchecked and unpunished, even though they can be just as damaging (sometimes even more so).

Serious violations and financial crime, in whatever form, should be treated with severity, not the leniency that has been so obvious over the years. Harsh financial and business penalties should be applied to those who think they are clever enough to get away with doing the wrong thing. Regulators (and the courts, where applicable) have a duty to make punishment swift and meaningful and must enforce the process; discipline should be frequent, and the penalties stiff. Not only does harsh discipline place the burden of transgression where it belongs, it sends a very powerful message to other would-be evildoers contemplating similar infractions: do the wrong thing and you'll pay the price.

While we're on the topic of infractions, it's time for regulators to stop allowing no-contest plea bargains. Authorities have too often been willing to let the Street slide through problems by writing checks and agreeing to some minor (often meaningless) reforms, but not admitting to any wrongdoing. This lets banks escape the taint of bad publicity (and possibly a few lawsuits) and cheapens the process. Why is Wall Street never guilty of anything, even though the evidence indicates just the opposite? Why isn't the act of pulling out the (shareholder-funded) checkbook to resolve a problem not taken to be what it is, an admission of guilt? (Bank executives say that they write those checks only to avoid lengthy and costly litigation in which they would undoubtedly prevail, but which would be distracting to business. Right.) It's a given that all parties are innocent until proven guilty. But if a bank doesn't believe it's done anything wrong, it shouldn't be writing checks—it should simply defend itself against the prosecutor's charges. And regulators shouldn't be cutting any more deals.

Which failures does this essential item help solve? Most of the ones associated with doing the wrong thing. Though we've seen that stumbling can lead to problems and losses, the stumbles often aren't associated with regulatory breaches; doing the wrong thing, however, generally involves violating rules and regulations. The abuses that occur in such cases, if dealt with through proper fines and discipline, might finally send the right message to others contemplating similar behavior and almost certainly help lower the frequency and severity of abuse. And who's responsible for implementation? The enforcement arms of regulators and, in cases leading through the courts, attorneys general and the legal system. They have the collective power to come down hard on those who tamper with the rules.

Essential #6: Make sure stakeholders act responsibly. Of course banks have lots of house cleaning ahead of them, and regulators and auditors have some shoring up to do as well; the combination of the two, if done in earnest, might well yield good results. But other external stakeholders—clients and bank investors, in particular—have a part to play in the repair job as well. They have to take greater responsibility for their own actions.

• *Clients.* If we think about some of the failures that have appeared over the years, it's pretty clear that clients have to stand up and take their share of the blame. It they weren't as susceptible to Wall Street's aggressive pitches, it's likely that problems wouldn't always get quite as bad as they do; if they weren't as gullible or greedy, the losses wouldn't be as spectacular. Again, we're not looking for scapegoats: the failures that we've discussed in this book are primarily of the Street's own making. But sometimes clients are too eager to believe the hyped research and buy the latest hot stock or bond so they can strike it rich; they are too eager to borrow more than they should, float their companies before they're ready, or buy derivatives that are riskier than they can handle. These behaviors make it far easier for the Street to fail to do the right thing.

Let's look at retail and institutional investment as an example. It's pretty easy to see when investment clients are only seeing dollar signs (or potential dollar signs) and ignoring warning signs: they invest in transactions that are increasingly speculative, unstable, or questionable, they take on more leverage (margin, bank borrowing, repurchase agreement financings), they ignore the risk disclosure in those hard-to-read prospectuses, they listen far too intently when researchers say that the next IPO company really can trade at 250 times expected 2025 earnings—all because they want a shot at the pot of gold. But they're forgetting that traversing the rainbow is fraught with danger, and that the pot of gold may just be an illusion. Clients get greedy, just like Wall Streeters. It tends to happen during strong markets when every day is an up day, when all the day trading is profitable, when the IPOs and add-ons skyrocket, and credit spreads come screaming in. Caution is thrown to the wind. But everyone is just setting up for some disappointment, because it always comes crashing down—the markets tank, the day trading sours, the shares plummet, and the credit spreads blow out. Then everyone tallies up the losses and tax carry-forwards, and some even call up their lawyers to schedule arbitration or court time. The same thing is true in every other facet of Wall Street business we've discussed: in hopes of making lots of dollars, clients participate in too much unwise borrowing, too much ill-advised equity issuance, too many risky derivatives or structured notes, or too many bad corporate finance transactions.

Clients have to check their behavior and not fall into the greed trap. They shouldn't forget the lessons of history, how good times (and then leveraged good times) are always followed by bad times. They shouldn't forget that there isn't any easy money to be made on the Street: every return has its risk, and there just aren't any outsize profit opportunities available for exploitation. If something looks too good, it is too good. If something's got huge returns, it can't be risk free, no matter what the bankers, brokers, and research analysts might say. Clients should remember not to get caught up in the spin and hype and frenzy and the promise of quick riches. All of this is easy to say, of course, but much harder to put into practice, especially at the tail end of a hot market cycle. Financial history shows us that speculative bubbles have existed for centuries because human nature is what it is; "more" is a preferred state, and this has been true for many, many years: the Tulip bubble of the seventeenth century, the South Sea bubble of the eighteenth century, the cotton and railroad frenzies of the late nineteenth century, the leveraged trusts of the 1920s, the go-go stocks of the 1960s, the emerging market carry trades of the 1990s, the TMT bubble of the millennium. Clients should exercise restraint, caution, and skepticism, and try to suppress (or at least manage) the powerful greed instinct.

*   *Shareholders.* Shareholders have to step up to the plate, too. They've got to take more control of their investment capital by making sure directors are doing what they're supposed to. Shareholders are the key external stakeholders in the process, certainly from a legal perspective (more important, even, than clients). As we've already said, each share they own conveys legal rights, and they've got to exercise these rights by being much more active and forceful watchdogs. We alluded to some of this in the previous chapter: shareholders have some ability to select and vote for directors, their representatives. This means they have to be involved in the process, finding out which current directors are good or bad, contributing or detracting, which candidates are on the shortlist for future directorships, the track record and experience they bring to bear, and so forth. Then they need to vote their proxies. Those following the "my vote is too small to count" approach relinquish their responsibilities and no longer have a right to complain when things turn sour. Those taking an active and involved stance can actually make a difference—this is especially true at the institutional level. And the process extends beyond director selection to cover other areas of corporate interest. Mechanisms allow agenda items to be tabled for a vote—these can cover compensation policies, acquisitions, expensing of stock options, and so forth (i.e., issues that shareholders should care about, as they affect the value of the firm they've invested in). It is incumbent upon each and every Street shareholder to help shore up the defenses through informed action.

Which external failures does this essential solve? Those that can put clients in harm's way and, by extension, lead to shareholder losses. Knowledgeable and prudent clients who deflect the latest pitch for bad financing deals, questionable acquisitions, or frothy investments are protecting themselves and their financial interests. They are saying "no" to the Street's overly exuberant deals/sales calls and the financial losses that can follow if they happen to be bad ones. And bank shareholders ultimately fare better as a result: when they aren't caught up in the latest Street scandal or failure, they save themselves some aggravation and dollars. And who's responsible for implementation? The two groups, obviously: clients have to take care of their responsibilities, investors theirs.

Essential #7: Remember that it's still caveat emptor. And in the end, everyone still has to be warned to watch out. There's always a risk that investors, clients, and other stakeholders will be lulled into complacency when things quiet down, when the Street has gone on for a few weeks or months without some major blowup, or when the bull market is back in town and clients are feeling wealthy again. That's actually one of the most dangerous scenarios because it sets everyone up for another fall when the next Street failure rolls around.

Stakeholders have to be on the lookout for any kind of behavior that doesn't look or sound right (e.g., overly aggressive investment bankers, institutional salespeople, or brokers pushing a hot deal, transaction or investment, analyst research ratings that are way too skewed toward "buy," good rankings in the deal league tables but poor rankings in disclosed fees, long delays in getting valuations on derivatives or other complex instruments, and so on). It's vitally important for regulators, auditors, and other external watchdogs to remind folks that the Street fails in key areas and, despite efforts at internal and external "fixing," more such failures are likely to occur in the future—though with greater awareness and some real repairs, the instance of failure should decline. But the bottom line is that everyone needs to conduct his or her Wall Street dealings with eyes wide open, vigilant toward shortcomings, conflicts, or bad behavior.

Chapter 12

SUMMARY: WHAT'S NEXT?

We've walked through Wall Street over the past few chapters and taken a look at aspects of business that don't always work out right, we've considered why they don't go right, and we've discussed what might be done to improve the situation. Let's now summarize some of our thoughts by asking, semi-rhetorically, "What's next?"

What's next depends on how Wall Streeters and the Street's stakeholders view all of the transgressions we've highlighted.

Do Wall Streeters believe there are problems with the way business is conducted, or do they think things are good enough? Are they happy to continue with the status quo? Can they convince themselves that their behavior is acceptable because it's the same type of behavior that's existed for the past 10, 20, or 100 years? Can they argue that things are okay because business works out [pretty well/perfectly well] 50 percent, 75 percent, or 95 percent of the time? If they think things are satisfactory—that the mistakes and malfeasances we've described are par for the course and really not too damaging in the grand scheme of things—then the answer to the question of "what's next?" is simple: a continuation of the past. For a while, at any rate. If the Street doesn't see too much wrong with the way things work, there will be no change from within.

And do stakeholders believe that the misbehaviors we've noted are bad enough to take a stand and demand change? Are regulators, auditors, clients, and investors willing to insist on fair play, reforms, new (and hopefully wise) regulations, and accountability? Some have shown their mettle by fighting the tough battles, and their efforts certainly help the broader constituency. But what about the rest of the stakeholders? If they aren't willing to make some of the difficult decisions by reallocating capital, disintermediating business, imposing new rules, voting their proxies, or insisting on new behaviors, then the answer to "what's next?" is again simple: more of the same. Without meaningful external pressure there can be no change.

What's next also depends on how the Street and its stakeholders recall past events.

When the sun is shining, markets are strong, corporate profits buoyant, investors doing well, and deals flowing smoothly, there is a tendency for Wall Streeters to forget about the dark days. We don't have to look too far back to see how quickly problems and failures are glossed over when the Street is back on top. When money is being made, it's all right to forget about the times when money was lost (however it was lost: trading, lending, bad controls, client settlements). This takes us back to the fundamental problem we've mentioned several times: the Street ignores the lessons of history. Unfortunately, many stakeholders suffer from the same amnesia: when the next bull market appears and there are M&A deals to be done, capital to be raised, assets to be invested, and new hot stocks or bonds to buy, stakeholders have a tendency to forget all about the dark days, too. So it's almost a given that when the storm clouds gather during future market cycles, there will be more failed deals, irate customers, and client and investor losses, because problems appearing during the last market dislocation haven't been properly addressed. The clients will start screaming and shouting, and the next round of mea culpas and sword falling will commence; some checks will be written, some no-contests pleaded, and the regulators will wake up and do a little wrist slapping or try to push through some new (after-the-fact) rules. But perhaps only a small amount of permanent, meaningful improvement will occur. So what about the next one? Will Wall Street and the Street's stakeholders remember all of the problems from the last gray days or will they forget? Will they take action in the present to avoid problems in the future?

"What's next" depends ultimately on what Wall Streeters and their stakeholders want to do. If the parties recognize that some relatively significant changes are required in order to improve things for everyone (regardless of market cycle), then some of the "essentials" we've summarized in chapters 10 and 11 can form the basis of discussion. If not, then let's all prepare for more replays of history.

THE IMPLICATIONS OF THE STATUS QUO

If the Street is unwilling to change its stripes (or doesn't believe that it has to, to any significant degree) the status quo remains. That means we shouldn't be surprised to see more of the same mistakes and misbehavior discussed in this book. They may take somewhat different form, but they will just be variations on an all-too-familiar theme. Internal and external stakeholders will continue to be hurt. At some point, though, the Street risks damaging some (much?) of what has been painstakingly created by many people and firms over many decades. Recall the comment from chapter 1 about the importance of Wall Street as a financial conduit and financial innovator. Its role is unique and vital, and it does a good amount of business fairly. But with each new instance of failure, scandal, or treachery, the fantastic mechanism that is Wall Street is damaged further; the resilience it has shown over time is threatened. Like the boxer taking repeated blows, it is a question of time before the Street is on the ropes and then on the mat. Absent change, the damage might become so severe that aspects of the function will be permanently destroyed. Stakeholders can only be hurt so many times before they lose confidence in the system and process. That, of course, would have significant consequences for many aspects of economic and financial progress.

Let's imagine that the status quo persists, meaning failures such as we've discussed continue to appear at regular intervals. Irate clients will start disintermediating Wall Street, looking to other mechanisms to obtain the services they require. It won't be easy (and in some cases it will be impossible, as there simply are no good substitutes), but it will almost certainly happen to some degree. Consider that a number of large corporations already handle most of their own capital-raising requirements. Firms like GM, GE, Ford, UPS, and others have direct-to-investor programs that let them issue securities without going through the Street. Others, like Vodafone and BAT, put together their own loans by organizing "syndicate club deals" on their own terms. These programs can't yet accommodate all of their funding requirements, but they prove that it is possible to raise funds without direct bank participation. So if the Street does a poor job in raising capital, capital disintermediation may accelerate. The same might occur in M&A business. Big firms such as GE, Pepsi, Viacom, Berkshire Hathaway, and Johnson & Johnson (again, among many others) have sourced, arranged, and executed multibillion dollar acquisition programs in recent years using their own internal "bankers," disintermediating Wall Street from its traditional investment banking role. So if the Street does a poor job in its M&A duties (e.g., bad advice, bad due diligence, bad fairness opinions, letting companies overpay), M&A disintermediation may accelerate. Trading and execution may also begin to shift from traditional conduits to the electronic platforms that have developed in recent years. Again, it doesn't mean wholesale abandonment of traditional organs like established stock and futures exchanges, but it might mean some redirection of business to alternative conduits. In the retail sector it's increasingly possible for

Moms and Pops to establish their own financial plans/targets, set up their own IRAs and savings plans, access independent research electronically, and execute their own trades (indeed, only 30 percent of wealthy private investors use a full-service broker as their primary advisor, down from 40 percent at the turn of the millennium; more have come to rely on their own skills or those of independent financial advisors, and the trend may spread to average-wealth investors). So if the Street does a poor job in handling its retail responsibilities, private client disintermediation can easily accelerate. Again, disintermediation won't occur across the board, with every company, client, or transaction; the markets are too complex for that to occur. But sticking with the status quo and not handling clients and deals properly will almost certainly lead to some loss of business, and that is obviously bad for the Street. It may also be damaging to broader economic and financial growth.

Preserving the status quo might also mean a dearth of bank capital for business expansion and risk activities. If investors continue to be mistreated, will they want to continue investing in Street firms? If it's clear that failures are taking real dollars out of their pockets, why not withdraw and invest elsewhere? In fact, that might occur. Lack of capital would have a serious impact on Street banks, particularly as they try to do more business or take more risks. They would be forced to pay more for capital funds, compressing their own profitability and making marginal investment or funding activities less attractive. They would have less of a cushion to take risks, meaning loss of business to others who might have greater capitalization. And they would have less risk capacity and a much smaller appetite for offering risk services to clients, which would also affect broader economic progress.

THE IMPLICATIONS OF CHANGE

What's the flip side? Abandoning the status quo and attempting to reform aspects of business presents an additional cost (and, perhaps, a bit of confusion) in the short run, but a far more profitable and secure business environment for all stakeholders in the medium term. Firms recognizing the need for change and willing to enact essentials such as we have proposed (or others that lead to some of the same end goals) can create an atmosphere in which quality business is done continuously and clients win; other stakeholders—investors, regulators, communities—come out ahead as well. Let's not pretend that this is some magical world and that the Street, in reforming its ways, will bring peace and harmony to all things. No such world exists—the Street will always have problems of one sort or another, and stakeholders will always suffer some losses.

That, as we've said, is the nature of free markets and a flexible system of capitalism. We simply mean to reemphasize what we noted in chapter 10: that diligence in doing the right things—promoting the right business in the right way—brings gains to all stakeholders and strengthens the industry. The contributions that Wall Street has provided over the years remain valuable and continue to expand and strengthen. While aspects of disintermediation might still occur, it will be for positive reasons (e.g., the search for corporate or retail efficiencies and cost savings) rather than negative ones (e.g., the search for alternatives so as not be abused by the Street). And capital will continue to flow: bank investors won't turn off the spigot because they will be earning fair returns and won't be faced with the prospect of ongoing accidents or problems that detract from the bottom line.

As noted, change involves a cost. Many of the internal and external essentials we've summarized have a price tag: hiring better businesspeople, auditors, and regulators, implementing more robust technology and controls, creating new (wise!) regulations, attracting more seasoned and diligent directors, rationalizing operations where needed, and so on, cost money. But the costs must be viewed as an investment and evaluated in a net present value framework. By balancing the dollar cost allocated today (and every year thereafter) to enact proper essentials against the gains reaped over time from more and better business, plus savings from a smaller number of mistakes and client mishandlings (lawsuits, arbitration, settlements), the result will undoubtedly be strongly positive. And this excludes the intangible benefits that will undoubtedly accrue: goodwill, integrity, trust and reputation can work to the Street's benefit by generating more business.

In 1972 then–Merrill Lynch Chairman and CEO Don Regan predicted that "by 1980 Wall Street will have lost lots of its distinctive flavor . . . the Street will be the scene of a lot less colorful action than we have witnessed in the past few years."[1] That, of course, hasn't proved to be the case. The Street has become exceptionally colorful over the past three decades, and there seems no doubt that it will become even more colorful in the future—that is the nature of financial business in a dynamic world. The question is whether the picture that emerges will have the hues of progress and reform.

Notes

CHAPTER 1—WALL STREET AND ITS ROLE

1. W. Ripley, *Main Street and Wall Street* (Whitefish, MT: Kessinger Publishing, 2003 [reprint of 1929]).
2. Address before the Securities Industry Association, October 2003.
3. J. Revell, "Levitt Speaks Out," *Fortune,* November 24, 2003.
4. F. Rohatyn, "Free, Wealthy, and Fair," *Wall Street Journal,* Op-ed, November 16, 2003.

CHAPTER 2—WHEN THE INTENDED ROLE FAILS

1. Former SEC official and Stanford University law professor Joseph Grundfest has put it very nicely: "There is no securities fairy paying the settlements. We're simply moving money from investors' right pocket to investors' left pocket." From N. Varchaver, "Winona, Martha and the Securities Fairy," *Fortune,* August 11, 2003.

CHAPTER 3—PROBLEMS RAISING CAPITAL

1. J. Creswell, "Too Good to Last," *Fortune,* March 13, 2003.
2. Morgan Stanley, *Technology IPO Yearbook,* March 2002.
3. Figures from J. Ritter, "Money Left on the Table," University of Florida working paper, 2003.
4. Figures from J. Ritter, "Some Factoids about the IPO Market," University of Florida working paper, 2002.

CHAPTER 4—BAD CORPORATE ADVICE

1. D. Henry, "Felix Rohatyn on Wall Street's Corruption," *Business Week,* May 3, 2002.
2. D. Henry, "Why Most Big Deals Don't Pay Off," *Business Week,* October 14, 2002.
3. A *Financial Times* op-ed, written shortly after the Bank of America/Fleet merger, captures the scenario nicely: "The prospect of investment bankers pocketing millions for advising clients to do what turns out to be a lousy deal is unappetizing. Several academic studies published in the past couple of years have suggested that two-thirds of deals fail." Lex, *Financial Times,* October, 29, 2003.
4. In L. Endlich, *Goldman Sachs: A Culture of Success* (New York: Touchstone, 2000), p. 11.

5. All references from U.S. Bankruptcy Court, In Re Enron, Third Interim Report, Neal Batson, 2003.
6. "Enron's Getaway Drivers," *Wall Street Journal*, July 29, 2003.

CHAPTER 5—BAD PERSONAL ADVICE

1. S. Syre, "Instant Incrimination," *Boston Globe*, August 12, 2003.

CHAPTER 6—BREACHING TRUST

1. G. Zuckerman, "Gutfreund King of the Street Returns to Less Exalted Post," *Wall Street Journal*, November 14, 2001.
2. T. Lauricella, "For Staid Mutual Fund Industry, Growing Probe Signals Shake-up," *Wall Street Journal*, October 1, 2003.
3. SEC v. Merrill Lynch 2003 filing.
4. P. Beckett, "Banks Raise Pressure to Get Loans," *Wall Street Journal*, March 19, 2003.
5. G. Farrell, "UBS Analyst Quits," *USA Today*, July 3, 2003.
6. In SEC v. CSFB, 2002.
7. From proceedings of Merrill Lynch Annual General Meeting 2003.
8. Goldman Sachs 2002 Annual Report.
9. Citicorp 2002 Annual Report.
10. G. Crecsi, "Spitzer Sternly Rebukes ML CEO O'Neal," *Forbes*, April 2003.
11. PBS Frontline, "The Wall Street Fix," 2003.
12. P. Sellers, "The Trials of John Mack," *Fortune*, July 2003.
13. Alaska Journal of Commerce, May 5, 2003.
14. M. Goldstein, "CalPERS Sues WorldCom Bond Underwriters," *The Street*, July 16, 2003.
15. PricewaterhouseCoopers, "Operational Risk" (New York: PwC, 2001).
16. Institutional Investor, ed., *The Way It Was* (New York: Institutional Investor, 1988), p. 75.
17. Ibid., p. 43.
18. Ibid., p. 311.
19. Ibid., p. 473.
20. Ibid., p. 583.
21. Ibid., p. 175.

CHAPTER 7—BAD RISK MANAGEMENT

1. Institutional Investor, ed., *The Way it Was* (New York: Institutional Investor, 1988), p. 87.
2. In J. Brooks, *The Go-Go Years* (New York: Ballantine, 1974), p. 259.
3. J.P. Morgan Chase, Annual Report 2002.
4. In F. Partnoy, *Infectious Greed* (New York: Times Books, 2003), p. 31.
5. Institutional Investor, ed., *The Way it Was* (New York: Institutional Investor, 1988), pp. 418–419.

CHAPTER 9—EXTERNAL WEAKNESS

1. M. Maremont and D. Salomon, "Behind the SEC's Failings," *Wall Street Journal*, December 24, 2003.

2. Berkshire Hathaway Annual Report, 2002.
3. M. Maremont and D. Salomon, "Behind the SEC's Failings," *Wall Street Journal,* December 24, 2003.

CHAPTER 12—SUMMARY: WHAT'S NEXT?

1. In J. Brooks, *The Go-Go Years* (New York: Ballantine, 1973), p. 348.

Index

ABN Amro, 155–156
A.G. Edwards, 14, 96, 113, 165
Aiding and abetting, 124–128
Allfirst, 192, 196–199, 226–227, 241
Alliance Capital, 15, 95, 123
Allied Irish Bank, 198–199
American Express, 171, 174
American Stock Exchange (AMEX), 3,
    15, 234, 238
Ameritrade, 212
AMEX, See American Stock Exchange
AOL Time Warner, 56–57

Bad corporate advice, 51–85
Bad due diligence, 151–157
Bad personal financial advice, 87–109
Bad management, 209–224
Bad risk management, 165–199
Bank of America, 14, 32, 94, 95, 123,
    129–130, 154–156, 179, 198–199,
    211, 222
Bank One, 123, 170
Bankers Trust, 14, 21, 28, 62–63, 74–78,
    83, 183, 186, 210, 214–215
Barclays, 34, 60, 126
Barings, 191, 193, 196–199, 226–227, 241,
    261
Bear Stearns, 14, 63, 82, 87, 123, 143,
    145, 149, 159–160, 173, 187–189,
    191, 205, 236
Blodget, H., 140–141, 148
Breaching trust, 111–163
Buffett, W., 74, 120, 170, 188, 234

Canadian Imperial Bank of Commerce
    (CIBC), 60, 126, 154, 179, 211
Capek, H., 141
CBOT, See Chicago Board of Trade

Chase [Manhattan] Bank, 139, 195, 212,
    215, 218
Chemical Bank, 183, 192
Chicago Board of Trade (CBOT), 116
Chicago Mercantile Exchange (CME),
    116
Chinese walls, 114–115
CIBC, See Canadian Imperial Bank of
    Commerce
Citibank, 13–14, 32, 34, 36, 56, 59–61, 78,
    87, 97, 99, 121, 123, 126, 129,
    131–132, 140–144, 146–147,
    153–156, 165, 167, 169, 179,
    188–189, 198–199, 205, 210–213,
    215, 218, 221, 223
Citron, R., 70–73
CME, See Chicago Mercantile Exchange
Commodity Futures Trading Commission
    (CFTC), 230
Corrigan, G., 120
Credit Lyonnais, 167
Credit Suisse First Boston (CSFB), 14, 47,
    60, 71–73, 78, 83, 87, 95, 97, 99,
    113, 122, 126, 129, 132–134, 140,
    142, 148, 150–151, 165, 167, 170,
    172, 174–175, 179, 184, 189–190,
    207, 211, 213, 215, 218, 222
CSFB, See Credit Suisse First Boston
CFTC, See Commodity Futures Trading
    Commission

Daiwa Bank, 192, 227
Derivatives and other instruments, 73–85
Deutsche Bank, 14, 34, 60, 63, 78, 87,
    113, 149, 155–156, 165, 167, 173,
    210–211, 213–215
Dillon Read, 66, 113
DLJ, See Donaldson, Lufkin, and Jenrette

Donaldson, Lufkin, and Jenrette (DLJ), 14, 32, 87, 172, 210, 211, 212, 215
Donaldson, W., 16, 144
Dresdner, 122, 189, 211–2113, 215
Dreyfus, 92
Drexel Burnham Lambert, 15, 28, 32, 54, 121, 136–139, 171–172, 190, 218
Drysdale Securities, 195

E.F. Hutton, 220
Enron, 59–61, 62–63, 125–126, 150, 153, 180
Etoys, 48–49
Etrade, 212
External weakness, 239–244

Failure of intended role, 17–28
Flawed governance, 204–209
FleetBoston, 60, 177, 211, 221
Front running, collusion, insider trading, fraud, 115–124

Galvin, W., 123, 233
Garn-St.Germain, 66
Getting the house in order, 247–264
Gibson Greetings, 76–78
Giuliani, R., 233
Glass-Steagall, 13
Goldman Sachs, 3, 13–15, 24, 34, 37, 46, 48–49, 53, 56, 66, 69, 83, 87, 100, 113, 121–122, 130, 133, 142, 144, 146, 152–154, 165, 167, 173, 179–180, 183–184, 188, 190, 194, 205, 208, 211, 215, 217, 236
Goldman Sachs Trust Corporation, 66
Gramm-Leach-Bliley, 13
Grasso, D., 235–236
Greenberg, A., 173
Grubman, J., 140–141, 146–147
Gruntal, 15, 219–220
Gutfreund, J., 119–121
Guth, W., 163

Hannan Investment Trust, 81
HSBC, 223

Ignoring conflicts of interest, 135–151
Internal breakdown, 203–288

Janus Capital, 15, 123
Jett, J., 192–194
J.P. Morgan Chase, 13–15, 21, 32, 34, 36–37, 59–61, 66, 71, 78–81, 99, 118, 122, 126, 128, 131, 133–134, 142, 145, 154, 160, 165, 167, 169, 174–177, 179–180, 184, 205, 211, 218

Kidder Peabody, 15, 82, 121, 170, 190, 192–194, 208, 218, 226–227, 241
Kohlberg Kravis Roberts, 54

Late trading, 122
Lazard, 14, 113, 165
Leeson, N., 191, 193, 196–199, 208, 226
Legg Mason, 92
Lehman, 3, 14–15, 54, 87, 113, 140, 143, 153, 160–161, 165, 167, 171, 195, 205, 210, 211, 222
Leverage, 67–73
Levitt, A., 16, 124
Limited partnerships, 95
Loeb, J., 163
Long Term Capital Management (LTCM), 27, 40, 149, 187–190
Loomis Sayles, 123
LTCM, See Long Term Capital Management

Mack, J., 151
Mahonia, 59–61
Margin, 100
Meeker, M., 140, 145
Mercury Asset Management, 211, 214, 223
Meriwether, J., 119–121
Merrill Lynch, 3, 13–14, 21, 32, 34, 56, 63, 69, 71–73, 82–85, 87, 95–97, 100, 113, 118, 125–126, 128, 140–144, 148–150, 153, 155,160, 165, 167, 175, 179, 182–184, 187, 189–191, 195, 205, 208, 210–215, 217–218, 221–224, 261
MFS, 123–124
Milken, M., 136–139
Mitchell, C., 139
Morgan Stanley, 13–14, 32, 54, 56, 69, 71–73, 83, 94, 97, 106–108, 113,

117, 133, 140, 142–145, 165, 167, 171, 173, 184
Morgenthau, R., 61, 207
Mozer, P., 119–121
Mutual funds, 90–92

NASD, See National Association of Securities Dealers
Nasdaq, 15, 117–118
National Association of Securities Dealers (NASD), 98, 104, 107, 117–118, 134
National Australia Bank, 192, 241
National City, 31, 139
New York Stock Exchange (NYSE), 3, 15, 98, 116, 134, 161, 234–238
Nomura, 71–73
NYSE, See New York Stock Exchange

Olde Discount, 97
Orange County, 69–73

Paine Webber, 14, 87, 95, 113, 118, 189, 211, 215
Payment for order flow, 100, 150
Phelan, J., 162–163
Pilgrim and Baxter, 123
Piper Jaffray, 14, 95, 113, 143, 145, 211, 221
Prepaid swaps, 59, 61
Problems raising capital, 29–49
Procter & Gamble, 74–76
Prudential, 14, 28, 87, 95–96, 113, 210, 220
Putnam, 15

Quattrone, F., 132, 150–151

Retail infractions, 134–135
Risk,
   Mispricing, 182–190
   Not controlling, 190–199
   Not understanding, 169–182
   Why take, 166–168
R.J. Reynolds, 54
Robertson Stephens, 134, 211, 221
Rockefeller, D., 162
Rohatyn, F., 16, 52, 163
Role of Wall Street, 3–16
Royal Bank of Scotland, 126, 186, 192

Rubin, H., 182–183, 191
Rubin, R., 58, 186
Rusnak, J., 196–199, 226

Salomon, 113, 118–121, 169, 173, 183, 179, 195, 208, 210, 241
Salomon, B., 173
Schwab, 14, 100, 123, 165, 205–206, 212, 222
Scottrade, 212
SEC, See Securities and Exchange Commission
Securities and Exchange Commission (SEC), 107, 118, 123, 125, 134, 149, 152, 160–161, 230, 234, 236–238
Securities Investor Protection Corporation (SIPC), 88
Self-regulatory organization, 90, 134, 236, 238
S.G. Cowen, 160–161
Shinsegi Investment Trust, 81
Shoring up the defenses, 265–278
SIPC, See Securities Investor Protection Corporation
SK Securities, 80–81
Societe Generale, 122, 160
Soros, G., 74
Spitzer, E., 123, 142–143, 147, 233
SRO, See Self-regulatory organization
Strong Capital, 15, 123
Sumitomo Corporation, 127–128

TD Waterhouse, 212
Tying, reverse tying, spinning, laddering, 128–134

UBS, See Union Bank of Switzerland
Union Bank of Switzerland (UBS), 14, 34, 87, 97, 122–123, 130, 140–141, 143, 145, 149, 160, 165, 167, 170, 179, 181–182, 187, 189, 196, 211, 213, 215, 218, 227, 241

Van Kampen, 92, 106–108
Vanguard, 92
Violating regulations, 114–124

Wachovia, 14, 87, 211

Wall Street
  Bad corporate advice, 51–85
    Bad corporate finance advice, 51–64
      Mergers and acquisitions, 52–58
      Special purpose entities, window-
        dressing, tax deals, 58–64
    Bad investment advice, 64–85
      Derivatives and other instruments,
        73–85
      Leverage, 67–73
  Bad personal financial advice, 87–109
    Risky instruments, 93–101
    Bad behavior, 101–109
      Churning, unauthorized trading,
        selling away, 101–103
      Lies, cold-calls, favoritism, 103–109
    Brokers sell, 89–90
  Bad risk management, 165–199
    Mispricing risk, 182–190
    Not controlling risk, 190–199
    Not understanding risk, 169–182
      Building risky relationships, 178–182
      Investing badly, 174–178
      Trading and originating risky things,
        169–174
    Why take risk, 166–168
  Breaching trust, 111–163
    Bad due diligence, 151–157
    Ignoring conflicts of interest, 135–151
    Jeopardizing customer assets, 157–163
    Violating regulations, 114–124
      Aiding and abetting, 124–128
      Chinese walls, 114–115
      Front running, collusion, insider
        trading, fraud, 115–124
      Retail infractions, 134–135
      Tying, reverse tying, spinning,
        laddering, 128–134
  External weakness, 239–244
    Stumbling auditors, 238–244
      Conflicts of interest, 241–244

      Technical inadequacies, 240–241
    Stumbling regulators, 230–239
      Checking the boxes, 231–233
      Closing the barn door, 238–239
      Conflicts, 235–238
      Status quo is okay, 233–235
      Too green, 231
  Failure of intended role, 17–28
  Internal breakdown, 203–288
    Bad management, 209–224
      Bad execution, 214–220
      No strategic focus, 209–214
      Time to reverse, 220–224
    Flawed governance, 204–209
    Poor skills and controls, 224–228
  Problems raising capital, 29–49
    Excessive debt, 31–37
    Excessive equity, 37–39
    Not enough money, 39–41
    Wrong price, 41–49
  Role of, 3–16
    Giving corporate advice, 8–9
    Giving personal financial advice, 9–10
    Key players, 12–16
    Managing risks, 11–12
    Performing fiduciary tasks, 10–11
    Raising capital, 6–7
Wasserstein Perella, 54, 56, 58, 211, 215
Weill, S., 147, 189
Wells Fargo, 175–177
West Virginia Consolidated Investment
    Fund, 69
WestLB, 129
Whitehead, J., 162
Whitney and Co., R., 160
Wiggin, A., 139
WorldCom, 34, 36–37, 155–156
Wriston, W., 37

Yosemite, 59–61
Young, P., 141